S O C I A L I S T
R E G I S T E R
2 0 1 4

SOCIALIST REGISTER 2014

REGISTERING CLASS

Edited by LEO PANITCH, GREG ALBO and VIVEK CHIBBER

THE MERLIN PRESS
MONTHLY REVIEW PRESS
FERNWOOD PUBLISHING

First published in 2013
by The Merlin Press Ltd.
99B Wallis Road
London
E9 5LN

www.merlinpress.co.uk

British Library Cataloguing in Publication Data is available from the British
Library

ISSN. 0081-0606

Published in the UK by The Merlin Press
ISBN. 978-0-85036-643-3 Paperback
ISBN. 978-0-85036-642-6 Hardback

Published in the USA by Monthly Review Press
ISBN. 978-1-58367-431-4 Paperback

Published in Canada by Fernwood Publishing
ISBN. 978-1-55266-593-0 Paperback

Printed in the UK on behalf of LPPS Ltd., Wellingborough, Northants.

CONTENTS

CONTRIBUTORS

Bastiaan van Apeldoorn is a reader in International Relations at the VU University, Amsterdam.

William K. Carroll is a professor in the Department of Sociology at the University of Victoria, Canada.

Vivek Chibber is an associate professor in the Department of Sociology at New York University.

Madeleine Davis is a lecturer in the School of Politics and International Relations at Queen Mary, University of London.

Virginia Fontes is a professor of history at the Fluminense Federal University in Rio de Janiero, Brazil.

Ana Garcia teaches international political economy at the International Relations Institute of Pontificial Catholic University of Rio de Janeiro (PUC-Rio) and is a researcher at the Institute for Political Alternatives in the South Cone (PACS).

Arun Gupta is a founding editor of the Indypendent magazine and was a founding editor of the Occupy Wall Street Journal.

Ursula Huws is director of the research consultancy Analytica and professor of labour and globalization at the University of Hertfordshire Business School.

Colin Leys is a professor emeritus in the Department of Political Studies at Queen's University, Canada.

Ian MacDonald is a visiting fellow at the Cornell Institute of Labour Relations in New York City.

Lecio Morais is an economics adviser to the Brazilian Chamber of Deputies.

Andrew Murray is Chief of Staff for the British trade union Unite.

Bryan Palmer is a professor in the Department of History at Trent University, Canada.

Leo Panitch is professor of political science at York University, Canada.

Alfredo Saad-Filho is a professor of political economy in the Department of Development Studies at the School of Oriental and African Studies, University of London.

Claude Serfati is a professor of economics at the University of Versailles-Saint-Quentinen-Yvelines.

PREFACE

The preface to the first volume of the *Socialist Register* in 1964, in announcing 'a series of annual volumes of socialist analysis and discussion', expressed the belief that 'the possibility of fruitful discussions is now greater than for a long time past. It is now better realized among socialists that dogmatic reiteration cannot, any more than crass empiricism, provide answers to the problems of the present.' It is in the same spirit that we have conceived this volume, the *Register*'s fiftieth. Our decision to focus on the theme of class not only reflects an abiding concern of the *Register* since the beginning, but also the fact that the spread and deepening of capitalist social relations around the globe has been increasingly marked by growing social inequality. And as the global economic crisis that capitalism has spawned in the early twenty-first century has been deployed to extend the class struggle from above so determinedly waged in the neoliberal era, so have the many resistances that have arisen been explicitly cast in terms of class struggles from below.

In the *Register*'s first volume, its founding editors Ralph Miliband and John Saville acknowledged it was not easy to identify strategies that might, within the existing balance of class forces, advance working-class organization and political reforms 'in socialist directions'. They nevertheless immediately added: 'But a beginning, or rather a new beginning, must be made somewhere; and the time to begin is surely now'. Almost four decades later, the 2001 volume, *Working Classes, Global Realities*, marked the new millennium with a critical survey of the global working class and the prospects for revitalization – another new beginning – of the socialist movement. As the preface put it: 'The global proletariat is not vanishing but expanding at a rate that has doubled its numbers since 1975. It is not the absence of proletarian numbers that is the defining feature of the age so much as the unprecedented combination of old and new proletariats in face of global capital'.

This is increasingly recognized today. And this calls for a return to class analysis, especially to the kind of *relational* class analysis that Andre Gorz advanced in his landmark essay on 'Reform and Revolution' in the 1968

Register: '... the power to initiate a policy of reforms is not conquered in Parliament, but by the previous demonstration of a capacity to mobilize the working classes against current policies; and this capacity can only be durable and fruitful if the forces of opposition can not only effectively challenge current policies, but also resolve the ensuing crisis; not only attack these policies, but also define other policies which correspond to the new balance of forces: or rather – since a relation of forces is never a static thing – to the new dynamic of struggle that this new relation of forces makes possible'.

This now requires a sharpened conceptual apparatus to apprehend the changing composition of both capitalist and working classes in recent decades. The major shifts in capitalism's financial, industrial and occupational profile, as the last quarter century has unleashed a profound restructuring of accumulation both technologically and geographically, has entailed a major restructuring of capitalist classes themselves while at the same time bringing about the unprecedented combination of old and new proletariats in the interstices of global capital. The deep crisis since 2008 has accelerated all of these changes.

In the light of this, a key question that needs to be posed by class analysis concerns how the restructuring of capitalist classes is changing the shape of political rule. And the changing structure and composition of the working classes requires probing what are their divergent and collective interests. On the presumption that socialism cannot happen unless working classes make it happen, how do socialists make the link between the working class today and strategies for developing the class as a transformative agency? In other words, what is the real working class that socialists have to work with in the twenty-first century?

The immensity of these questions is such that they will command the attention of both the fiftieth and fifty-first volumes of the *Register*. The 2015 *Register* will attempt to assess further the organizational foundations of the ruling classes today, in both their corporate forms and their national and regional settings. And it will also investigate further the changing face and prospects of working-class organization and politics. The geographical range will be extended to include China and India, as the central places in Asia where both capitalist and working classes are being remade. The volume will also feature contributions on the potential for a breakthrough in working-class organization and politics in the capitalist heartland of the USA, and will continue to explore the transformations taking place within working-class families. The restructuring of the sphere of reproduction, with its important implications for migration and gender relations, is as vital as the restructuring of the labour process for understanding contemporary working-class lives and politics.

The essays for these two volumes on class analysis emerge out of a workshop held in Toronto in February 2013. There are a number of people to thank for providing support in facilitating the meetings – Frederick Peters, Eric Newstadt, Steve Maher, Jared Gampel and Khashayar Hooshiyar. We are grateful to our contributors for their participation, for the stimulating dialogue and debate that ensued, and for the attentiveness they paid to the comments we supplied on their drafts. The workshop encouraged a variety of approaches to the issues at hand, and we hope that our readers will appreciate the differences and tensions across the essays, which we believe is an absolute requirement for advancing socialist theory and strategy today. We want to thank Alan Zuege for his insights on theoretical and strategic issues related to planning both the volumes on class analysis, as well as Adam Hilton for his outstanding editorial assistance. We are also grateful to Louis Mackay for presenting us with an especially evocative cover. Finally, with this fiftieth volume, we want to extend the greatest appreciation to Tony Zurbrugg and Adrian Howe at Merlin Press for the long-standing and unfailing support given to the *Register* over the years, including this one.

Our co-editor Vivek Chibber has decided that with the completion of the *Register*'s fiftieth volume he would prefer to return to the position of associate editor, where he will continue to play an active supporting role. As we embark on the next fifty years, we also look forward to our continuing collaboration with the *Register*'s editorial collective, to which we are very pleased to welcome Madeleine Davis and Ray Kiely as new members.

LP
GA
VC
August 2013

THE WALMART WORKING CLASS

ARUN GUPTA

In April 2012 my partner, Michelle Fawcett, and I were preparing to embark on a road trip around the United States. We were planning to visit Occupy Wall Street camps as a follow-up to our journey in late 2011 that took us to Occupations in 27 different cities. Wanting to avoid eating overpriced, greasy restaurant food, we decided to purchase a cooler, plates, glasses, cutlery, and cleaning supplies to prepare meals out of a car. As many retailers now carry these items, we popped into a CVS in a strip mall outside San Diego. I was struck by how expensive all the items were, which would strain our budget earned from freelance journalism. We decided to try our luck elsewhere, and upon exiting we noticed a Walmart in the distance. 'No', I said. 'I've never been in a Walmart, and I'm not about to start now'. We found a Walgreens and futilely repeated the exercise. 'OK', I muttered as we exited and the Walmart loomed closer. 'Let's just check it out'. Inside it was a consumer wonderland as everything was half or even a third the price at the other retailers. Soon we were piling our cart with goods. Michelle remarked as we grabbed 25-cent forks and spoons, 'It's so cheap it might as well be free'. The whole process was efficient, and we spent $50 for dozens of items, less than a cooler would have cost at the other chain stores.

This was confirmed by my visits to five other Walmart stores since then. Intellectually, I knew Walmart ruthlessly rationalized global supply chains, pushed the flight of US manufacturing and normalized precarious low-wage jobs. But as a consumer I discovered that Walmart is unmatched for the low cost and ease of social reproduction. Or as one worker put it, 'Walmart is cheap as shit and it's convenient'.

Walmart accounts for about 13 per cent of the $2.53 trillion US retail market, and 140 million Americans shop at Walmart weekly, more people than voted for Barack Obama and Mitt Romney combined in 2012. It employs almost 1 per cent of the US workforce with 1.3 million workers, and claims another 3 million US jobs are dependent on it. At 3 per cent of

US GDP ($466 billion in fiscal year 2013), its net sales were on par with GM's postwar peak. Almost 80 per cent of its $27.8 billion in operating profits came from domestic sales ($274.5 billion, plus $56.4 billion for over 600 Sam's Club outlets). In 2007 the Walmart family wealth was greater than the combined wealth of the bottom 30 per cent of American families, and by 2010 it had grown to more than 41.5 per cent of all families, making Walmart an unambiguous measure of class polarization in US society.[1]

Walmart aims to offer the lowest-priced goods, relying on high volume to compensate for razor-thin margins, so from the start its model has been to maximize labour productivity by minimizing pay, benefits and workplace rights. This process has intensified during the economic downturn that began in 2007 as Walmart has cut an average of 57 employees per US outlet.[2] Even as same-store sales have stagnated since 2008, it is increasing profits by cutting staff and benefits, forcing the remaining workers to speed up their work pace through strict time-management software. Internal Walmart memos reveal poorly stocked stores and for six years it has been 'placed last among department and discount stores in the American Customer Satisfaction Index'.[3] Indeed, Walmart may no longer be able to maintain a significant price advantage over other grocery stores and discount retailers and is being pressured by Amazon in e-commerce. Walmart is a victim of its own success as it has eliminated 'a raft of salesmen, jobbers and other supply-chain middlemen, squeezed the manufacturers by shifting every imaginable cost, risk, and penalty onto their books, and taught the entire retail world how the bar code and data warehouse could finally put real money on the bottom line'.[4] To add just 24 full-time employees per US store would cost it $2.1 billion, or 10 per cent of its domestic profits.

This is the context in which a new struggle by Walmart workers – the national campaign led by Organization United for Respect (OUR Walmart) and the Chicago-based Warehouse Workers for Justice (WWJ) and its organizing arm, the Warehouse Workers Organizing Committee (WWOC) – has emerged since 2009. It was very much on the minds of the eleven Walmart retail and warehouse workers with whom I conducted in-depth interviews in May and June 2013. While the only workers I found willing to talk were disgruntled – using terms like 'prison', 'serfs', and 'company town' – and expressed contempt for Walmart as an employer and shopping destination, evidence indicates discontent is widespread. As if confirming what interviewees told me about being 'overworked', and 'pulled in too many directions', one former Walmart store manager explained to *The Huffington Post*: 'People don't line up for those jobs. You can make the same thing at a 7-Eleven or flipping burgers but you don't have to work nearly as hard'.[5] A 2011 survey of 501 'associates' (as Walmart calls its workers) found '84 percent say they would take a better job if they could find one'.[6]

Despite having been told or believing that any attempt to unionize or even discuss unions at work would result in being fired, all eleven workers are pro-union. One is organizing his workplace as part of OUR Walmart, and all four warehouse workers participated in a semi-successful 2012 strike against Walmart and its subcontractors in massive distribution facilities outside of Chicago. OUR Walmart and WWOC coincide with organizing efforts in Walmart warehouses in New Jersey and California, the Walmart supply-chain along the Gulf Coast, and the national 'Fight for 15' campaign – an unabashed drive by the Service Employees International Union (SEIU) to unionize low-wage workers with the slogan, '$15 and a union'. One burning question before the left today is whether these campaigns in the low-wage sectors can revitalize the American labour movement, especially after the Occupy Wall Street movement injected class politics back into popular discourse with talk of the 99 per cent and the 1 per cent.

THE WALMART EFFECT

Walmart's uniqueness as a general discount merchandiser by the beginning of the twenty-first century could be measured by its annual revenue – more than the next four largest global retailers combined.[7] Founded as a discount retailer in 1962 – the same year as more than 20 other retail chains began discount operations, including Kmart and Target – it soon compelled 'many competitors and suppliers ... to adjust their business models to conform to Walmart'.[8] It 'forced its suppliers to cut costs, made it more difficult for companies to compete on any terms other than price, and made it close to impossible for manufacturers and service providers to pass on the cost of improvements in products and services to consumers in the form of price increases'.[9]

Taking advantage of new technology, as well as 'concentration in the retail sector and the rise in global competition in suppliers' industries', Walmart pioneered the late twentieth century merchant-led 'drive to rationalize market institutions'.[10] This logistics revolution induced a shift from a 'push' system 'dominated by large consumer-goods manufacturers [with] long production runs in order to gain efficiencies of scale and minimize unit costs' to a 'pull' system in which retailers used bar codes, scanners and computers to scrutinize point-of-sale consumer behaviour and share that information with vendors to 'coordinate production with actual sales, minimizing inventory buildup anywhere in the chain ... which cuts costs for both manufacturers and retailers'. By acting as a monopsony, which can set prices for vendors, and by becoming an operations specialist with 'core competencies' in 'purchasing, warehousing, distribution, trucking', Walmart devised an answer (along the lines of Japan's just-in-time production system) to capitalism's chronic 'disjuncture between production and distribution, or supply and demand'. It has 'organised and rationalized global supply chains; established trade standards and logistics solutions, and even ventured into product development'.[11]

Given Walmart's role as a motor force in 'American-led globalization' and as the largest private-sector employer of African Americans, with 255,000 associates in 2013, the origins of its proletariat and ideology are steeped in irony. Walmart was founded in the Ozarks, the populist 'heartland of anti-monopolism' and movement against chain stores. Sam Walton tapped into populist discontent by promising to keep 'Ozarks dollars in the Ozarks', and later positioning Walmart as 'a populist multinational'. While the nineteenth century Populist movement was anti-corporate to the bone, it supported government largesse to promote economic activity, 'so long as it acted on behalf of the mythic original citizen, the yeoman'. Walmart benefited from this history, as well as the New Deal, which served as a welfare state for whites by excluding 'African Americans from the new federal bounty [like] Social Security, minimum wages, healthcare, education'. New Deal credit programmes 'subsidized free enterprise' in the underdeveloped South, a process that spread during the Cold War as federal money flowed to employers that were allowed to deny social claims. And the Labor-Management Relations Act of 1947, known as Taft-Hartley, encouraged Sun Belt states to pass anti-union 'right-to-work' legislation, with Arkansas becoming one of the first to pass such a law.[12]

Along with these elements, Walmart benefited from a racially homogenous Ozarks that witnessed anti-Black pogroms around the turn of the twentieth century. Walmart was founded in the early '60s in Benton County, Arkansas, 'which had but 23 blacks, most elderly servants'. This helped it dodge civil rights protests targeting anti-integration businesses. Almost all of its first hundred stores were in this 'homogenous homeland' that 'precisely coincided with the territory that had generated so many sundown towns' starting in the 1890s. Walmart was an economic and cultural lifeline for 'farm wives and daughters displaced by the agricultural revolution', not unlike the 'Lowell Mill girls of the early nineteenth century'. Combined with the dominant Christian and patriarchal culture, Walmart enclosed 'a rural Protestant family ideology and a female work culture based on "people skills"'. It replaced the male-dominated industrial economy with a 'patriarchal organization of work' that extended from the store floor to apparel sweatshops. 'The industrial economy's scorn for women's work skills meant they could be had for a bargain price.' By offering social value to rural women entering the workforce, while emphasizing 'Every Day Low Prices' for the same women looking to economize in service to their family, Walmart generated unusual loyalty while exploiting underpaid female workers. From the start Walton squeezed labour costs by creating shell companies to evade minimum-wage laws in the 1960s.[13]

During its explosive growth in the 1970s and '80s, Walmart took advantage of inflation spikes to attract newly price-conscious consumers, as well as global trends towards waning union strength and labour process restructuring, including the 'deskilling' and 'reskilling' of jobs.[14] Walmart is also a virtuoso in manipulating regulation. It benefited from the 1970s property-tax revolt as local governments turned to siting big-box retailers to increase tax revenue, and it aggressively sought development subsidies, with one study uncovering more than $1 billion in public largesse by 2004, while systematically challenging property-tax assessments to reduce payments to local governments.[15] At the heart of Walmart's model are Distribution Centers (serving up to 150 retail stores to keep 'commodities in motion' as quickly as possible from manufacturer to stores) which are 'built deep in the countryside where wages are low and workers largely anti-union'; and it supplemented this with a profit-sharing system (eliminated in 2011) as a means of not only 'linking the employees to the fate of the company, but also justifying the self-exploitation that was integral to the Walmart culture'.[16] Its 'well-organised anti-unionization policy [which] set the standard for other retailers and industrialists' involves taking such union avoidance so seriously that it 'maintains a staff of 200 in its labour relations department, many available to fly to any store' whenever the 'Union Probability Index' (keyed to 'factors measuring morale, complaints, turnovers and other problems') hits a prescribed level.[17] The success of this was such that an independent Walmart effect on the economy – and the working class – could be discerned, 'where the jobs are traps: low wages, miserly benefits, stultifying work, no respect, no future'.[18]

THE WALMART PROLETARIAT

Some economists contend the Walmart effect is positive because benefits accrue to all of society, particularly to low-income households that can save up to 25 per cent on food costs from lower prices offered by supercenters and increased competition with other supermarkets.[19] It was also claimed that Walmart was single-handedly responsible for much of the late 1990s surge in US productivity because its 'success forced competitors to improve their operations'.[20]

Whatever the accuracy of such claims, they sidestep the role Walmart has played in shifting working-class employment from stable medium-wage jobs to a precarious low-wage service sector. Walmart's assertion that it 'create[s] quality jobs', or any jobs for that matter, does not hold up to scrutiny.[21] The most detailed study of Walmart's effects on local labour markets found that each Walmart job cost 1.4 retail-sector jobs, or nearly 150 jobs on average in affected counties. There was 'a 2.7 percent reduction in retail employment attributable to a Walmart store opening', as well as 'declines in county-level retail earnings of about $1.4 million, or 1.5 percent'.[22] The Walmart effect is especially pronounced among supermarkets whose unionization rates were traditionally much higher than general merchandisers like Walmart. In 1988 Walmart opened its first grocery store and discount supercenter to capture more revenue as consumers 'shop for food on average about 2.5 times a week' compared to once a month at a drugstore or retailer. By 2012 groceries accounted for 55 per cent of Walmart's US sales, and by one estimate it has acquired a breathtaking 33 per cent market share. One Walmart study revealed that it paid supercenter workers up to $3.50 an hour less than unionized supermarket workers.[23] Thus if Walmart has reduced consumer good prices for the entire US economy, it has also reduced wages and benefits for entire sectors. If a state had 50 Walmarts, which was the average in 2000, wages dropped 10 per cent and health insurance coverage shrank 5 per cent among all retail workers in that state.[24]

Even if an average family buys all its food, clothing, electronics and furnishings from Walmart, they will still spend twice as much on healthcare, education, transportation and housing.[25] Plus, consumers are not purely rational agents who will buy the same amount of goods if they switch to Walmart and pocket the savings. Some vendors discovered their sales increased dramatically after becoming Walmart suppliers with no other explanation than consumers were buying more products, replacing them more often, and consumption was being 'driven strictly by price and impulse'.[26] By one estimate Walmart has directly pushed 20,000 families into poverty nationwide.[27] At the same time, and by no means unrelated, Walmart has been fingered as responsible for 10.5 per cent of the rise in obesity from 13 per cent to 34 per cent among Americans from 1960 to 2006 due to innovations 'in *distribution* technology that lower the prices of food and other consumer goods'.[28]

With its anti-union, low-wage strategy, Walmart exploited neoliberal 'attacks on the welfare state, deregulation, and increased international free trade that began in the 1970s'.[29] Just like nineteenth century industrialists who pitched free trade as a boon for workers,[30] Walmart fiercely pushed NAFTA and subsequent free trade agreements claiming this would lower prices and create jobs. Instead it accelerated the loss of US manufacturing and middle-income jobs.[31] The relation between lower-cost goods and lower wages is symptomatic of an era that's 'a golden age' for corporate profits. During the third quarter of 2012, corporate profits' share of national income reached 14.2 per cent, 'the largest share at any time since 1950, while the portion of income that went to employees was 61.7 percent, near its lowest point since 1966'.[32]

No less than 26 per cent of US private sector jobs, held by 29.1 million workers, pay less than $10 an hour, and most of these jobs are precarious.[33] The low-wage workforce includes both the poor and 'near poor' – those who earn up to 200 per cent of the poverty threshold – which together number 106 million Americans, or 34 per cent of the US population. Of 10.2 million families (47.5 million people) classified as working poor, an estimated 61 per cent 'had a high housing cost burden', meaning they spent more than 33 per cent of their income on housing, while low-income families spent 8.6 per cent of their income on gasoline as opposed to 2.1 per cent for higher-income families. As of 2011 48.6 million Americans lacked health insurance, including 28 million workers.[34]

Walmart associates average $8.81 an hour, more than cashiers average at Target and Kmart, $7.96 and $7.59 respectively.[35] An internal wage guide dated February 2012 'details a rigid pay structure for hourly employees that makes it difficult for most to rise much beyond poverty-level wages'.[36] The wage guide was developed to cut costs and provide objective measures for pay 'as a response to a landmark class action lawsuit, *Dukes v. Walmart Stores Inc.*, which accused the company of discriminating against women in pay and promotion'.[37] (That suit was dismissed by the US Supreme Court in 2011.) The guidelines create an incentive to push out higher-waged workers. Walmart acknowledged this in a 2006 internal memo: 'the cost of an Associate with 7 years of tenure is almost 55 percent more than the cost of an Associate with 1 year of tenure, yet there is no difference in his or her productivity'.[38]

In 2013 Walmart admitted 'disproportionately' hiring part-time workers without fixed hours, possibly to circumvent the Affordable Care Act that will, starting in 2015, require businesses with more than 50 workers to offer health insurance to employees who work at least 30 hours a week.[39] In fact, a Walmart memo from 2005 explicitly laid out a strategy for slicing healthcare costs by 'hiring more part-time workers and discouraging unhealthy people from working at Walmart'.[40] This memo exposed the fact that in 2004 the number of Walmart associates and their children on Medicaid was about 25 per cent higher than the national average. They spent 8 per cent of their income on healthcare, 'nearly twice the national average', and 38 per cent of enrolled employees spent more than one-sixth of their income on healthcare. It noted Walmart 'workers are getting sicker than the national population, particularly with obesity-related diseases' like diabetes and heart disease.[41] Ironically, the Supplemental Nutrition Assistance Program benefits (food stamps) – which one in seven Americans receive and amounted to $74.6 billion in 2012 – is a vital source of revenue for Walmart, which admits that a 'significant percentage of all SNAP dollars are spent in our stores'; nine of its supercenters in Massachusetts received $33 million in SNAP in one year; and in Oklahoma it raked in 42 per cent of all SNAP monies ($506 million) over one 21-month period.[42] In Wisconsin, it has been estimated that a worker in a 300-employee Walmart supercenter requires at least $3,015 and up to $5,815 in public aid once subsidized school meals, childcare, housing, energy assistance, food stamps, healthcare and tax credits are taken into account.[43] The shreds of social welfare that backstop millions of service sector workers thus also subsidize Walmart as well as other big global corporations like McDonalds, Wendy's and Burger King. 'Walmart transfers income from the working poor and from taxpayers through welfare programs directed at the poor to stockholders and the heirs of the Walmart fortune, as well as to consumers.'[44]

Ultimately, 'Walmart management may well have more power than any other entity to "legislate" key components of American social and industrial policy'.[45] And this includes shaping a workforce that serves its interests – one that is precarious, on the cusp of poverty, lacks any semblance of workplace rights and minimal social solidarity, and above all, lives in fear.

WALMART WORKERS SPEAK

Interviews with seven current and former Walmart retail workers and four warehouse workers (six of whom are 26 years old or younger) flesh out what life is like for this segment of the proletariat.[46] Everyone said a Walmart store or warehouse is the one place nearly anyone can get work, and often it's a job of last resort. The retail workers earned between $7.85 and $9.50 an hour, apart from one with 11 years' experience who makes $12 an hour. The warehouse workers made $9 to $11.50 an hour. Their time in the labour force ranges from 4 to 36 years. Each of the retail workers has had at least five jobs, mainly in fast food, retailing, bookstores, supermarkets, convenience stores, telemarketing and drugstores, while the warehouse workers lean toward physical labour, equipment operators or trades, though one is currently working in fast food. One former retail worker now earns $35 an hour as a part-time unionized stagehand, one warehouse worker once made $17.50 an hour as an apprentice electrician, but none of the others ever made over $15 hourly. Most earned under $15,000 annually and only one makes above $20,000. All describe 'anxiety about financial issues'. When asked how much they think they should be paid, the range was one to four dollars an hour extra.

One former retail worker and all four warehouse workers lack healthcare, the rest have it through family, spouses or the government, and one through Walmart. Five retail workers live in multi-generational households of adults, indicative of the 22.3 million shared households, an increase of 13 per cent since 2007.[47] Among workers with more than one year tenure, only one receives any paid vacation; two say they are working injured because of the inability to take time off; and three report attempts at wage theft involving managers demanding cashiers stay later to check out customers because of chronic understaffing, and then at the end of the pay period managers pressure workers to delete the overtime and work off the clock. Others say managers would tell them to go home early or take longer lunches to eliminate overtime. One said managers told him to follow the example of other workers who 'skip breaks to get their products in the shelves'. Five say they were 'coached' repeatedly, or written up. Nearly all say they're overworked as a result of understaffing, and that managers can be verbally abusive or condescending, especially in the warehouses. Other than the bakery worker, retail workers know their schedules only two weeks in advance and shifts are unpredictable, which affects their ability to plan their lives. If they take unpaid leave for even a day their hours may be cut. In essence Walmart treats labour as another just-in-time commodity.[48] Steve, 44, successfully managed to get his job back after being fired by appealing to higher levels of management on the basis of Walmart's vaunted 'open door' policy of listening to employee complaints; but he says he had never been fired in more than 25 years of working prior to that, and there was a 'constant threat of losing your job. They tolerate bad behavior so they can fire them when they don't need them anymore. The whole purpose is not to have to pay unemployment.'

Aaron, who lives in St. Petersburg, Florida, says human resources staff at his former Walmart store 'made sure to tell everyone if you needed help with housing assistance or food stamps they would help you get that stuff'. He echoes other workers when he says employees and customers are captive of Walmart: 'It's like the old company town. The minute workers get their paycheck they spend their money right there.' Many are frustrated at being perceived as 'stupid' or 'dumb' for working at Walmart. 'Low wages don't mean low intelligence', says one. Tim Adams, a 'Marxist and pro-union' cashier and college student in Columbus, Ohio, says about his co-workers, 'there's not much energy, or excitement or happiness. … It does seem like a lot of workers are depressed about their conditions'.

Perhaps because they are hidden from public view, the warehouse workers, known as 'lumpers', live and toil in particularly onerous conditions. The four I interviewed were all temps, classified as 'material movers', and none had paid time off, healthcare or other benefits. This is the norm in Chicago-area according to the Warehouse Workers for Justice (WWJ) study, 'Bad Jobs in Goods Movement': 63 per cent of warehouse workers are temps; 78 per cent are male; the average wage is $9 an hour, $3.48 an hour less than those who work directly for Schneider Logistics, Walmart's warehouse management firm; and 'only 5 percent of temps had sick days and 4 percent health insurance'. The four men I talked with are all single and rent houses with other single men or live in a Catholic Worker house, which has aided the organizing effort. Phillip, 38, said some workers squat in abandoned homes and one lived in a tent in the woods for a few weeks.[49] All four earned under $20,000 in 2012, and say on workdays lumpers survive on fast food because 'you can eat for $5 or $6 a day'. One said, 'You see a lot of people in the break rooms not eating, and that's the saddest thing you could ever see'. Mike, 35, says managers would eliminate breaks 'if they said our cartons per hour were too low. I've never seen the quota so vigorously enforced as in Walmart. You'd be working a 14-hour day and they would come by your trailer and say, "You're 8 minutes off pace"'. At age 38, Phillip has left the industry because 'the pace was pretty fast and brutal. It's back-breaking. During the summer it's 120 or 130 degrees in the back of the truck trailer. People routinely fall out in the summer from dehydration or exhaustion. They would pass out, they would have heat strokes … I'm too old. You're in serious pain every day you do that.' Joseph, 25, says minor injuries happen every day: 'your shin gets cut, jam fingers, sprain something, neck pulls, back pulls'. Nor was management sympathetic, according to James, 26: 'The supervisors would basically say, "You need a job, here's how many boxes you have to throw an hour. You can't do it, we'll find somebody else"'. WWJ's study found one-third of workers were fired or disciplined for reporting injuries.

In any case, few report the injuries, says James, because 'they immediately take you for a drug test, and if you fail it you're fired and they don't pay your medical bills'. Indeed, James and others say drug use is pervasive. 'At least 80 percent do drugs. Most people smoke weed, a lot of people take prescription painkillers on the docks, some people do coke. Adderall was really common. It would focus you and keep you awake.' Because of high unemployment and high turnover, warehouse jobs attract everyone from paroles, former union plumbers, carpenters and machinists to university graduates. Mike, who's worked in warehousing since 1996, says employers 'feed off people who are on their last legs, who are struggling. These jobs are easy to get if you have a criminal background. I'd say close to 50 percent of temps have a criminal record. One temp agency specialized in paroles, they bussed all of them in. There's guys who've worked there five years and are temps, they're perma-temps. There's no such thing as a raise, no such thing as vacation, no such thing as benefits.' All claim wage theft is systematic. Mike says, 'Every pay period people would complain about being shorted hours. Sometimes people were missing a whole day on their check. One guy was missing a whole weekend.' One of the chief complaints was irregular hours. James says, 'You would come in at 6 am and sometimes you'd be sent home in a couple of hours or sometimes you'd be there for 14 hours'. Some temp agencies use a morning 'shape up' and regularly send home workers 'who drove there from wherever with no pay', which is illegal. He says, 'These management tactics are letting you know that you don't have any rights'.

This especially applies to women who work in the warehouses, who are not only often paid less but also subject to sexual harassment, assault and battery by coworkers and supervisors. Warehouse Workers for Justice spokesperson Leah Fried says, 'We surveyed 53 women and found about 50% reported sexual harassment, and 82% reported gender discrimination'. When women would report the incidents to management, responses allegedly ranged from, 'I didn't see that', to assigning them the most-difficult jobs, to supervisors asking the worker 'out on a date', to one company allegedly retaliating by accusing a 19-year-old woman of criminal acts with the result she was imprisoned for 16 days.[50]

Retail workers face their own set of difficulties. Ally is a married 26-year-old female who has worked at a Kentucky Walmart for more than two years. She began working at age 16, and makes $8 an hour for 34 hours a week, while her husband works in a factory at $17.50 an hour. She's worked in supermarkets and pharmacies, and the most she ever earned was $12.75 an hour. They pay $600 for housing and her husband pays another $600 a month in student loans.

My husband and I argue a lot because we don't have enough money for the bills to go around. We've had to go to McDonald's and take napkins to use as toilet paper for the last week. My shoes fell apart and I had to rubber-band the soles back on. For the two of us we spend $50 a week on groceries, sometimes $25. For lunch I'll bring a Michelina frozen dinner, it costs 98 cents. I would like to eat healthier, but we can't afford to eat healthier. Almost everything we eat is a frozen TV dinner or canned food. Every work shirt has holes in them.

Ally has considerable credit card debt and says 10 creditors are demanding $1,000 a month in payments total, but she can't afford to hire a lawyer to discharge the debt. 'The stress in my life is ridiculous. [The job] is making me mentally exhausted, emotionally exhausted. It sucks you into such a deep rut you can't look for another job.' In terms of the workplace,

Walmart is the first place I've worked where no one ever tries to stab you in the back because Walmart does it enough for you. It feels like a prison movie. It feels like the Walking Dead. ... Every day when I go in I dread going into work because I have to deal with crap. I don't hate the customers. I hate Walmart because they're an evil corporation. I work my butt off every single day and they tell you if you work hard we'll promote you, and that's not true.

As for workplace issues, Ally has an irregular schedule, often works weekends and holidays, and has not accrued vacation time in two years. She can take unpaid days, but says when 'I requested one day off, they scheduled me only for two days the next week'. She pulled a muscle in her arm at work and has been working injured for two months because her schedule conflicts with doctor's appointments. She complains about understaffing, poorly stocked shelves and broken equipment around the store. The work is monotonous, 'All you do is stand in one spot; you don't do anything'. But at the beginning of the month 'you're lucky to get your break. We live in a poor part of town, a lot of people on welfare, WIC, food stamps. There's a big rush when they get their aid. When I ring up other employees almost everyone uses food stamps.'

Ally says, 'A lot of customers complain' about Walmart's dependence on goods from China, while co-workers complain about schedules, low pay, working on holidays and the cost of healthcare. Once or twice a month Ally is forced to work through a paid 15-minute break. Management has 'told us if any employees are heard talking about a union they will be fired'. She describes management as abusive, 'I've never been at a job where a manager can call you stupid, calls you retarded, screams at people'.

Ally previously worked in a unionized supermarket and didn't like paying dues. 'I don't think I would get better benefits with a union because I made minimum wage there.' But she adds, 'I'd rather pay union dues and be treated like a human, rather than being treated like an insect. I support OUR Walmart whether they help or not. I'd like knowing someone is standing up to Walmart. We can't just be treated like crap forever.' As for the possibility of organizing, coworkers are 'afraid of losing their job. Walmart would need to come to some kind of standstill. I don't see it happening because they know they are too big to do that.'

Janet, a 50-something mother, has worked for Walmart in Missouri for 11 years, currently as a baker earning $12 per hour. She applied to more than 100 businesses but says no one else would hire her because of her age. Her husband Brad's $3,000 monthly pension is their main source of income. But he is in failing health and says, 'If I can last until Janet's 65, then she will get my pension'. Janet earns about $2,000 a month. After out-of-pocket medical expenses, deductions for healthcare, and taxes, her take-home pay is about $900 a month. The couple, who live with an adult child who works sporadically, paid off their mortgage and 'wiped the slate clean' after Brad's father, a unionized auto worker, left them an inheritance when he died in the early 2000s. Janet's been working with an injured leg for more than a month and is afraid to take sick days to recover after a coworker with 20 years on the job was replaced because she missed her scheduled return date after surgery.

> The work is horrible, and the pay's no good. You have to push hard to get everything done. It makes me feel stressed. There's a lot of pressure put on the people that can be tracked by the computers. Anything that can be monitored they monitor. The fact that it's not paying that much makes you feel worthless. Walmart is like a company town. We're entering a new stage of feudalism. It's the corporation that's the baron and the workers are the serf. To be honest I can't afford the meat anymore. We have a garden that helps. Our idea of meat anymore is bacon, hotdogs, canned meat.

The store is 'understaffed continually' and workers are 'pretty dissatisfied with what's going on. We don't get the equipment we need. We're trying to do too much. Everyone feels overworked.' She says people work there mainly for the healthcare and the paycheck, and want to be paid more.

> My coworkers don't have any hope in government, not anymore. They're pretty sure government is in the pocket of corporations. I brought up the

factory collapse in Bangladesh, and no one heard about it. They said, 'You've got it be kidding. I'll believe it if it's Walmart'. They are so fixated on their survival. They talk about how Walmart is essentially a sweatshop operation. 'They should bring it back and be made in America'. A lot of my coworkers shop at Walmart. They don't have a choice about it. A lot of younger woman with small children talk about money problems. None of them have any hope of getting into a house unless their husbands have a really good job. Most are on food stamps, and get childcare from the state. They get a lot of state-based assistance. Everything is a strain for them. They have to wait weeks to get their cars fixed. They get together and if one of them gets into a jam they loan them money, and they pass it around.

Janet is adamantly pro-union. 'When I was growing up, my dad belonged to the union. It was called "the union", and it did good things for workers. The union gave my dad a well-paying job that took care of five kids and my mom. We had good medical because of them.' Her coworkers' opinions vary. 'A lot of my coworkers are very conservative. They don't want to give their money to a union, taking money out of their mouths to give it to a union to influence political rallies.' She says that in terms of participating in OUR Walmart strike actions:

Many workers wished they could just go ahead and walk out. They thought it would serve Walmart right, but they're terrified of losing their jobs. We're talking about people who literally live from paycheck to paycheck. These discussions would take place very quietly at the cash register. To try to organize a union they would have to be assured they had a job if Walmart fired them. It's economic fear above all else. I don't think there's anti-union sentiment nearly as badly as anyone thinks among Walmart employees.

For her part, Janet dismisses Walmart's famous 'open door' policy which allegedly allows any worker to 'take their complaint straight to a top executive in Bentonville'.[51] '[It's] bullshit. If you use the open-door policy they will tell you why it's done the way it's done and then they close the door in your face.' She's still angry about an incident in which a male coworker revealed Walmart 'paid him $1.50 more an hour because he had a family to support. That really pissed me off. I was taking care of my brother's four children, my children and a husband.' And she claims the only way she gets a raise is through class-action suits. 'I got 40 cents per hour from one lawsuit.' But she also sees Walmart as part of any solution, 'Walmart could do so much good if they tried. I think it's just about profits. It's all about greed right now. Look at all the influence they got. They could green the world. If they gave everybody a raise the economy would boom. A lot of customers say unions have outlived their usefulness.' Though they ask, '"Why can't they buy stuff made in America, why can't they support American jobs?" But a lot of times customers are in the same boat as us and they have no choice. When you're poor you go to the lowest price place period.'

Gabriel is a 31-year-old resident of Apple Valley, Minnesota working on a B.S. in math communications, and in addition to working at Walmart he's a DJ. He's worked there since August 2011, is an electronics associate earning $9.00 an hour, and is involuntarily part-time at 20 to 25 hours per week. He's worked since he was 14, previous employers include Kmart, Best Buy and a bank, and the most he's ever earned is $11.75 an hour as a manager of Game Crazy. Gabriel lives with his two parents, who are homeowners with a remaining mortgage of approximately $50,000. He receives low-income healthcare and food stamps, and has $20,000 in student loans in deferral.

Gabriel sought employment at Walmart because, 'It was a hard time, I needed the money, and I was having trouble finding work'. His weeklong orientation included a 'full day of discussion and video about how unions take your money and do nothing for you. Managers used scare tactics, "You could lose health benefits. Unions cause business to go down, so we will have to cut back on hours".' The orientation included 'role-playing and skits, where someone would play an organizer and the employees were taught how to respond. It was a lot of words and training in our heads.' Gabriel says at first he didn't care about the anti-union ideology. 'I was raised Republican, not to be fond of unions.'

He says, 'I don't have money to buy clothes, and I'm ashamed. I have a '92 Dodge Caravan I call Big Bertha, and if she breaks down we have to see if we can do without things to pay for repairs'. In terms of benefits, 'I don't get any paid vacation from Walmart. If I take vacation, I take unpaid leave. I don't get any sick days. That's how Walmart saves money, by keeping us part-time.'

Gabriel's decision to join OUR Walmart began after he was on the job three months and was having difficulty learning the stocking system.

A manager started yelling at me in front of the customers because I was working slower. First I took it, and was very upset. That night I looked for chat boards or groups to see if there were other associates being treated this way. And I happened upon OUR Walmart. I started reading the testimonials. I clicked the link to be contacted, and I left my number but a fake name. They called back after a few days. At first I was very scared and worried. We had it drilled into our heads you don't go outside to organize. We have the 'open door'.

Then in December 2011 while at work he started urinating blood and nearly collapsed because of 'major kidney stones'. As a coworker helped him a manager said, '"You can leave whenever you want, but we can't okay the absence." I was very surprised.' These incidents and discussions with an organizer convinced him to join OUR Walmart. He's taken part in two walkouts in 2012, and two worker-led protests in Bentonville. He says in October 2012 when he went on strike to travel to Bentonville to protest an investors' meeting:

> I saw a bunch of passionate people who were trying to make things better for our fellow co-workers, so they don't have to rely on food stamps and housing assistance. When I went on strike everybody thought I was going to get fired. When I came back I thought people would be upset, angry. They gave me handshakes and said, 'This is a long time coming, thank you for standing up for us'. I had one manager pull me aside who said, 'I totally believe in what you're doing, keep it up, Gabe. A couple of other managers believe the same thing'. Everybody at Walmart knows how bad it is.

During breaks and afterhours he talks extensively with other workers: 'We talk about wages, being underpaid, understaffed, how do you pay the bills and mortgage, or do you buy food. We talk about people who feel like they're being retaliated against or mistreated. Given too much work knowing it's not going to get done so a write-up ensues, on the floor being micro-managed and critiqued.' Gabriel says some workers told him after he went on strike, 'You leave more work for the rest of us', and that instead he 'should talk to management and use the open door'. He responded, 'If Walmart staffed the way it should we wouldn't have this problem, but it wants to use the least workers possible'. He also told them, 'The open door can't get more pay for us. The open door can't make staffing better and get us more hours. The open door can't get better healthcare for us. We need a stronger fix.'

He claims, 'Everyone that's joined has come to me. They say, "We saw how you went on strike, and you weren't fired." I was the only worker that went on strike. The way people are joining I can guarantee next time it will be 10 to 15 workers on strike.' But he also acknowledges 'Until we educate the public they're not going to care, and Walmart's going to keep pushing'.

Perhaps one of the most important effects of the organizing campaign is the sense of meaning and self-worth workers derive from their involvement. Gabriel says the 'strategy is to have associates stand up and live better', a play on Walmart's slogan, 'Save Money, Live Better'. 'You can go talk to your boss without fear of retaliation. You can have better pay, better health benefits, better schedules so you can attend your son's baseball games.'

And he adds:

God sent me down for a reason. He's got a path laid out for us. I'm very proud to be part of this movement. I now have people looking up to me. When my kids read in the history books about this, I'll be able to tell them I was there, and that makes me feel good. I want to be able to go into work with my head held high, do my job and provide for my family. That's all any of us wants to do.

OUR WALMART

The United Food and Commercial Workers launched Organization United for Respect at Walmart in 2011 through social media and personal outreach by about 100 staff and union members. It builds on an attempt launched in 2005 to build a workers' association in Florida by UFCW, SEIU and the now-defunct ACORN association of community groups. The campaign hindered Walmart's expansion in the state, and the national attention, including from the Federal Reserve, it drew to its demands for better hours and pay for its workers apparently motivated Walmart to raise wages in more than 500 stores in 2006. Yet, the same year the workers association collapsed in part due to union infighting.[52]

OUR Walmart began with a flurry of optimism, with organizers saying 'they have more than 50 members at some stores, and they hope to soon have tens of thousands of members'. Its first action was one-day strikes at stores in October 2012 involving 88 workers across 28 stores. The impetus was to protest Walmart firing and punishing OUR Walmart members, and came on the heels of strikes in September at Walmart warehouses in Mira Loma, Calif., and in Elwood, Ill., as well as a strike by eight 'guestworkers' at a Walmart supplier, CJ's Seafood in Louisiana in June 2012.[53] In November OUR Walmart organized community-based protests in 100 cities in 46 states on Black Friday, the annual shopping frenzy at US retail stores, that drew thousands of demonstrators including 500 striking workers. It has also organized three protests in Bentonville, Arkansas during Walmart shareholder and investor meetings in 2012 and 2013.[54] Smaller actions have taken place, and in April 2013 a meeting was held in Los Angeles bringing together Walmart supply chain workers from Chicago warehouses, the Gulf seafood industry and Bangladeshi garment factories.[55] By the summer of 2013 at least a thousand workers (including some former workers) were dues-paying members (at $5 or more a month), while perhaps five times that many were active in OUR Walmart. Yet, the effort was slow going. As one union staffer put it: 'It's extremely difficult to organize low-wage workers period, much less low-wage workers who are working among an extremely hostile company with a sophisticated union avoidance strategy'.

This difficulty is also a product of the weakness of US labour law. A survey of 1,004 NLRB elections from 1999 to 2004 found 'employers threatened to close the plant in 57 percent of elections, discharged workers in 34 percent, and threatened to cut wages and benefits in 47 percent of elections'.[56] A 2007 Human Rights Watch report explained US laws allowed for 'a wide range of employer tactics that interfere with worker organizing', while imposing only 'weak' penalties to 'deter employers from breaking the laws', allowing them to 'violate their employees' basic rights with virtual impunity'. Walmart, the report stated, 'takes full advantage' of that process.[57] This highlighted how far 'the welter of laws, board decisions, judicial decisions, and contractual obligations... ensnared the modern labor organization' since the passage of Taft-Hartley. That act banned secondary strikes, excluded foremen and supervisors from labour law, legalized 'employer free speech' and right-to-work laws, and stoked internal warfare against the labour left by requiring union officers to file 'non-Communist affidavits'.[58]

Once Taft-Hartley reversed successful organizing among black workers in the South, most unions proved ill-equipped to embrace African-American workers seeking an equal footing in core industries. While public-sector unionism grew dramatically starting in the '60s, unions largely ignored the growing private service sector that relied on part-time female workers. Slow to embrace rank-and-file democratic movements, or to respond effectively to the neoliberal counterattack, yet desperate to stay relevant, organized labour has banished most talk of the working class in favor of the poll-tested middle class. Its call for 'good jobs', 'fair wages' and 'a level playing field' romanticize a corporatist past where national capital can be cajoled to bring good-paying jobs back home.

Walmart's anti-union strategies smashed earlier attempts at unionization. In 1978 the International Brotherhood of Teamsters found a receptive audience of workers fed up with low pay, a high rate of injury and unresponsive management at a Walmart distribution center in Searcy, Arkansas. Nearly half of the 415 employees at Searcy signed union cards. On the eve of the vote, after delaying it for years, Sam Walton and his brother Bud parachuted into the facility and threatened to fire workers, eliminate profit sharing and close the facility (all in violation of labour law). The Teamsters lost the vote by a more than 3-to-1 margin, and pro-union employees were fired.[59] But having been spooked, Walmart elevated its drivers 'to something resembling a labor aristocracy' by paying them union-scale wages, giving them high-quality equipment and no longer requiring them to load and unload their trailers. As a result, annual turnover among Walmart truckers declined to single digits and it achieved an 'astounding' on-time store delivery rate of 99.8 per cent.[60]

In 2000, when UFCW organized nine butchers in a Texas Walmart into a bargaining unit, the company eliminated all meat cutters at several hundred US supercenters, which was 'almost certainly a form of illegal retaliation'. The same year when UFCW filed a petition to prepare an NLRB election for 18 tire-and-lube workers in a Kingman, Arizona store, Walmart dispatched a labour team within 24 hours, eventually flooding the store with more than 20 outside managers. Regular staff 'watched anti-union videos and attended near-daily captive meetings', a new set of cameras were trained on the tire-and-lube shop, and hourly managers were told they were part of management and required to report any union activity despite repeated NLRB rulings against this tactic. After the 'UFCW organizing drive collapsed in inglorious defeat … the labor board eventually ruled, at Kingman and elsewhere, that Walmart had systematically harassed and spied upon numerous workers, that it had threatened employees with a loss of benefits and raises if they supported the union, and that the company had fired key labor partisans outright'.[61] In 2005 another UFCW organizing drive in a Colorado store wilted after Walmart 'employed its sophisticated array of anti-union tactics that go to the very brink of what weak U.S. labour law allows'.[62]

The Walmart effect on unionized workers was clearly seen after it announced in 2002 it would build 40 supercenters in California. Since Walmart has 'a decisive competitive advantage' over supermarkets when it comes to labour costs, wages and benefits, Safeway and Kroger used the mere announcement as an excuse 'to chop wages, and reduce retirement and healthcare benefits'. In October 2003 more than 59,000 workers with the UFCW went on strike or were locked out for 145 days. The strike leaders 'made a hash of the epic confrontation', which ended 'in a decisive defeat' after the union accepted a two-tier wage structure, smaller pensions and higher healthcare premiums and expenses. The lesson for the entire labour movement was ominous: 'union organizing and collective bargaining …

were ineffective, if not obsolete, in that huge sector of the economy where Walmart cast such a large shadow'.[63]

OUR Walmart is thus the third phase of UFCW attempts to organize Walmart workers, incorporating lessons from past union drives and recent corporate campaigns. One source explained why the union has scrapped traditional organizing, 'We would lose, and even if we won Walmart would close the store, fire the workers and thumb its nose at the rulings'. OUR Walmart avoids the trap of a traditional NLRB election by striking over 'unfair labour practices', the same innovative tactics used by the United Electrical, Radio and Machine Workers of America (UE) involvement in the Warehouse Workers Organizing Committee to unionize Walmart warehouses west of Chicago and SEIU's 'Fight for 15' campaign to organize low-wage workers in cities nationwide. Labour law allows companies to 'permanently replace' workers who strike over economic issues or for union recognition, but not those who picket over unfair labour practices. Although all three campaigns admit companies have fired pro-labour workers, particularly after the walkouts, this tactic has nevertheless enabled workers to conduct strikes in which they returned to their jobs, establishing credibility among co-workers that collective on-the-job action is possible without immediate retaliation, thereby increasing the possibility of larger actions in the future. Notably, all three campaigns are influenced by community-level workers centres and Occupy Wall Street.[64]

The UFCW along with SEIU broke from the AFL-CIO to form the Change to Win labour federation in 2005, and OUR Walmart includes former SEIU organizers who were hired because of their experience with corporate campaigns, which is 'a multidimensional campaign that attacks an adversary from every conceivable angle, creating relentless pressure on multiple individual and institutional targets'.[65] One union staffer says that when the UFCW and SEIU organized corporate campaigns in the mid-2000s like Walmart Watch and Wake-Up Walmart, this was designed to force the company to 'agree to some form of organizing conduct, or at least tarnish their brand and make it harder for them to expand into other markets. Those campaigns were geared toward public-relations strategies, anti-trust work, targeting the company's vulnerabilities in relation to the gender discrimination lawsuit. Unfortunately there was not enough of a worker base.' By contrast,

OUR Walmart is a non-traditional model using traditional union tactics with lots of union resources but it's not creating a dynamic where the company can call for an election and then crush the organizing attempt in that store. There are corporate campaign elements targeting the company's expansion into urban markets, its attempts to rebrand itself as green and socially responsible. It's counter-marketing that benefits significantly from workers who can carry that message. Workers are organizing but they're not seeking to gain majority recognition status in any worksite. They're calling on the company to hear the concerns that they're raising, but they have to be very careful about not making union demands around economics. The strikes over the last year are unfair labour practice strikes based on retaliation against workers who are exercising their rights to speak out about those issues.

Spread across hundreds of stores, OUR Walmart is a classic example of 'minority unionism', in which a core of passionate, militant workers can exert pressure across the whole company, win demands and attract more workers to their movement, slowly building their ranks until they can win an election. To this point, it's been more effective than previous unionization drives. One union staffer says: 'It's succeeded in placing Walmart at the center of the debate about the low-income economy, worker rights, fairness and equity in the workplace and just what it's like trying to be a low-income worker in today's economy'. The strikes are historic as there's 'never been a group of workers at Walmart that have engaged in this type of action. It has been very important in capturing the imagination of the Walmart workforce and the public', and it appears to have had an impact, along with the Bangladesh factory collapse and fires, in Walmart's declining reputation among consumers. Despite lacking 'anywhere the numbers to affect retail operations', this union staffer says that OUR Walmart 'continues to be a thriving organization that can engage with company officials in a public way and raise issues that resonate with a significant part of the workforce'.

OUR Walmart faces an uphill climb, however. Walmart treated the first strike cautiously in October 2012, circulating a memo that told salaried managers strikes were generally 'protected concerted activity', and not to discipline associates for walking off the job or discussing work stoppages on break time.[66] In advance of Black Friday, Walmart filed charges with the NLRB to stop OUR Walmart picketing, claiming the UFCW was engaged in illegal representational actions. In January 2013, in order 'to avert likely charges from regulators that it engaged in weeks of illegal picketing at Walmart stores', the UFCW announced it was not trying to unionize Walmart.[67] Since then all its communications have included a disclaimer like: 'UFCW and OUR Walmart have no intent to have Walmart recognize or bargain with UFCW or OUR Walmart as the representative of Walmart employees'.[68] Because labour law 'requires the NLRB to prioritize employers' allegations of illegal picketing over other charges', injunctions against picketing are usually issued within days while workers who are fired for union activity usually languish months without remedy.[69]

Around the time of the June 2013 shareholder meeting, Walmart started firing and disciplining OUR Walmart members, and by late June the worker organization claimed the company had retaliated against 36 members, including 11 who were fired.[70] As a UFCW source put it: 'We're now going to have a new test of the NLRB to see if they respond in a timely fashion and reinstate workers who appear to have been illegally fired, and if they don't then this more adaptive tactic of striking over ULP and U.S. labour law may prove ineffective in the face of Walmart's aggression. ... We've yet to see the board do anything substantive to protect Walmart workers.' There's also the issue of top-down organizing strategy. While OUR Walmart foot soldiers like Gabriel are on the front lines recruiting and organizing other workers, it's doubtful they have input in a strategy determined by lawyers, pollsters, senior union officials and outside consultants like ASGK Public Strategies, 'the media and branding firm started by David Axelrod, a senior political adviser to President Obama'. According to *Bloomberg Businessweek*, ASGK conducted 'opinion research about how to effectively reach Walmart employees', decided to use social media, 'helped name the movement and craft' the logo, and determined that the campaign should recruit 'dedicated employees' whose chief complaints included a lack of respect from managers and low wages.[71]

ORGANIZING THE WAREHOUSE

Like OUR Walmart, the Chicago-area Warehouse Workers for Justice (WWJ) was set up by a union, in this case UE. Unlike OUR Walmart, WWJ is explicitly a workers centre that aims to educate workers about 'workplace rights, unite warehouse workers to defend their rights on the job, build community support for the struggles of warehouse workers and fight for policy changes to improve the lives of warehouse workers and members of our communities'.[72] The union established WWJ after UE Local 1110 successfully occupied a windows factory in 2008, winning back pay owed to more than 200 workers. The Warehouse Workers Organizing Committee, with about 300 active members, is also backed by UE and since 2009 has served as the labour-organizing arm to WWJ's community activism. Leah Fried, spokesperson for Warehouse Workers for Justice, explains that UE (for whom she is a staffer) is taking a long-haul approach in working with the WWOC. The UE-led campaign is also noteworthy for its commitment to developing rank-and-file organization, leadership and democracy, with workers deciding the tactics and broader strategy. The UE's decision to create a strike fund for non-unionized workers is a very rare and especially important step in the North American labour movement.

WWOC focuses on organizing in the warehouses located in Will County, Illinois, where some 30,000 clerks, truck drivers, material movers and package handlers work. The Chicago-Naperville-Joliet metropolitan area is the only place in North America where six class I railroads converge along with four interstate highways. Walmart relies on two intermodal facilities with 3.4 million square feet of space to process a phenomenal 70 per cent of its imported goods sold in the United States.[73] The four warehouse workers I interviewed all temped in a Walmart warehouse in Will County, IL. James, who helped organize workers there, says Walmart uses subcontractors to shield it from liability: 'Walmart owns the warehouse, Schneider Logistics runs it, subcontracts for labor to Roadlink Workforce Solutions, and Roadlink will then subcontract some workers to other temp agencies'. He says, 'The strategy is to build a militant minority union, and over many years to build density because of the high turnover'. Joseph says they want to eliminate the temp agencies and get directly hired by Schneider because 'it's much more vulnerable to a union drive. It's much more difficult for Walmart to cut their ties with them.' Workers say after UE first started organizing 'Schneider raised wages and improved benefits'.

Matters came to head in 2012 with a 21-day strike by 38 workers, about 10 per cent of the workforce there. James says it began 'in mid-September when about 40 to 50 workers from two docks were delivering a petition to Roadlink. A supervisor charged with a forklift, cut off half the group and threatened to fire the rest if they kept going. The petition had basic things like living wage, safety, face masks and shin guards, set hours per day.' After a confrontation with management, the workers went out on strike, which was unplanned, but eventually drew substantial support, including a march of 600 people followed by civil disobedience in early October. The combination of bad publicity for Walmart as well as claims that $8 million was lost as a result of management's decision to close the warehouse led Roadlink to agree to let the workers return.[74]

Prior to this, rank-and-file organizers built a core group with tactics like handing out 'know your rights' flyers, which Mike says helped 'people get over scared of being fired'. Joseph, who was active in Occupy Wall Street, took a position in the warehouse specifically for the purpose of organizing. He says 'Pointing to space heaters that cost $65 each, talking about how many there are, how much Walmart makes is a really effective way to explain you're being stolen from. "So in five minutes we've unloaded enough for a day's pay".' Organizing softball games provided an opportune place to bend coworkers' ears outside the workplace. Once the strike occurred UE, in a highly unorthodox gesture, gave 'picket pay' of $200 a week to workers not even in the union. Bailey says, 'We considered ourselves union, but were not part of a recognized union. None of it would have been possible without WWJ being there.'

James says while few workers were 'actively anti-union', the company used plants and spies to sow fear and disrupt organizing. Mike says rank-and-file organizers would 'share notes on people we thought were spies. We really watched what we said around them.' James says 'the real problem is most people have so much shit on their plate they don't have time to organize. They're dealing with children, taking care of parents, paying off a mortgage, the car just broke down. They're homeless, recovering from an addiction.' Another issue says Mike, 'More than anti-union, there's a lot of ignorance and misinformation about unions'.

Joseph says the strike 'was a huge bonding experience, there was a lot of pride. We had consolidated and done something, the bosses were afraid of us.' After they returned to work they were put on the same dock. As the workforce is over 80 per cent Black and Latino, and strikers were mostly white, managers tried to divide workers along racial lines. Mike says, 'We're already divided, so there was definitely a sense from Black workers that it's those crazy white kids on strike'. Joseph adds, 'Schneider keeps the line divided. They don't like the temps talking to the direct hires.' But returning gave the strikers credibility. Joseph says, 'We went in with another petition and it went faster. People were much more aware of their rights and were not afraid to sign their names like the first time. We should have taken our time when we went back in to develop the conversations, but we were also under pressure. For those not striking there was lots of confusion, questions, misunderstandings, fear.'

Ultimately, says Joseph, the warehouse is 'still the same shop floor. You're in physical confrontation with your bosses. There's someone breathing down your neck telling you to work faster all the time. You're all mad together. It could lead to the kind of militancy that you don't get in other sectors.' But he argues workers internalize precarity: 'The job creates a feeling of insecurity, dispensability. You have to accept that I work here in this warehouse and I'm going to make this job better no matter how long it takes. The general attitude among workers is the job is temporary.'

James notes, 'There is rudimentary class consciousness. The workers are aware of their own conditions, and how economic forces affect them. But expanding it to how this affects all the working class, and I should unite with them, not even close.' Mike adds, 'A majority of the workers see management as the enemy. I was surprised by how many people would say, "Fuck the Waltons". But they … don't realize what could be accomplished with collective bargaining. They feel powerless in their own country, what can they do across the ocean?' In his view militant solidarity gives labour its power. 'You can't wait on the NLRB to reinstate your jobs. You have to organize the shop floor so if anyone gets fired or threatened for organizing everyone should walk off the job. That's the way it's always been done. It's a cat-and-mouse game.' After returning to work the four were among nine workers illegally fired for union activity in November by Roadlink. The NLRB ruled in their favor, but Roadlink had not settled the case as of July 2013. As Roadlink's contract with Schneider ended April 30, Bailey points out it has to compensate workers only for back pay up to April 30, and if anyone found a job in the meantime that's when the back pay ends. 'Labor law is extremely weak. It's a completely rigged system in the favor of the employer.' he laments. Most are also part of a separate class-action suit charging wage theft.[75] Mike says, 'For now it appears the company won. They got the organizers out of the warehouse. Even if we win and get our back pay and jobs reinstated, they put an end to the organizing for a while.'

Joseph is more optimistic. 'I don't feel defeated. In the warehouse it's like organizing sand. We learned a lot from the first attempt. You have to build relationships and trust' before you build class solidarity. Indeed, Joseph is essentially reviving an old form of labour organizing known as 'colonizing' or 'salting', in which militant pro-labour activists take jobs 'organizing the unorganized' from the inside. This strategy was used effectively in the '30s and to a lesser degree in the '70s in heavy industry. As Steve Early notes in a forthcoming book, nothing can replace salting 'in teaching young organizers, largely from a non-working-class background, what the working class is about and how to talk and especially listen to workers. Salting needs to become fashionable again for young people politically committed to reinvigorating the labor movement.'[76]

'FIGHT FOR 15'

The SEIU's 'Fight for 15' campaign kicked off in November 2012 when about 200 workers joined 'a day of walkouts and rallies at dozens of Burger King, Taco Bell, Wendy's, McDonald's and other fast-food restaurants' in New York City and by the summer of 2013 similar walkouts had spread to 10 cities total with a coordinated national strike planned for July 2013.[77] According to *Labor Notes*, the campaign is 'part of a coordinated effort by SEIU, which has been providing funds as part of its two-year-old project "Fight for a Fair Economy"'. The Fight for 15 campaign mobilizes community groups, clergy, politicians and unions in the same manner as corporate campaigns and worker centres. Most target cities have a 'Workers Organizing Committee' that brings the workers together, but SEIU provides strategic direction, funding and hires the paid organizers, 8 to 12 per city, except in New York, which has 40 organizers devoted to the effort. Reports claim the New York Communities for Change (a successor to the ACORN community group in that city) is organizing workers. But SEIU is behind this, with NYCC and funds the organizers. In fact, one labour organizer in New York confided that the organizers themselves were discussing forming their own union because of low wages and 60-hour work weeks.[78]

SEIU organizers say after finding 'large majorities' in favor of unionization in New York and Chicago, the first two cities targeted, the project was expanded and similar one-day walkouts have occurred in Detroit, St. Louis, Milwaukee, Washington, D.C. and Seattle, while similar campaigns were being nurtured in Arizona, Colorado and South Carolina. In addition to agitating for $15 an hour, more than double the federal minimum wage of $7.25 in 2013, the campaign wants to ensure workers can organize without fear of retaliation and to stop the employer practice of shorting workers hours or overtime pay, common forms of 'wage theft'. A report by the SEIU-funded Fast Food Forward found 84 per cent of 500 workers surveyed in New York City were victims of wage theft.[79] SEIU is using an industrial union approach that welcomes any low-wage workers who work for chains in apparel, retail, drug stores, convenience stores, discounters or similar enterprises.

Fight for 15 draws on a December 2009 SEIU proposal, 'A Plan for Organizing Post-Labor Law Reform'.[80] After spending $450 million during the 2008 election cycle, unions were banking on Obama to secure passage of the Employee Free Choice Act, which would have legalized card-check unionization, imposed binding mediation if contract talks stalemated and enhanced penalties against employers who illegally retaliated against workers.[81] Eyeing 40 million low-wage workers, SEIU saw EFCA as 'the best opportunity the union has had in decades to once and for all turn the tide in favor of America's workers', but the act died in the Senate in 2010 after being sidelined by Obama.[82] Nonetheless, the 2009 plan appears to guide current strategy. It proposed concentrating on one or two geographic areas before expanding. Cities were chosen for 'favorable local political environment and workforce composition', and targets limited to 7 to 10 of the largest chains. The campaign aimed to build support for workers via extensive community outreach and work 'with prominent local elected officials, deploying the call for 'a living wage' as a vehicle to build momentum, including by building worker lists and identifying potential leaders who would potentially support collective bargaining. One SEIU organizer outlines the thinking behind the drive:

> The labor movement is dying. The only way to turn it around is by organizing the low-wage sector. How do we organize outside the traditional NLRB model? How do we build minority unions to fight? Rather than sitting back and waiting for the government to say you're a union, we say we're a union. Labor is often afraid of using the strike, we're using the strike to try to win. Can we create a crisis? Let's set the bar high: $15 an hour and the right to form a union without retaliation. Post-Occupy, how do we start something in cities like New York, Seattle, Chicago, Detroit, can we inspire other cities as well? Can we build a toolkit for a small town in Kansas to do a strike themselves?

SEIU has apparently devoted the equivalent of 100 to 200 full-time staff to the project, which is in line with the 2009 proposal. There's an attempt to try to create an Occupy-like uprising, which is one reason why SEIU is not taking centre stage. Given the ambitious scope of the campaign and SEIU's top-down organizing style where strategy is kept under wraps, there is considerable speculation as to the real goals. No one believes wages will suddenly leap to $15 an hour. One organizer says workers know this. 'They want to make $15 an hour, but they realize that's not going to happen overnight. It doesn't hurt that President Obama has talked about raising the minimum wage, but not a single worker thinks $9 is nearly enough.' Some organizers think 'SEIU will strike a deal like in the healthcare industry where they agree to organize one city, but nowhere else'. But another organizer responds, 'That would be a high-quality problem. We're not even close to that'. Steve Early, the author of *The Civil Wars in US Labor*, points out that it was the SEIU model to unionize nursing homes, but only because it could convince employers, 'We can add value, we're going to be a corporate partner by lobbying for more money in the state legislature'.[83]

Bill Fletcher Jr., who heads the National Retail Justice Alliance, a UFCW-backed think tank and advocacy group, hints the $15 an hour slogan is misleading: 'If the objective is really to raise the minimum wage, it's important that workers know that that's what they're fighting for'.[84] Indeed, Fight for 15 revives criticisms of SEIU, such as its disdain for internal democracy. One organizer describes the cross currents:

A lot of these folks are pissed off and have been struggling for all of their lives, for some it's a generational thing. This campaign is giving them a spark of hope for a better life in America. We've had over a hundred workers in the room. Enthusiasm is high, but everyone's on edge. The workers have day-to-day issues, family stuff, paying rent. They're all scared if they lose their bread and butter they'll be out on the street in two weeks. The agenda is pretty top-down, such as strike dates. The organizers say, 'All the other cities have decided to go on strike on this date, do you want to join them?' And the workers are like, 'Yeah!' Do I think it's ideal? No. But do I have any better ideas? No, and that's the problem.

Speaking of protests at fast-food shareholder meetings the same organizer says, 'They shuffle the workers in, shuffle them out, tell them what to say, what makes the best story for the media, not necessarily what the truth is'. SEIU organizers say the union campaign 'is looking at models of minority unionism and worker centers with the workers driving the fight'. But even more than UFCW, SEIU treats minority unionism as a tactic, rather than a strategy, taking a bureaucratic, even corporate approach. Workers' centers and a few unions send 'salts' into workplaces to build rank-and-file democracy, worker consciousness and organic leaders. This contrasts with SEIU which is 'very quick to hire organizers and turn them into full-time doorknockers'.[85] This creates a disconnect as organizers are often unaware of day-to-day issues facing workers or downplay them in favour of strategy determined by a remote leadership. The fact that organizers were guessing as to the strategy shows how removed they are from the decision-making, and workers even more so.

There is obvious overlap between the Fight for 15 campaign and SEIU's earlier Fight for a Fair Economy initiative in 2011 to mobilize 'mostly low-wage minority workers in 10 to 15 cities' with high numbers of SEIU members and threatened by cuts to the public sector. Steve Early explained that Fight for a Fair Economy never achieved much visibility. 'The campaign looked good on paper, but was top-down, staff-driven and [had] a consultant-shaped message that was boilerplate union rhetoric'.[86] Early also criticized SEIU's tendency to jump from one campaign to the next, while one former SEIU organizer who praised the low-wage worker campaign nevertheless fretted that the union was 'fickle', and 'subject to entering and leaving a project at whim, given its panic and lack of anything like consistent social vision, its internecine fights exemplary of paranoia, its fear of its own membership and failed track record of cultivating member consciousness'. One organizer is worried the union will call off the campaign if it isn't working, leaving the workers in the lurch, and another organizer indicates SEIU may pull the plug within two years if it's not meeting expectations: 'The money going into this is a gamble. These workers aren't paying dues; they're not financing this right now.'[87] At the same time, workers have notched victories in cities like Chicago, where workers report pay increase of 10 cents to $2 an hour, more regular scheduling, increased hours, improved break rooms and better treatment from managers.[88]

A LABOUR RENAISSANCE?
BEYOND WORKERS CENTRES AND OCCUPY

It is notable that in all three campaigns discussed above, the unions place themselves in the background, downplaying their involvement. While unions have a 51 per cent favourability rating in polls, only 20 per cent of the public expresses confidence in them, slightly behind banks, televised news and big business. At the same time, Blacks and Hispanics combined are twice as favourable toward unions as unfavourable, and women nearly 50 per cent more favourable, while men and whites are almost exactly evenly split.[89] In this light it's logical to organize sectors that are disproportionately female and people of colour.[90] There is no doubt, in this respect, that the new union campaigns reflect the influence of workers' centres. These are new types of community-based, rather than workplace-based, organizations that support low-wage workers by raising wages, improving working conditions, advocating for immigration reform and addressing issues like housing, education and healthcare for immigrant communities, which can be considered a revival of social unionism.[91] They've grown from five nationwide in 1992 to 139 by 2005, 88 per cent of which work 'specifically with immigrants', and emphasize 'leadership development and democratic decision-making'.[92] Worker centres also organize across borders, often through the supply chain of a corporation, and ally with religious, governmental, community and labour organizations. Seeing the growth and opportunity afforded by workers centres, 'the AFL-CIO has formal partnerships with the National Day Worker Organizing Network, Interfaith Worker Justice, the Domestic Workers Alliance and the National Guestworkers Alliance'.[93]

But workers' centres are a far cry from the type of labour organization that can unionize millions of workers, as the CIO did in the 1930s. At a time when their proportion of the workforce has fallen to under 12 per cent, the lowest in almost a century, Early says if the 14.3 million US workers in unions had 'a movement worth its salt [there wouldn't] be any need for foundation-funded worker centers'.[94] He sees an inherent problem with them: 'They have very high turnover. People pay dues, get active for a while, but then they get another job. If people aren't paying dues to a workers center, how is it their organization? The organizations workers do pay dues to are hard enough to control'. However, Early also notes that one advantage of workers' centres is that they 'organize without regard to employer, industry wide'. Insofar as big initiatives like Fight for 15 are 'following the worker center model', Early says, 'unions are finally taking a creative approach ... but it's also a recognition that traditional labor organizing is all but dead'. Unions have an advantage in being able to marshal money, organizers and public support to allow for these strike waves. 'It allows workers to walk out for a day and there's enough community pressure so that the workers keep their jobs.'

One of the most significant influences on new labour organizing has been Occupy Wall Street as it opened space for militancy and creative actions. When activists occupied Zuccotti Park near Wall Street on 17 September 2011, organized labour was absent, but unions quickly climbed aboard as Occupy spread like wildfire. Unions provided Occupy camps around the country with camping supplies, office space and even a small park for the Charleston, West Virginia group. Jackie DiSalvo, a New York labour activist and retired professor, said labour gave 'Occupy a broader constituency than the young people sleeping in Zuccotti who were precarious workers, unemployed or students'. When New York Mayor Michael Bloomberg attempted to shut down the camp in October 2011, hundreds of union members joined the thousands who showed up to successfully defend the park. In numerous cities organizers say Occupy influenced labour talks, such as in Philadelphia, where 1,000 staff at a major arts centre and 2,500 office cleaners in 100 corporate hi-rises won better-than-expected contracts. In New York City, Occupy activists joined with Teamsters to thwart union busting by the Sotheby's auction house and participated in the Laundry Workers Center campaign that helped 23 mostly undocumented workers at the Hot and Crusty bakery chain win union recognition after they briefly occupied their workplace and the sidewalk in front of a Manhattan outlet. Most dramatically, Occupy Oakland in 12 days went from its first public action to drawing tens of thousands of people into the streets for a general strike endorsed by local unions.[95]

Labour groups and workers also adopted the tactic of occupying public space in continuous protest. In Freeport, Illinois, Sensata Technologies workers, aided by SEIU organizers, erected an Occupy-style camp outside their factory during the 2012 election campaign. Protesting the transfer of 170 jobs and the physical factory to China by the private equity firm

Bain Capital, which Mitt Romney co-founded, the workers drew national support and backing from dozens of unions and Occupy movements. In West Virginia, retirees with an average age of 70 have set up an 'Occupy Century Aluminum' outpost in two consecutive years, first for 75 days in the winter of 2012, to protest the company's cancellation of their health benefits. A more radical approach has been taken by the SEIU-backed 'We Are Oregon' community organization, which supports homeowners in foreclosure who stay in their homes, and has even helped families re-occupy homes after being evicted. In fact, it was a labour struggle that presaged the Occupy movement. In 2008 workers with UE Local 1110 in Chicago illegally occupied their window-making factory after being laid off without proper notice, and again in 2012, eventually forming the worker-owned New Era Windows Cooperative. After their 2008 occupation became a national sensation, a group of workers embarked on a national tour to spark more militant labour action, but as local 1110 president Armando Robles admits they found that other workers were reluctant to engage in any actions that might be illegal.[96]

A few high-profile incidents soured many Occupiers on working with labour. In West Coast cities attempts by Occupiers to stage actions at ports led to conflicts with West Coast longshore workers. In Los Angeles many Occupiers claimed labour organizers tried to hijack the movement by setting up an alternative occupation. And in New York City on 17 November 2011, days after police evicted the Occupation, unions led a march of 30,000 protesters into Brooklyn while Occupiers wanted to use the numbers to march on Wall Street and potentially retake the park. But Occupy also failed to create an organizational infrastructure that could mobilize a mass constituency around inequality or labour issues.

If organized labour is to have a renaissance it has to go far beyond selectively picking from a buffet of activist tactics. It needs to revive tactics like sit-down strikes that enabled a new labour formation such as the CIO to exploit the organizing possibilities of the '30s and '40s, whereas the conservative AFL fumbled numerous opportunities. Of course, it was spurred by pressures from below reflecting greater rank-and-file democracy, and further aided by broad public support, sympathetic politicians and media, and new labour laws like the NLRA. There is all too little like this visible today. This is not to say organized labour is doomed, but its resurrection is unlikely to come from unions that have presided over more than half a century of decline. It will depend on the rebirth of a strong left in large enough numbers, with a vision that points the way beyond wages and consumption to economic democracy, to spur militant class consciousness and create the social space for it to spread.

NOTES

1   The data in this paragraph were gleaned from Walmart *2013 Annual Report*, pp. 17-20; *Walmart U.S. Stores*, available at corporate.walmart.com; 'Supply Chain Graphic of the Week: A Detailed Look at Walmart Statistics in Chart Form', *Supply Chain Digest*, 1 August 2012, available at www.scdigest.com; Linton Weeks, 'Is Walmart a Magnet for American Mayhem?', National Public Radio, 14 September 2011, available at www.npr.org; 'NRF Forecasts Retail Industry Sales Growth of 3.4 Percent in 2012', National Retail Federation, 16 January 2012, available at www.nrf.com; Elizabeth Flock, 'Walmart heirs net worth equals total of bottom 30 percent of Americans', *The Washington Post*, 9 December 2011; Charles Fishman, *The Walmart Effect: How the World's Most Powerful Company Really Works – and How It's Transforming the American Economy*, New York: Penguin, 2011, p. 7; Josh Bivens, 'Inequality exhibit A: Walmart and the wealth of American families', Economic Policy Institute, 17 July 2012, available at www.epi.org.

2   Stephanie Clifford, 'Walmart Strains to Keep Aisles Fresh Stocked', *The New York Times*, 3 April 2013.

3   Renee Dudley, 'Walmart Faces the Cost of Cost-Cutting: Empty Shelves', *Bloomberg Businessweek*, 28 March 2013. *The New York Times* reported that other confidential memos indicated similar problems such as poor stocking, poor quality and low consumer confidence: see Clifford, 'Walmart Strains'.

4   Nelson Lichtenstein, *The Retail Revolution: How Walmart Created a Brave New World of Business*, New York: Metropolitan Books, 2009, p. 35. See also 'Comparable Store Sales', Walmart, June 2013, available at stock.walmart.com.

5   Alice Hines and Christina Wilkie, 'Walmart's Internal Compensation Documents Reveal Systematic Limit on Advancement', *The Huffington Post*, 16 November 2012, available at www.huffingtonpost.com.

6   John Marshall, 'The High Price of Low Cost: The View from the Other Side of Walmart's "Productivity Loop"', *Making Change at Walmart*, 2011, p. 10, available at makingchangeatwalmart.org.

7   Misha Petrovic and Gary G. Hamilton, 'Making Global Markets: Walmart and Its Suppliers', in Nelson Lichtenstein, ed., *Walmart: The Face of Twenty-First Century Capitalism*, New York: The New Press, 2006, pp. 110-5.

8   Anita Chan, ed., *Walmart in China*, Ithaca: Cornel University, 2011, p. 2; see also Anthony Bianco, *Walmart: The Bully of Bentonville*, New York: Currency, 2006, p. 13.

9   Edna Bonacich and Jake B. Wilson, *Getting the Goods: Ports, Labor and the Logistics Revolution*, Ithaca: Cornell University Press, 2008, p. 7.

10   Petrovic and Hamilton, 'Making Global Markets, p. 110.

11   See Nelson Lichtenstein, 'Walmart's Long March to China', in *Walmart in China*, pp. 21-2; Bonacich, *Getting the Goods*, pp. 4-5; Petrovic and Hamilton, 'Making Global Markets', p. 111; Fishman, *The Walmart Effect*, p. 83.

12   Bethany Moreton, *To Serve God and Wal-Mart: The Making of Christian Free Enterprise*, Cambridge, MA: Harvard University Press, 2009, pp. 24-40; Lichtenstein, *The Retail Revolution*, pp. 53-84.

13 For Blacks, a 'Sundown town' was literally a town where they may have been in physical danger if still there after sundown. Many towns literally had signs posted at their limits reading, 'Nigger, Don't Let The Sun Go Down On You In ___'. Lichtenstein, *The Retail Revolution*, pp. 39, 62-4, 89-90. See also James W. Loewen, *Sundown Towns: A Hidden Dimension of American Racism*, New York: The New Press, 2005; and Moreton, *To Serve God and Walmart*, pp. 49-65, 84. Walmart also claims to employ more than 169,000 'Hispanic associates'. See 'Our People', Walmart, available at corporate.walmart.com.

14 Arindrajit Dube, Barry Eidlin and Bill Lester, Institute of Industrial Relations Working Paper Series, 'Impact of Walmart Growth on Earnings throughout the Retail Sector in Urban and Rural Counties', University of California at Berkeley, 2005, p. 3, available at economics.ucr.edu.

15 Clarence Y. H. Lo, *Small Property Versus Big Government: Social Origins of the Property Tax Revolt*, Berkeley: University of California Press, 1990; Barnaby J. Feder, 'Walmart's Expansion Aided by Many Taxpayer Subsidies', *The New York Times*, 24 May 2004; David Cay Johnston, 'Study Says Walmart Often Fights Local Taxes', *The New York Times*, 10 October 2007.

16 See Lichtenstein, *The Retail Revolution*, pp. 36-9; 125-6, 141; Matthew Boyle and Duane D. Stanford, 'Walmart to End Employee Profit-Sharing in February', *Bloomberg Businessweek*, 9 October 2010.

17 Wade Rathke, 'A Walmart Workers Association? An Organizing Plan', in *Walmart*, pp. 268-70.

18 Fishman, *The Walmart Effect*, pp. 3-9.

19 Jerry Hausman and Ephraim Leibtag, 'Consumer Benefits from Increased Competition in Shopping Outlets: Measuring the Effect of Walmart', National Bureau of Economic Research, Working Paper 11809, December 2005, available at www.nber.org. Hausman and Leibtag also claim a bias against using Walmart in inflation data causes the US government to overstate increases in the Consumer Price Index by 15 per cent. Jerry Hausman and Ephraim Leibtag, 'CPI Bias from Supercenters: Does the BLS Know that Walmart Exists?', National Bureau of Economic Research, August 2004, p. 29. Another analysis concludes prices decline 1.5-3 per cent in the short run and 7-13 per cent in the longer run, Emek Basker, 'Selling a Cheaper Mousetrap: Walmart's Effect on Retail Prices', *Journal of Urban Economics*, 58(2), September 2005.

20 Michael Schrage, 'Walmart Trumps Moore's Law', *MIT Technology Review*, 1 March 2002, available at www.technologyreview.com.

21 'Walmart U.S. to Create more than 22,000 Jobs in 2009', Walmart.com, 4 June 2009, available at news.Walmart.com.

22 David Neumark, Junfu Zhang and Stephen Ciccarella, 'The effects of Walmart on local labor markets', *Journal of Urban Economics*, 63, 2008, available at socsci. uci.edu. See also Dube, Eidlin and Lester's 'Impact of Walmart Growth', esp. pp. 1, 28-30.

23 Tim Sullivan, 'In bitter strike, grocery workers lost ground', *High Country News*, 7 June 2004, available at www.hcn.org; Stephanie Clifford, 'Big Retailers Fill More Aisles With Groceries', *The New York Times*, 16 January 2011.

24 Arindrajit Dube, T. William Lester, Barry Eidlin, 'A Downward Push: The

Impact of Wal-Mart Stores on Retail Wages and Benefits', UC Berkeley Center for Labor Education and Research, December 2007, pp. 6-7, available at laborcenter.berkeley.edu.

25   Jared Bernstein, L. Josh Bivens, and Arindrajit Dube, 'Wrestling with Walmart: Trade-offs Between Profits, Prices and Wages', Economic Policy Institute, 15 June 2006, pp. 4-5. For example, median gross rents rose 45 per cent from 1970 to 2000 in inflation-adjusted dollars. 'Historical Census of Housing Tables: Gross Rents', available at www.census.gov.

26   Fishman, *The Walmart Effect*, pp. 69-70.

27   Fishman, *The Walmart Effect*, pp. 163-6.

28   Charles Courtemanche and Art Carden, 'Supersizing Supercenters? The Impact of Walmart Supercenters on Body Mass Index and Obesity', 10 September 2010, p. 29, available at papers.ssrn.com, emphasis in original.

29   Bonacich, *Getting the Goods*, p. 5.

30   Friedrich Engels, 'History of the English Corn Laws', *Telegraph für Deutschland*, December 1845, available at www.marxists.org.

31   Moreton, *To Serve God and Walmart*, pp. 248-63.

32   Nelson D. Schwartz, 'Recovery in U.S. Is Lifting Profits, but Not Adding Jobs', *The New York Times*, 3 March 2013.

33   'Big Business, Corporate Profits, and the Minimum Wage: Executive Summary', National Employment Law Project, July 2012, available at nelp.org. It's unclear if NELP includes farmworkers, and seasonal migrants in the United States, who are an integral part of the Walmart supply chain. One estimate puts their numbers at more than 3 million, with one of the highest poverty rates of any sector at 23 per cent. 'Table B-1. Employees on nonfarm payrolls by industry sector and selected industry detail', Bureau of Labor Statistics, June 2013, available at www.bls.gov. 'Farmworker Health Factsheet', National Center for Farmworker Health, Inc. August 2012.

34   The most precise data are in Carmen DeNavas-Walt, Bernadette D. Proctor, and Jessica C. Smith, 'Income, Poverty and Health Insurance Coverage in the United States: 2011', U.S. Census Bureau, September 2012, pp. 17-24, available at www.census.gov. See also Sabrina Tavernise and Robert Gebeloff, 'New Way to Tally Poor Recasts View of Poverty', *The New York Times*, 8 November 2011; Jason DeParle, Robert Gebeloff and Sabrina Tavernise, 'Older, Suburban, and Struggling, "Near Poor" Startle the Census', *The New York Times*, 18 November 2011; 'Low-Income Working Families: The Growing Economic Gap', The Working Poor Families Project, winter 2012-2013, p. 3, available at www.workingpoorfamilies.org.

35   Courtney Gross, 'Is Walmart Worse?', *Gotham Gazette*, 14 February 2011, available at old.gothamgazette.com.

36   See Alice Hines, 'Walmart's Internal Compensation Documents Reveal Systematic Limit on Advancement'; Sam's Club, 'Field Non-Exempt Associate Pay Plan FY 2013', *The Huffington Post*, 11 February 2012.

37   Hines, 'Walmart's Internal Compensation Documents'.

38   Susan Chambers, 'Reviewing and Revising Walmart's Benefits Strategy: Memorandum to the Board of Directors', Walmart Stores, Inc. Financial Year

2006.

39   Dhanya Skariachan and Jessica Wohl, 'Walmart Only Hiring Temporary
     Workers In Many U.S. Stores', *Reuters*, 13 June 2013.

40   Steven Greenhouse and Michael Barbaro, 'Walmart Memo Suggests Ways to
     Cut Employees Benefit Costs', *The New York Times*, 26 October 2005.

41   Chambers, 'Reviewing and Revising Walmart's Benefits Strategy'

42   Michele Simon, 'Food Stamps: Follow the Money. Are Corporations Profiting
     from Hungry Americans?', *Eat, Drink, Politics*, June 2012, pp. 15-7, available at
     www.eatdrinkpolitics.com. See also Leslie Dach, 'Partnership for a Healthier
     America Remarks', 29 November 2011, available at www.news.Walmart.
     com.

43   Democratic Staff of the U.S. House Committee on Education and the
     Workforce, 'The Low-Wage Drag on Our Economy: Walmart's low wages
     and their effect on taxpayers and economic growth', May 2013, available at
     democrats.edworkforce.house.gov.

44   Stephan J. Goetz and Hema Swaminathan, 'Walmart and County-Wide
     Poverty', Department of Agricultural Economics and Rural Sociology,
     Pennsylvania State University, 18 October 2004, p. 12. This study was later
     published in *Social Science Quarterly*, 87(2), 2006.

45   Lichtenstein, *The Retail Revolution*, p. 8.

46   The interviews were conducted over the phone, with the exception of two
     in person. Most workers asked for anonymity due to fear of losing their
     job or being blacklisted, as such identifying information has been changed.
     Some of the quotes are edited and condensed from the transcript. Nearly two
     dozen other Walmart workers were contacted, including many who said 'I'm
     interested in telling my story', but who did not make or keep appointments
     for interviews. From discussions with interviewees and some who backed out,
     many workers fear retaliation by Walmart or other employers, even though
     they were promised full anonymity.

47   DeNavas-Walt, 'Income, Poverty and Health Insurance Coverage in the
     United States: 2011', pp. 18-9.

48   Jenny Brown, 'In Walmart and Fast Food, Unions Scaling Up a Strike-First
     Strategy', *Labor Notes*, 23 January 2013, available at www.labornotes.org.

49   Paul Harris 'Walmart supply chain: warehouse staff agencies accused of theft',
     The Guardian, 18 October 2012. Bailey told me the same anecdotes when I
     interviewed him by phone.

50   'Women at Work, Women at Risk: Sexual Harassment and Assault in Will
     County Warehouses', Warehouse Workers for Justice, 8 March 2012.

51   Lichtenstein, *The Retail Revolution*, p. 66.

52   Brown, 'In Walmart and Fast Food'; Steven Greenhouse, 'Walmart Workers
     Are Finding a Voice Without a Union', *The New York Times*, 3 September 2005;
     Liza Featherstone, 'Walmart Workers Walk Out', *The Nation*, 17 October
     2012, see also 'Meeting of the Federal Open Market Committee', 10 May
     2006, available at www.federalreserve.gov. The entire Board of Governors,
     including Chair Ben Bernanke and Vice Chair and Treasury Secretary Timothy
     Geithner, were present during the discussion where it was revealed Walmart

was raising wages 'because of all the controversy about Walmart'.

53   Steven Greenhouse and Stephanie Clifford, 'Protests Backed by Union Gets Walmart's Attention', *The New York Times*, 18 November 2012; Josh Eidelson, 'Walmart strikes spread to more states', *Salon*, 9 October 2012; and his 'Walmart punishes its workers', *Salon*, 26 July 2012, available at www. salon.com. See also Featherstone, 'Walmart Workers Walk Out'; and Gabriel Thompson, 'The Big, Bad Business of Fighting Guest Workers Rights', *The Nation*, 3 July 2012.

54   Alice Hines and Kathleen Miles, 'Walmart Strike Hits 100 Cities, But Fails to Distract Black Friday Shoppers', *The Huffington Post*, 23 November 2012; Greenhouse and Clifford, 'Protests Backed by Union Gets Walmart's Attention'; Susan Berfield, 'Walmart vs. Union-Backed OUR Walmart', *Bloomberg Businessweek*, 13 December 2012.

55   'Global Supply Chain Workers Pressure Walmart to Get Serious About Labor Conditions', Warehouse Workers United, 9 April 2013, available at www. warehouseworkersunited.org.

56   Kate Bronfenbrenner, 'No Holds Barred: The Intensification of Employer Opposition to Organizing', Cornell School of Industrial and Labor Relations, 20 May 2009.

57   Carol Pier, 'Discounting Rights: Walmart's Violations of US Workers' Right to Freedom of Association', Human Rights Watch, May 2007, p. 3, available at www.hrw.org.

58   A good summary of how Taft-Hartley Act reshaped organized labour is Rich Yeselson, 'Fortress Unionism', *Democracy*, Summer 2013, available at www. democracyjournal.org.

59   Bianco, *Walmart*, pp. 111-2.

60   Lichtenstein, *The Retail Revolution*, pp. 128-31.

61   The preceding quotes in this paragraph are from Lichtenstein, *The Retail Revolution*, pp. 137, 143-7.

62   Pier, 'Discounting Rights', pp. 100-11.

63   Lichtenstein, *The Retail Revolution*, pp. 135, 230-1. Sullivan, 'In bitter strike, grocery workers lost ground'. *High Country News*, www.hcn.org/issues/276/14795

64   This was confirmed by a dozen union staffers (including ones from all three unions in question) and close observers of the US unions (including Steve Early, Jenny Brown and Ari Paul) that I interviewed.

65   Corporate Campaign, Inc., 'What We Do', available at www. corporatecampaign.org.

66   Walmart, 'Response to Walkout/Work Stoppage – Salaried Management Talking Points', *The Huffington Post*, 8 October 2012.

67   Josh Eidelson, 'Walmart Asks a Judge to Block Historic Strikes', *The Nation*, 19 November 2013; Steven Greenhouse, 'Labor Union to Ease Walmart Picketing', *The New York Times*, 31 January 2013.

68   Organization United for Respect at Walmart, available at www.forrespect.org.

69   Eidelson, 'Walmart Asks a Judge to Block Historic Strikes'.

70   Josh Eidelson, 'Walmart Fires Eleven Strikers in Alleged Retaliation', *The*

Nation, 22 June 2013; Ned Resnikoff, Walmart workers' campaign targets Yahoo's Marissa Mayer', 27 June 2013, MSNBC, available at tv.msnbc.com.

71 Berfield, 'Walmart vs. Union-Backed OUR Walmart'.

72 Warehouse Workers for Justice, available at www.warehouseworker.org.

73 'NAI Hiffman/NAI Global Logistics assists Wal-Mart with a 3.4 Million Square Foot MEGA Distribution Center', available at www.hiffman.com.

74 Micah Uetricht, 'Strike Supporters Shut Down Illinois Walmart Warehouse', *Labor Notes*, 2 October 2012.

75 Josh Eidelson, 'Labor Board Alleges Repeated Retaliation at Walmart's Top US Warehouse', *The Nation*, 20 March 2013; Alexandra Bradbury, 'Walmart Warehouse Strikers Return to Work With Full Back Pay', *Labor Notes*, 9 October 2012. Information on the NLRB case and class-action suit is from a follow-up phone interview with Phillip Bailey, 5 July 2013.

76 Excerpt from *Save Our Unions: Dispatches from a Movement in Distress*, New York: Monthly Review Press, 2014.

77 Steven Greenhouse, 'With Day of Protests, Fast-Food Workers Seek More Pay, *The New York Times*, 29 November 2013.

78 Jenny Brown, 'Fast Food Strikes: What's Cooking?', *Labor Notes*, 24 June 2013; Josh Eidelson, 'In rare strike, NYC fast-food workers walk out', *Salon*, 29 November 2012; 'Strike Wave by Fast Food and Retail Workers Spreads to Chicago', Workers Organizing Committee of Chicago, 24 April 2013, available at www.commondreams.org. An SEIU organizer provided information on the planned national strike. The labour organizer who claims NYCC organizers want to unionize is involved in a different fast-food worker campaign in New York. The Association of Community Organizations for Reform Now was born during the '60s welfare-reform movement and grew into a national organization known for direct-action style campaigns around housing, living-wage and social-welfare issues as well as voter-registration drives. ACORN founder Wade Rathke drafted the initial plan for a Walmart Workers Association. ACORN collapsed in 2010 after a right-wing media sting operation presented flimsy video evidence that low-level employees were advising clients on how to hide criminal financial activity, but this came right after news that ACORN had hushed up nearly $1 million in embezzlement by Rathke's brother Dale in 1999 and 2000. Rathke, 'A Walmart Workers Association? An Organizing Plan'; Stephanie Strom, 'Funds Misappropriated at 2 Nonprofit Groups', *The New York Times*, 9 July 2008.

79 Josh Eidelson, 'Fast food walkout planned in Chicago', *Salon*, 23 April 2013. Fast Food Forward, 'Wage Theft and NYC's Fast Food Workers: New York's Hidden Crime Wave', 2013. Saki Knafo, 'Seattle's Fast-Food Workers Strike as National Movement Begins to Claim Small Victories', *The Huffington Post*, 30 May 2013.

80 'Recommendation to the Property Services Division Leadership Board: A Plan for Organizing Post-Labor Law Reform', SEIU, December 2009.

81 Steven Greenhouse, 'After Push for Obama, Unions Seek New Rules', *The New York Times*, 8 November 2008.

82 Adam Turl, 'Who Killed EFCA', *Socialist Worker*, 23 July 2009.

83   Author interview with Steve Early, 29 May 2013.

84   Brown, 'Fast Food Strikes: What's Cooking?'

85   Steve Early interview, 29 May 2013.

86   Author interview with Steve Early, January 27, 2012.

87   Kris Maher, 'Big Union to Step Up Recruiting', *The Wall Street Journal*, 11 February 2011. Arun Gupta, 'What Occupy taught the unions', *Salon*, 2 February 2012. The email note from the former SEIU organizer was sent to a listerve and the author was forwarded a copy.

88   Ellyn Fortino, 'Chicago Fast Food and Retail Workers Win Victories After April Strike', Progress Illinois, 10 July 2013, available at www.progressillinois.com.

89   Pew Research Center for the People and the Press, 'Favorable Views of Labor, Business Rebound', 27 June 2013, available at www.people-press.org; Elizabeth Mendes and Joy Wilke, 'Americans' Confidence in Congress Falls to Lowest on Record', Gallup Politics, 13 June 2013, available at www.gallup.com.

90   SEIU organizers note that in many cities the percentage of the workforce and strikers who are African American is as high as 90 per cent, and women make up two-thirds of the fast-food workforce. As for Walmart, data turned over in the gender discrimination class-action suit on 3.9 million personnel employed from 1996 to 2002 found that by the end of 2001 sixty-four per cent of active retail positions were filled by women. See Richard Drogin, 'Statistical Analysis of Gender Patterns in Wal-Mart Workforce', Drogin, Kakigi & Associates, February 2003.

91   Charles Post, 'Social Unionism Without the Workplace?', *New Politics*, Winter 2013, available at www.newpol.org.

92   Janice Fine, 'Workers Centers: Organizing communities at the edge of the dream', Economic Policy Institute, 13 December 2005, pp. 2-5.

93   Steve Early, 'Can Workers Centers Fill the Union Void', *New Labor Forum*, Summer 2006, available at www.newlaborforum.cuny.edu; John Garvey, 'The New Worker Organizing', *Insurgent Notes*, 11 March 2013, available at insurgentnotes.com.

94   Author interview with Steve Early. See also Steven Greenhouse, 'Share of the Work Force in a Union Falls to a 97-Year Low, 11.3 percent', *The New York Times*, 23 January 2013.

95   Gupta, 'What Occupy taught the unions'; Steven Greenhouse, 'Occupy Movement Inspires Unions to Embrace Bold Tactics', *The New York Times*, 8 November 2011; Gabriel Thompson, 'Occupy Oakland Calls for a November 2 General Strike', *The Nation*, 1 November 2011; Gayge Operaista, 'The Oakland General Strike, The Days Before, The Days After', Autonomous Struggle of the Glitteriat, 6 November 2011, available at glitteriat.blogspot.com; Nick Pinto, 'Hot and Crusty Bakery Employees Go from Lockout to Victory in One Week', *The Village Voice*, 10 September 2012, available at blogs.villagevoice.com.

96   Arun Gupta, 'What Happened to the Green New Deal, *Truthout*, 16 November 2012, available at www.truth-out.org; Zach Roberts, 'Corporate Giant vs. Retirees in West Virginia', *The Mudflats*, 1 May 2013, available at www. themudflats.net; Arun Gupta, 'Freeport is Not a Democrat vs. Republican Issue', *The Progressive*, 2 November 2012.

RECONSIDERATIONS OF CLASS: PRECARIOUSNESS AS PROLETARIANIZATION

BRYAN D. PALMER

> The positing of the individual as a *worker*,
> in this nakedness, is itself a product of *history*.[1]
>
> Karl Marx

The experience of class conflict, proletarian mobilization, and class consciousness – so clearly visible in 1917-21, 1934-37, and 1946-48 – was very much on the 20th century's calendar again in the mid-1960s, when the *Socialist Register* was founded. Shop stewards movements and discussions of workers' control animated much of the left in the United Kingdom. With the Labour Party in power there was spirited debate aimed at developing a programme for socialist advance, as opposed to the reformist inclination of collapsing strategic sensibility into the cul-de-sac of an incomes policy.[2] In the United States and Canada rising discontent in labour circles took many forms. A mid-1960s wildcat wave was eventually tamed,[3] but was soon followed, into the early 1970s, by much talk of 'blue collar blues' at General Motors plants like the sprawling assembly-line complex in Lordstown, Ohio.[4] Detroit gave birth to the League of Revolutionary Black Workers.[5] The Ben Hamper-designated 'Rivethead' phenomenon of counter-planning on the shop floor was governed less in this period by an individualist credo of escape from work than it was by an edgy class antagonism.[6] May 1968 had witnessed the coming together of workers and students in massive protests in France,[7] while Edward Heath's governing Tories across the channel were toppled in 1974. An upsurge of class conflict in the first four years of the decade beat back anti-union legislation, broke a wage freeze and unleashed militant factory occupations in opposition to plant closures. Two miners' strikes – one in 1972, another in 1974 – finally sealed the fate of the Conservatives. They helped bring the Labour Party back into government, with the militant rhetoric of a 'fundamental shift in class power' advanced by those in its ranks a source of visible discomfort to its tepid leadership.[8]

This 'moment' of class struggle, reaching from 1965-74 was, arguably, labour's last stand in the faltering economic climate of the post-World War II 'long boom' that was obviously winding down. For by the mid-1970s, the terms of trade in the class war had shifted. Working-class victories, registering in militant extra-parliamentary mobilizations of class struggle as well as the incremental creep of union densities that saw, over time, the percentage of the non-agricultural workforce associated with labour organizations climb to 35 per cent even in that bastion of ostensible 'exceptionalism', the United States, slowed, stalled, and sputtered. Oppositional political formations – Militant Tendencies, anarchist collectives and aspiring vanguards of 'new communists' – came into being, made their voices heard and then, all too often, disintegrated. The routine tempo of class conflict downshifted into a climacteric that would, over decades, see union densities plummet to one-third the percentage of earlier, better, times. Working-class combatants almost everywhere had the lifeblood of militancy sucked out of them, and confidence in labour circles waned as the advantage was seized by class adversaries. From 1975 to the present capital has rewritten the script of class relations in the developed capitalist economies of the west, using to good effect a series of deepening and ongoing crises to discipline not only labour, but all dissident forces, drawing on the myriad powers of the state and unleashing material and ideological assaults of unprecedented vigour.

The result: declining material standards of the working class as a whole; the domestication of a once combative trade unionism to a machinery of concession bargaining; a generation of young workers robbed of a sense of class place, its future marked by insecurity, with employment prospects understood to be precarious. Working-class defeats have, after decades of retrenchment, taken on a cumulative character, and the result is a class too often stripped of its seeming capacity to fight, its leadership increasingly characterized by caution and the sensibilities of an ossified officialdom. To be sure, there are, on a global scale, indications of class mobilizations that threaten to break out of these doldrums. Mike Davis writes, for instance, that 'two hundred million Chinese factory workers, miners and construction labourers are the most dangerous class on the planet. (Just ask the State Council in Beijing.) Their full awakening from the bubble may yet determine whether or not a socialist Earth is possible'.[9] Davis's optimism is refreshing, but a certain pessimism may well also be in order. The class consciousness and appetite for militancy within the Chinese proletariat is subject to a number of constraints, including limitations on working-class agency characteristic of class relations forged in the cauldron of a Stalinist-Maoist state moving away from its planned economy roots towards integration into a global capitalist order with which it has yet to fully align.

In any case, the developing world and the nature of its class formations certainly reinforces the contemporary significance of proletarian precariousness. The International Labor Organization has recently estimated that what might be called the global reserve army of labour is now larger than the approximately 1.4 billion workers who are totally dependent on wage labour for subsistence. This reserve now extends well beyond the roughly 218 million unemployed, an astronomical 1.7 billion workers being designated 'the vulnerably employed'. A significant portion of this reserve is undoubtedly wageless, composed of members of marginal domestic economies who eke out material being through unpaid labours, scavenging and other illicit endeavours of the kind associated with life in the favelas, barrios and shanty towns of Latin America, Asia and Africa. Often this segment of the dispossessed scratches its day-to-day remunerations out of an *informal* economy where the struggle for subsistence relies as much on the trappings of petty, self-exploiting entrepreneurialism as on anything approximating waged labour.[10] Precariousness is axiomatic. What Davis calls the 'global informal working class' – a socio-economic stratum that he sees 'overlapping with but non-identical to the slum population' – now surpasses one billion in number, 'making it the fasting growing, and most unprecedented, social class on earth'.[11]

But does precariousness, per se, constitute a *separate and distinct class formation*? If it does, then precarious employments, across a spectrum of almost infinite possibilities, are, in their fragmentations, constitutive of specific and particular classes, which then necessarily occupy different class places, with counterposed class interests, from those in other employment sectors. It is the purpose of this essay to suggest that this kind of thinking, which has of late gathered momentum, is antagonistic to foundational Marxist understandings and will, inevitably, have consequences in terms of struggle and practice which are divisive and counterproductive.[12]

PRECARIOUSNESS AS SOCIAL CLASS

Leading the analytic charge to declare precarious workers a *new class force*, one that must be reckoned with in the social struggles of our times, is Guy Standing. Standing, for instance, insists that in our current reconfigurations of work and everyday life 'the precariat is in the front ranks, but it has yet to find the voice to bring its agenda to the fore. It is not the "squeezed middle" or an "underclass" or "the lower working class". It has a distinctive bundle of insecurities and will have an equally distinctive set of demands.'[13] Such claims rest on understandings of a *hierarchy of differentiated class formation* in which a new neoliberal global economy has forever gutted both the old, drab, Fordist regime of factory-driven accumulation and the routine conception of employment as a nine-to-five undertaking, defined by continuous work relations which were ordered, in part, by union protections. Stable working-class identities have been swept aside; a sense of proletarian power as a transformative agent of social relations of exploitation and oppression is now ended.

This new instalment to what is by now over a three decades-old 'retreat from class'[14] is ironically centred on insisting that old class structures and agencies have been replaced by new ones, albeit class formations that are defined by their distance from structures of class place and the many destabilizations that separate this new precarious class from all previous touchstones of working-class identity. Standing posits the existence of a ladder of stratification that orders the lower classes of contemporary society into distinct components: the manual working class; the army of the unemployed; the social misfits living a thoroughly marginalized existence; and the youth-dominated precariat.

Beyond the intellectual grid of Standing's Weberian/Lloyd Warnerian classifications lie a graveyard of political implications, in which are buried the possibilities of a past written off as *finis*. A sclerotic labourist politic, according to Standing, is simply antiquated in modern times, a residue of a tired social democracy, its affiliation with a dying labour movement little more than a hangover of a previous era. As a separate youth-led precariat emerges as a distinct class force, according to Standing, it will scale the heights of new mobilizations, creating struggles and corresponding slogans that leave older injunctions, such as 'Workers of the World, Unite!', discarded as useless impediments. The precariat is now the truly dangerous class, threatening disorder, a body of nomads coalescing under the banner, 'Denizens, Unite!' Insisting that with the dismantling of the public sector, the rising significance of black markets and generational tensions associated with the young resenting their elders living off of state subsidies, such as lavish pensions, the precariat is a unique and distinct class entity, Standing urges this powerful force to make the turn to utopianism, calling on all right-thinking advocates of multiculturalism to rally to its standard as a matter, almost, of natural selection. 'The precariat is not victim, villain, or hero', he writes, 'it is just a lot of us.'

Standing's response to capitalist crisis, the intensification of expropriation, the dismantling of working-class entitlements and the assault on the material well-being of the working class that manifests itself in a growing insecurity of waged employment – all of which, and more, constitute a revived class war from above – is nothing less than an *ideology*. It is, to be sure, appealing in its simplified identification of the young, the restless and the insecure as the foundation of a new movement of resistance. Nonetheless, for all of its attractiveness to an increasingly volatile global sector of the working class, the end result of being drawn into this ideology will be to fragment the potential power of an amalgamation of the dispossessed by hiving off a sector of this class from all other components with whom this contingent might ally, thereby weakening the forces of anti-capitalism. The suggestion that class, its composition and its strategic importance, has somehow changed in the recent past, because work is no longer secure, represents a retreat into fragmentation, rather than a creative response to it. It is also a fundamentally ahistorical argument, for work has never been anything but a precarious foundation of life lived on the razor's edge of dispossession.

Claims of a new precariat class grow logically out of the 'post-Marxist postmodernism' that has, since the 1980s, revelled in study of marginality, repudiating the 'totalizing' master narratives of class and class struggle that animate the desire, not only to interpret the world, but to change it. The tragedy is that this ideological posture is likely to gain traction precisely because the established trade union leaderships have ossified to the point that they cannot reclaim the sensibility that prodded the labour movement into being, the understanding that 'An Injury to One is an Injury to All'. With the revolutionary left largely moribund, moreover, there are precious few forums in which class mobilizations are hailed as stepping stones in the creation of new organizations, parties and structures of opposition that can truly become 'tribunes of the people', expressions of the need to resist capitalist encroachments in the name of a wide-ranging, socialist agenda. Instead, there are European examples, like Portugal and Spain, where the marginally, casually and insecurely employed are an expanding and increasingly significant percentage of the working class (upwards of 40 per cent), exhibiting organizational initiatives (such as the formation of the *Precári@s Inflexiveis* Movement) that reflect this reality.[15]

For Marxists, the existence of such organization of the precariously employed is heartening. Yet this is no substitute for a powerful coming together of *all* components of the working class, which must be united in their struggles against capitalism and staunch in their refusals of division, driven by capitalism's conveniences rather than the needs of socialized humanity. In this sense, resisting the ideology of *precariousness as class formation* is a theoretical point of departure. Doing this necessitates going back to the original theoretical foundations of historical materialism, and addressing the extent to which dispossession (from which flows all manner of insecurities and all manner of precariousness in the wage relation) has always been *the fundamental feature of class formation* rather than the material basis of a new, contemporary class, with an agenda silent on the necessity of socialism.

DISPOSSESSION AS SOCIAL CLASS: THE ORIGINS OF HISTORICAL MATERIALISM

In the 1873 Afterword to the second German edition of *Capital*, Marx declared that 'the contradictions inherent in the movement of capitalist society impress themselves upon the practical bourgeois most strikingly in the changes of the periodic cycle, through which modern industry runs, and whose crowning point is the universal crisis. That crisis is once again approaching, although as yet but in its preliminary stage; and by the universality of its theatre and the intensity of its action it will drum dialectics even into the heads of mushroom upstarts'.[16] Capitalist progress was thus premised on capitalist destruction. 'The growing incompatibility between the productive development of society and its hitherto existing relations of production expresses itself in bitter contradictions, crises, spasms', Marx wrote in the *Grundrisse*, concluding that, 'the violent destruction of capital not by relations external to it, but rather as a condition of its self-preservation, is the most striking form in which advice is given it to be gone and give room to a higher state of social production'. [17]

Socialism, Marx and Engels reasoned, was necessary if humankind was ever to transcend the destructive logic of the profit system, which was 'too narrow to comprise the wealth' that it created:

> And how does the bourgeoisie get over these crises? On the one hand, by enforced destruction of a mass of productive forces; on the other, by the conquest of new markets, and by the more thorough exploitation of the old ones. That is to say, by paving the way for more extensive and more destructive crises, and by diminishing the means whereby crises are prevented.[18]

Class formation, about which Marx wrote relatively little, was never separable from this understanding of *capitalism as crisis*. Earlier epochs had seen society fragmented into 'various orders, a manifold gradation of social rank [composed of] ... patricians, knights, plebeians, slaves ... feudal lords, vassals, guild-masters, journeymen, apprentices, serfs'. Capitalism, in contrast, 'simplified the class antagonisms'. Under the revolutionizing drive of the bourgeoisie, civil society was split into 'two great hostile camps, into two great classes directly facing each other: Bourgeoisie and Proletariat'. This was, for Marx and Engels, the fundamental socio-political fact of the human relations of capitalism. As much as the working classes, pluralized in the mainstream language of the epoch, were fragmented by identities of nationality, religion, morality and status, Marx and Engels insisted that the proletarians, recruited from all previous classes of the population, were finally brought together in inevitable association because of what they lacked: property. An original expropriation, generalized (sometimes over generations) to dispossession, defined the mass of humanity as inherently opposed to the propertied and powerful minority, and the isolations of labouring life would eventually give way 'to revolutionary combination'. Capitalism and the bourgeoisie had produced their 'own gravediggers'. This was fundamental to what Marx and Engels insisted was a process, spawned in all that was once solid melting into air, of men and women at last being 'compelled to face with sober senses' their 'real conditions of life'.[19]

In hindsight, and with an historical appreciation of the *longue durée* of class formation, it is clear that Marx and Engels wrote at a specific juncture, preceded by the dissolution of feudal relations and followed by the consolidation of increasingly structured capitalist social relations, of which differentiated labour markets were an integral part. To be sure, Marxist analysis of class relations necessarily addresses value, extraction of surplus and regimes of accumulation, but the prior (and always historically ongoing[20]) process, on which all of this is premised, is necessarily expropriation and, in the long term, the continuity of dispossession. Thus, in Chapter 23 of *Capital*, Marx declares, in his discussion of simple reproduction and the relations of seigneurs and serfs, 'if one fine morning the lord appropriates to himself the land, the cattle, the seed, in a word, the means of production of this peasant, the latter will thenceforth be obliged to sell his labour power', while in Chapter 25, on 'the general law of capitalist accumulation', Marx criticized (but drew upon) Sir Fredrick Morton Eden's book, *The State of the Poor: Or, an History of the Labouring Classes of England* (1797). Against Eden's view that those emerging capitalists who commanded the produce of industry owed their exemption from labour 'to civilization and order', Marx argued that,

the reproduction of a mass of labour-power, which must incessantly re-incorporate itself with capital for that capital's self-expansion; which cannot get free from capital, and whose enslavement to capital is only concealed by the variety of individual capitalists to whom it sells itself, this reproduction of labour-power forms, in fact, an essential of the reproduction of capital itself. Accumulation of capital is, therefore, increase of the proletariat.

Marx quoted the eighteenth-century satirist, philosopher and political economist, Bernard de Mandeville, who noted, 'it would be easier, where property is well secured, to live without money than without the poor; for who would do the work?' Dispossession, then, is the basis of all proletarianization, which orders accumulation. Only socialism can end this cycle of dispossession/accumulation/crisis/disorder, the partial and temporary resolution of which, under capitalism, can only be achieved by the bloodletting of another round of violent dispossession.[21]

DISPOSSESSION AS SOCIAL CLASS: WHAT'S PAST IS PRECARIOUSNESS

From the vantage point of Marx, schooled by Eden's marshalling of evidence and other sources, proletarianization flowed historically, a trickle that commenced in antiquity and had grown to a stream by the seventeenth century. Christopher Hill describes the masterless masses who provided the shock troops of Digger and Leveller contingents in the 1640s, the 'surplus' population that created the surplus out of which the capitalist class would coalesce. He refers to a

> seething mobility of forest squatters, itinerant craftsmen and building labourers, unemployed men and women seeking work, strolling players and jugglers, pedlars and quack doctors, vagabonds, tramps: congregated especially in the big cities, but also with footholds wherever newly-squatted areas escaped from the machinery of the parish or in old-squatted areas where labour was in demand.

It was from this 'underworld' that ships' crews and armies were recruited, and out of which the migratory settlement that peopled the New World was fashioned.[22]

By the mid-nineteenth century this stream of dispossession had become a torrential river of class formation, fed by underground currents of enclosures, wars, technological displacements of handicraft labours and other forces of expropriation and displacement. Marx and Engels can perhaps be excused for seeing proletarianization at this time as a maturing process, rather than one that was, in fact, only coming into its adolescence. In the decades that would follow, class formation would consolidate, indeed harden. Yet this would be an extremely uneven project, and never one in which anything approximating 'stabilization' occurred. Dispossession was always disorderly: the old jostled with the new, layers of labour were structured into seemingly contradictory locales, with their designations running from the aristocratic (the black-coated worker) to the derogatory (the dangerous classes, the residuum).[23] And complicating this chaotic making and remaking of class experience was the potent disruption of capitalism's persistent underside: crisis.

A working class conceived as forged out of the process of dispossession is thus central, not only to the thought of Marx and Engels, but to the monumental achievement of E.P. Thompson's *The Making of the English Working Class* which, in 2013, celebrated a fiftieth anniversary of its original date of publication. Indeed, Thompson explored the crucible of class formation in England in the years 1790-1830 by accenting how a mass of previously differentiated *employments*, in which variegated occupational labours evolved, had come, through struggle and crisis, to be *a working class*. He drew on Henry Mayhew, whose writings on London labour and the poor emerged at roughly the same time as the commentaries of Marx and Engels. Mayhew had suggested the extent to which the capitalist employment marketplace was structured in a series of arbitrary ways. It was dependent on work that could only be conducted seasonally, reliant on fashion and accident, ordered by over-work and scamp-work in the cheap trades, constantly reconfigured by the dilution of skills that saw women and children introduced into specific handicrafts in order to depress wages and restructured by machinery and managerial innovations. Recruited to the metropolis by the dissolution of landed relations and the destruction of village handicrafts, waged workers struggled, through time, with impersonal disciplines of a labour market always cramped by acute limitations. Mayhew concluded that regular employment was available to roughly 1.5 million labourers, while half-time work might accrue to a further 1.5 million, with 1.5 million more either wholly unemployed or working occasionally only by displacing those who considered specific jobs to be their terrain.

This might seem to be anything but a coherent grouping, the 'working classes' that it designated a 'bundle of discrete phenomena'. Thompson nevertheless argued that it was *a working class* that was indeed made in the cauldron of the Industrial Revolution and the counter-revolution of property, both historical processes either ridden forcefully or instigated by the bourgeoisie, and both either dependent upon or directed against those who were, increasingly, dispossessed of property and power over their lives. Class constituted an 'identity of interests ... of the most diverse occupations and levels of attainment', and it was forged in antagonism to the attempts to make of all of these components 'a sort of machine'. If class was composed of various parts, drawn from a plethora of experiences of dispossession, both Marx's and Engels' and Thompson's understandings converged: all of these layers of class formation were drawn together, not so much because they had come from or were embedded in absolute sameness, but because their life courses were being determined by ultimately similar processes and outcomes.[24]

The point, as a rich historiography reveals, and as is evident in Thompson's *Making*, with its accounts of proto-industrialization and outworkers, field labourers, declining crafts, 'Church and King mobs', opaque societies of machine-breakers, the denizens of 'Satan's Strongholds' and metropolitan artisans, is that there is nothing new about fragmentations of class experience. Class has always embodied differentiation, insecurity and precariousness. Just as precariousness is historically inseparable from class formation, there are invariably differentiations that seemingly separate out those with access to steady employments and secure payments from those who must scramble for work and access to the wage. Expropriation, then, is a highly heterogeneous experience, since no individual can be dispossessed in precisely the same way as another, or live that process of material alienation exactly as another would. Yet dispossession, *in general,* nonetheless *defines proletarianization.* It is the metaphorical mark of Cain stamped on all workers, regardless of their level of employment, rate of pay, status, waged placement or degree of wagelessness.[25]

This has been a premise of much Marxist analysis, evident, for instance, in the (admittedly gendered) title of Martin Glaberman's essay on the American working class in the 1960s, 'Be His Payment High or Low'. Glaberman noted, decades ago, that 'what is involved in industry after industry is not simply the replacing of men by automated machines but the discarding of men, the moving of others and the bringing of still others into the industrial working class and the reorganisation of the work process'.[26] This kind of constant restructuring is precisely what animated Harry Braverman's concern with the degradation of work in the twentieth century.[27] Although, as Braverman argued, the process of change in the relations of production intensified in the twentieth-century age of monopoly, it had been around for decades. It astounded even early capitalists, who could not quite fathom the 'moral economy' of Adam Smith. 'It is vain to read his book to find a remedy for a complaint which he could not conceive existed, vis. 100,000 weavers doing the work of 150,000', wrote one humane English employer early in the nineteenth century. This man's inability to understand 'that the profits of a Manufacture should be what one Master could wring from the hard earnings of the poor, more than another' led to his ruin.[28]

It is in this context that capitalist crisis has become something of a fountainhead from which spring all manner of theoretical musings on new class formations. Capitalist crisis, for instance, ushered into being new class struggle initiatives on the part of the bourgeoisie. It has often called forth new tactics and strategic reassessments on the part of the working class. The *ahistorical* claim that the precariousness of modern labour is something dramatically new, necessitating a revision of all that has been solid in the Marxist approach to class, however, must be refused. Acknowledging the extent of precariousness in the contemporary trends of global class formation does *not* necessitate a conceptual and political rupture with understandings of the possibilities of a unity of the dispossessed, which remains the only hope for a socialist humanity.

PROLETARIAN SURPLUS, PRECARIOUSNESS AND PAUPERIZATION

A stable working class identity or, dichotomously, a precarious one – these are not the defining features of class difference, one designated *proletarian,* the other defined as *precariat.* Rather, as a deep structure of being, dispossession itself is fundamental, and throughout history has been a continuous thread that ties together exploitation *and* oppression. Marx noted this in *Capital,* writing that capitalist enrichment was premised on 'the condemnation of one part of the working class to enforced idleness by the over-work of the other part', accelerating 'the production of the reserve army on a scale corresponding with the advance of social accumulation'. Every proletarian can thus be categorized, not so much according to their waged work, but to the possible forms of surplus population, which Marx labelled 'the floating, the latent, and the stagnant'. This is why the accumulation of capital is also the accumulation of labour, but the Malthusian multiplication of the proletariat does not necessarily mean the working class will, in its entirety, be waged. As Marx wrote:

> The lowest sediment of the relative surplus-population finally dwells in the sphere of pauperism ... the quantity of paupers increases with every crisis. ... Pauperism is the hospital of the active labour-army and the dead weight of the industrial reserve army. Its production is included in that of the relative surplus population, its necessity in theirs; along with the surplus population, pauperism forms a condition of capitalist production, and of the capitalist development of wealth. It enters into the *faux frais* of capitalist production.[29]

As John Bellamy Foster, Robert W. McChesney and R. Jamil Jonna note in a recent issue of *Monthly Review,* Marx's way of seeing class formation was much ahead of his time, anticipating how modern imperialism and the relentless march of capital accumulation on a world scale would result in the quantitative expansion and qualitative transformation of the global reserve army of labour.[30] This massive reserve, from which capital draws such sustenance for its accumulative appetite, now numbers in the billions, and as it has grown so too have the dimensions of misery of the dispossessed expanded, as Marx predicted.[31] Jan Breman, writing of exploitation, expropriation and exclusion in India, declares 'a point of no return is reached when a reserve army waiting to be incorporated into the labour process becomes stigmatized as a permanently redundant mass, an excessive burden that cannot be included now or in the future, in economy and society. This metamorphosis is, in my opinion at least, the real crisis of world capitalism.'[32]

What this suggests is that in any analytic grappling with the historical record of class formation, it is mandatory to see proletarianization whole. Historians are beginning to appreciate, as indicated by the interpretive excursions of Michael Denning into wagelessness and Mike Davis into slummification, that it is imperative not to centre our studies of labour in the logic of capital's validations. The working class does not only achieve visibility and become invested with political relevance to the extent that it is *waged*. Expropriation is being, and even in the throes of dispossession work is necessary for the vast majority of humanity, regardless of whether or how it is remunerated. Indeed, as feminists have long insisted in their accounts of unpaid reproductive labour, a perspective on class formation bounded only by the wage will inevitably be blinkered in all kinds of ways.[33]

PRECARIOUSNESS AND THE LUMPENPROLETARIAT: THE POLITICS OF CLASS AFFILIATION

In circles uninfluenced by Standing's approach to the precariat as a separate social class there is nonetheless a congruent, if seemingly unrelated, interest in Marx's ostensible dismissiveness of precariousness, especially as it manifested itself in jaundiced comments on the lumpenproletariat. There is no doubt that, writing as a Victorian, Marx often lapsed into moralistic judgement with respect to the most marginalized, often criminalized, subcultures of the dispossessed. The further one gets from the core capitalist economies of the advanced capitalist western nations, the more apparent it is that class formation is often structured around wagelessness and subcultures of the marginally employed: transitions in and out of penny capitalism, criminality and hybrid existences in which peasant subsistence and temporary proletarianization congeal are almost routine.

Historians interested in class formation on a world scale, and especially the importance of wagelessness in the developing world, have necessarily confronted the prejudice in selective comments by Marx on a class stratum he was prone to denigrate as the lumpenproletariat.[34] Nonetheless, for all that Marx (and Engels) can be castigated for the 'political incorrectness' of their comments on the lumpenproletariat, it is crucial to recognize that this loose term of abuse was situated within a particular context and was not necessarily a way of separating out one portion of the dispossessed from others in class terms. Given that Marx's coining of the term lumpenproletariat was as much metaphorical trope as it was a rigorously developed analytic category, claims that Marx erred in writing out of the proletariat the criminalized and destitute who were divorced from the productive relations of developing capitalism may well be overstated. Indeed, a close reading of the entire oeuvre of Marx and Engels suggests four things.[35]

First, even within the political writings of the 1840s, where there is no doubt that the term *lumpenproletariat* is used to designate derogatorily sectors of the dispossessed that cast their political lot with the project of reaction and restoration of class privilege, it is obviously the case that use of the prefix *lumpen* is meant to convey debasement rather than a hardened class place. This is evident in how Marx affixes the lumpenproletarian adjective to Bonaparte himself, who is the principal object of Marx's revulsion in 'The Eighteenth Brumaire of Louis Bonaparte' and *Class Struggles in France*. Bonaparte was metaphorically castigated as the princely *'chief of the lumpenproletariat'*, a scoundrel who recognized in the 'scum, offal, refuse of all classes the only class upon which he [could] base himself unconditionally'.[36] One literary theorist has commented that 'Marx must have lived the history of France from 1848 to 1852 – the revolution careening backwards – as resembling nothing so much as a latrine backing up'.[37] Understanding this, it would seem, might temper the ways in which contemporary scholarship evaluates the birth of a term such as lumpenproletariat, which truly did enter the world amidst the death agonies of revolutionary possibility. As Hal Draper has suggested, Marx's utilization of the prefix 'lumpen' was a way of labelling an individual or a social grouping as knave-like or odious,[38] and this means, I would suggest, that the term is far less a rigorous classification of analytic substance than it is an adjective of vitriol. This surfaces in Marx's pillorying of a particular kind of mid-nineteenth-century French financial aristocracy, a rakish layer of bourgeois society that is presented as having risen to commanding, parasitic heights, gorging itself on wealth produced by others, exhibiting an 'unbridled display of unhealthy and dissolute appetites'.

Such an aristocratic layer, characterized by pleasure becoming '*crapuleux*, where gold, dirt, and blood flow together', was, in Marx's view, 'nothing but the resurrection of the lumpen proletariat at the top of bourgeois society'.[39]

Second, in as much as this debasement is, in the passions of an 1848-51 defeat of working-class revolution, Marx's way of locating how sectors of the dispossessed opted to struggle in ways that secured the privileges of power and money rather than challenging them, the central issue in approaching the lumpenproletariat must be a consideration of how the lowest of the low act in moments of class struggle. Even Fanon – whose validation of the 'pimps, the hooligans, the unemployed, and the petty criminals' as a revolutionary contingent seems at odds with Marx's less salubrious approach to people identified in this way – understood that colonial authority might well be 'extremely skilful in using [the] ignorance and incomprehension of the *lumpenproletariat*'. Unless organized by revolutionary activists, Fanon feared that the lumpenproletariat would 'find itself fighting as hired soldiers side-by-side' with the troops of reaction, and he cited instances in Angola and the Congo where precisely this had indeed happened.[40]

Third, even when he is, as in the writings relating to France between 1848-51, disparaging the lumpenproletariat as a force of reaction, Marx hints at the extent to which the sectors of the dispossessed were not so much acting as a distinct class apart from the proletariat, but were, rather, individuals *directed* in this way by bourgeois forces. When Marx writes in *The Class Struggles in France* that the 24 battalions of the Mobile Guards were set up by the Provisional Government, and that they were (rightly or wrongly) composed of young men from 15 to 20 years of age who 'belonged for the most part to the *lumpenproletariat*', he prefaces this reading of historical development with the statement that it came about because of bourgeois need.[41] With the bourgeoisie no 'match for the proletariat' in 1848, it embarked on establishing 'a hundred different obstacles' to curb working-class power. When these efforts failed 'there consequently remained but one way out: to set one part of the proletariat against the other', a conclusion that can certainly be interpreted as acknowledgement that Marx did not consider the lumpenproletariat and the proletariat as irreconcilably divided, but part of a continuum of the same dispossessed class. But consciousness of class place/interests is never simply a fait accompli. Because this must be built, and is part of the project of making socialism by making socialists, it is possible, in periods of intense struggle to see individuals cross class lines and act in ways that pit them against members of their class. The language of antagonism is then often quite harsh, as the designation 'scab' reveals.

Fourth, in as much as Marx never wrote the decisive volume on labour that might well have at least addressed, if not clarified, the meaning of lumpenproletarianization, it is surely critical to acknowledge that Marx's perspective shifted gears through and over time. His assessment of the lumpenproletariat reached, to be sure, something of a nadir with Bonaparte's coup d'etat, orchestrated by the so-called Society of December 10, composed, in Marx's words, of

> ruined and adventurous offshoots of the bourgeoisie ... vagabonds, discharged soldiers, discharged jailbirds, escaped galley slaves, swindlers, mountebanks, *lazzaroni*, pickpockets, tricksters, gamblers, *maquereaus*, brothel-keepers, porters, *literati*, organ-grinders, rag-pickers, knife grinders, tinkers, beggars – in short, the whole indefinite, disintegrated mass, thrown hither and thither, which the French term *la bohème*.[42]

This rhetoric of revulsion notwithstanding, there are passages in both earlier and later writings, distanced from the immediacy of Marx's 1848-51 political disappointment, that exhibit a more analytic understanding. As Peter Haynes suggests, Marx recognized well the ways in which the dispossessed were victimized by capitalism's capacity to criminalize and punish the poor. In later writings, Marx drew explicitly on Thomas More, for instance, whose *Utopia* was a source utilized in the writing of *Capital*, and who had represented the dispossessed as 'dryven to this extreme necessitie, firste to steale, then to dye'.[43]

For all that Marx and Engels could write in the pejorative language of their times about what would later be called 'the underclass',[44] they were also not unaware of how the 'residuum' was reciprocally related to the stalwart proletarians on whom they based their hope for socialism. Engels' *The Condition of the Working-Class in England in 1844* had much of moralistic condemnation in it, especially with respect to immigrant Irish labour, but this did not mean that he saw the most downtrodden sectors of the proletariat as irredeemably separated out from the working class. Indeed, in an 1892 preface to his Manchester study, Engels recorded with considerable optimism the extent to which socialism's advance in England had registered even in a former bastion of lumpenproletarianization, London's East End. 'That immense haunt of misery is no longer the stagnant pool that it was six years ago', Engels wrote. 'It has shaken off its torpid despair, has returned to life, and has become the home of what is called the "New Unionism"', he continued, adding, 'that is to say the organisation of the great mass of "unskilled" workers'.[45]

Marx understood well, as Michael Denning has recently noted, that political economy … does not recognize the unemployed worker, the workingman, insofar as he happens to be outside this labour relationship. The rascal, swindler, beggar, the unemployed, the starving, wretched and criminal workingman – these are *figures* who do not exist *for political economy* but only for other eyes, those of the doctor, the judge, the grave-digger, and bum-bailiff, etc.; such figures are spectres outside its domain.[46]

Marx, of course, also had considerable empathy for what was *done to* the dispossessed, as is more than evident in his condemnation of the 'barbarity in the treatment of the paupers' and his recognition of the 'growing horror in which the working people hold the slavery of the workhouse', which he dubbed a 'place of punishment for misery'.[47] In his 1842-43 *Rheinische Zeitung* articles on the debates in Germany over the law on the theft of wood, moreover, there is ample suggestion that Marx appreciated the ways in which capitalism's socio-economic trajectory tended in the direction of wider criminalization of behaviours of the poor that were themselves critical to the survival of the dispossessed. Separated first from nature, the dispossessed then found themselves expropriated from the institutionalized protections of civil society.

State formation, in Marx's view, proceeded on this basis: ruling-class power and institutions subservient to such authority's ends made the law into a vehicle driving forward the expanding nature of dispossession, turning the apparatus of governance into a mailed fist of privileged interests. As Peter Linebaugh pointed out in the mid-1970s, Marx's writings on the thefts of wood provide a jumping off point for a discussion of class formation that necessitates analysis of the meaning of Marxist understandings of the lumpenproletariat, a term that can only be interrogated when 'the principle of historical specification' and 'the concept of class struggle' are central to analysis.[48] In discussing the issue of access to the fallen wood of the forest, Marx contended that 'just as it is not fitting for the rich to lay claim to alms distributed in the street, so also in regard to these *alms of nature*', and he insisted on the need for a universal set of 'customary rights of the poor'.[49] Needless to say, nothing of the sort materialized in the cauldron of capitalist class formation, and Marx concluded that the state had been turned into a servant of property.

Marx thus addressed proletarianization as a dual process, the creation of labour as both 'free' *and* outlawed.[50] But if there is honour among *some* thieves, not all who have been placed beyond the boundary of respectability exhibit admirable traits.[51] Marx appreciated, in a way that many contemporary scholars who romanticize segments of society driven to incorrigibility fail to discern, that extreme and long-term dispossession could well deform a section of the proletariat politically, reducing it to an adjunct of reaction. This matter was still being posed in the 1930s, with activists and Left Book Club authors such as Wal Hannington, a founding member of the Communist Party of Great Britain and organizer of the National Unemployed Workers' Movement, asking worriedly, 'Is there a Fascist danger amongst the Unemployed?'[52]

Debates over lumpenproletarianization, like discussions of precariousness, highlight the reality of status differentiation within the dispossessed, illuminating the importance of conscious identifications on the plane of class struggle politics among sectors of the working class. As difficult as is the project of uniting the expropriated, many of whom can be incorporated into the hegemonic and ideological edifice of acquisitive individualism, this can never be the foundation of a materialist separation of layers of the dispossessed into distinct classes.

CLASS POLITICS AND PRECARIOUSNESS

Expropriation is not in and of itself a guarantee of behaviours that will advance humanity. It is in uniting the dispossessed in struggles that can realize a new social order, one premised not on expropriation, exploitation and oppression, but on collective productions for the use and benefit of all, that constitutes the only possibility for meaningful progress.

On a global scale, dispossession is accelerating. A crisis-ridden capitalism necessarily intensifies expropriation and expands the boundaries of immiseration. The necessity of orchestrating a collective response to this quickening pace of material alienation is most urgent, yet analytic thought in our times trends in the direction of accenting the fragmentations and divisions that incapacitate the working class, in all its gradations, rather than forging it into a fighting tribune for all of the world's exploited and oppressed. At its most populist, such thought, articulated most clearly by Guy Standing, stresses the unique constellation of a new class force, the *precariat*. Radical revisionists, animated by the need to address class formation on a global scale and cognizant of the importance of marginalization in the making of the world's proletariat, have turned away from some of Marx's insights, fracturing the experience of the waged and the wageless, questioning Marx's failure to create a sense of class premised on inclusivity.

These developments, largely confined at this point to theoretical discussions and academic treatises, are nevertheless paralleled in the actual world of class politics and praxis by a deepening structural and institutional separation of the fragments of the working class. Trade unions atrophy, both in terms of their capacity to organize labour, and with respect to their willingness to put forward a politics of class that extends past the constrictions of business unionism, which focuses narrowly on specific occupational jurisdictions of waged employments. The revolutionary left, never weaker over the course of the last century than it is now, is a tragically understated presence in contemporary class relations, and has been usurped, as a critical political voice, by identity-driven social movements that reproduce the fragmentations inherent in capitalism's tendency to divide the better to conquer. And the working class appears as more and more fractured, divided against itself, and less and less able to utilize the precarious conditions of its material life to sustain structures of resistance.

Understanding this tragic set of parallel trajectories, it is imperative that those on the socialist left – as well as those working in unions, social movements, and all manner of campaigns that see themselves challenging capital and the state in the interests of the dispossessed – reassert what is most solid in the Marxist tradition. What is more than ever needed is a politics of class that speaks directly to the betterment of humanity through insistence that the expropriated are as one in their ultimate needs. The reciprocal powers (however subjectively and seemingly different) of the waged and the wageless must be organized and utilized to speak to the debilitating consequences of precariousness as well as the exploitative nature of all productions, payments and prohibitions. Transcending an imposed and ultimately artificial difference is central to breaking the chains that keep workers separated from their collectivity, and bind them to the isolations that seal their subordination. In the recent words of the East European dissident, G.M. Tamás, 'Vive la difference? No. Vive la Commune!'[53]

Once it is grasped that all proletarians suffer precariousness, and all of those constrained by precariousness in their working lives are indeed proletarians or have interests that coincide directly with this class of the dispossessed, it is clear that there are expanding possibilities for more effective politics based on class struggles in our times. And it is indeed class struggle – rooted in expropriation and forged in the increasingly agitated crises of capitalism – that remains the ultimate basis for changing the world through a transformative politics.

NOTES

1   Karl Marx, *Grundrisse: Foundations of the Critique of Political Economy*, Harmondsworth: Penguin, 1973, p. 472.

2   See, for instance, the discussions of 'Incomes Policy' by A.J. Topham, 'Background to the Argument', Ken Coates, 'A Strategy for the Unions', and Ralph Miliband, 'What Does the Left Want', *Socialist Register 1965*, New York: Monthly Review Press, 1965, pp. 163-94; as well as Richard Hyman, 'Workers' Control and Revolutionary Theory', *Socialist Register 1974*, London: Merlin Press, 1974, pp. 241-78.

3   Bryan D. Palmer, 'Wildcat Workers: The Unruly Face of Class Struggle', *Canada's 1960s: The Ironies of Identity in a Rebellious Era*, Toronto: University of Toronto Press, 2009, pp. 211-41.

4   Barbara Garson, 'Luddites in Lordstown', *Harper's Magazine*, June, 1972, pp. 68-73; Judson Gooding, 'Blue-Collar Blues on the Assembly Line', *Fortune*, July, 1970, pp. 112-3; Jefferson Cowie, *Stayin' Alive: The 1970s and the Last Days of the Working Class*, New York and London: New Press, 2010.

5   James A. Geschwender, *Class, Race, and Worker Insurgency: The League of Revolutionary Black Workers*, Cambridge: Cambridge University Press, 1977.

6   Bill Watson, 'Counter-planning on the Shop Floor', *Radical America*, May-June, 1971; and Ben Hamper, *Rivethead: Tales from the Assembly Line*, Boston: Warner, 1991.

7   Daniel Singer, *Prelude to Revolution: France in May 1968*, Boston: South End Press, 2002; Kristin Ross, *May '68 and Its Afterlives*, Chicago: University of Chicago Press, 2002.

8   On class conflict see Richard Hyman, 'Industrial Conflict and the Political Economy', *Socialist Register 1973*, London: Merlin, 1973, pp. 101-54, which surveys the 1960s and early 1970s. Note, on the 1972 miners' strike, E.P. Thompson, 'A Special Case', *Writing by Candlelight*, London: Merlin, 1980, pp. 65-76. See also, L. Panitch, *Social Democracy and Industrial Militancy*, Cambridge, UK: Cambridge University Press, 1976, 204-34.

9   Mike Davis, 'Spring Confronts Winter', *New Left Review*, 72(November-December), 2011, p. 15. See also Kwan Lee, *Against the Law: Labour Protests in China's Rustbelt and Sunbelt*, Los Angeles: University of California Press, 2007.

10   Early comment on the growing significance of the informal economy appeared in Manfred Bienefeld, 'The Informal Sector and Peripheral Capitalism', *Bulletin of the Institute of Development Studies*, 4, 1975, pp. 53-73; and the importance of this informal sector in terms of African class formation is much discussed in Bill Freund, *The African Worker*, Cambridge: Cambridge University Press, 1988.

11   Mike Davis, *Planet of Slums*, New York and London: Verso, 2006, p. 178.

12   Not all recent writing on precariousness is wrong-headed. Although approaching the issue from an entirely different vantage point than the current essay, addressing precarity from a cultural studies perspective and placing far more emphasis on 'the knowledge economy', 'creative industries' and 'cultural revolutions', Andrew Ross refuses both the suggestion that a precariat is necessarily a cross-class formation and that there is nothing to unite those in

work sectors associated with the traditional, unionized proletariat and those who find themselves in more precarious employments. See his *Nice Work If You Can Get It: Life and Labor in Precarious Times*, New York and London: New York University Press, 2009.

13   Guy Standing, *The Precariat: The New Dangerous Class*, London and New York: Bloomsbury Academic, 2011. For the quotations in this and the following paragraphs, see esp. pp. vii, 8-9, 154, 159, 183.

14   Note, for instance, Ellen Wood, *The Retreat from Class: A New 'True' Socialism*, London: Verso, 1986; and Leo Panitch, 'The Impasse of Working Class Politics', *Socialist Register 1985/6*, London: Merlin, 1986; as well as the subsequent essays on 'The Retreat of the Intellectuals', *Socialist Register 1990*, London: Merlin, 1990.

15   See Ricard Antunes, 'The Working Class Today: The New Form of Being of the Class Who Lives from its Labour', *Workers of the World: International Journal on Strikes and Social Conflict*, 1(2), January, 2012.

16   Karl Marx, *Capital: A Critical Analysis of Capitalist Production*, Volume 1, Moscow: Foreign Languages Publishing House, n.d., p. 20.

17   Marx, *Grundrisse*, pp. 749-50.

18   Karl Marx and Frederick Engels, 'Manifesto of the Communist Party', in Karl Marx and Frederick Engels, *Selected Works*, Moscow: Progress, 1968, pp. 36-46.

19   Marx and Engels, 'Manifesto'.

20   See Bryan D. Palmer, 'Social Formation and Class Formation in Nineteenth-Century North America', in David Levine, ed., *Proletarianization and Family History*, New York: Academic Press, 1984, pp. 229-308.

21   Marx, *Capital*, pp. 568, 612-6. See also, Marx, *Grundrisse*, esp. pp. 483-509.

22   Christopher Hill, *The World Turned Upside Down: Radical Ideas during the English Revolution*, New York: Viking, 1972, p. 39.

23   The literature that could be cited is immense, and for London alone is benchmarked between 1850 and 1890 by the pioneering sociological inquiries of Henry Mayhew and Charles Booth. See, for other useful commentary, Raphael Samuel, 'Workshop of the World: Steam Power and Hand Technology in Mid-Victorian Britain', *History Workshop Journal*, 3, 1977, pp. 6-72; Gareth Stedman Jones, *Outcast London: A Study in the Relationship Between Classes in Victorian Society*, Oxford: Oxford University Press, 1971; and for France, Louis Chevalier, *Laboring Classes and Dangerous Classes in Paris During the First Half of the Nineteenth Century*, New York: Howard Fertig, 1973; Robert Stuart, *Marxism at Work: Ideology, Class and French Socialism during the Third Republic*, Cambridge: Cambridge University Press, 1992, pp. 127-79.

24   E.P. Thompson, *The Making of the English Working Class*, Harmondsworth: Penguin, 1968, esp. pp. 9-11, 276-7, 887-8. This is not to deny what Thompson would later stress, and that is congruent with subsequent writings of Michael Lebowitz and David Harvey, that Marx, in his fixation on creating an *anti-structure* counterposed to the structure of conventional Political Economy, failed to adequately theorize class formation as something other than the object of capital's accumulative appropriation of surplus. See E.P. Thompson, *The*

Poverty of Theory & Other Essays, London: Merlin, 1981, pp. 60-5; Michael Lebowitz, *Beyond 'Capital': Marx's Political Economy of the Working Class*, Basingstoke, UK: Palgrave Macmillan, 2003; Lebowitz, *Following Marx: Method, Critique, and Crisis*, Leiden and Boston: Brill, 2009, pp. 308-11; David Harvey, *The Limits to Capital*, Chicago: University of Chicago Press, 1982, p. 163.

25   For a useful attempt to wrestle with the ever-present tension between 'universalist' and 'exceptionalist' understandings of labour see Dipesh Chakrabarty, *Rethinking Working-Class History: Bengal, 1890-1940*, Princeton: Princeton University Press, 1989, esp. pp. 219-30.

26   Martin Glaberman, 'Be His Payment High or Low: The American Working Class in the Sixties', *International Socialism*, 21(Summer), 1965, pp. 18-23. Glaberman, of course, drew directly on Marx: 'It follows, therefore, that in proportion as capital accumulates, the lot of the labourer, be his payment high or low, must grow worse'. *Capital*, p. 645.

27   Harry Braverman, *Labor and Monopoly Capital: The Degradation of Work in the Twentieth Century*, New York and London: Monthly Review Press, 1974.

28   Quoted in Thompson, *Making*, p. 309.

29   Marx, *Capital*, pp. 641, 643-4.

30   John Bellamy Foster, Robert W. McChesney and R. Jamil Jonna, 'The Global Reserve Army of Labor and the New Imperialism', *Monthly Review*, 63(November), 2011, available at http://monthlyreview.org.

31   Marx, *Capital*, p. 644-5.

32   Jan Breman, *The Labouring Poor in India: Patterns of Exploitation, Subordination, and Exclusion*, New York: Oxford University Press, 2003, p. 13.

33   Particular contributions to this literature were made by Canadian feminists. See Meg Luxton, *More Than a Labour of Love: Three Generations of Women's Work in the Home*, Toronto: Women's Press, 1980; Bonnie Fox, *Hidden in the Household: Women's Domestic Labour Under Capitalism*, Toronto: Women's Press, 1980; Michèle Barrett and Roberta Hamilton, eds., *The Politics of Diversity: Feminism, Marxism, and Nationalism*, London and New York: Verso, 1986.

34   See, for instance, Michael Denning, 'Wageless Life', *New Left Review*, 66(November-December), 2010, pp. 79-87; Marcel Van der Linden, *Workers of the World: Essays Toward a Global Labor History*, Leiden and Boston: Brill, 2008, pp. 10, 22-7, 267, 298; Van der Linden, 'Who are the Workers of the World? Marx and Beyond', *Workers of the World: International Journal on Strikes and Social Conflicts*, 1, January, 2013, pp. 55-76. Unease with Marx's seeming dismissiveness of the so-called lumpenproletariat has long been evident among Africanists, and was posed forcefully in Peter Worsley, 'Frantz Fanon and the "Lumpenproletariat"', *Socialist Register 1972*, London: Merlin, 1972, pp. 193-229.

35   See especially Hal Draper, 'The Lumpen-Class versus the Proletariat', *Karl Marx's Theory of Revolution: The Politics of Social Classes, Volume II*, New York: Monthly Review, 1978, pp. 453-80. Draper's discussion is informed and invaluable, and contains many important insights and analytic nuances. Nonetheless, while I draw on this account I also depart from some of its claims.

36 Karl Marx, 'The Eighteenth Brumaire of Louis Bonaparte', in Marx and Engels, *Selected Works*, p. 44.

37 Jeffrey Mehlman, *Revolution and Repetition: Marx/Hugo/Balzac*, Berkeley and London: University of California Press, 1977, pp. 24-5.

38 Draper, *Marx's Theory of Revolution*, esp. pp. 628-34.

39 Karl Marx, *The Class Struggles in France (1848-1850)*, New York: International, n.d., p. 36.

40 Quoted in Stuart Hall et al., *Policing the Crisis: Mugging, the State, and Law and Order*, London: Macmillan, 1978, p. 385, which has a useful discussion of 'The Wretched of the Earth', pp. 381-9. See Frantz Fanon, *The Wretched of the Earth*, New York: Grove, 1966, pp. 103-9.

41 Marx, *Class Struggles in France*, p. 50.

42 Marx, 'Eighteenth Brumaire', p. 138. On Marx, the lumpenproletariat and the economic analysis of *Capital*, see Draper, *Marx's Theory of Revolution*, pp. 469-71.

43 Peter Hayes, 'Utopia and the Lumpenproletariat: Marx's Reasoning in "The Eighteenth Brumaire of Louis Bonaparte"', *The Review of Politics*, 50(Summer), 1988, esp. p. 458.

44 The 'underclass', an early twentieth-century sociological designation that would be excavated in Robert Roberts, *The Classic Slum: Salford Life in the First Quarter of the Century*, Manchester: Manchester University Press, 1971, is not unrelated to the continuity of precariousness in proletarian life.

45 Frederick Engels, *The Condition of the Working-Class in England in 1844*, London: Swam Sonnenschein, 1892. Six years earlier Engels had written in correspondence to Laura Lafargue and August Bebel in ways that suggested a problem in seeing 'barrow boys, idlers, police spies, and rogues' as sources of support for socialism. He referred to 'numbers of poor devils of the East End who vegetate in the borderland between working class and lumpen proletariat'. Engels to Laura Lafargue, 9 February 1886; Engels to August Bebel, 15 February 1886, in Karl Marx and Frederick Engels, *Collected Works, Volume 47, 1883-1886*, New York: International, 1995, pp. 403-10. See, also, Stedman Jones, *Outcast London*; and Arthur Morrison, *A Child of the Jago*, London: Methuen, 1896.

46 Karl Marx, 'Economic and Philosophic Manuscripts of 1844', in Karl Marx and Frederick Engels, *Collected Works, Volume 3, 1843-1844*, New York: Lawrence and Wishart, 1975, p. 284.

47 Among many passages that might be cited see Marx, *Capital*, pp. 653-4; as well as the following discussions of 'The Badly Paid Strata of the British Industrial Working Class', pp. 654-63, 'The Nomad Population', pp. 663-7, and 'The British Agricultural Proletariat', pp. 673-712.

48 See Karl Marx, 'Proceedings of the Sixth Rhine Province Assembly. Third Article Debates on the Law on Thefts of Wood', in Marx and Engels, *Collected Works, Volume 1: 1835-1843*, Moscow: Progress, 1975, pp. 224-63; Teo Ballvé, 'Marx: Law on Thefts of Wood', 12 July 2011, available at http://territorialmasquerades.net; Peter Linebaugh, 'Karl Marx, the Theft of Wood, and Working Class Composition: A Contribution to the Current Debate',

Crime and Social Justice, 6(Fall–Winter), 1976, pp. 5-16; Erica Sherover-Marcuse, *Emancipation and Consciousness: Dogmatic and Dialectical Perspectives in the Early Marx*, New York: Blackwell, 1986.

49   See also Peter Linebaugh, *The Magna Carta Manifesto: Liberties and Commons for All*, Berkeley: University of California Press, 2008.

50   Marx, *Capital*, p. 733; and Van der Linden, *Workers of the World*, p. 27.

51   For sober cautionary assessment of the extent to which precarious work in the informal sector, so obviously central to the developing global South, and not unrelated to understandings of lumpenproletarianization, might well prove an 'unlikely source of sustained or coherent resistance to an unjust order', see Freund, *African Worker*, pp. 79-81; Robin Cohen and D. Michael, 'Revolutionary Potential of the African Lumpenproletariat: A Sceptical View', *Bulletin of the Institute of Development Studies*, 5, 1976, pp. 31-42.

52   Wal Hannington, *The Problem of the Distressed Areas*, London: Victor Gollancz, 1937, pp. 233-50.

53   G.M. Tamás, 'Words from Budapest', *New Left Review*, 80(March–April), 2013, p. 26.

CAPITALISM, CLASS AND UNIVERSALISM: ESCAPING THE CUL-DE-SAC OF POSTCOLONIAL THEORY

VIVEK CHIBBER

After a long, seemingly interminable hiatus, we appear to be witnessing the re-emergence of a global resistance to capitalism, at least in its neoliberal guise. It has been more than four decades since anti-capitalist movements exploded with such force on a global scale. To be sure, there were tremors every now and then, brief episodes that temporarily derailed the neoliberal project as it swept the globe. But not like that which we have witnessed in Europe, the Middle East and the Americas over the past two years. How far they will develop, how deep will be their impact, it is still impossible to predict. But they have already changed the complexion of left discourse. Suddenly, the issue of capital and class is back on the agenda, not as an abstract or theoretical discussion, but as an urgent political question.

But the re-emergence of movements has revealed that the retreat of the past three decades has exacted a toll. The political resources available to working people are the weakest they have been in decades. The organizations of the left – unions and political parties – have been hollowed out or worse yet, have become complicit in the management of austerity. But the left's weakness is not just political or organizational – it also extends to theory. The political defeats of the past decades have been accompanied by a dramatic churning on the intellectual front. It is not that there has been a flight away from radical theory or commitments to a radical intellectual agenda. Arguably, self-styled progressive or radical intellectuals are still very impressive in number at a good many universities, at least in North America. It is, rather, that the very meaning of radicalism has changed. Under the influence of post-structuralist thinking, the basic concepts of the socialist tradition are either considered suspect or rejected outright. To take but one example, the idea that capitalism has a *real* structure which imposes real compulsions on actors, that class is rooted in real relations of exploitation, or that labour has a real interest in collective organization – all these ideas, which were the common sense of the left for almost two centuries, are taken to be hopelessly outdated.

Whereas these criticisms of materialism and political economy came out of the post-structuralist milieu generally, they have found a particular sharp expression in the most recent product of that current, which has come to be known as postcolonial theory. Over the past couple of decades, it is not the Francophone philosophical tradition that has been the flag-bearer of the attack on materialism or political economy. It is, interestingly enough, a clutch of theorists from South Asia and other parts of the Global South that have led the charge. Perhaps the most conspicuous and influential of these are Gayatri Chakravarty Spivak, Homi Bhabha, Ranajit Guha and the *Subaltern Studies* group, but it also includes the Colombian Anthropologist, Arturo Escobar, the Peruvian sociologist Anibal Quijano and the Argentine literary theorist Walter Mignolo, among others. The most common target of their criticism is Marxist theory, of course; but their ire extends to the Enlightenment tradition itself. Of all the weaknesses of Enlightenment radicalism, what most agitates postcolonial theorists is its universalizing tendencies, i.e. its claims for the validity of certain categories, regardless of culture and of place. Marxism figures in their analysis as the theory that most pointedly expresses this aspect of the Enlightenment's deadly intellectual inheritance.

Marxists insist that certain categories like class, capitalism, exploitation and the like have cross-cultural validity. These categories describe economic practices not just in Christian Europe, but also in Hindu India and Muslim Egypt. For postcolonial theorists, this kind of universalizing zeal is deeply problematic – as theory, and just as important, as a guide for political practice. It is rejected not just because it is wrong, but also because it supposedly deprives actors of the intellectual resources vital for effective political practice. It does so in two ways: because in being misleading, it is a questionable guide to action – any theory that is wrong will perform poorly in directing political practice. But also, because it refuses to recognize the autonomy and the creativity of actors in their particular location. Instead, these universalizing theories shoehorn the local and the particular into the rigid categories that are derived from European experience. They deny local agents recognition of their practice, and in so doing, marginalize their real agency. This worry about the use of universalizing categories is so strong that it often appears, not as a criticism of illicit or unwise generalizations, but as a general injunction against universalisms.

Postcolonial theory presents itself as not just a criticism of the radical enlightenment tradition, but as its replacement. In this essay I will critically examine the basis of postcolonial theory's claim to be a guiding framework for radical politics. I will show that, ironically, it is the very elements of its framework that postcolonial theorists present as genuine advances that count it out as a serious political theory.

I am going to argue, in particular, that the strictures against universalizing categories ought to be rejected. I will show that they are both incorrect and contradictory. My argument is not, of course, that all universalizing claims are defensible. They may or not be, and some of them will be quite problematic. My argument, rather, is that there are some universal categories that are defensible. More importantly, I will suggest that certain of the key concepts that postcolonial theorists question or reject are not only legitimate, but are essential for any progressive politics. These are concepts that have been at the very heart of radical politics since the birth of the modern left – and are the ones that have, after a long hiatus, reemerged in the global organizing against austerity in the past few years.

THE TURN AGAINST UNIVERSALISM

In one of the most widely used texts on postcolonial studies, the editors explain the motivation behind the turn against universalizing categories. It turns out that European domination of the colonial world was based in part on just these sorts of concepts. 'The assumption of universalism', we are told, 'is a fundamental feature of the construction of colonial power because the "universal" features of humanity are the characteristics of those who occupy positions of political dominance.' The mechanism through which universalism abets colonial domination is by elevating some very specific facts about European culture to the status of general descriptions of humanity, valid at a global scale. Cultures that do not match these very specific descriptions are then consigned to the status of being backward, needing tutoring in civilization, incapable of governing themselves. As the editors describe it, 'the myth of universality is thus a primary strategy of imperial control ... on the basis of an assumption that "European" equals "universal"'.[1]

We see in this argument two of the most commonly held views by postcolonial theorists. One is a formal, meta-theoretical idea – that claims to universality are intrinsically suspect because they ignore social heterogeneity. This is why, in postcolonial texts, we often find critiques of universalism cashed out in terms of its homogenizing, leveling effects. The worry is that it ignores diversity, and in so doing, it marginalizes any practice or social convention that does not conform to what is being elevated to the universal.

And the act of marginalization is an act of suppression, of the exertion of power. The second view is a substantive one – that universalization is complicit with European domination in particular. This is so because in the intellectual world, Western theories are utterly dominant. Insofar as they are the frameworks that guide intellectual inquiry, or the theories that inform political practice, they imbue it with an enduring Eurocentrism. The frameworks and theories inherited from the Enlightenment bear the mark of their geographical origin. But the mark is not easily discerned. It operates insidiously, as the hidden premise of these doctrines. The task of postcolonial criticism is to expunge it, by exposing its presence and highlighting its effects.

Owing to its assigned complicity with colonial domination, anti-universalism has become a watchword among postcolonial theorists. And because of the enormous influence of postcolonial theory in academic culture, it has become the common sense of many on the left. So too the hostility to the 'grand narratives' associated with Marxism and progressive liberalism. The action these days is in 'the fragment', the marginal, the practices and cultural conventions that are unique to a particular setting and cannot be subsumed into a generalized analysis – as Dipesh Chakrabarty describes them, the 'heterogeneities and incommensurabilities' of the local.[2] This is where we are directed to search for political agency.

The hostility to universalizing theories carries some interesting implications. The radical tradition since Marx and Engels' time has relied on two foundational premises for all of its political analysis. The first is that as capitalism expands across the globe, it imposes certain economic constraints – one might even call them compulsions – on the actors that come under its sway. Hence, as it takes root in Asia, Latin America, Africa and elsewhere, economic production in all these regions is forced to abide by a *common* set of rules. How the regions develop, what the tempo of growth is, will not be identical – it will proceed unevenly, at different rates, with considerable institutional variation. They will not all look the same. But their differences will be worked out in response to a common set of compulsions, coming from the underlying capitalist structure. On the other side of the analysis, it is taken for granted that as capitalism imposes its logic on actors, as it exercises its economic and political domination, it will elicit a response from labouring groups. They will resist its depredations in order to defend their well-being. This will be true regardless of the cultural or religious identity of these groups. The reason for their resistance is that, whatever the facts about their local culture, whatever its 'incommensurabilities' with respect to other ways of being, capitalism generates an assault on some basic needs that all people have in common. So just as capitalism imposes a common logic of reproduction across regions, it also elicits a common resistance from labour. Again, the resistance will not take the same form, it will not be ubiquitous, but the potential for its exercise will be a universal one, because the wellspring that generates it – workers' drive to defend their well-being – is common across cultures.

These two beliefs have been foundational to much of radical analysis and practice for more than a century. But if we accept postcolonial theory's injunctions against universalism, they must both be rejected, for they are both unabashedly universalistic. The implications are profound. What is left of radical analysis if we expunge capitalism from its theoretical tool kit? How do we analyze the global depression since 2007, how do we make sense of the drive for austerity that has swept the Atlantic world, if not by tracing the logic of profit-driven economies and the relentless struggle to maximize profits? And what do we make of the global resistance to these impositions, how do we understand the fact that the same slogans can be found in Cairo, Buenos Aires, Madison and London, if not through some universal interests that are being expressed in them? Indeed, how do we generate *any* analysis of capitalism without recourse to at least some universalizing categories?

THE UNIVERSAL COMPULSIONS OF CAPITAL

The stakes being rather high, one would think that postcolonial theorists might grant amnesty to concepts like capitalism or class interests. Perhaps these are examples of universalizing categories that have some justification, and might therefore escape the charge of Eurocentrism. But as it happens, not only are these concepts included in the list of offenders, but they are singled out as *exemplars* of all that is suspect in Marxist theory. Gyan Prakash expresses the sentiment well in one of his broadsides against Enlightenment (e.g. Marxist) thought. To analyze social formations through the prism of capitalism, or capitalist development, he suggests, inevitably leads to some kind of reductionism. It makes all social phenomena seem as if they are nothing but reflexes of economic relations. Hence, he argues, 'making capitalism the foundational theme [of historical analyses] amounts to homogenizing the histories that remain heterogenous within it'.[3] This tendency blinds Marxists to the specificity of local social relations. They either fail to notice practices and conventions that are independent of capitalist dynamics, or simply assume that whatever independence they have will soon dissolve. Even more, the very idea that social formations can be analyzed through the lens of their economic dynamics – their mode of production – is not only mistaken, but also Eurocentric and complicit with imperial domination. 'Like many other nineteenth-century European ideas', Prakash notes, 'the staging of the Eurocentric mode-of-production narrative as history should be seen as an analogue of nineteenth-century territorial imperialism.'[4]

Dipesh Chakrabarty has given this argument some structure in his influential book, *Provincializing Europe* (2007). The idea of a universalizing capitalism, he argues, is guilty of two sins. The *first* is that it denies non-Western societies their history. This it does by squeezing them into a rigid schema imported from the European experience. Instead of respecting the autonomy and specificity of regional experiences, Marxists turn regional histories into so many *variations on a theme*. Every country is categorized on the extent to which it conforms with, or departs from an idealized concept of capitalism. In so doing, regional histories never are able to escape from being footnotes to the European experience. The telos of all national histories remains the same, with Europe as their endpoint. The *second* error associated with the idea of capitalism is that it evacuates all contingency from historical development. The faith that Marxists repose in the universalizing dynamic of capitalism blinds them to the possibility of 'discontinuities, ruptures, and shifts in the historical process', as Chakrabarty puts it.[5] Freed from interruption by human agency, the future becomes a knowable entity, drawing toward a determinable end.

Chakrabarty is crystallizing a view held by many postcolonial theorists, that if they allow categories like capitalism a central place in their tool kit, they also commit to a historical teleology. Taken together, the two criticisms I have outlined suggest that the universalizing assumptions of concepts like capitalism are not just mistaken, but politically dangerous. They deny non-Western societies the possibility of their own history, but they also disparage the possibility of their crafting their own futures. In so doing, they impugn the value of political agency and struggle.

The fact that postcolonial theorists include the concept of capitalism in their list of offending ideas bequeathed by the Enlightenment would seem to generate a conundrum. Surely there is no denying the fact that, over the course of the past century, capitalism really has spread across the globe, imbricating itself in most all of the postcolonial world. And if it has taken root in some areas, whether in Asia or Latin America, it must also have affected the actual institutional make-up of those regions. Their economies have been transformed by the pressures of capital accumulation, and many of their non-economic institutions have been changed to accommodate to its logic. There is, therefore, a common thread that runs through these regions, even though they remain highly diverse, and this thread does bind them together in some way. Because it speaks directly to this, the category of capitalism surely has some purchase in the analysis of their economic and political evolution. For any such analysis to be taken seriously at all, it has to recognize this simple and basic fact – because it *is* a fact. But the rhetoric of postcolonial theory seems perilously close to denying this very fact, when it castigates Marxists for abiding by 'universalizing' concepts like capitalism. The conundrum, then, is this: postcolonial theory seems to be denying the reality of capitalism having spread across the world; and if it is not denying it, then what are the grounds on which it can criticize Marxists for insisting that the concept has cross-cultural validity?

In *Provincialzing Europe* Chakrabarty affirms that capitalism has in fact globalized over the past century or so. But while he acknowledges the fact of its *globalization*, he denies that this is tantamount to its *universalization*.[6] This allows him, and theorists who follow this line of thinking, to affirm the obvious fact that market dependence has spread to the far corners of the world, while still denying that the category of capitalism can be used for its analysis.[7] For Chakrabarty, a properly universalizing capitalism is one that subordinates all social practices to its own logic. A capitalism that spreads to any particular corner of the world can be said to have globalized. But it cannot have universalized unless it transforms all social relations to reflect its own priorities and values. In so far as there are practices or social relations that remain independent, that interrupt its totalizing thrust, its mission remains incomplete. Indeed, it can be judged to have failed. 'No historic form of capital, however global in its reach', Chakrabarty argues, 'can ever be a universal. No global, or even local for that matter, capital can ever represent the universal logic of capital, for any historically available form of capital is a provisional compromise' between its totalizing drive, on the one hand, and the obduracy of local customs and conventions, on the other.[8] The basic idea here is that the abstract logic of capital is always modified in some way by local social relations; in so far as it is forced to adjust to them in some way, the description of capitalism that is contained in abstract, general theories, will not map onto the way in which people are actually living their lives on the ground. There will be a gap between the description of capitalism in the abstract, and the really existing capitalism in a given region. This is how it can globalize, but without ever universalizing itself – it could be said to have universalized only if it properly universalized certain *properties*.

In purely formal terms Chakrabarty's arguments are sound. It is an entirely justified argument to insist that an object should be classified as belonging to a certain kind of thing, or a category, only if it exhibits the properties associated with that kind of thing. If what we call capitalism in its Peruvian instance does not have the same properties as in its classic examples, then we might justifiably say that to classify what we find in Peru as 'capitalist' is misleading, and that the category is potentially misleading. The question, of course, is whether or not the properties we are identifying with the universal can be justified. It could be that Chakrabarty is formally correct, but substantively mistaken. He is right to insist that capitalism must properly transmit certain properties to new regions if it can be said to have universalized – but he might be mistaken in the properties on which he bases his judgments. And this is in fact what I will show in what follows.

Chakrabarty's entire case rests on one question: is it in fact justified to require that all social relations become subordinated to capitalism, for us to be able to use the category of capital? Chakrabarty's argument is not all that idiosyncratic. He is drawing on a tradition within Marxian theorizing itself, which has consistently described capitalism as a totalizing system, driven to expand, to subordinate all social relations to its own logic. But it is one thing to point to capitalisms corrosive effect on social conventions. It is quite another to build the strongest version of that observation into ones definition of capitalism itself. Postcolonial theorists make a subtle, but crucial error. They accept the description of capitalism by Marx, in which he characterizes it as having an internal drive for self-expansion. Thus Ranajit Guha summarizes Marx as arguing the following:

> This [universalizing] tendency derives from the self-expansion of capital. Its function is to create a world market, subjugate all antecedent modes of production, and replace all jural and institutional concomitants of such modes and generally the entire edifice of precapitalist cultures by laws, institutions, values, and other elements of a culture appropriate to bourgeois rule.[9]

Marx is making two claims here: first, that capitalism is driven to expand, and it is this relentless pressure to press toward ever new regions that is behind its universalization; second, that the universalizing drive also impels it to dismantle any legal or cultural conventions that are inimical to its dominance. Postcolonial theorists tend to focus on the second clause in this passage – the idea that capitalism, as it universalizes, will replace 'the entire edifice' of pre-capitalist values and laws with new ones. This is what is behind Chakrabarty's denial that capital has universalized, since it is clear to him that there are many institutions in capitalism, especially in non-Western societies, that cannot be derived from the logic of capital, and indeed, which have a reproductive integrity of their own. That being the case, is it not legitimate to conclude that universalization has failed?

Now it could be that there is an overly narrow fixation here on Marx's characterization. One way to proceed, if we wanted to reject Chakrabarty's argument, is to simply set aside Marx's passage and argue for a new criterion for successful universalization. But a case can be made that even this passage does not lend itself to postcolonial theorists' reading of it. Marx is not arguing that capital requires a root-and-branch transformation of all institutions, but that the institutions in place will be those that are 'appropriate to bourgeois rule'. It is true that this might call for a dismantling of very many parts of the pre-capitalist legal and normative conventions – but whether or not it does, and how far the call for dismantling goes, will be decided by what is needed for capitalism to reproduce itself – for its self-expansion to proceed. It is entirely possible that this expansion of accumulation could proceed while leaving intact a great many aspects of the *ancien regime*. At least, this is one reading of the passage.

It is also a more plausible way to understand what is involved in capitalism's expansion. Nobody, including Chakrabarty, Guha and other postcolonial theorists, disputes that capitalism is, in the first instance, a way of organizing economic activities – the production and distribution of goods. In an economy organized along capitalist lines, economic units are compelled to focus single-mindedly on expanding their operations, in an endless cycle of accumulation. Capitalists pursue profits because if their firms fail to do so, they are overtaken by their rivals in the market. Wherever capitalism goes, so too does this imperative. This is what Marx was referring to in the first part of the passage quoted above and neither Guha nor Chakrabarty questions it. All that is required for capitalism to reproduce itself is for this imperative to be followed by economic actors – the imperative for firms to seek out greater markets, more profit, by out-competing their rivals.

Now, if capitalists are single-mindedly driven to accumulate, then their attitude toward cultural and legal institutions will be instrumental toward the achievement of this goal. If the institutions in place inhibit the accumulation of capital, if they do not respect private property or if they insulate labour from having to seek out waged work, then those institutions will most likely come under attack, as Marx suggests. Capital will carry out a campaign to overturn them. But what if existing institutions do not come into conflict with accumulation? What if they are neutral with respect to capitalist interests? This is the crucial question, which Chakrabarty simply ignores. In his argument, a universalizing capitalism must internalize all social relations to its own logic. It must be a totalizing system, which refuses to allow any autonomy to other social relations. Chakrabarty does produce a reason for this. So long as social practices refuse to conform to the direct needs of capital, so long as they refuse to reflect capital's own values and priorities, they carry the threat of disrupting its reproduction. They embody 'other ways of being in the world' than as a bearer of labour power, or a consumer of commodities.[10] Capital cannot tolerate the possibility of 'ways of being in the world' that are not aligned with its own logic. It therefore seeks what he calls their 'subjugation/destruction'.[11]

This whole argument rests on the assumption that if a practice does not *directly* advance capitalism's reproduction, by being part of what Chakrabarty calls its 'life-process', it must elicit a hostile response from capital. But we might ask, why on earth would this be so? Returning to the question I posed in the preceding paragraph, if a practice is simply neutral with respect to accumulation, wouldn't the natural response from capital be one of indifference? Chakrabarty makes it seem as though capitalist managers walk around with their own political Geiger counters, measuring the compatibility of every social practice with their own priorities. But surely the more reasonable picture is this: capitalists seek to expand their operations, make the best possible returns on their investments, and as long as their operations are running smoothly, they simply do not care about the conventions and mores of the surrounding environment. The signal, to them, that something needs to be changed is when aspects of the environment disrupt their operations – by stimulating labour conflict, or restricting markets, and such. When that happens, they swing into action, and target the culprit practices for change. But as for other practices – which may very well embody other 'ways of being in the world' – capitalists simply would be indifferent.

As long as local customs do not inhibit or undermine capital accumulation, capitalists will not see any reason to overturn them – this is the conclusion we have reached. This has two immediate implications. The first has to do with Chakrabarty's grounds for denying the universalization of capital. On his argument, the reason we cannot accept that it has universalized is that the pure logic of capital is modified by the local customs of the regions into which it spreads. But we have just seen that a mere modification of a practice does not constitute grounds for rejecting its viability. As long as its basic rules and compulsions remain intact, we are justified in regarding it as a species of its earlier, unmodified, ancestor. It therefore follows – and this is my second point – that if what has been globalized really is capitalist economic relations, than it makes little sense to deny that those relations have also been universalized. We can reject Chakrabarty's claim that globalization does not imply universalization. How could it not? If the practices that have spread globally can be identified as capitalist, then they have also been universalized. It is the fact that we can recognize them as distinctively capitalist that allows us to pronounce capital's globalization. If we can affirm that they are in fact capitalist, and that they therefore have the properties associated with capitalism, how can we then deny their universalization? The very idea seems bizarre.

THE UNIVERSAL GROUNDS FOR RESISTANCE

Capitalism spreads to all corners of the world, driven by its insatiable thirst for profits, and in so doing, in bringing an ever-increasing proportion of the global population under its sway, it creates a truly universal history, a history of capital. Postcolonial theorists will often give at least some lip service to this aspect of global capitalism, even if they deny its substance. What makes them even more uncomfortable is the second component of a materialist analysis, which has to do with the sources of resistance. There is no dispute around the idea that as capitalism spreads it meets with resistance – from workers, from peasants fighting for their land, from indigenous populations, etc. Indeed, the celebration of these struggles is something of a calling card for postcolonial theorists. In this, they would seem to be of a piece with the more conventional Marxist understanding of capitalist politics. But the similarity in approaches is only at the surface. Whereas Marxists have understood resistance from below as an expression of the real interests of labouring groups, postcolonial theory typically shies away from any talk of objective, universal interests. The sources of struggle are taken to be local, specific to the culture of the labouring groups, a product of their very particular location and history – and not the expression of interests linked to certain universal basic needs.

The hostility to analyses that see resistance as an expression of common universal drives is that they impute to agents a consciousness that is peculiar to the developed West. To see struggles as emanating from material interests is 'to invest [workers] with a *bourgeois rationality,* since it is only in such a system of rationality that the 'economic utility' of an action (or an object, relationship, institution, etc.) defines its reasonableness'.[12] All of this is part of the escape from essentializing categories handed down by Enlightenment thought, initiated by post-structuralist philosophy. As Arturo Escobar explains, 'with poststructuralism's theory of the subject we are … compelled to give up the liberal idea of the subject as a self-bounded, autonomous, rational individual. The subject is produced by/in historical discourses and practices in a multiplicity of domains.'[13]

So, whereas traditional Marxist and materialist theories hew to some conception of human needs, which constitute the basis on which resistance is built, current avatars of post-structuralism – postcolonial theory being the most illustrious – reject this idea in favour of one in which individuals are entirely constituted by discourse, culture, customs, etc. In so far as there is resistance to capitalism, it must be understood as an expression of local and very particular conceptions of needs – not only constructed by geographically restricted histories, but working through a cosmology that resists translation. In Chakrabarty's expression, what drives the struggle against capital is the 'infinite incommensurabilities' of local cultures[14] – something that he posits outside of the universalizing narratives of Enlightenment thought.

The question, then, is whether it is unwarranted to assign some universal needs and interests to agents, which span across cultures and across time. There is no doubt that, for the most part, the things that agents value and pursue are culturally constructed. In this, postcolonial theorists and more traditional progressives are of one mind. But is Escobar right in arguing that agents are not just influenced, but entirely *produced* by discourse and custom? Surely we can recognize the cultural construction of many, even most, of our values and beliefs, while also recognizing that there is a small core of the latter that humans hold in common across cultures. To give one central example, there is no culture in the world, nor has there ever been one, in which agents did not give regard to their physical well-being. A concern for certain basic needs – for food, shelter, safety, etc. – is part of the normative repertoire of agents across localities and time. There has never been a culture that has endured over time which erased or ignored the valuation of basic needs, since the fulfillment of these needs is a precondition for the culture's reproduction. Hence, we can affirm that there are some aspects of human agency that are not entirely the construction of local culture, if by that we mean that they are specific to that culture. These aspects are rooted in aspects of human psychology that extend across time and space – they are components of our human nature.

Now to say that social agents are oriented to give due regard to their physical well-being is not to insist that culture has no influence in this domain. What they consume, the kinds of dwellings they prefer, their sartorial inclinations – all these can be shaped by local custom and the contingencies of history. It is common to find cultural theorists pointing to the variability in forms of consumption as evidence that needs are cultural constructions. But this is a bogus argument. The fact that the *form* of consumption is shaped by history – which it might be to some extent – is no evidence against the view that there is a need for basic sustenance. They are, after all, presented as forms *of* something. The language is a signal to the common factor – to label them forms of consumption is to say that they are species of a common genus. The question is whether the higher-order need for sustenance is itself a cultural construction. Or, correspondingly, whether culture can erase the recognition of basic needs. To even pose the question shows how absurd it is.[15]

It is the agential concern for well-being that anchors capitalism in any culture where it implants itself. As Marx observed, once capitalist relations are in place, once agents are subsumed under its imperatives, the 'dull compulsion of economic relations' is all it takes to induce workers to offer themselves up for exploitation. This is true regardless of culture and ideology – if they are in the position of being a worker, they will make themselves available for work. This claim presumes the facts about human nature I have just defended, namely, that agents in any culture are motivated to defend their physical well-being. The reason they make their labour-power available to employers is that this is the only option that they have open to them if they are to maintain their well-being. They are free to refuse of course, if their culture tells them that such practices are unacceptable – but as Engels pointed out in his earliest writings, this only means that they are free to starve.[16] I belabour this point only for the following reason – postcolonial theorists cannot affirm the globalization of capital, the spread of wage labour across the world, while also denying the reality of basic needs and people's regard for their physical well-being. If they continue to insist on a thoroughly constructionist view, they must explain why the 'dull compulsion of economic relations' can be effective wherever capitalist class relations are secured, regardless of culture or ideology or religion.

Now, while this one aspect of human nature is the foundation on which exploitation rests, it is also a central fount for resistance. The same concern for well-being that drives workers into the arms of capitalists also motivates them to resist the *terms* of their exploitation. Employers' remorseless drive for profits has, as its most direct expression, a constant search for minimizing the costs of production. The most obvious such cost, of course, is wages. But the reduction of wages, while a condition for increased profit margins, necessarily means a squeeze on workers' standards of living – and hence an assault, in varying degrees of intensity, on their well-being. For some workers in high-end or unionized sectors, the squeeze can be contained within tolerable limits, so that it amounts to struggle around their standard of living, but not necessarily around their basic needs. But for much of the Global South and an increasing range of sectors in the developed world, the stakes are much higher. Now add to this the drive the need for employers to manage other costs associated with production – trying to squeeze out extra time from outdated machinery, hence increasing the risk of injury to workers, the drive to speed-up the pace and intensity of work, the lengthening of the working day, the raids on pensions and retirement benefits, etc. – and we can see that accumulation comes up systematically against workers' interest in their well-being. Workers' movements are often going to be geared simply at securing the basic conditions for their reproduction, not just higher standards of living.

The concern for their well-being, then, is the reason why proletarians offer themselves up for exploitation, and why, having done so, they proceed to struggle around its terms. This particular aspect of their human nature locks them in a condition of *antagonistic interdependence* with capital. It is in their interest to seek out employment, in order to reproduce themselves; but the condition for securing employment is that they must submit to the authority of their employer, who is driven to undermine their well-being, even while he uses their labouring activity. The first dimension of this process – their submission to the labour contract – explains why capitalism can take root and secure itself in any and all corners of the globe. The second dimension – of fighting around the terms of their exploitation – explains why class reproduction begets class *struggle* in every region where capitalism establishes itself.[17] The universalization of capital has as its dual the universal struggle for workers to defend their well-being.

We have derived both of these universalisms from just one component of human nature. This does not in any way suggest that that is all there is to it. Most progressive thinkers have believed that there are other components to human nature, other needs that span across regional cultures. Thus, for example, there is the need for autonomy or freedom from coercion, for creative expression, for respect – just to name a few. My point is not that human nature can be reduced to one basic, biological need. It is, rather, that this need does exist, even if it is less exalted than some others; and, more importantly, that it can account for a startling range of practices and institutions that radicals are concerned with. It is a sign of how far left thinking has fallen, how degenerate the intellectual culture has become, that it would even be necessary to defend its reality.[18]

CONCLUSION

Whatever their many disagreements may have been over the past century or so, radicals and progressives have almost always agreed on two basic postulates – that as capitalism spreads, it subordinates all parts of the world to a common set of compulsions; and that wherever it spreads, those whom it subjugates and exploits will have a common interest in struggling against it, regardless of culture or creed. Has there ever been a time when both of these claims are more obviously true? For more than five years now, a tremendous economic crisis has roiled global markets and convulsed national economies from the United States to East Asia, from Northern Europe to Southern Africa. If there was ever a doubt that capital has universalized, surely we can put it to rest now. Correspondingly, movements against neoliberalism have broken out across the globe, organized around a set of demands that converge around a strikingly small set of concerns – for economic security, greater rights, for protecting basic services, and for respite from the unrelenting demands of the market. This is perhaps the first time since 1968 that there is a real glimmer of a global movement emerging again. It is only a hint, of course, of what many of us hope it can become. But it is more than we have had in quite some time.

It seems quite bizarre, at a time like this, to find ourselves saddled with a theory that has made its name by dismantling some of the very conceptual pillars that can help us understand the political conjuncture, and to devise effective strategy. Postcolonial theory has made some real gains in certain domains, especially in its mainstreaming of literature coming out of the global south. Over the 1980s and 1990s, it played an important role in keeping alive the idea of anti-colonialism and anti-imperialism; and of course it has made the problem of Eurocentrism a watchword among progressive intellectuals. But these achievements have come with a steep price tag. Giving up on the concept of universalism, as many of the leading lights of this theoretical movement have, is hardly a step toward a more adequate theorization of the times in which we live.

I have shown that the arguments against universalism – at least the ones that have greatest currency – are without merit. The two most salient universalisms of our time – the spread of capitalist social relations and the interest that working people have in resisting this spread – stand affirmed. Postcolonial theorists have spilled a great deal of ink tilting against windmills of their own creation. In so doing, they have also given license to a massive resurgence of nativism and Orientalism. It is not just that they emphasize the local over the universal. Their valorization of the local, their obsession with cultural particularities, and most of all, their insistence on culture as the well-spring of agency, has given license to the very exoticism that the left once abhorred in colonial depictions of the non-West.

Throughout the twentieth century, the anchor for anti-colonial movements was, at least for the left, a belief that oppression was wrong wherever it was practiced, because it was an affront to some basic human needs – for dignity, for liberty, for basic well-being. But now, in the name of anti-Eurocentrism, postcolonial theory has resurrected the very cultural essentialism that progressives viewed – rightly – as the ideological justification for imperial domination. What better excuse to deny peoples their rights than to impugn the very idea of rights, and universal interests, as culturally biased? But if this kind of ideological manoeuvre is to be rejected, it is hard to see how it could be, except through an embrace of the very universalism that postcolonial theorists ask us to eschew. No revival of an international and democratic left is possible unless we clear away these cobwebs, thereby affirming the two universalisms – our common humanity, and the threat to it posed by a viciously universalizing capitalism.

NOTES

1   Bill Ashcroft, Gareth Griffiths, and Helen Triffin, eds., *The Postcolonial Studies Reader*, London: Routledge, 1995, p. 55.

2   Dipesh Chakrabarty, *Provincializing Europe*, Princeton: Princeton University Press, 2007, Second Edition, p. 95.

3   Gyan Prakash, 'Postcolonial Criticism and Indian Historiography', *Social Text*, No. 31/32, 1992, p. 13.

4   Prakash, 'Postcolonial Criticism', p. 14.

5   Chakrabarty, *Provincializing Europe*, p. 23.

6   Chakrabarty, *Provincializing Europe*, p. 71.

7   Chakrabarty's is not the only argument for the failure of capital's universalization or for the suspect nature of Marxism's universalizing framework. But it is one of the most influential. For a more detailed analysis of Chakrabarty's work, and of other theorists associated with the *Subaltern Studies* project, see my *Postcolonial Theory and the Specter of Capital*, London: Verso, 2013.

8   Chakrabarty, *Provincializing Europe*, p. 70. This argument is embedded in a complicated discussion of two different kinds of histories – History1, which embodies the universalizing drive of capital, and History2, which embodies those practices that manage to retain their own integrity. I have refrained from using this jargon because it would needlessly complicate the exposition, without adding any content. For a discussion and extended critique of the conclusions that Chakrabarty draws from the History1/History2 dual, see my *Postcolonial Theory*, especially Chapter 9.

9   *Dominance without Hegemony*, Princeton: Princeton University Press, 2000, pp. 13-14.

10   Chakrabarty, *Provincializing Europe*, p. 66.

11   Chakrabarty, *Provincializing Europe*, p. 67.

12   Dipesh Chakrabarty, *Rethinking Working Class History: Bengal 1890-1940*, Princeton: Princeton University Press, 1989, p. 212, emphasis added.

13   Arturo Escobar, 'After Nature: Steps to an Anti-essentialist Political Ecology', *Current Anthropology*, 40(1), February 1999, p. 3.

14   Chakrabarty, *Provincializing Europe*, p. 254.

15   Another argument against basic needs is that we typically consume a great deal that has no connection with our needs. This is of course true, but even sillier than the objection I have described in the main text. The fact that much of what we consume is unnecessary, or is culturally shaped, hardly overturns the

fact that we still need to have some basic needs met in order to survive.

16   Frederick Engels, *The Condition of the Working Class in England*, New York: Penguin Books, 1987 [1844].

17   To be precise, what it begets is the *motivation* to struggle. Whether or not the motivation generates actual resistance, in the form of collective action, depends on a host of additional and contingent factors.

18   What is most shocking of all is to find self-styled Marxists denying the universality of basic needs as a component of human nature. This was a subject of some controversy in the 1980s, and one might be forgiven for thinking that the matter had been settled. But, perhaps owing to the continuing (and rather baffling) influence of Althusser, especially among younger intellectuals, the denials persist. For the definitive textual evidence on Marx, see Normal Geras' *Marx and Human Nature: Refutation of a Legend*, London: Verso, 1983. More recently, see on the young Marx, the superb study by David Leopold, *The Young Karl Marx: German Philosophy, and Human Flourishing*, Cambridge: Cambridge University Press, 2007; more globally, see John McMurtry, *The Structure of Marx's World-View*, Princeton: Princeton University Press, 1978. The only serious recent attempt I know of to raise doubts about Marx's commitment to a human nature is Sean Sayers, *Marxism and Human Nature*, New York: Routledge, 1998, but Sayers qualifies his argument by categorically denying the case for an anti-humanist Marx (the Marx of Althusser) and affirming that 'Marxism... does not reject the notion of a universal human nature' (p. 159).

THE UNDERPINNINGS OF CLASS IN THE DIGITAL AGE: LIVING, LABOUR AND VALUE

URSULA HUWS

As Marxism has segued in and out of vogue, there is hardly a Marxian concept that has not at some time been questioned as anachronistic, in the light of the transformations in economic and political conditions that have occurred over the last century and a half. The current renewal of interest in Marx's ideas is no exception. It is indeed no easy task to apply theoretical concepts developed in the mid nineteenth century to a world where capitalism has penetrated every region and every aspect of life, where the pace of technological change is so rapid that labour processes are obsolescent within months of being introduced and where the division of labour is so intricate that no single worker has any chance of grasping it in its full complexity. Divisions between manual and non-manual work dissolve and are reconstituted, the boundaries between production, distribution and consumption melt away, and, whilst some paid work morphs into unpaid work, new jobs and new economic activities are generated from areas of life which were traditionally seen as beyond the scope of any market. In the suck and blow of commodification, the abstract becomes concrete and the concrete abstract, casting doubt on conceptual categories that formerly seemed self-evident. It may seem that we need new definitions of the most basic concepts used by Karl Marx, including 'class', 'commodity' and 'labour'.

One current idea that has attracted considerable support, especially among the young, is the notion that the idea of a working class defined by its direct relationship to production is outmoded. Since all aspects of life, such arguments go, have been drawn into the scope of the capitalist cash nexus in some way, all those who are not actually part of the capitalist class must be regarded as part of an undifferentiated 'multitude'. In Michael Hardt and Antonio Negri's formulation, this 'multitude' takes the place of a working class, while according to Guy Standing, a 'precariat' constitutes a new class in and for itself alongside the traditional proletariat.[1] Standing does not attempt to locate this 'precariat' with any precision in relation to capitalist production processes. However, many of the followers of Hardt and Negri have engaged in elaborate attempts to do so in relation to the 'multitude'. Two questions in particular, have puzzled them: what sorts of commodities are being produced by members of this multitude?[2] And how does the value produced by this labour accrue to capital?

In these debates particular attention has been paid to the value created online by 'virtual' or 'digital' labour. In the field which is becoming known as 'Internet studies', there have recently been energetic discussions about 'digital labour' and how it should be conceptualised.[3] These debates have addressed the increasingly blurred boundaries between 'work' and 'play' (encapsulated in the term 'playbour'[4]) and between production and consumption ('prosumption'[5] and 'co-creation'[6]); discussed the problematic category of 'free labour'[7] and questioned whether such labour, paid or unpaid, can be regarded as producing surplus value and whether it is 'exploitative' or 'alienated'. With the exception of Andrew Ross, few of these authors have drawn parallels with other forms of labour carried out offline. Yet, many of the questions they raise apply much more generally to labour under capitalism. These debates thus provide a useful starting point for investigating the labour theory of value itself, and how – or, some would wonder, even if – it can be applied in twenty-first century conditions.

This essay argues that it is still possible to apply Marx's theory in current conditions, to define what is, or is not, a commodity, to identify the point of production of such commodities, whether material or immaterial, and to define the global working class in relation to these production processes. In order to do so, however, it is necessary to re-examine the labour theory of value in all its dimensions. I pay particular attention to 'digital' or 'virtual' labour not only because it is currently attracting so much attention, but also because online labour is particularly difficult to conceptualise. It is thus a fertile source of cases against which to test more general hypotheses. If a theory can apply here, then it should be more generally applicable. The aim of doing this is to enable a mapping of the working class across the whole economy by applying the theory more broadly (as Marx did). This is an important task, in my view, because without a clear sense of which workers are engaged directly in the antagonistic relation to capital that characterises commodity production, and without identifying where that point of production is located, it is impossible to identify strategies that will enable labour to confront capital where it is possible to exercise some power to shape the future in its own interests.

LABOUR AND CAPITALISM

The labour theory of value is the knot at the heart of Marx's conceptualisation of capitalism as a social relationship. It integrally links three things: workers' need for subsistence, their labour, and the surplus value expropriated from the results of that labour, without which capital cannot be accumulated or capitalism perpetuated. The expropriation of labour is the act of violence at the heart of this relationship. It is the worker's labour time which constitutes the bone which is fought over in this relationship, so an understanding of how and under what circumstances this expropriation takes place is critical to an understanding both of capitalism as a system and of which workers can be said to belong to the working class. The knot cannot be undone: each rope is essential to holding the system together. Nevertheless it seems necessary to examine it, strand by strand, so that we can grasp how it is put together, what tightens it, and what enables new threads to be drawn in or existing ones more elaborately entangled.

In its basic form, the argument is remarkably simple: the worker, obliged to do so in order to subsist, works a given number of hours for the capitalist, producing a certain value as a result. Some of this value is essential to cover the cost of subsistence, and the hours worked to produce this value ('necessary labour time') are (usually) reimbursed. The remainder ('surplus value') is appropriated by the capitalist to distribute as profit and invest in new means of production. On close examination, however, just about every element of this simple story turns out to be open to question. What, exactly, is 'labour'? And, more particularly, what labour is productive of surplus value? How is 'subsistence' to be defined? Does it include only what the individual worker needs to keep going, or does it also include what is required for the sustenance of his or her entire household? If we cannot define subsistence precisely, how can we possibly calculate necessary labour time? And, just because all value within capitalism ultimately derives from the results of human labour applied to the earth's raw materials, does this mean that all value that accrues to individual capitalists is necessarily surplus value?

The current debates around 'digital labour' skim past some of these questions and oversimplify others. This essay will not attempt to rewrite Marx's entire theory, as that would be both hopelessly over-ambitious and misguided. Rather, it will take some of the questions raised in these debates about digital labour as starting points for examining the factors that will have to be taken into account in any modern elaboration of Marx's theory, an elaboration that will, in my view, be an essential precondition for understanding the new class formations that are emerging in the twenty-first century in all their complex and contradictory dimensions. I will do this by attempting to unravel the three strands – *living* (or subsistence), *labour*, and *value* – in order to categorise their separate components. I will do this in reverse order, reflecting the priorities of current debates in this field. These concepts are all well used and difficult to re-employ without bringing along a large freight of associated meanings, both intended and unintended. So it is perhaps useful to begin with two explanatory notes.

The first concerns the terminology. In advanced capitalist societies, not only is the division of labour extremely complex but so, too, is the distribution of wealth. Workers' subsistence is achieved not only as a direct result of waged labour but also via redistribution through the financial system (in the form of credit, private insurance and pension schemes, etc.) and through the state (in a monetary form through tax and social security systems, and in kind by means of state-provided services). In such a context, the direct connection between labour and value can be obscured. It is common for analysts to follow Marx in classifying labour as 'productive' or 'unproductive'. The approach I adopt in this essay draws on insights from feminism and makes a slightly different distinction. This is a distinction between labour which is productive for capitalism as a whole (which can be termed 'reproductive') and labour which is directly productive for individual capitalists (which, for lack of a better term, I have named 'directly productive'). I draw a further distinction between work that is paid and work that is unpaid. I argue that (dependent though it is on other forms of labour for its reproduction) the quintessential form of labour that characterises capitalism is labour that *both* produces value for capital *and* produces the income that is necessary for the worker's survival. This is work whose very performance contains within itself the contestation of labour time between worker and capitalist at whose heart lies the wrench of expropriation, the experience of which Marx described as 'alienation' (a term which has, unfortunately, become so contaminated with other meanings that it can no longer be used with the precision with which Marx employed it). And this is therefore the work that lies at the centre of the accumulation process. The workplace is not, of course, the only place that labour confronts capital. But, because capital cannot be accumulated without workers' consent, it is the site at which labour has the greatest potential power to wrest concessions from capital (without resorting to bloodshed).

Table 1 Labour: A Schematic Typology

	Paid labour	Unpaid labour
Reproductive (productive for society / capitalism in general)	**A** Public administration and public service work (including NGOs); individually provided private services.	**B** Domestic labour (childcare, household maintenance, etc., including non-market cultural activities).
Directly productive (for individual capitalist enterprises)	**C** Commodity production, including distribution.	**D** Consumption work.

The term 'waged labour' encompasses work which Marx would have designated as both productive and unproductive. It also excludes various forms of labour (piecework, freelance work, etc.) paid in non-wage forms, which contribute directly both to capital accumulation and workers' subsistence. Defining labour only in terms of whether it is productive or not, in Marx's sense, ignores the reality that (as will be discussed below) there is a considerable amount of unpaid labour which produces value directly for capital without contributing to the worker's subsistence. Conversely, of course, there is paid labour which contributes to subsistence without creating value directly for capital. After spending some time considering a range of alternatives (including 'contested productive labour', 'alienated productive labour', 'directly productive labour' and 'productive waged labour'), I have, for the purposes of this essay, decided to use a shorthand term to distinguish this form of labour from other forms of productive and waged labour. Drawing on the metaphor I have used to describe the labour theory of value, I therefore refer to it below as labour which is 'inside the knot' (Quadrant C in Table 1).

Labour 'inside the knot', in this definition, is labour carried out directly for a capitalist employer by a worker who is dependent on this labour for subsistence and is therefore a front-line adversary in the struggle between capital and labour over how much labour time should be exchanged for how much money. This may seem like a somewhat narrow definition. It is indeed the sort of definition that was much criticised in the 1960s and 1970s for excluding large groups of workers who often saw themselves as part of the working class, including public sector workers and some service workers, whose relationship to production was indirect. In using it here,

I am not arguing that such workers are not productive. On the contrary, many of the tasks they perform are essential for the reproduction of labour. However, these workers' exposure to the coercive logic of capitalism may be somewhat mitigated, either because they are working under older forms of employment (for instance as domestic servants or as petty commodity producers), or because they are employed by the state to provide as yet uncommodified services.

These forms of labour still exist, of course, but, as I have argued elsewhere, in the current wave of commodification, these forms of work are diminishing and the workers who carried them out are rapidly being drawn 'inside the knot'.[8] In other words, the commodification of public services has produced a major shift of labour from Quadrant A in the diagram above to Quadrant C.

This is not the only movement that is occurring.[9] The more general commodification of consumer goods and services has also involved large shifts from Quadrant B to Quadrant D, transforming the nature of some unpaid work from the direct production of use values for household members to the purchasing of commodities in the market, involving a direct relationship with capitalist production and distribution activities. In a further twist, there has also been a shift of labour from Quadrant C to Quadrant D as capitalist production and distribution companies have reduced their labour costs, increasing the exploitation of their paid workers by externalising more and more tasks onto consumers who have to carry them out as unpaid self-service activities. In a parallel process, austerity measures are also leading to a shift of activities from Quadrant A to Quadrant B, which in turn puts more pressure on the further shift from B to C. Thus whilst labour 'inside the knot' constitutes a sub-set of all labour, it is a sub-set that is rapidly expanding to become the overwhelming majority of paid labour.

My second cautionary note concerns the danger of extrapolation from a typology of labour to a typology of workers and hence to a class typology. Whilst part of my aim is to classify different forms of *labour* in their relation both to capital accumulation and workers' subsistence, I do not intend in so doing to produce a classification of *workers* that can be read off in any simple manner from this typology. Most workers engage in several different kinds of labour, paid and unpaid, both simultaneously and over the course of their lives, crossing these simple categories. Even more importantly, most workers live in households where different kinds of labour are carried out by different household members, some of whom, at any given time, may be unemployed. Whether or not members of such households perceive themselves, or can be perceived by others, as belonging to the working class is a large question. In my conclusion I will attempt to sketch out some of the ways that it might be possible to map working classes in the twenty-first century drawing on this analysis. But the analysis of labour constitutes only a small first step in that larger process and this exercise is necessarily speculative.

'DIGITAL LABOUR' IN A MATERIAL WORLD

Before embarking on this analysis, it is worth noting that digital labour cannot be regarded as a discrete form of labour, separated hermetically from the rest of the economy. As I argued in these pages, the existence of a separately visible sphere of non-manual labour is not evidence of a new 'knowledge-based', 'immaterial', or 'weightless' realm of economic activity.[10] It is simply an expression of the growing complexity of the division of labour, with a fragmentation of activities into separate tasks, both 'mental' and 'manual', increasingly capable of being dispersed geographically and contractually to different workers who may be barely aware of each other's existence. This is a continuing process, with each task subject to further divisions between more creative and/or controlling functions on the one hand, and more routine, repetitive ones on the other.

Furthermore, whilst there has clearly been an enormous expansion in non-manual work, both routine and deskilled and otherwise, it remains a minority of all labour. As I have argued previously, the growing visibility of apparently dematerialised labour, dependent on information and communications technologies to observers in developed economies has sometimes served to obscure the reality that this 'virtual' activity is dependent on a highly material basis of physical infrastructure and manufactured commodities, most of which are produced out of their sight, in the mines of Africa and Latin America, the sweatshops of China and other places in the developing world. Without the generation of power, cables, satellites, computers, switches, mobile phones and thousands of other material products, the extraction of the raw materials that make up these commodities, the launching of satellites into space to carry their signals, the construction of the buildings in which they are designed and assembled and from which they are marketed, and the manufacture and operation of the vehicles in which they are distributed, the Internet could not be accessed by anyone.

Whilst 20 per cent of the world's 100 largest transnational corporations are now service companies, it should not be forgotten that 80 per cent are not.[11] And, according to UNCTAD, in 2012 it was manufacturing companies that were expanding their foreign investment the fastest.[12] The physical production of material commodities is still capitalism's preferred method for generating profit; it is still growing; and it seems likely to continue to employ the largest proportion of the world's workforce. There is, moreover, a continuum between tasks that mainly involve the exercise of physical strength or dexterity and those that involve mental agility, engagement or concentration. There are few jobs that do not require workers to bring their own knowledge, judgement and intelligence to the task in hand, and even fewer that do not involve some physical activity, even if this just entails speaking, listening, watching a screen or tapping keys.

That said, a large and growing proportion of the workforce *is* involved in performing 'digital labour' whose products are intangible, much of it low-paid and menial. And many members of this workforce are descended from or cohabiting with workers who would by any definition be assigned to the working class. It is therefore important to understand what role their labour plays in global capitalism, what the composition of this workforce is, how it is changing and what class allegiances these workers might express.

VALUE

Put simply, it could be said that there are three main ways that enterprises generate profit under capitalism, the first two of which also existed under other systems. These are rent, trade and the generation of surplus value through commodity production. Because it is the paradigmatic form of value generation under capitalism, it is commodity production that receives the most attention from Marxian analysts. If value is observably being generated from some activity, the tendency is to search for the commodity at its source. If a commodity cannot easily be identified, or if it does not appear to be produced by extracting surplus value from paid workers, then it is sometimes concluded that this means that Marx's labour theory of value does not apply and is either outmoded or in need of adaptation. However, before leaping to the conclusion that entirely new theories are needed to explain online activities, it is worth analysing them in relation to traditional forms of value generation to see whether they fit these categories.

Rent

The ways in which commercially-mediated online activities seem to encroach indiscriminately on work, leisure, consumption and personal relationships draws attention to the extent to which capitalist relations have spread into all aspects of life, or as Marx put it, 'in the modern world, personal relations flow purely out of relations of production and exchange', encouraging broad-ranging speculation about how the monetisation of online exchanges can be understood and theorised.[13] The starting point for many of the current discussions about the value that is generated on the Internet is the indisputable reality that online companies like Google and Facebook are hugely profitable. If they are making profits, it is then argued, this must be because some commodity is being produced, which in turn begs the question of what precisely these commodities might be and whose labour is producing them. In the case of Google and Facebook, the main source of income is revenues from advertising, which can be targeted with great precision as a result of the ever-more sophisticated analysis of data generated by users. Here, Dallas Smythe's concept of the 'audience commodity'[14] has been seized on by a number of commentators, including Christian Fuchs.[15] Originally developed as part of a Marxian attempt to understand the economics of advertising in commercial radio and TV, this concept portrays the media audience as the commodity which is sold to advertisers to generate revenue: 'Because audience power is produced, sold, purchased and consumed, it commands a price and is a commodity.'[16] Fuchs applies this logic to the Internet: 'the productive labour time that is exploited by capital ... involves ... all of the time that is spent online by the users'. He goes on to say that 'the rate of exploitation converges towards infinity if workers are unpaid. They are infinitely exploited'. Other contributors to the digital labour debate suggest that 'reputation'[17] or even life itself (produced by 'bio-labour')[18] have become commodities.

Whilst Smythe's concept has undoubtedly opened up useful insights into the nature of the mass media, it has also led to much confusion. The underlying assumption among Smythe's followers seems to be that the term 'commodity' can be used to refer to anything that can be bought and sold. There is a certain circular logic operating here. Since Marx declares that 'commodities are nothing but crystallised labour' and that 'a good only has a value because labour is objectified or materialised in it', then it must follow, according to this logic, that anything described as a commodity must be the result of productive labour.[19] But how useful is such a broad conception of the term?

It seems to me that in order to understand the distinctive nature of the commodity form under capitalism a somewhat different definition needs to be used. I have defined commodities elsewhere as 'standardised products or services for sale in a market whose sale will generate profits that increase in proportion to the scale of production' (all else being equal).[20] This definition singles out capitalist commodities as fundamentally different from those produced under other systems. A traditional carpenter making chairs and selling them directly to the public makes more or less the same profit on each chair. The capitalist who opens a factory and employs workers to mass-produce chairs has to make an investment in machinery, buildings and so on and will not make a profit on the first chair, but the more chairs that are produced in that factory, the greater will be the profit on any given one. This gives the chairs produced in the factory a fundamentally different character from those produced individually by a single artisan in relation to their value. There are a number of services, including intangible ones (such as insurance policies or software programs) which have the same character as commodities. It is the social relations under which they are produced (the coerced labour of waged workers, under the control of the capitalist) that gives them this character.[21] Such a definition of commodity inverts the logic of Smythe's followers. It takes as its starting point the nature of the capitalist–labour relationship rather than the fact that something is being sold.

If they do not derive from the sale of commodities, how can we understand the profits made by online social networking or search engine companies? There is an alternative explanation, and it is one that has long antecedents in the offline world: they derive from rent. A simple historical example of a similar way of generating income could be provided by a street market where the rent charged for a stall-space is higher in areas where the most customers (or the richest customers) will pass by. Bricks-and-mortar examples can be found in New York's Fifth Avenue, London's Oxford Street, or any other street with a large and lucrative footfall: the more well-trafficked the site, the higher the rent. For well over a century, properties that border busy highways have been able to make money by renting space for billboards. Don't these online companies simply follow the same model, albeit with sites that are virtual rather than paved and rather more sophisticated means of identifying the most lucrative customers and gaining intelligence about their desires? The value that accrues to the social networking and search engine sites does indeed ultimately derive from surplus value produced by labour. But this is the labour of the workers who produced the commodities that are advertised on these sites, not the labour of the people who use the sites.[22]

Some participants in the digital labour debate, such as Adam Arvidsson and Eleanor Colleoni, dispute Fuchs's notion that social media users are producing surplus value.[23] They, too, argue that the value that is generated can be more properly regarded as rent. However, they use the term 'rent' to refer to the value that accrues to financial investors in these companies. But in this respect they do not say what it is that makes online companies different from any other companies that are quoted on stock exchanges and attract financial investments. In attempting to classify what, precisely, it is that generates the value that attracts such investors, they develop an explanation whereby 'social media platforms like Facebook function as channels by means of which affective investments on the part of the multitude can be translated into objectified forms of abstract affect that support financial valuations'. They further argue that such companies gain their share of 'socially produced surplus value' through 'the ability to attract affective investments ... from the multitude or the global public'.[24] This somewhat convoluted model sidesteps the rather more prosaic question of who is paying whom for what in order to generate the return on investment for the shareholders. It can, in my opinion, be rather simply answered by saying that it is the advertisers (producers of commodities for sale) who are paying the social media or search engine companies for the opportunity to advertise to their users. This is not to deny that social media sites do not incidentally also facilitate other forms of labour which could be regarded as more directly productive. These will be discussed below.

There are, of course, a number of ways that value is generated online other than through the use of search engine or social media sites. There are many other online activities that rely on rent for the generation of income. These include a variety of other sites that rely on advertising revenue, but also sites that charge rents to their users for access to information (such as online databases), sites from which copyright music or videos can be downloaded (such as *iTunes)*, companies that sell software licenses online, and online games for which subscriptions have to be bought (on the same principle as software licenses).

Other sites can be regarded as essentially online equivalents of offline businesses that generate income from rent. These include online marketplaces (such as *eBay*), dating sites (such as *eHarmony* or *Match.com)*, online employment agencies which match freelance workers to employers (such as *oDesk* or *Elance*), price comparison sites, online travel booking or accommodation finding sites (such as *Opodo* or *Expedia)* or various forms of peer-to-peer services allowing people to find bed-and-breakfast accommodation (such as *Airbnb*) or car shares (such as *Lyft)*. The connection with offline businesses is often evident here. For example, one of the largest of the online peer-to-peer car rental services, *RelayRides*, was launched with funding from GM Ventures (the investment arm of General Motors) in 2011 and has now been acquired by Zipcar, which in turn was acquired by Avis in January 2013.[25]

Whatever the specific mix of sources of revenue, most of the profit of such enterprises comes from some combination of charging usage or commission fees to service providers and/or service users and/or advertisers – in other words, rent. It is interesting to note that some of these sites seem to be enabling the development of new forms of petty commodity production and *rentier* activity or allowing older forms to survive offline. *Etsy*, for example, makes it possible for individuals to sell craft products in the online equivalent of a crafts market. *Airbnb* lets them make an income from renting out rooms in their homes for bed and breakfast (taking a percentage of the cost). Peer-to-peer car rental services enable people to provide taxi services or charge others to borrow their cars.

Trade

Trade involves acquiring something at one price (including stealing it) and selling it a higher price, making a profit in the process. Some forms of stealing, such as the appropriation of other people's intellectual property, may take place online. These include the reselling of captured images or music or the plagiarism of text for sale or some more elaborate forms of theft which are currently emerging, such as the exploitation of the unpaid labour of language learners to obtain free translation of web content by the website *Duolingo.com*, or *reCAPTCHA'* s reuse of users' attempts to decode distorted images of letters and numbers (required for security on many sites 'to ensure that you are not a robot') that cannot be recognised by automatic optical scanning systems.[26]

However, there are also a very large number of companies that sell online (Amazon being probably the most famous) in a manner that replicates offline commercial trade. Indeed many established merchants now buy and sell both online and offline. Although there may be some blurring of traditional boundaries between the distribution activities of manufacturers, wholesalers and retailers, and some labour processes may be rather different, there is nothing mysterious about how value is generated by such companies. The scale of many of these companies, and the fact that they have had to put extensive infrastructure in place for processing payments internationally, has meant that some of them have been able to diversify into rental activities which have in turn created the basis for new forms of commodity production, discussed in the next section.

Commodity production

This brings us to the final category: value which is generated from the production of commodities. Here, the analyst seeking to isolate the role of digital labour in value creation is faced with considerable challenges. The spread of computing across most sectors of the economy, combined with the near-universal use of telecommunications, means that there are few economic activities that do *not* involve some element of digital labour, whether they take place in farms, factories, warehouses, offices, shops, homes or on moving vehicles. Furthermore, these activities are linked with each other in complex chains which cross the boundaries between firms, sectors, regions and countries. Tracing the connection of any given activity back to its origins, or forward to the final commodity to whose production it has contributed, is no easy task. Nevertheless, it is by no means impossible. One useful approach here is to analyse economic activities in functional terms.[27]

The functions of research and development and design, for instance, clearly make direct inputs to the development of new commodities (or the adaptation of older ones). Much of the labour involved in these activities nowadays comes into the category of digital labour in that it involves computer-based tools and/or is delivered in digital form to the workers who will take it forward to the production stage. The same goes for activities whose purpose is to develop content for books, films, CDs or other cultural products. Here, some activities may be more directly 'digital' than others: actors or musicians, for instance, may be performing in a manner that is 'live', but if the end result is going to be incorporated into a reproducible commodity then their functional relation to capital is the same as that of fellow workers sitting at screens or mixing desks.[28] Digital labour is also involved in a variety of ways in production processes, whether this involves the operation of digitally-controlled tools, the maintenance of software, the generation of immaterial products or the supervision of other workers engaged in these processes.

When it comes to 'service' activities it is useful – though increasingly difficult – to make a general distinction between those that contribute directly to production (such as cleaning the factory floor or servicing the machines); those that contribute to the maintenance or management of the workforce (such as processing payroll data or staff recruitment or training); those that contribute to the more general management of the enterprise (including financial management); those that are involved in activities connected with purchasing, sales and marketing; and those that are involved in distribution. All of these categories include activities that are carried out online and/or using a combination of information and communications technologies. They are, however, becoming more and more difficult to tell apart, for several interconnected reasons.

The first of these is the increasingly generic nature of many labour processes. Workers inputting numerical data on a keyboard, for instance, may be doing it for a bank, a government department or a manufacturing company, for purposes entirely unknown to them. Call centre operators may be using standard scripts to deal with sales, customer services, debt collection, government enquiries, fund raising or a variety of other functions, cutting across any neat classification scheme that would allow them to be sorted into different categories by function. Software engineers may be working on the development of new products, or the maintenance of existing ones.

Closely linked with this form of standardisation is the growing propensity of such activities to be outsourced, often to companies that bundle together a number of different functions for different clients into clusters of activities carried out in shared service centres. The possibility for these and other services to be carried out online has further blurred the distinction between services provided to businesses and those provided directly to final customers. If everyone can order goods online, to be delivered to the door from a central warehouse, then the distinction between 'wholesale' and 'retail' becomes an artificial one. Similarly, there is a growing range of standardised immaterial products, ranging from software licenses to bank accounts to insurance policies that can be sold as readily to individuals as to companies.

The existence of online platforms through which labour can be co-ordinated has led to the development of an extreme form of subdivision of tasks, sometimes known as 'micro-labour', 'crowd work'[29] or 'crowd-sourcing'.[30] These include 'pay-per-click' work whereby workers are paid by commercial companies to 'like' their Facebook posts or blog entries, or platforms like Amazon's *Mechanical Turk,* whose users are paid a few cents to perform a variety of very small tasks, so fragmented that they are very unlikely to understand what relation any given task has to the final commodity to which it contributes.

If such activities, however dispersed, are carried out by paid workers, in the employ of enterprises set up to make a profit, then they can unproblematically be assigned to the category of work that directly produces surplus value for capital – labour 'inside the knot'. However, as the borderlines between production, distribution and consumption become increasingly fuzzy and the same activity can be carried out interchangeably by paid and unpaid workers, this simple position needs some modification. Marx was somewhat ambivalent about distribution labour, regarding transport workers as productive but not retail workers. However, at one point in the *Grundrisse*, he asserted that the whole process of bringing a product to market should be regarded as productive labour: 'Economically considered, the spatial condition, the bringing of the product to the market, belongs to the production process itself. The product is really finished only when it is on the market'.[31] Following this logic, a wide range of functions to be found in a modern corporation can be assigned to this directly productive category, including marketing, logistics management, distribution, transport, customer service, retail and wholesale sales (whether online or offline) and delivery – in short, the whole value chain from factory gate (or software development site) to the final consumer should be regarded as productive labour. But what happens when the customer's unpaid labour is substituted for that of the productive waged worker? What if, for instance, you go and fetch a purchase yourself from the store or warehouse? Or design your own product, selecting a unique combination of standard features from a website? And what, exactly, is the difference between booking your own holiday via a website, keying in your own data, and doing so over the phone to a (paid) call centre operator who keys it in on your behalf? In the latter case, the labour falls comfortably into what is traditionally regarded as the 'productive' category. But what about the former? In my view, all these activities should be regarded as productive. However, only those carried out by paid workers fall 'inside the knot' whereby their relationship to capital is both direct and, actually or potentially, contested.

LABOUR

Any attempt to categorise different forms of labour has to begin by confronting the extraordinarily difficult question of what labour actually is. The word itself covers a vast spectrum of meanings from the physical exertion of giving birth at one extreme to formal participation in employment, or the political representation of people who do so, at the other. If we take it to refer to activities which are actually or potentially reimbursed by wages in a 'labour market' then we have to include a large range of activities which most people carry out without pay, including sex, caring for children, cooking, cleaning, gardening, singing, making people laugh and holding forth on topics that interest us.

If we apply a more subjective filter and try to exclude activities that are carried out for pleasure, then we are confronted with the awkward reality that the same activity may be experienced as a chore or a joy under differing circumstances and, furthermore, that some activities, paid or unpaid, may be both onerous and enjoyable simultaneously. The baby, for instance, may give you a beaming smile whilst its smelly diaper is being changed; a truck driver's long lonely journey may suddenly bestow a heart-stoppingly beautiful glimpse of landscape; hard physical work in harsh surroundings may engender a camaraderie between workers that leaves a warm glow long after the muscle ache has subsided; solving a tricky problem may release a sudden gush of satisfaction, even if the problem is not one's own.

Another dimension that might help to distinguish between 'labour' and 'pleasure' is whether or not the activity is carried out voluntarily or by coercion, under the direction of another person or organisation. Here again what seems a simple distinction becomes remarkably difficult to apply in practice. One difficulty results from the historically determined ways in which such things as gender roles, concepts of duty or even caste-based divisions of labour are internalised, rendering patterns of power and coercion invisible to all parties and, indeed, giving many acts of service the subjective quality of freely offered gifts of love even when objective analysis might suggest that they involve the exploitation of one person's labour by another. Coercion may also be exercised in more indirect ways. An addicted gambler, for instance, may perceive his or her compulsion as internally generated, not recognising the societal pressures that impel it. The same could, perhaps, be said of many of the online activities that people spend so much time on, including online gaming and interacting with others on social media sites. It is perhaps some inkling of these social pressures that leads so many commentators in the digital media debates to insist that these unpaid activities are a form of 'free' labour.[32]

Unpaid labour is not, of course, a new phenomenon. It has however received only rather fitful attention from Marxian scholars, except as a kind of vestigial repository of pre-capitalist social relations from which waged labour later emerged. Apart from debates about slavery among historians, most of the attention paid to unpaid labour until recently was in the context of what could loosely be called 'reproductive labour', in particular in feminist debates during the 1970s. In these discussions, the main question raised was whether unpaid domestic labour or 'housework' could be regarded as producing surplus value because without it capitalism could not exist. The reproduction of the workforce depended crucially, it was argued, on unpaid labour in the home, not only for bringing up the next generation of workers but also to provide the nutrition, cleaning and bodily maintenance services that allow the current workforce to perform effectively in the labour market. In 1976, Batya Weinbaum and Amy Bridges published a ground-breaking article in which they argued that, under monopoly capital conditions, much of this labour did not only involve producing services in the home but also consuming commodities produced in the market.[33] The concept of 'consumption work', in which unpaid labour is substituted for what was formerly the paid labour of distribution workers, is one that I developed further in the late 1970s and, I argue here, is relevant for understanding some of the new forms of unpaid labour that take place both on and offline.[34] Drawing on some of this work, I propose here a somewhat rough-and-ready typology of unpaid labour in the hope that it can provide a starting point for a categorisation that will bring some clarity to these debates.

The first category is the labour that is carried out independently of the market to produce use values in the home, the category of labour located in Quadrant B in the diagram above. It is 'unproductive' in the sense that it produces no direct value for capital in the form of surplus value from somebody's direct labour, but 'reproductive' in the sense that it is necessary for the reproduction of the workforce. It includes many of the tasks traditionally carried out in subsistence agriculture and housework. If someone is employed to do this kind of work by the direct user of the service (e.g. a domestic servant, nanny, cleaner or gardener) that worker is, in Marx's opinion, an unproductive worker, although if they are employed via a capitalist intermediary (e.g. a commercial childcare, cleaning or gardening company) then they move into the category of productive worker (in terms of the diagram above, from Quadrant A to Quadrant C).[35] However, we are concerned here with unpaid labour. To the extent that maintaining the emotional health of a family and sustaining the social networks in which it is embedded is a necessary part of ensuring the survival of a household, then a range of non-physical activities can be included in this category, including such seemingly trivial tasks as remembering birthdays, writing letters of condolence or arranging social get-togethers which help to produce and reproduce the solidaristic bonds that may be necessary for survival in times of crisis. It also includes acquiring the skills and habits that enable someone to be employable. Even courtship can be regarded as a necessary prelude to this family maintenance project. Many of these activities are carried out online these days; thus at least a part of online social networking activity could be assigned to this category (represented by Quadrant B). Whether or not the person carrying out this labour is exposed to advertising in the process of carrying it out is as incidental to the productivity of the labour as whether or not they might pass a billboard on the way to visit a sick grandmother or be exposed to cinema commercials whilst on a date.

The second category of unpaid labour is what I have referred to above as 'consumption work' (Quadrant D). This involves the consumer taking on tasks in the market that were previously carried out by paid workers as part of the distribution processes of commodity production. Since these tasks are necessary to the distribution of these commodities, and increase the profits of the commodity-producing companies by eliminating forms of labour that were formerly paid for, there are strong arguments for categorising this kind of work as 'productive', even when it is unpaid. However, because it does not generate income directly for the worker it has to be treated differently from paid labour in relation to its contribution to subsistence, a topic to which I will return below. It is in other words 'outside the knot'. As already noted, increasing amounts of consumption work are carried out online, with the Internet having opened up a range of new ways of externalising labour over distance.[36]

The third category involves creative work. Here, Marx made his position clear:

Milton, for example ... was an unproductive worker. In contrast to this, the writer who delivers hackwork for his publisher is a productive worker. Milton produced *Paradise Lost* in the way that a silkworm produces silk, as the expression of *his own* nature. Later on he sold the product for £5 and to that extent became a dealer in a commodity. ... A singer who sings like a bird is an unproductive worker. If she sells her singing for money, she is to that extent a wage labourer or a commodity dealer. But the same singer, when engaged by an entrepreneur who has her sing in order to make money, is a productive worker, for she directly *produces* capital.[37]

According to this conception, to the extent that it is carried out for the purposes of self-expression, unpaid artistic work, such as blogging or posting one's photographs, music or videos on the Internet comes straightforwardly into Marx's category of 'unproductive' labour (which I would prefer to regard as unpaid reproductive labour, producing social use values). If the product of this labour is subsequently sold, or stolen, to become the basis of a commodity, then this does not change that status. It is only if the worker is hired to do the work for a wage that it becomes productive labour in Marx's sense of the term (i.e. it moves from Quadrant B to Quadrant C). As Ross has pointed out, many artistic workers may oscillate between these forms: 'Creatives have been facing this kind of choice since the eighteenth century when the onset of commercial culture markets offered them the choice of eking out a living with the scribblers on Pope's Grub Street or of building a name-recognition relationship with the fickle public'.[38] The fact that the same person does both kinds of work does not, however, invalidate the distinction between them. Creative work thus has to be seen as straddling a number of different positions in the labour market including self-employment, paid employment and petty commodity production, leading, very often, to contradictory identities for creative workers.[39]

The same logic applies even in the much-discussed case of the 'free labour' that built the Internet, much of which was designed by idealistic software developers who donated their labour for nothing in the belief that they were creating a common benefit for humankind (in other words they were producing social use value without pay, placing them in Quadrant B). As Marx said, 'labour with the same content can be both productive and unproductive'.[40] In this case, it seems that although the results of their labour were appropriated by capital to incorporate into new commodities, their original unpaid labour cannot be regarded as productive in the sense of producing surplus value for capital under coercive conditions (i.e. it is not 'inside the knot'). Rather, the value that was produced from it should more properly be put into the category of trade, which, as I noted above, also includes theft.

A fourth – but overlapping – form of unpaid labour, which is increasingly discussed, is the widespread use of unpaid internship or 'voluntary' labour.[41] This, too, seems to have precedents in various forms of apprenticeship labour, such as the production of 'show pieces' to impress potential employers. Situated ambiguously between education and self-promotion it is undoubtedly used in highly exploitative ways by employers as a direct substitute for paid work. Sometimes, direct coercion is involved to oblige the worker to undertake unpaid 'work placements', for instance by state job search agencies which threaten the withdrawal of unemployment benefit from those who refuse to take them. Nevertheless, like the unpaid consumption labour already discussed, whilst clearly contributing value to commodity production, this form of labour plays no part in generating present income for the worker and must therefore be regarded as 'outside the knot', even if it is producing value indirectly for the unpaid worker in the form of 'employability'. It is clear that in order to make sense of the relationship of unpaid labour to capital we have to take into account the third rope in the knot that constitutes the labour theory of value: the worker's subsistence, or 'living'.

LIVING

The question of how the worker pays for the cost of subsistence is surprisingly absent from most of the debates about 'free' digital labour. Perhaps because they themselves often have secure academic jobs, the majority of the authors who have contributed to these discussions fail to ask how those dedicated workers who built the Internet with their free labour actually made a living. Nor, among those who advocate a 'Creative Commons' on the Internet, to which all authors are supposed to donate their work for free, is it ever made clear how these authors are supposed to pay their rent and provide for their families.

Yet, the labour theory of value cannot be operationalised without this information. In order to know how much surplus value is generated, and how, from any given unit of labour, we need to know the cost of that worker's reproduction, and how much of his or her working time is the 'necessary labour time' required to sustain life. Only then can we see how much of the remainder is left over to be appropriated as surplus value and begin to formulate demands for its redistribution. This is not, of course, a mechanical calculation. It is perfectly possible for workers to be employed below the cost of subsistence. What does the employer care if they die, if there are plenty more where they came from? Equally, it is possible for well-organised groups of workers with scarce skills to punch above their weight and claim back from capital a higher wage than that required for bare survival – even one which allows them to employ other workers as servants. Nevertheless, capitalism as a system, in Marx's model, requires a working class that is compelled to sell its labour in order to survive, just as it requires capitalists who are able to employ that labour to produce commodities whose collective value on the market exceeds the total wages of the workforce required to produce them. And it is the direct experience of being obliged to contest ownership of their labour time with the employer that produces the alienation likely to lead to class consciousness. The question of 'necessary labour time' cannot therefore be ducked.

But even in Marx, this is quite a problematic concept. One reason for this is that although workers normally enter the labour market as separate individuals, their subsistence takes place in households where several people may co-habit.[42] Because these households vary considerably in size and composition and in the number of members who engage in paid work, the same wage may have to stretch to cover the subsistence of varying numbers of people. Marx and Engels discuss the 'natural' (sic) division of labour in the family, which they regard as a form of 'latent slavery' that can even be regarded as the origin of all property.[43] From their premise that women and children are the property of the male head of household it is possible for them to conclude that, when women and children enter the workforce, 'Formerly, the sale and purchase of labour-power was a relation between free persons; now, minors or children are bought; the worker now sells wife and child – he becomes a slave-dealer'.[44]

In the twenty-first century, when women make up nearly half the workforce in most developed countries and only a minority are economically inactive, such an explanation will not suffice. Every worker who enters employment needs to be separately accounted for as an individual with his or her own cost of subsistence to be raised. The fact that people co-habit with other workers can, however, mean that this 'necessary labour time' should be regarded as producing a fraction, rather than the whole, of any individual's cost of subsistence. Or, in other words, that the concept of a 'family wage' is redundant in most circumstances. A number of other factors have also intervened to make it difficult to identify a simple correspondence between what a person earns and what it costs them to survive, at least in situations where that person is co-habiting with, or responsible for, economic dependents. These complicating factors include societal transfers in the form of pensions, welfare benefits or tax credits, intergenerational transfers within families, remittances from migrants working abroad and other forms of subsidy for some (or drains on the resources of others). Tax credits, the favoured neoliberal model of social transfer, have played a particularly pernicious role in disguising not only the extent to which many jobs pay wages that are well below subsistence level but also in concealing from public awareness the reality that a large and growing proportion of social benefit payments go not to unemployed 'scroungers' but to workers in employment.[45] Such transfers could thus be seen as having played an important role in blunting class-consciousness and diverting workers' energy away from direct conflict with their employers.

Despite very real difficulties of precise calculation, it is possible to analyse the income of any given individual in any given household and produce some estimate of how this is generated. In the case of 'free labour' on the Internet, it is likely that a number of different income sources may be involved. Some of this labour may be contributed by people who are economically dependent on their parents, some by people drawing pensions or receiving some other form of welfare benefit, some by people with regular salaries from jobs that leave them with enough leisure time to blog, surf the net or write Wikipedia entries; some might be done by people (such as freelance journalists, consultants, or academics) whose jobs require them to engage in self-promotion. And others might be being supported from rents, gambling, the proceeds of trade, crime or other activities. What is clear, however, is that these unpaid contributors could not engage in this unpaid activity without some kind of subsidy from somewhere. Otherwise, how would they eat? Arguments that postulates the production of surplus value at a societal level from their labour seem untenable. Such arguments could also be seen as playing a similar role to societal financial transfers in diverting workers' attention away from confronting the employers directly expropriating their labour towards expressing their anger and sense of exploitation towards abstract targets (such as 'globalisation'). In failing to organise at the point of production, they give away their strongest weapon: the power to withdraw their labour.

CLASS CONFIGURATION IN THE TWENTY-FIRST CENTURY

We live in a society where capital is highly concentrated, with most commodity production carried out by companies whose fates are largely shaped by financial investors. The commodities that they produce, whether material or immaterial, are made available to us in a global marketplace, delivered through complex value chains in whose operation our own unpaid labour as consumers is increasingly implicated. Information and communications technologies have so affected the spatial and temporal division of labour that for many of us the boundaries between work and private life are inextricable muddled and few relationships are unmediated by them. In such a situation, are not the kinds of distinctions made in this essay not ridiculously nit-picking? Should we not just accept that all of us are, in some way or another, part of a huge undifferentiated workforce, producing undifferentiated value for an undifferentiated capital?

I argue that we should not. Capitalism is a social relationship in which workers play specific roles in relation to the production of specific commodities. This relationship relies crucially on workers' consent. If we cannot understand this relationship in its specificity, we cannot identify the critical points in the processes of production and distribution where workers' agency can be implemented to some effect. And if we cannot identify these, workers cannot understand their powers to consent to, or refuse, the specific deal that is on offer to them. This prevents them from actively renegotiating the terms of the deal – their only option for improving their situation. Neither, without this knowledge, can we see which groups of workers have interests in common, how these common interests might become mutually visible or how their labour may be interconnected.

Each of the different forms of unpaid labour described above has an impact on paid labour, opening up the potential for tensions and fissures within the working class. Interns, working for nothing to make themselves employable, erode the bargaining position of paid workers in the same roles. Carrying out unpaid consumption work affects service workers by reducing overall employment levels and intensifying work through the introduction of new forms of standardisation and Taylorisation, leading to deteriorating working conditions. Writing Wikipedia entries, blogging or posting video clips or photographs online without payment threatens the livelihoods of journalists, researchers or other creative workers who lack a subsidy from an academic salary or other source and rely on their creative work to provide an income. In many cases, the same people occupy several of these paid and unpaid roles in different capacities. Even more commonly, different members of the same household may be doing so. To regard unpaid workers as scabs who are undermining paid workers is of course much too simplistic, ignoring the imperatives that propel these behaviours and the broader reality that exploitation takes place in all of them, albeit in different forms. But an analysis that equates a common exploitation with an identical role in the generation of surplus value, and collapses all these separate positions into a common collective identity as a 'multitude' makes it impossible to identify the point of production: the point where workers have the power to challenge capital; the centre of the knot.

Starting from a detailed analysis of how value chains are structured, it is possible to begin to sketch out the lineaments of the class configuration that might confront us in coming years. However, this exercise has to be embarked on with extreme caution because, as noted earlier, many of us are engaged simultaneously or consecutively in a number of different forms of labour, with different relations to capital, or live in households where multiple forms of labour take place.

Leaving aside the rural populations that still subsist, at least in part, from their own direct labour on the land, in this emerging labour landscape the largest, and by far the most rapidly-growing group is that of workers 'inside the knot': those who are employed by capitalist enterprises producing commodities, both material and immaterial. Many of these have been sucked into directly capitalist labour relations comparatively recently, coming to this work as migrants from the countryside or from other countries, being transferred from public sector employment, or recruited from a previous existence in petty commodity production. Not all of these workers have the status of permanent employees, with many paid by piece rates or employed on a casual or temporary basis. They are, nevertheless, productive workers, directly producing surplus value. However, the ways in which their labour processes connect with each other are not obvious.

A product like a smart phone contains within it the results of the labour of miners, assembly-line workers, chemical workers, designers, engineers, call centre workers, invoice clerks, cleaners and many more. Scattered in different countries, with different occupational and social identities, these workers may not perceive themselves as having anything whatsoever in common. Indeed they may believe their interests to be directly opposed to each other. If and when they organise themselves this might be on the basis of skill, occupation or the company they work for, but it might also be on the basis of a shared regional, linguistic or cultural identity, a shared political history or a response to a shared form of discrimination. What forms of solidarity or shared consciousness might emerge from these forms of organisation is an open question.

Another open question is the extent to which managerial, professional and technical workers within these value chains will identify with other workers rather than aligning themselves with the employer. These are volatile groups, made up of people who, in the accelerating speed of technological change and economic restructuring, find many of their labour processes undergoing standardisation and deskilling even whilst new opportunities to become managers are emerging. On the one hand their employers want to nurture them as sources of innovation; on the other they want to cheapen their labour and drive up their productivity. Caught between these two contradictory imperatives, these intermediate workers may be put into a position where they have to decide whether to continue to internalise management priorities and take the pain, to leave, to look for individualistic solutions or to throw in their lot with other workers and resist.

Alongside, and overlapping with, this explosively growing body of workers 'inside the knot' of capitalism are other groups less directly involved in capitalist social relations. These include people patching together a living out of petty commodity production, small-scale rent or trade, a class which Marx assumed would die out but which appears to have been given a new lease of life by the Internet, although it is doubtful whether such sources of income can ever supply a sustainable livelihood for more than a minority of the population. In many cases, it seems likely that this way of earning a living, often cobbled together from several different kinds of economic activity, is a transitional one, adopted by people who have been displaced from the formal labour market, or have not yet managed to enter it. It is not new. Working-class biographies have always thrown up many examples of people making ends meet by taking in lodgers, child-minding, pet-breeding or making small items for sale. But it cannot be taken for granted that all such people will necessarily identify their interests with those of workers 'inside the knot'.

Groups that are 'outside the knot' also include people involved in paid reproduction work: public sector workers working in the increasingly rare fields of service provision that remain uncommodified; domestic servants; and other forms of service work that are not directly involved in the market (such as work in the voluntary sector). Their work is, of course, necessary for the reproduction of capitalism, but it is 'outside the knot' according to my earlier definition. Again, these groups cover a diverse range of social identities and may not perceive themselves as having interests in common, either with each other or with workers 'inside the knot'.

Added to these are large numbers of people who are not paid workers but who nevertheless also produce value, either in the form of reproduction, such as unpaid childcare or housework, or (externalised) production, in the form of consumption work. Many of these will be women, and their unpaid status may place them into relations of dependency on paid workers or on the state. History has given us many examples of reproduction workers throwing in their lot with the production workers to whom their lives are linked (for instance in the organisation of miners' wives in the UK coal-miners' strike in the 1980s) and of consumption workers acting in solidarity with production workers, for instance in the consumer-based Clean Clothes Campaign which organises petitions and boycotts to improve working conditions for garment workers.[46]

These are broad categories and a much more detailed mapping of the composition of these groups and their interrelationships with each other will be necessary to predict the class configuration that will confront us globally in the twenty-first century. Tedious though it may be to unravel the complexities of global value chains and position our labour processes in relation to them, this seems to be an absolutely necessary task if we are to learn how this system might be changed, act collectively to change it, and start to imagine what alternatives might be possible.

NOTES

1   M. Hardt and A. Negri, *Multitude: War and Democracy in the Age of Empire*, New York: Penguin, 2004; G. Standing, *Precariat: The New Dangerous Class*, London and New York: Bloomsbury, 2011.
2   Hardt and Negri, *Multitude*; T. Terranova, 'Free Labor: Producing Culture for the Digital Economy', *Social Text*, 18(2), 2000, pp. 33-58.
3   See for instance, M. Andrejevic, 'Exploiting YouTube: Contradictions of User-Generated Labor', in P. Snickers and P. Vonderau, eds., *The YouTube Reader*, Stockholm: National Library of Sweden, 2009; A. Arvidsson and E. Colleoni, 'Value in Informational Capitalism and on the Internet', *The Information Society,* 28(3), 2012, pp. 135-50; J. Banks and S. Humphreys, 'The Labor of User Co-Creators', *Convergence,* 14(4), 2008, pp. 401-18; C. Fuchs, 'Labor in Informational Capitalism and on the Internet', *The Information Society*, 26(3), 2010, pp. 179-96; C. Fuchs, 'With or Without Marx? With or Without Capitalism? A Rejoinder to Adam Arvidsson and Eleanor Colleoni', *Triple C*, 10(2), 2012, pp. 633-45; D. Hesmondhalgh, 'User-Generated Content, Free Labour and the Cultural Industries', *Ephemera*, 10(3/4), 2011, pp. 267-84; A. Ross, 'On the Digital Labour Question', in T. Scholz, ed., *The Internet as Playground and Factory*, New York: Routledge, 2012; and Terranova, 'Free Labor,' in Scholz, *Internet as Playground and Factory*.
4   J. Kücklich, 'Precarious Playbour: Modders and the Digital Games Industry', *The Fibreculture Journal*, Issue 5, 2005.
5   Alvin Toffler coined this term in his 1980 book *The Third Wave*, published by Bantam Books. It has since been taken up by a number of other writers working in a Marxist framework, including Christian Fuchs and Ed Comer.
6   Banks and Humphreys, 'The Labour of User Co-creators', using a term derived from C.K. Prahalad and V. Ramaswamy, 'Co-Opting Customer Competence', *Harvard Business Review*, (January/February), 2000.
7   A term coined by Tiziana Terranova in her influential article, 'Free Labor'.
8   U. Huws, 'Crisis as Capitalist Opportunity: The New Accumulation through Public Service Commodification', *Socialist Register 2012*, Pontypool: Merlin, 2011, pp. 64-84.

9   U. Huws, 'Domestic Technology: Liberator or Enslaver?', in U. Huws, *The Making of a Cybertariat: Virtual Work in a Real World*, New York: Monthly Review Press, 2003, pp. 35-41.

10   U. Huws, 'Material World: The Myth of the Weightless Economy', *Socialist Register*, 1999, pp. 29-56.

11   UNCTAD, *World Investment Report*, Geneva, 2008.

12   According to UNCTAD, 60 per cent of manufacturing TNCs were planning to increase their FDI in the next year, compared with 45 per cent of firms in the primary sector and 43 per cent of those in services. See *World Investment Report*, 2012, p. 19.

13   Karl Marx, *Grundrisse*, 'Chapter on Money' Part II, available at http://www.marxists.org.

14   D. W. Smythe, 'Communications: Blindspot of Western Marxism', *Canadian Journal of Political and Social Theory*, 1(3), 1977, pp. 1-27.

15   C. Fuchs, 'Dallas Smythe Today – The Audience Commodity, the Digital Labour Debate, Marxist Political Economy and Critical Theory. Prolegomena to a Digital Labour Theory of Value', *Triple C*, 10(2), 2012, pp. 692-740.

16   D. W. Smythe, 'On the Audience Commodity and its Work', in M.G. Duncan and D.M. Kellner, eds., *Media and Cultural Studies*, Malden, MA: Blackwell, 1981, p. 233.

17   A. Hearn, 'Structuring Feeling: Web 2.0, Online Ranking and Rating, and the Digital "Reputation" Economy', *Ephemera*, 10(3/4), 2010, pp. 421-38.

18   C. Morini and A. Fumagalli, 'Life Put to Work: Towards a Life Theory of Value', *Ephemera*, 10(3/4), 2010, pp. 234-52.

19   K. Marx, *Capital*, Chapter 1, available at http://www.marxists.org.

20   Huws, *Making of a Cybertariat*, p. 17.

21   This point is made a little differently in a discussion of the distinction between productive and unproductive labour by Marx in *Capital*, Chapter 4.

22   Except in some special circumstances, such as when workers are paid to go on Facebook and click 'like' on commercial websites in the 'pay per click' model. But here they are not employed by Facebook but by companies linked to these commercial websites which have some commodity to sell, so they should more accurately be regarded as belonging to the value chain of these commodity-producing companies.

23   Arvidsson and Colleoni, 'Value in Informational Capitalism'.

24   Arvidsson and Colleoni, unpublished manuscript.

25   'All Eyes on the Sharing Economy', *The Economist*, 9 March 2013.

26   I am indebted to Kaire Holts for drawing my attention to this explanation of the business model of *reCAPTCHA* by its originator, who also founded *Duolingo*, available at http://www.willhambly.com. See also the related video, available at http://www.inmyinnovation.com.

27   I have discussed the concept of the 'business function' and its relation to Marxist analysis in several publications. See for instance, U. Huws, 'The Restructuring of Global Value Chains and the Creation of a Cybertariat', in Christopher May, ed., *Global Corporate Power: (Re)integrating Companies into International Political Economy* (International Political Economy Yearbook Volume 15),

Lynne Rienner Publishers, 2006, pp. 65-84; and U. Huws, 'The Emergence of EMERGENCE: The Challenge of Designing Research on the New International Division of Labour', *Work Organisation, Labour and Globalisation*, 1(2), 2007, pp. 20-35.

28   I have analysed the relationship of creative labour to capital elsewhere. See, for instance, U. Huws, 'Expression and Expropriation: The Dialectics of Autonomy and Control in Creative Labour', *Ephemera*, Volume 10(3/4), 2010.

29   Kittur et al., 'The Future of Crowd Work', 2013, available at http://hci. stanford.edu.

30   K. Holts, 'Towards a Taxonomy of Virtual Work', Hertfordshire Business School Working Paper, 2013.

31   Marx, *Grundrisse*, Notebook V. It should be noted that this interpretation of this passage is disputed. Marx is often considered to be making a special exception of transport workers (perhaps because they were a group with strong potential trade union organisation – a potential that was more-than-realised in the twentieth century when transport workers played a key role in industrial action). It is my view that his argument applies equally to other forms of labour involved in getting products to market, many of which were inconceivable at the time when he was writing.

32   Terranova, 'Free Labor'.

33   B. Weinbaum and A. Bridges, 'The Other Side of the Paycheck: Monopoly Capital and the Structure of Consumption', *Monthly Review*, 28(3), 1976.

34   See for instance Huws, 'Domestic Technology'.

35   See K. Marx, *Economic Manuscripts*, Chapter 4, available at http://www. marxists.org.

36   I use the term 'externalising' here to refer to the ways in which employers increase the productivity of paid staff by transferring some or all of their unpaid tasks to unpaid consumers in the form of self-service, whether through the operation of machines such as ATMs or self-service supermarket or online activities such as booking tickets, filling in tax returns or ordering goods.

37   Marx, *Economic Manuscripts*, Chapter 2.

38   A. Ross, 'In Search of the Lost Paycheck', in Scholz, *Internet as Playground and Factory*, p. 15.

39   I have anatomised these in greater detail in Huws, 'Expression and Expropriation', pp. 504-21.

40   Marx, *Economic Manuscripts*, 'Productive and Unproductive Labour'.

41   See, for instance, R. Perlin, *Intern Nation: How to Earn Nothing and Learn Little in the Brave New Economy*, London: Verso, 2011.

42   I have written more extensively about this in U. Huws, 'The Reproduction of Difference: Gender and the Global Division of Labour', *Work Organisation, Labour and Globalisation*, 6(1), 2012, pp. 1-10.

43   K. Marx, 'Division of Labour and Forms of Property – Tribal, Ancient, Feudal', Part 1, A, *The German Ideology*, 1845, available at http://www.marxists.org.

44   F. Engels, *On Marx's Capital*, Moscow: Progress Publishers, 1956 [1877], p. 89.

45   For more on this, see my blog post on 'Hunger in a Supermarketocracy', available at http://ursulahuws.wordpress.com. In the UK, according to HM

Revenue and Customs, 'the numbers of families without children receiving Working Tax Credits-only has risen over time, almost doubling from 235,000 in April 2004 to around 455,000 in April 2009 and now at just over 580,000 in April 2012' and 'the numbers of families benefiting from the childcare element has consistently risen over time, from 318,000 in April 2004 to around 493,000 in April 2011'. By this date tax credits (paid to workers in employment) already accounted for 27 per cent of all benefit spending – by far the largest single component. By comparison Job-seekers Allowance (paid to the unemployed) accounted for only 4 per cent. In the USA, similarly, many large companies rely on government-provided benefits, such as food stamps and Medicaid, to subsidise below-subsistence wages. For instance, Wal-Mart employees are estimated to receive $2.66 billion in government assistance every year, or about $420,000 per store. See HM Revenue and Customs, *Child and Working Tax Credits Statistics*, Office of National Statistics, 2012; and P. Ryan, 'Walmart: America's Real "Welfare Queen"', *Daily Kos*, 2012, available at http://www.dailykos.com.

46   See http://www.cleanclothes.org.

THE BRITISH RULING CLASS

COLIN LEYS

The arrival of global capitalism has created a new problem for the ruling classes of post-industrial liberal-democratic countries such as Britain. National ruling classes find it harder and harder to resolve the tension between the requirements of global capital and the interests of the population whose votes they need to stay in power. The British ruling class is a particularly telling case for two main reasons: the fact that the UK has been a de facto protectorate of the US since at least 1945, if not 1917, and serves as a key base for US influence in Europe; and the fact that London's financial district (the City of London) is the world's leading financial centre.[1] Both features make the UK economy exceptionally open to pressures from global capital, transmitted both by the global financial markets concentrated in London and by the US government. When these pressures impose policies that are electorally unpopular, the British ruling class faces serious difficulties, and it is how these are being dealt with that is the focus of this essay.

RULING CLASSES: GLOBAL AND BRITISH

To tackle this question it isn't essential to enter into the debate over the existence or otherwise of a global or transnational capitalist class, but the pressures coming from the US state and global markets are not disembodied forces, so a brief clarification of terms is needed. For Marx, the class that possesses the means of production is necessarily also the politically ruling class – the class whose interests must prevail over time, regardless of surface appearances, such as concessions made to the working class (social security provision, for example), or governmental alliances made with elements of other classes.[2]

In this sense there is certainly a British ruling class. But is there also a global ruling class? Do the owners of increasingly globally integrated capital constitute a global or transnational ruling class? So long as their interests prevail, they clearly do. How far they conceive of themselves as a global ruling class is another matter. As Bill Carroll and others point out, this consciousness is intermittent, stronger in some sectors or countries than in others, and still very imperfectly institutionalized; but these are normal features of all classes. There are always leaders and followers. The American businessmen who in 1942, contemplating the fact of Soviet power, published 'An American Proposal' for reshaping the postwar world on capitalist lines, were acutely conscious that their class interest was now global.[3] Over the following decades various sectors of US business would seek to retreat into nationalism, and less developed and powerful countries took time to produce a cadre of capitalists who recognized that their national class interest too was ultimately identical with that of capitalists everywhere. Nonetheless there has been a steady development of capitalist class solidarity on a global plane, manifested in the construction of a global regime of regulation and a successful series of responses to global crises, paid for by the world's working classes. It is through engaging in such activities and coping with crises that the global capitalist class becomes conscious that it is one.

How does the British ruling class intersect with and relate to the global capitalist class? There is first of all the fact that the British ruling class is part of the global ruling class. Many British capitalists, and certainly the country's 2,000-plus multi-millionaires and all the shareholders in UK-based transnational companies, own capital in other countries. Conversely, a large part of the capital invested in Britain is owned by foreigners. Many if not most of the biggest corporations operating in the UK are owned and headquartered elsewhere, mainly in the US (not just famous American companies like Ford, Kellogg, Starbucks, Amazon, Google, etc., but also British household names like Cadbury's and Vauxhall that are now subsidiaries of US firms). Moreover in 2010 the companies listed on the London Stock Exchange (LSE) were 42 per cent foreign-owned,[4] and the biggest ones were largely foreign-managed (around a third of the top 100 had foreign CEOs;[5] in early 2013 only six of the 20 chairmen and CEOs of the 10 biggest companies were British).

This doesn't mean that most British capitalists see themselves as part of a global capitalist class. Owners of small or medium enterprises, or companies with purely domestic markets, often have a nationalist outlook. They will support policies that aim to defend property everywhere, but they may call for 'buy British' policies on the part of the state, and other forms of protection, and may have working-class support when they do so. Politicians have to try to reconcile such demands with the demands of global capital – for maintaining the free flow of capital across national borders, limiting government deficits and borrowing, privatising the infrastructure and public services, low taxes and 'light touch' regulation. These demands are enforced through corporate threats to move elsewhere and by pressure from the bond markets and credit rating agencies, supplemented by pressure from the OECD, the IMF, the WTO, the EU, etc., as well as through lobbying, party funding, and the media.

Retaining political legitimacy while complying with these demands is now more and more problematic for the ruling classes of northern countries, because corporate access to low-paid workforces in the global 'south' means that average wages in the north tend to be depressed, undermining consumerism and the belief in growth. A nation with a weak economy in long-term recession could eventually become very hard to manage under even the 'thinnest' kind of democracy.

We could simply call the British ruling class the British section of the global ruling class. But its political capacity to enforce global ruling-class interests in Britain depends heavily on its social and cultural 'Britishness'. It seems better to accept that it is both a British ruling class and part of the global ruling class, involving an often-visible political tension.

THE BRITISH RULING CLASS AND THE UK ECONOMY

The distinctive problem confronting the British ruling class is the weakness of the UK economy. The manufacturing sector had already become uncompetitive before the First World War and the two wars, followed by a failure to adapt to the country's post-imperial status, weakened its external position further still. From 1945 to 1980 a fragile balance of payments led to a series of currency crises and devaluations without solving the problem. Then, in the 1980s, the Thatcher government's policy of high interest rates and removal of barriers to overseas competition led to the elimination of two thirds of what was left of the country's uncompetitive manufacturing industry. Two crucial factors prevented this policy leading to economic bankruptcy and potentially unmanageable political unrest: the discovery of oil in the North Sea, and the 'Big Bang' of 1986, which opened up the London Stock Exchange and other exchanges to foreign banks and led to the City of London's re-emergence as the world's largest centre for currency transactions and international business services.

Revenues from oil production almost exactly covered the cost of paying social security benefits to the 1.5m workers made redundant by the contraction of the manufacturing sector in the 1980s (another two million manufacturing jobs would go by 2010). But oil self-sufficiency, plus the rapid growth of export earnings by the financial services sector, offset the collapse of manufactured exports. The balance of payments returned briefly to surplus (in 1995 and again in 1997-98), and between 1980 and 2007 GDP per capita increased dramatically, momentarily equalling the US level.[6] The distribution of this income, however, became much more unequal: the Gini coefficient rose from 25 in 1980 to 36 in 2009, reflecting dramatic income increases for the top 10 per cent, substantial gains for the next four deciles and very limited increases for the bottom 50 per cent. Working-class living standards did rise, though mainly due to tax credits (state income support), a steep increase in household debt (up from 105 per cent of income in 1997 to 170 per cent in 2008) and women taking jobs, which offset higher male unemployment.

But the policy of exposing the economy as fully as possible to global market forces failed to correct the familiar underlying weakness of the economy. Since 1999 North Sea oil production has been declining, making Britain once again a net oil importer. By 2006, the last full year before the global financial crash, the deficit on trade in goods had risen to be more than twice the size of the surplus on services. From 1999 onwards, the balance of payments returned to deficit on an ever-growing scale: In 2006 it was £45 billion, equivalent to 3 per cent of the country's GDP..

The export earnings of financial and business services also grew, but could not keep up; the gap was unsustainable in the long run and the US-generated financial crisis of 2007-08 made the fragility of the UK economy, by now the most open in the OECD, painfully clear. Between 2007 and 2012 the value of the pound dropped dramatically, but in spite of the big price advantage this gave to British manufacturing exports they remained virtually flat. The country's dependence on a largely foreign-owned financial centre, which had played a leading part in causing the crash, had left it extremely vulnerable. A banking collapse was averted by massive government borrowing, quadrupling public debt from 36 per cent of GDP in 2006-07 to almost 150 per cent in 2010-11. No contribution was demanded from the banks' shareholders, whose investment was thus saved, or from the banks' global debtors. Instead the rescue was to be paid for by the British working class in the form of unemployment and the loss of social services and social security, as the government cut spending drastically to reduce the fiscal deficit that the bank rescue had opened up, which in 2012 was £100 billion. The much-trumpeted objective was to balance revenue and expenditure by 2016. But as cuts reduced public sector employment and so the level of consumption, economic activity flatlined, tax revenues fell and the fiscal deficit kept tending to rise rather than fall.

The spending cuts served an unacknowledged political purpose as much as the official economic one. They were aimed at a drastic reduction in the scale and coverage of social security and social services, weakening what remained of the political strength of the unions, and increasing still further the share of national income going to capital. For this reason they were persisted with, even though they were making the fiscal deficit more intractable, to the growing concern of the global ruling class (signalled by unprecedentedly public calls from both the OECD and the IMF to change course, and the loss of the government's cherished triple-A credit rating). If the price was a heightened risk of social disorder, it was one the government was for the moment ready to pay.

But in the long run a solution to the economy's weakness must be found, or a severe reduction in working-class living standards will have to be accepted. The official response is to call for a 'rebalancing' of the economy by a revival of manufacturing. The problem is that no one knows how to achieve this – at least not within the existing framework of ownership and economic power. The major companies are largely foreign-owned. In early 2013 they had cash reserves of £7 billion, but showed no sign of intending to invest it in Britain.[7] Investment as a percentage of GDP stayed around 15 per cent, compared with 18-20 per cent in the other major EU economies. The banking system remained unreformed and focused on the profits to be made from international transactions, not British industry. The Cambridge economist Ha-Joon Chang advocates an industrial strategy:

> The strategy should first carefully identify the industries, and the underlying technologies, that will be the future motor of the economy and then provide them with the necessary support. This could be in the form of subsidies for R and D, loan guarantees for small firms, or preferences in government procurement, and should be targeted at 'strategic' industries, although they could also be in the form of policies that are not industry-specific.[8]

But even if the will was there it is not clear that the government of a medium-sized country with an already weak economy can still pursue a national economic strategy, as opposed to continuing to adapt the national society to the requirements of the global economy.[9]

Yet a drastic lowering of living standards for the majority of the population would carry high political risks. In 2011, 22.7 per cent were already at risk of poverty or social exclusion.[10] An era of technocratic 'governments of national unity', buttressed by 'soft fascism' and charged with securing a big reduction in consumption by the 'unproductive' majority, is certainly conceivable, but it is not obvious that ruling-class hegemony would survive it.

THE HISTORICAL SOURCE OF THE PROBLEM

How did Britain's ruling class arrive at this impasse? In the 1960s a vast literature was devoted to trying to explain the country's relative decline (reading it today one is struck by how little the problem has changed). In a series of influential articles written between 1964 and 1976, Perry Anderson and Tom Nairn tried to explain it through a comprehensive historical analysis focusing on the distinctive history of the political and social dominance of a landed class with a pre- or even anti-industrial outlook.[11] After the French revolution, they argued, the rapidly expanding British bourgeoisie chose to accept the continued political hegemony of the landed class, which after 1846 placed few obstacles in the way of capitalist development, rather than challenge it with the support of a working class that was potentially revolutionary. The working class failed to define itself as a revolutionary class, and satisfied itself with a 'corporatist' ideology and role. All these features survived into the twentieth century, uninterrupted by invasion or tyranny. This distinguished Britain from its main rivals, especially Germany and France, both of which had been ravaged by the two world wars, but by the 1960s were forging ahead of Britain economically.

This crude summary is unjust to the richness and sophistication of Anderson's and Nairn's thesis, but in any case a key element of it was challenged fundamentally by the publication in 1981 of Arno Mayer's *The Persistence of the Old Regime*, which showed that down to 1914 all the major European countries were dominated economically and politically by their pre-industrial landed classes, and that their rising bourgeoisies were just as socially and politically subservient to them as the bourgeoisie in Britain.[12] Therefore the mere political dominance of Britain's landed class couldn't explain why in the 1960s Britain alone of the major west European countries had a poorly performing economy and a state seemingly unable to remedy this.

In his 1987 revision of the original analysis, Anderson shifted the focus away from the 'archaic nature of the ruling stratum' and more towards the structures – economic, state, social and cultural – produced by the particular balance of class forces in Britain from the seventeenth century onwards, and placed more emphasis on the significance of having avoided the rupture caused by wars in continental Europe.[13] Unlike the landed classes of continental Europe, British landowners had been essentially capitalist since the late eighteenth century, pursuing improved rents by encouraging investment by tenant farmers. Through their ownership of land they had also established themselves in coal mining and railways; and thanks to their control of the military, and their resulting imperial interests, they became strongly established in the financing of foreign trade. As a result, being more socially modernized, more open to entry, and much richer, the British ruling class hegemonized the industrial and commercial bourgeoisie in a way their continental counterparts couldn't. Enjoying both the benefits of free trade and preferential access to Britain's empire markets they saw no need for a state capable of pursuing the kind of national development strategy that later-industrialising countries were obliged to adopt.

And thanks to US intervention in the First World War (the origin of the 'special relationship' between the US and the UK), and again in the Second World War, the British state and social order inherited from the nineteenth century were not fatally disrupted and discredited, as those of continental Europe were. The continental monarchies, the pinnacles of aristocratic authority, had already been politically weakened by the impact of the French revolution and by their own backward culture, and were finally destroyed in the First World War (as Engels had predicted: 'crowns will roll into the gutters by the dozen, and no one will be around to pick them up'),[14] ending the legitimacy of aristocratic control of the state. And with the obvious exception of Germany after 1920, the devastation of the two wars also radicalized the continent's working classes, which were already more radical than Britain's.

The UK, by contrast, was damaged by bombing but not ravaged by fighting; society had not been polarized by occupation; the monarchy was not weakened but reinforced. The aristocracy was finally sidelined politically, but its institutional and social legacies had been so effectively normalized as to seem like inviolable principles of the (consequently still unwritten) constitution. (What became of its cultural power is more of a puzzle: the fundamental point is perhaps that all the distinctive pre-war class cultures, including that of the working class, were weakened and eventually marginalized by commercialization and consumerism.)[15]

So the state and dominant outlook of the British landed class remained potent long after its political eclipse. That outlook was not anti-capitalist, but it prioritized trade and finance over manufacturing, and had shaped the state and other public institutions accordingly. The senior civil service remained the preserve of men with a classical education, not engineers or scientists or economists. The Treasury remained focused on balancing budgets rather than on production, the education system remained stratified on class lines.

In the absence of a political elite which considered radical change essential, a state with the organizational capacity for radical change, and an administrative elite trained to carry it through, British manufacturing competitiveness continued its relative decline. A new kind of 'regulative intelligence' was needed, Anderson argued, equivalent to the institutions and cadres that had succeeded in reversing economic disadvantage elsewhere – the grandes écoles and the École Nationale d'Administration in France, the landesbanken in Germany, MITI and the keiretsu in Japan, the chaebols in South Korea, etc.

> Deregulation – of labour and capital markets – could only mean still more deindustrialisation, in pre-established conditions. The laws of comparative advantage have continued to work themselves out. The rectification of disadvantage requires another kind of social logic. For it to occur, a centralising force capable of regulating and counteracting the spontaneous molecular movements of the market must exist.[16]

This analysis still seems broadly valid. The Wilson government elected in 1964 briefly attempted to emulate the French model, creating a new civil service training school, establishing a new Department of Economic Affairs to formulate and promote a national plan for growth, and instituting special advisers drawn from outside the permanent civil service to inject a more technocratic thrust to government policy.[17] But the first two of these initiatives were neutered and finally strangled by the senior civil service and the Treasury (with remarkably little serious resistance from the Labour leadership, who were cowed by the power of the City). Special advisers survived, but instead of constituting a new kind of regulative intelligence within the state, they came into their own in the Blair years as a cadre helping to reduce the scale and power of the state and to subordinate policy ever more precisely to what were treated as the imperatives of adaptation to market forces.

For the most significant feature of the economic policy of all governments since Anderson published his 1987 article is sustained and maximum exposure to global market forces. Neoliberal theorists maintain that this has promoted competitiveness and growth and must be steadfastly pursued, in spite of the social costs involved for the domestic workforce, in spite of the evidence that from the late 1980s growth was enabled by non-recurring special factors (North Sea oil and the rise of the City of London as a global financial centre), and in spite of growing public alarm at the scale of foreign control of the economy.[18] The leaderships of all three main political parties remain committed to this. The question is how far they will continue to do so as the social costs increase in the wake of the financial crisis – especially if the promised revival of competitiveness fails to transpire.

Anderson and Nairn originally thought that Britain's economic decline portended an 'organic crisis' in which the existing order of class power would collapse and give way to a new one. That hasn't occurred, but the question of whether it might remains a good starting-point for thinking about the ruling class in Britain today.

THE BRITISH RULING CLASS IN ITSELF

Like any ruling class, the British ruling class has a core and a periphery, and a penumbra of other class fractions attached to it by a variety of ties: the monarchy and its functionaries, the judiciary, the police, the military, the security services, the established church hierarchy, the senior civil service, senior doctors and lawyers, etc. At the core of the core there is an intense class consciousness, and institutions that embody and reinforce class solidarity in the defence of property, such as public (i.e. private) schools, clubs, guilds, masonic lodges and exclusive sports (big game shooting, offshore sailing, horse-racing, polo). At the periphery there is less at stake and the consciousness is less intense, but still present. Everyone is connected to the core in one way or another.

Rebecca Cassidy's entertaining study of Newmarket, the Mecca of British thoroughbred horse racing and the beneficiary of three centuries of royal and aristocratic patronage, provides a useful paradigm of ruling-class coherence and hegemony. At the centre are extremely wealthy owners, served by a strict hierarchy of staff, from trainers through bloodstock agents to jockeys, stud hands and stable 'lads'. Around them clusters a racing 'community' of people who can claim a 'connection' to particular horses currently competing or in training: they are related to, or at least know, its trainer, or the trainer of one of its forebears, or a jockey who rode a famous ancestor of the horse, and so on. Where someone lacks such a link, but is sufficiently rich, an imaginary connection will often be accepted provided the person in question otherwise fits in – shares the values and at least some of the social style of the racing hierarchy. Connections – symbolized by a very precise and subtle dress code – are certificates of entry. At races only 'connections' may enter the paddock, and the other racecourse facilities are segregated according to users' closeness to or distance from the core. Meanwhile the entire industry is sustained by a levy on the estimated £5 billions' worth of bets placed every year on horse races by overwhelmingly working-class 'punters'.[19]

Peter Robbins, the author of a scathing unpublished exposé of the behaviour and power of the world's super-rich, points to the general function of all such ruling-class connections: to ensure that property and the privileges it confers are secure, there has to be a very strong level of trust between those who operate in it.[20] To be accepted you must be seen to be committed to the ruling class's interests and values, and the indicators of commitment are, precisely, connections, established through private schools, clubs, marriage, social links and spending patterns. Nicholas Shaxson describes the British bankers in offshore tax havens in similar terms:

> Offshore, legal frameworks that distinguish between the criminal and the legitimate have eroded away and been replaced by networks of trust that distinguish between the well established and respectable on the one hand, and the unknown and dubious on the other. These trust-based networks, deferential to the aristocracy of wealth and privilege and resistant to formal laws, are the ultimate comfort for the banks' wealthy clients.[21]

This passage refers specifically to tax havens such as the Bahamas and Jersey. But London is also a tax haven and operates on similar principles.

The nature of the internal connections of the ruling class, and the ties that bind other class fractions to it, are more interesting than numerical estimates of its size. That said, in 2013 the thousand richest people in Britain between them owned assets worth £450 billion.[22] Eighty-eight were billionaires, the rest mere multi-millionaires. The poorest ten multi-millionaires on the list owned assets worth an average of £33 million each, barely distinguishable among the 6,015 High Net Worth Individuals (people with over $30 million) living in London in 2012,[23] and quite possibly not even rich enough to make them interesting to Coutts, a private bank in London which targets 'thrillionaires' – people with annual *incomes* of £3 million, enough to afford 'a luxury 5 bedroom house, two servants, two luxury cars, an apartment or yacht in the South of France and... enough left over to dine out twice a week and have a couple of luxury holidays a year'.[24] Still, they are clearly part of the ruling class. We also know that in 2004-05 five per cent of UK adults – just under five million people – owned 40 per cent of all marketable assets, while in 2008 over 400,000 people declared annual incomes averaging £156,000 (42,000 of them declared incomes averaging £780,000).[25] It is probably safe to say that between one and two million people have enough money to be seen, and to think of themselves and their families, as connected to the ruling class.

Of the super-rich a significant proportion are foreigners – in 2013 all but five of the richest 20 were non-British, for example. They are concentrated in London. Of the apartments sold in central London (defined narrowly, as the west end, the City of London and Docklands) in 2010, only 21 per cent went to British buyers.[26] A striking 47 per cent were bought by 'Asian investors' (i.e. from Hong Kong, Singapore, Malaysia and the Middle East), primarily as investments or, in a quarter of the cases, for their children to live in while studying at universities in London. In the twelve months ending in April 2013 foreigners, led by Russians, bought more than half of all London properties costing more than £2 million, attracted by the low value of sterling and ultra-low interest rates.[27]

These facts underscore the way London and its surrounding counties (the 'home counties') are integrated into the global capitalist system, in certain respects more than into the rest of the UK, aggravating the central problem of class rule.

> London has effectively left the UK; it belongs instead to a loose international federation of global cities united by their economic dynamism and cosmopolitanism and the people who flit between them. This leads to a big problem... The politicians, civil servants and journalists who make up Britain's governing class have had their world view shaped by living in the capital and its wealthy satellites. They run the country, but effectively live in another.[28]

Of course, what the author has in mind here is not the parts of London where most of its 8.2 million inhabitants live, and which include some of the most deprived areas of Britain, but the parts of London lived in (or commuted to from the home counties) by the richest, globally-oriented, one or two per cent. And it is not so much these people's global links that influence the outlook of politicians, civil servants and journalists, as their sheer affluence, which does trickle down, by various mechanisms, to the milieu in which politicians, civil servants and journalists work, and makes them insensitive to what life is like for most Londoners, and even more, for most people outside the south-east of England.

The mechanisms of connection which ensure ruling-class solidarity are sometimes tested by the speed with which new fortunes can be made in today's global economy, often in new trades that sound questionable – plus the fact that so many of the richest people in Britain are now from somewhere else. How are the established members of the ruling class to know whether this gambling or porn publishing king, or that Russian oligarch, is trustworthy? The *Tatler* magazine, which celebrates the social life of the very wealthy and has a circulation of 90,000, is always ready with advice on etiquette ('Receiving guests at your country pile this weekend? Please, please follow these bedroom etiquette rules, says Violet Henderson'). But the main social solvent is undoubtedly consumption. The *Financial*

Times (circulation 316,000) has a weekly supplement called 'How to Spend It', on everything from resorts and clothing and restaurants to furniture and real estate. Its target readership is so obvious, its advice defies parody. Jewellery is described as showing 'a carefully edited eclecticism'. A fancy kitchen is said to fulfil a need for 'personalization in our globalized society where everything tends towards sameness... The intention is to create a room that radiates warmth even when not in use'. A small folding table costing 85 per cent of the average UK household's income 'would make a brilliant games table to be brought out at will in any household'.[29] The long-established British ruling class expresses its class-belonging through expensive but very conventional taste, which 'naturalizes class membership by making it apparently effortless'.[30] The new global capitalist class (British as well as foreign) is invited to establish its class credentials by the apparently effortless spending of enormous amounts of money.

But newcomers have always finally secured membership of the British ruling class by sending their children to an 'independent' (i.e. private) school, and the global ruling class are following suit: 5 per cent of the children in the UK's private schools come from non-resident foreign families, who pay average fees of £26,000 a year, equivalent to the average annual income in the UK.[31] These schools account for only 7 per cent of the country's school children, but in addition to securing social acceptance they are also key to securing entry into the public life of the ruling class. In 2011 44 per cent of prominent people had been to one of them;[32] 12 per cent had been to just ten elite schools; 4 per cent, including no fewer than 12 members of the Cameron government, had been to just one – Eton College. Private schools also supply 44 per cent of the students admitted to Oxford and Cambridge, and almost a third of the 'top people' studied in 2011 had been to one or the other of these two universities.

In short, numerous members of the global ruling class favour London as a location and like to educate their children there (and if possible get them residential status and British passports). It is also in London that the corporate executives, politicians, senior bureaucrats, lawyers, accountants, advertising and media personnel – the 'globalising' fractions of the British ruling class – are based.

THE CLASS FOR ITSELF:
THE HYPERTROPHY OF PSEUDO-DEMOCRACY

The way the British ruling class rules doesn't differ in essentials from the methods used in any other post-industrial neoliberal democracy: shifting the tax burden to the working class, shifting from universal benefits to workfare, paring down social services, think-tank dominance of policy debate, constant and shameless government spin, populism, displacement (royal events, military parades, reality TV, gay marriage, women bishops, immigration, 'Brussels', foreign 'wars of choice'). These, the consent-winning aspects of hegemony, are complemented by repressive surveillance (saturation cover of public space by CCTV, undercover policing of dissent) and coercion (heavy-handed policing of demonstrations), both justified as counter-terrorism. And the whole package is underpinned by the radical reshaping of society from one of producers to one of consumers.[33] None of this is peculiarly British.

Two general points should be noted, however. On the one hand many elements in the mix are under strain, especially since the onset of the financial crisis. For example, as austerity pushes more people into poverty, income inequality and tax avoidance and evasion have become public issues which have seriously eroded the ruling class's legitimacy. Austerity has also made consumerism problematic (young people can't afford housing, old people can't afford adequate heating, 350,000 are using food banks). Cuts in police spending have also upset the normally close relationship between the police and the ruling class. The drive to downsize the state has led to a series of major policy fiascos (the West Coast train line franchise, the 111 health phone help line, the Stafford Hospital disaster). And so on.

On the other hand inherited pre-modern aspects of the British state still insulate the ruling class from challenge. Archaic institutions such as the monarchy (marketed as 'the royal family') and the House of Lords (protected by titles and ermine from being seen as the unaccountable collection of political cronies it is) still underpin its rule. The plurality or 'first past the post' electoral system discriminates strongly against new parties and secures the Labour Party in place as an alternative instrument of ruling-class control (the two major parties have jointly seen off all proposals to change it). The so-called unwritten constitution makes much executive action the exercise of 'royal prerogative', unaccountable to parliament – a feature accentuated by the arrival of 'e-politics': 'servers suck in and store the imprints of dissent and protest so that liquid modern politics can roll on unaffected and unabated – substituting soundbites and photo opportunities for confrontation and argument... Bush and Blair could go to war under false pretences with no *dearth* of websites calling their bluff'.[34]

The combination of these factors allows the electoral process to be disconnected from the reality of rule with remarkably little penalty. Democracy is not just 'thin'; party politics have become a parallel political universe to the realities of rule. In the 2010 election most of the really important problems confronting the country were barely discussed, or were barely mentioned: the unwinnable war in Afghanistan, the causes of terrorism, regulating the financial sector, the scandalously regressive tax system, not to mention the impending environmental catastrophe. The reason was that these are issues for the global ruling class, not the British electorate – as City commentators in the aftermath of the election, when negotiations over the formation of a coalition were still ongoing, didn't hesitate to point out:

> Investors favour a government that focuses on cutting the budget deficit, paying back the country's debts in full and on time... The new government will have to follow the market's guidelines, investors warn. 'The bond market will rule the UK whoever's prime minister', said Gary Jenkins, a credit analyst at Evolution Securities.[35]

> Analysts at BILLIONP Paribas reckoned that a 'Lib-Lab government is the least liked option by markets and would almost guarantee a downgrade of the UK sovereign debt'... Analysts at Morgan Stanley reckoned that the pound could have fallen to $1.35 – from around $1.50 yesterday – if a Lab-Lib coalition had been formed.[36]

No mainstream media figure challenged this. By 2010 the initial furious public anger against the authors of the financial crisis seemed to have been overcome.[37] But by 2013, as politicians of all parties talked less and less of recovery, and more and more of a permanent future of austerity, the mood shifted again, and Britain's underlying economic predicament came under public scrutiny once more. In confronting this problem three distinctive features of the context deserve particular emphasis: the exceptional role of the financial sector, the problematic nature of the EU as a regional expression of global capital and the radical transformation that successive governments have wreaked in the British state.

THE CITY OF LONDON

While fast-expanding financial and business services have overflowed the City's original 'square mile' (chiefly down-river to Canary Wharf), the City remains the financial sector's political headquarters, with its own distinctive local government, the Corporation of London, representing the big firms based in the City, and its own police force. It also has a special permanent official in the House of Commons (going by the archaic and innocent-sounding title of 'Remembrancer'), with a staff of fifty who scrutinize all parliamentary business and lobby MPs and ministers in the interests of the financial sector.

The City is thus lodged in the heart of British government, yet it has become more global than British. While it is not as big a financial centre as New York in terms of total market equity, more investment funds are managed in the City, and more foreign shares are traded there, than in New York or anywhere else in the world. The huge scale of these operations is partly due to low levels of regulation and taxation: the City is 'offshore' in more senses than one. Already in the late 1950s it had begun to deal more in dollars than in sterling, encouraging most of the major US banks to establish offices and take advantage of the Eurodollar market. Since 1986 almost all the City's investment banks have been foreign-owned and largely foreign-staffed, and more than half the City's business is done for foreign customers.

Links to the rest of the British economy are weak. Even the four big British retail or 'high street' banks, which are also headquartered in the City, make most of their money from their international trading and investment activities (for example, 72 per cent of Barclays' total profits of £1.8 billion in 2012–13 came from investment banking), not from lending to companies in Britain; and they have so far successfully resisted post-crash pressure to separate their retail from their investment functions. Moreover most shares in UK companies are in managed funds (around half are managed by just 50 fund management groups) whose managers have no interest in preferring British to overseas companies when placing their clients' investments.[38] And in so far as they do invest in UK shares they have no interest in becoming involved in the management of the companies concerned, because the longer-run value of a company's shares is of no interest to the investors they are working for (in the words of a relatively sympathetic insider, 'the current quarter is what matters, perhaps the next quarter, certainly not next year's equivalent quarter').[39] Out of 22 fund managers interviewed by Aeron Davis in 2005, only two had any experience in industry and none had ever visited the site of a company in which their funds had shares.[40] The Coalition government's promised £1 billion government-funded 'business bank' to direct capital into industrial modernization remains on the drawing board.

City spokespeople constantly stress that the financial sector is a major employer, accounting for over a million jobs. This is true if all the country's local bank branches and insurance and accountants' offices and the like are included. Banking and financial services jobs in the City of London and at Canary Wharf total about 100,000, out of a total UK workforce of 31 million.[41] Where the City does make a critical economic contribution is in foreign exchange earnings. In 2011 the UK had a trade surplus in services of £76 billion, £39 billion of which were earned by banks and other financial institutions; and this surplus offset three quarters of the country's £100 billion trade deficit in goods. But this contribution gives the City enormous leverage with any Chancellor of the Exchequer; and this leverage is reinforced by the City's provision of a major share of political party funding. This was thrown into sharp relief as the City fought to resist reform of the banking sector after the 2007–09 crisis, in which two major British banks had to be rescued by the taxpayer at a cost of £66 billion, doubling the public debt as a proportion of GDP. In 2010 financial sector donations to the Conservative Party accounted for 25 per cent of its total funding. By 2012 the proportion had doubled to over 50 per cent.[42]

Since the financial crash, reformers have called for the UK's four big retail banks to be broken up, and for the state's implicit underwriting of the risk of failure to be confined to their retail functions, leaving the risks of their more profitable trading operations to be borne by their shareholders and creditors. And the risks do remain high: for example in 2012 Barclays alone had £1.8 trillion of gross credit risk, more than the entire UK GDP, consisting largely of Eurozone-linked derivatives; and all the banks are major creditors of dangerously over-leveraged private equity funds.[43] But the banks have succeeded in getting reform watered down and postponed: their retail lending functions will not be split off but only 'ring-fenced', and then only by 2019; and they have continued to lobby against measures to ensure more transparency, more effective regulation, and measures to limit the bonus system which is at the heart of risk-taking.

The financial sector has also mobilized politically on a range of other issues with equally problematic implications for the UK economy. One is tax reform. The UK tax burden is highly regressive: the top tenth of income earners pay 34 per cent of their incomes in direct and indirect taxation, compared with the lowest decile's 47 per cent – and that is only income that is declared. A great deal of the income of the rich is concealed through ingenious tax avoidance schemes: as a tax adviser told his clients back in 2009, for such taxpayers paying tax is really optional.[44] Another category of mainly wealthy tax avoiders are included among Britain's 120,000 'non-doms' – people who are resident in Britain but are 'domiciled' elsewhere for tax purposes and pay no tax in the UK on their overseas incomes. In 2008 the TUC estimated that of the £25 billion of tax revenues it estimated were lost through tax avoidance, nearly £13 billion were lost through tax avoidance by individuals, among whom non-doms were a significant element.[45]

As for multinational firms, their tax avoidance is on an appropriately industrial scale, using legal accounting devices to declare most of their profits in tax havens. In 2006 more than 60 per cent of the 700 biggest companies in Britain paid less than £10 million corporation tax apiece, and 30 per cent had paid nothing.[46] In 2011, on a total turnover of £2,250 million,

McDonald's, Google, Starbucks and Amazon paid a total of £8.8 million between them.[47] The tax rate on corporate profits for that year was 26 per cent. Starbucks, with 760 UK outlets, reported a £33 million loss. In 2013, faced with growing public resentment, Starbucks undertook to make a voluntary tax donation of £20 million, underlining the optional nature of corporate tax payment.

The reaction of these companies when threatened with the possibility of action against tax avoidance is revealing. Google's chairman explained to the House of Commons Public Accounts Committee that Google's tax affairs were what the law allowed and that it was a big employer in Britain, for which it should be appreciated.[48] Also revealing is the response of the Revenue and Customs Agency: 'The UK has an internationally competitive corporate tax system, which is designed to attract and retain economic activity here'.[49] Ernst and Young, which employs 2,081 tax experts in Britain, generating a quarter of its global profits, lobbied the Prime Minister against making global companies pay taxes on their local turnover when it seemed as if public fury was about to make this likely.[50]

Tax has become an issue where the interest of the global ruling class and the management of national politics are in open conflict, with the City at the centre of it. On the whole, the City seemed likely to win. Early in 2012 eleven Eurozone countries decided to impose a financial transactions tax on trades in shares, bonds and derivatives, calculated to raise €57 billion a year.[51] The City opposed it, fearing a diversion of business from London, where a large share of euro trades take place, to Asia and North America. In 2013 George Osborne, the Chancellor, entered a legal challenge to it at the European Court of Justice.[52]

The City's position is complicated – although, astonishingly enough, no more than complicated – by the fact that the big banks have been revealed as large-scale abusers of power, if not criminal fraudsters. It emerged that they had been making money by manipulating the London inter-bank lending rate (Libor), on which an estimated $370 trillion deals are based world-wide. HSBC and Standard Chartered had also gone in for large-scale money-laundering. Lloyds, HSBC, RBS and Barclays had gone in for cheating their customers by selling them payment protection insurance (PPI) on their loans which often didn't apply to their situation, and which the banks routinely failed to honour when it did; their average return on this swindle was an extraordinary 80 per cent, accounting in some years for a large part of their profits. The total liabilities of the banks for all this are staggering: in fines for manipulating Libor (Barclays, UBS and RBS), £1.65 billion, with the bill for four other major banks still to come in; in fines for money-laundering

(Standard Chartered and HSBC), $2.587 billion; in fines for helping US citizens evade tax (UBS) $780 million; in compensation to the victims of the PPI scandal and the victims of a related insurance scam for loans to small businesses (Lloyds, HSBC, RBS, Barclays), an estimated £26 billion.[53]

Two features of these extraordinary revelations should be stressed (in addition to the further demonstration they provide of the need for banking to be state-owned and managed). First, the offences were mainly committed by banks based in London, or by foreign-based banks' London offices. Second, it is not clear that they would have come to light had it not been for the crash, which drew in the US regulators. The City's weak regulatory regime has been a key factor in its continued global importance.[54]

And here too there have been no signs of contrition, or of a drastic change in regulation. In relation to both Libor and PPI one senior banker after another has claimed they had no knowledge of what had been going on; the chairman of Standard Chartered Bank even described the rigging of the Libor as 'clerical errors or mistakes'. The US regulators were angry enough with this remark to force a retraction, but in the UK the relationship between the financial sector and the regulators was too intimate even for an expression of irritation.[55]

This was made embarrassingly clear by a parliamentary review of what went wrong at HBOS (Halifax-Bank of Scotland), which had to be rescued by the government at a cost of £11.5 billion at the height of the crisis. The MPs found that the regulators in the Financial Services Authority had been content to trust the bank's own complacent view of itself, while it was in fact so incompetently managed that it was insolvent even before the 2007 crisis hit. The MPs repeatedly declared themselves astonished at the delusions of grandeur of the titled gentlemen who had run the bank into the ground: 'We are shocked and surprised that, even after the ship has run aground, so many of those who were on the bridge still seem so keen to congratulate themselves on their collective navigational skills.'[56] But the idea that the financial sector is run by people of exceptional talent whom only huge salaries and bonuses can secure has been shown again and again to be pure rhetoric. The regulators were manifestly lax and seem quite likely to remain so;[57] in the absence of serious regulation, incompetents can award themselves fortunes with no serious risk: 'No jail time, no financial penalties, not even a clawback of bonuses, even though these were based on profits that have proven illusory'.[58] James Crosby, the CEO of HBOS, resigned before the crash, cashed in two-thirds of his HBOS shares (when they still had some value), was knighted, and finally appointed to the board of the regulator (the FSA), even becoming its deputy chairman until 2009. You couldn't invent it.

Few features of British politics better illustrate the central problem of the British ruling class than its relationship with the City. On the one hand it depends on the City's contribution to the increasingly unsustainable UK balance of payments, and relies on it for party funding, while on the other it is obliged to meet the terms the City sets for these contributions, terms which reflect the City's need for a tax and regulatory regime that will allow it to remain at the epicentre of global finance, and be paid lavish rewards. But the ruling class actually sees the City's terms as rational and inevitable; and the class solidarity felt between the leaders of parties and the leaders of the City, reinforced by an inherited class culture of tradition and deference, tends to make any public questioning of the terms seem like vulgar bad manners. The problem of rule then becomes to a significant extent one of how to win elections while imposing on the electorate policies the City needs to maintain its position in the global economy.

THE BRITISH RULING CLASS AND THE EU

Britain's membership of the EU is a problem for the ruling class because it plays two conflicting roles. On the one hand it provides free access to the world's largest single consumer market of over 500 million relatively prosperous consumers, who between them take close to 60 per cent of UK exports. On the other it is a scapegoat for the weaknesses of the UK economy, blamed for bureaucratic red tape and interference in matters such as working hours, which the Conservative far-right resent, and for immigration from Eastern Europe, especially, which a significant number of unemployed British workers dislike. The problem is greater for the Conservative Party, because it relies heavily for electoral support on older white working-class men – the section of the electorate that is most susceptible to xenophobic appeals. Without working-class support the Conservative Party would be a permanent minority. Indeed it may already be one, having failed to win an outright majority in 2010 when the Labour Party – in office for 13 years – was riven by divisions, tainted by the invasion of Iraq, and paralysed by the worst economic crisis for 80 years. Retention of this segment of electoral support is therefore critical to the Conservatives' future.

In early 2013 the EU issue was forced, at least for a time, to the top of the political agenda by the right-wing United Kingdom Independence Party (UKIP). Formed only in 1993, UKIP's defining issues are exit from the EU and stiff limits to immigration. In early 2013 it came second in a parliamentary by-election, with 28 per cent of the votes, pushing the Conservatives into third place (the seat was retained by the Liberal-

Democrats), and in May 2013 it won 25 per cent of the vote across a swathe of local council elections in mainly rural areas of England. An opinion poll later in May showed UKIP with 18 per cent of the national vote, boosted by a switch to UKIP of 27 per cent of voters who had voted Conservative in the 2010 election.[59] This precipitated a crisis for the Conservatives: the right wing of the parliamentary party rebelled, demanding an early referendum on leaving the EU which Cameron could not grant, since his Liberal-Democrat coalition partners opposed it. The challenge threatened a split which could itself spell electoral defeat.

But the EU issue also represented a threat to Labour and the Liberal Democrats, which had lost 13 per cent and 12 per cent of their 2010 voters to UKIP, respectively. UKIP was capitalising on a widespread disaffection with all the major parties, which were seen as led by affluent professional politicians out of touch with the needs and feelings of the 'ordinary hardworking people' they constantly claimed to represent. Polls showed that EU membership was not in fact high on most voters' lists of concerns, but it had become an issue on which the British ruling class's capacity to serve the interests of the global ruling class while managing British electoral sentiment could be severely tested.

The wish of a large number of right-wing Conservative MPs to leave the EU is partly driven by electoral anxiety, but it also reflects their dislike of having to compromise with the social market ideas of Christian Democrats, Social Democrats, Greens, etc. in the other EU countries. The party's official policy is to stay in the EU provided various powers are 'repatriated' from Brussels to Westminster. The powers in question are never specified but chiefly concern employment, social security, and law and order. It seems very unlikely that the other EU countries would agree.

Some advocates of withdrawal argue that easy access to EU markets is serving to delay the needed radical renovation of the UK economy; leaving the EU would force Britain to tackle its fundamental internal problems. Boris Johnson, the Mayor of London and a strong candidate to replace Cameron as Conservative leader, expressed it in terms that explicitly harked back to the arguments about British decline of the 1960s, but with a neocon tinge:

If we left the EU, we would end this sterile debate, and we would have to recognise that most of our problems are not caused by 'Bwussels', but by chronic British short-termism, inadequate management, sloth, low skills, a culture of easy gratification and underinvestment in both human and physical capital and infrastructure. Why are we still, person for person, so much less productive than the Germans? That is now a question more than a century old, and the answer is nothing to do with the EU. In or out of the EU, we must have a clear vision of how we are going to be competitive in a global economy.[60]

This perspective raises the obvious question of how it would affect the City. The financial sector clearly did not want to be drawn into a fight inside the party it relies on to look after its interests; at the time of writing the silence emanating from the City was deafening. It was hard to believe City firms saw leaving the EU as a positive prospect. The BBC's economics editor Robert Peston seemed to have no doubt about the City's true feelings:

Those who run our biggest companies would tend to be horrified at the idea of withdrawal from the EU. Our multinationals, unlike those of Switzerland, increasingly think of themselves as global corporate citizens, as much as British citizens. And whether they started life as British or not, they have a mindset that they are in Britain because it is an attractive place to be located within the EU. Bosses of big banks and financial institutions would have this European mindset in spades. And many of them would take serious issue with Lord Lawson's idea that they would be liberated to thrive again, outside of the supposedly deadening clutches of EU financial reform and its planned new tax on financial transactions.[61]

Another question was whether Scottish voters would be more likely to support independence for Scotland in the referendum due to be held on that issue in October 2014, if they thought that government by Westminster might no longer be tempered by the institutions of the EU. An even more crucial question was the attitude of the US, for which the UK was a valuable entry-point to the EU. In January Obama's Assistant Secretary for European Affairs took the highly unusual step of publicly warning Cameron that 'there would be consequences for Britain if it either left the EU or played a lesser role in Brussels... Jacob Kirkegaard, of the Peterson Institute for International Economics in Washington, said: "This is essentially [the US] saying to the UK – 'you guys are on your own'. There is an element of pre-emption here and must be clearly intended to create waves".'[62]

What is at issue are two competing models of engagement in the global capitalist system: one as part of a trading bloc large enough to set terms for other countries to trade with it, which happens also to suit the strategic interests of the US; the other as an independent medium-sized economy willing to impose on its working class whatever social price is needed to compete against larger economies with lower wages and less social protection.

Whether the second option would prove compatible with even the thinnest kind of electoral democracy may be doubted.

THE OUTSOURCED STATE

Since the early 2000s successive governments have been outsourcing work that used to be done by the state. The civil service has been scaled back from a peak of 536,000 in 2005 to 460,000 in 2012, by which time the annual value of contracts held by private firms providing public services was £82 billion, accounting for 24 per cent of total government spending; and outsourcing was increasing so fast that by 2014 the total annual value was expected to exceed £140 billion.[63] The provision of these services is dominated by three very big companies, G4S, Capita and Serco, which depend entirely on government contracts and which are virtually risk-free, being both 'too big to fail', and providing services that are indispensable. This not only makes regulation of them unenforceable, but also puts them at the heart of policy-making for the sectors in which they are involved. In effect, policy for these sectors must now conform to corporate requirements.

But companies have been effectively put in charge of the policy-making process in other sectors too. For instance in 2010 the Conservative Secretary of State for Health invited Pepsico, Starbucks, McDonalds, Unilever, the Wine and Spirits Trade Association and other corporate interests in the food and drinks (and fitness) industries to help set public health policy[64] – and abolished the Food Standards Agency. In the field of trade and industry a so-called 'buddy' scheme, introduced for 38 companies in 2011 and expected to include a further 42 by 2013, gives them a 'direct line to ministers and officials'.[65] By the end of 2012 the original 38 companies – more than two-thirds of which are based outside the UK – had held a total of 700 face to face meetings with ministers. Throughout the 2000s the scale of lobbying, and a series of scandals arising from it, prompted the prime minister to commit himself to the idea of a register of lobbyists; in mid-2013 it seemed likely that industry opposition would finally be overcome, but that the legislation would offer few real obstacles to lobbyists' continued power.

An even larger breach in the boundary between the public and the private sector is arguably the recruitment of personnel from the private sector into the policy-making heart of the civil service. Of the 200 most senior civil servants in 2012, 41 per cent had been recruited from outside the service, primarily from the private sector,[66] while a steady stream of senior civil servants – and ministers – flowed into highly-paid corporate jobs in the sector covered by their former departments.[67] This 'revolving door' briefly became a cause of public concern, but was soon forgotten.[68] In early 2013, when the House of Lords voted to endorse regulations that effectively force commissioners of health services for the NHS to invite private firms to bid for them, it was noted that 145 peers had links to companies that stood to profit.[69] A third of them voted. As the famous Wall Street analyst Jack Grubman is said to have remarked, 'what used to be conflict of interest is now defined as a synergy'.[70]

As the civil service shrank, and its senior personnel were increasingly drawn from the private sector, outsourcing of policy-making itself became increasingly common. For example in 2007-08 three major policy reports setting out the future of the National Health Service were commissioned from three separate American think tanks.[71] Much that these reports recommended proved unworkable but yet another one, commissioned from McKinsey in 2009, was adopted without public discussion and has been undermining the financial viability of the NHS ever since.[72] In general, since the early 2000s the terms of policy debate have increasingly been set by industry-funded think tanks, to the point where in March 2012 the Cabinet Secretary, at the apex of the state's policy-making structure, speculated publicly that inviting external bids to provide policy was a 'perfectly legitimate challenge'.[73]

Is it possible to see all this as the early stages of development of a new kind of 'regulative intelligence' capable of solving Britain's chronic economic problems? It seems implausible, at least within the parameters of liberal-democratic democracy. At the heart of the most extreme neoliberal conception of local government, in which local councils meet once a year to award contracts, there has always been a crucial flaw: who, and on what basis of legitimacy, would form the council and make the annual decisions? The same problem now arises in the outsourced central state of the UK. The concept of a public interest, different from and superior to any constellation of private interests, is the indispensable bedrock of legitimacy, and needs to be sustained and developed by a cadre of people with the capacity, incentive and authority to do it, on whom elected politicians can rely. The senior civil service inherited from the Victorians has proved unequal to the task, but it is not a task that corporate executives, or the young 'policy-wonks' in corporate-funded think tanks, are trained or incentivized to perform. Perhaps a small stratum of career civil servants could still emerge who would be capable of inducing corporate interests to collaborate in generating long-term solutions to the country's increasingly urgent economic needs, but given the true power imbalance between senior civil servants and the CEOs of transnational companies it seems an improbable scenario.

The ruling class should be praying that it will happen, but as yet shows few signs of even being aware of the problem. So far from seeing the financial crisis as a wake-up call for radical reform of both the state and the economy, the coalition government has seen it primarily as an opportunity to intensify the rollback of the state and the compression of wages. For its part, the Labour Party leadership has failed abysmally to counter the right-wing media view that the crisis was due to the profligacy of the Blair and Brown governments, and that austerity is the price to be paid for it. Dependent on an inherited cohort of Blairite MPs, and desperate to win the next election, it endorses fiscal rectitude and 'radically pruning central government'.[74]

Of course, to end with this allusion to the pitiable situation of the Labour Party leadership is to remind the reader that no attention has been paid in this essay to the British working class, whose political weakness has been such a key premise of ruling-class practice since at least the early 1990s. Mainstream opinion doesn't yet hold that everyone in Britain except the super-rich is 'middle class' — that British society, like America's, 'by definition contains no lower classes'.[75] But it does think that workers no longer see themselves as forming a class with shared political interests that they are ready or able to fight for. In keeping with this view, just as this essay was being written, a team of academics announced on the basis of 160,000 interviews that Britain now has not two or three but seven classes: an 'elite' (6 per cent), an 'established middle class' (25 per cent), a 'technical middle class' (6 per cent), 'new affluent workers' (15 per cent), a 'traditional working class' (14 per cent), 'new emergent service workers' (19 per cent), and a precariat (15 per cent).[76] The 'elite', which evidently corresponds roughly to the ruling class described here, was defined as having 'very high economic capital (particularly savings), high social capital, and very high highbrow cultural capital' — but not as having class interests opposed to those of other classes, or a project for defending them. But as this essay has shown, that is a travesty; the recurrent effort to treat classes as if they have no politics invariably ends in the same absurdity. Establishing how British workers see their interests, and what kind of political project may prove able to enforce them, calls for a different kind of enquiry that urgently needs to be undertaken.

NOTES

1   London ranked first above New York and then Hong Kong in 2011, according to Z/Yen, The Global Financial Services Index, Qatar Financial Centre Authority, June 2011, cited in Ranald Michie, 'The City of London as a Global Financial Centre: An Historical and Comparative Perspective', presentation to the TP Annual Conference 2012. In 2010 London handled 18 per cent of the world's interbank activity, 37 per cent of foreign exchange turnover and 46 per cent of interest rate derivatives turnover.

2   Göran Therborn, *What Does the Ruling Class Do When It Rules?*, London: Verso 1978, pp. 144-61.

3   Leo Panitch and Sam Gindin, *The Making of Global Capitalism: The Political Economy of American Empire*, London and New York: Verso, 2012, pp. 67-9.

4   *Statistical Bulletin: Ownership of UK Quoted Shares, 2010*, Office for National Statistics February 2012, available at http://www.ons.gov.uk.

5   Jane Simms, 'Selling off Britain', *Director Magazine,* March 2010, available at http://www.director.co.uk. The FTSE is the leading index of shares on the London Stock Exchange.

6   At $46,000 each. Data available at http://data.worldbank.org.

7   Jeremy Warner, 'Trillion Pound Cash Mountain to the Rescue? It's Unwise to Bank on It', *The Telegraph*, 25 February 2013.

8   *Guardian*, 8 March 2013.

9   Royal Academy of Engineering, *Competing in the Global Economy, A Series of Debates*, May 2011, available at http://www.raeng.org.uk.

10   Office for National Statistics, *Poverty and Social Exclusion in the UK and EU, 2005-2011*, available at http://www.ons.gov.uk. Thirty-seven per cent said they were unable to meet unexpected expenses and 30 per cent said they could not afford an annual holiday. Five per cent were experiencing severe material deprivation.

11   Perry Anderson, 'Origins of the Present Crisis', and Tom Nairn, 'The British Political Elite', *New Left Review*, I/23(January/February), 1964. Six other *NLR* articles by Anderson or Nairn between 1964 and 1976 filled out the analysis.

12   Arno Mayer, *The Persistence of the Old Regime: Europe to the Great War*, London: Verso, 1981.

13   Perry Anderson, 'The Figures of Descent', *New Left Review*, I/161(January/February), 1987, pp. 20-77.

14   'And, finally, the only war left for Prussia-Germany to wage will be a world war, a world war, moreover of an extent and violence hitherto unimagined. Eight to ten million soldiers will be at each other's throats and in the process they will strip Europe barer than a swarm of locusts. The depredations of the Thirty Years' War compressed into three to four years and extended over the entire continent; famine, disease, the universal lapse into barbarism, both of the armies and the people, in the wake of acute misery; irretrievable dislocation of our artificial system of trade, industry and credit, ending in universal bankruptcy; collapse of the old states and their conventional political wisdom to the point where crowns will roll into the gutters by the dozen, and no one will be around to pick them up; the absolute impossibility of foreseeing how it will all end and who will emerge as victor from the battle. Only one consequence is absolutely certain: universal exhaustion and the creation of the conditions for the ultimate victory of the working class'. Introduction to S. Borkheim, *Zur Erinnerung fur die deutschen Mordspatrioten 1806-1807* [To the Memory of the German Arch-patriots of 1806-07], Hottingen-Zurich, 1888.

15   See Richard Hoggart, *The Uses of Literacy*, London: Chatto and Windus, 1957; and Raymond Williams, *The Long Revolution*, London: Chatto and Windus, 1961; also Ross McKibbin, *Classes and Cultures: England 1918-1951*, Oxford:

OUP, 1998, chapter 1.

16   Anderson, 'Figures', p. 73.

17   The French example was hugely influential. The Europeanist Brian Chapman was bleakly envious of the impatience, briskness and efficiency of the 'young men concentrating on influencing the real sources of power in the State. They believed in rational planning, expansion, efficiency. They were products of the French educational pattern which... instils a belief that human affairs can be better organised by reason rather than by instinct'. *British Government Observed: Some European Reflections*, London: George Allen and Unwin, 1963, p. 22.

18   This concern was shared by many leading business figures, as revealed in a series of interesting debates of the Royal Academy of Engineering (see note 9), where it was noted that 'in some sectors, including water and power utilities, the automotive industry and national newspapers, well over 50 per cent of UK-based companies and corporations are controlled by foreign owned groups'. Interestingly, a 'small majority' of the 100 'senior engineers and business people' participating in this debate voted *against* the motion that the advantages of foreign ownership outweighed the disadvantages.

19   Rebecca Cassidy, *The Sport of Kings: Kinship, Class and Thoroughbred Breeding in Newmarket*, Cambridge: Cambridge University Press, 2002, p. 6. The financial data are from 1999-2000, and so understate the scale.

20   I am very grateful to Peter Robbins for the opportunity to read 'Filthy Rich'. Completed in 2009, the book has still to find a publisher for fear of libel actions, even though every fact cited in it is referenced to an already published source. British libel law protects the very rich from criticism to an extent unmatched elsewhere and until 2013 it had become common for non-British members of the global ruling class to bring libel actions in London. A new Defamation Act, expected to come into force by the end of 2013, should put an end to this, but it is not clear that it makes the fact that a statement is true a good defence against a libel action.

21   Nicholas Shaxson, *Treasure Islands: Tax Havens and the Men Who Stole the World*, London: The Bodley Head, 2011, p. 220. Shaxson adds: 'The similarities with Mafia codes of behaviour are no coincidence at all'.

22   *The Sunday Times Rich List* 2013.

23   Frank Knight Research, *The Wealth Report 2013*, London: Think Publishing, 2013, p. 9, available at http://www.knightfrankblog.com.

24   Robbins, 'Filthy Rich'.

25   Mike Brewer, Luke Sibieta and Liam Wren-Lewis, *Racing Away? Income Inequality and the Evolution of High Incomes*, Institute of Fiscal Studies 2008, available at http://www.ifs.org.uk.

26   *The Implications of Global Capital Flows on the London Office Market*, prepared for the City of London Corporation and the City Property Association by Jones Lang LaSalle, March 2012, p. 26, available at http://www.cityoflondon.gov. uk.

27   Rupert Neate, 'Foreign Buyers Behind Half of £2m+ Home Sales in London', *Guardian*, 7 May 2013.

28   Neil O'Brien, 'Another Country: London's Separateness from the Rest of

Britain Becomes More Pronounced Every Year', *Spectator*, 14 April 2012.

29   *Financial Times*, 'How to Spend It', 5 January 2013.

30   Cassidy, *Sport of Kings*, p. 27.

31   Independent Schools Council Annual Census, Table 9.

32   The Sutton Trust, *The Educational Backgrounds of the Nation's Leading People*, 2012, available at http://www.suttontrust.com. The study covered 7.637 people educated at secondary schools in the UK whose names appeared in the birthday lists of *The Times*, *The Sunday Times*, *The Independent* or *The Independent on Sunday* during 2011.

33   Zygmunt Bauman, *Consuming Life*, Cambridge and Malden: Polity Press, 2007.

34   Bauman, *Consuming Life*, pp. 108-9.

35   Elena Moya, *Guardian*, 12 May 2010.

36   Jill Treanor, *Guardian*, 12 May 2010.

37   See Julie Froud, Michael Moran, Adriana Nillson and Karel Williams, 'Opportunity Lost: Mystification, Elite Politics and Financial Reform in the UK', *Socialist Register 2011*, Pontypool: Merlin, 2010, pp. 98-119.

38   Office for National Statistics, *Statistical Bulletin: Ownership of UK Quoted Shares, 2010*, released 28 February 2012. Eleven per cent of UK quoted shares are owned by UK individuals: foreigners owned 41 per cent. Forty five per cent were owned through managed funds, 8 per cent belonged to insurance companies and 5 per cent to pension funds.

39   Tony Golding, *The City: Inside the Great Expectation Machine*, 2nd edition, London: FT Prentice Hall, 2003, p. 181.

40   Aeron Davis, *The Mediation of Power*, London: Routledge, 2007, p. 86.

41   City of London Department of Planning and Transportation, April 2010. Data are for 2008. See http://www.cityoflondon.gov.uk.

42   Bureau of Investigative Journalism, 'Tory Party Funding from City Doubles Under Cameron', 25 October 2011. Individual donors of £50,000 or more were entitled to membership of the Leader's Group who 'are given numerous opportunities to meet "David Cameron and other senior figures from the Conservative Party at dinners, post-PMQ lunches, drinks receptions, election result events and important campaign launches"'. See http://www.thebureauinvestigates.com.

43   Larry Elliott, 'Takeover Boom of Last Decade May Lead to Another Crash, Bank Warns', *Guardian*, 14 March 2013.

44   Jill Treanor, 'Tax is Optional, Says Advisor with Links to Rescued Bank', *Guardian*, 6 October 2009. In polite circles using legal loopholes to escape tax is avoidance, not evasion, but a great deal is in fact evaded. In 2009 a whistleblower leaked details of over 100 British residents who had undeclared offshore accounts, which constitutes evasion. Just why it took until May 2013 for the authorities to make this public is unexplained, other than by the likely eminence of some of the evaders. The language used by the revenue authorities when the story became public is interesting: they said they *encouraged* 'early disclosure of tax irregularities. Failure to do so may result in a criminal prosecution or significant financial penalties *and the possibility of their identities being published*'. Rupert Neale and James Ball, *Guardian*, 9 May 2013; italics

added.

45 Trades Union Congress, *The Missing Billions: The UK Tax Gap*, 2008. HM Revenue and Customs estimated the gap in corporation tax at between £3.7 billion and £13 billion. The Commons Public Accounts Committee estimated it at £8.5 billion. Will Hutton thinks the loss from all tax avoidance/evasion is equivalent to about one per cent of UK GDP. 'Behind Tax Avoidance Lies an Ideology that Has Had Its Day. We Must End It', *Guardian*, 14 February 2009.

46 'Firms' Secret Tax Avoidance Scheme Cost UK Billions', *Guardian*, 3 February 2009, the first of a series of investigative reports on the issue.

47 *Guardian*, 17 October 2012.

48 Charles Arthur, 'Google Chief Defends Low Tax Payments', *Guardian*, 23 April 2013.

49 *Guardian*, 17 October 2013, p. 9.

50 Simon Bowers and Phillip Inman, 'Tax Advisers Lobby Cameron to Avert New Rules for Companies', *Guardian*, 8 May 2013. Cameron had announced that it would be a priority during his impending chairmanship of the G8.

51 *Guardian*, 23 April 2013.

52 Ernst and Young have estimated that if the tax is imposed the City will be raising an estimated 60 per cent (£21billion) of it, none of which will presumably be spent in Britain so long as the government opposes it. This situation would clearly be electorally hard to sustain. See http://www.tuc.org.uk.

53 The banks' 'barely believable behaviour' is ably summarized by John Lanchester in 'Are We Having Fun Yet?', *London Review of Books*, 4 July 2013, pp. 3–8. He also notes that in addition to rescuing the banks at the cost of ten years of austerity taxpayers are now also paying for the fines and compensation costs of Lloyds and RBS, which are still largely owned by the public. Moreover the potential scale of the banks' liabilities for manipulating Libor is far higher than the fines they have paid or have yet to pay, as many institutions around the world are instituting or contemplating lawsuits for resulting losses.

54 It also helps account for the fact that two of the biggest bank losses since the 2008 crisis – £1.4 billion lost by a 'rogue trader' at the Swiss bank UBS, and $6.2 billion lost by a trader (the 'London Whale') at JP Morgan Chase – occurred in these banks' London branches.

55 Jill Treanor, 'Standard Chartered Refuses to Claw Back Bonuses', *Guardian*, 29 March 2013.

56 Parliamentary Commission on Banking Standards – Fourth Report: *'An Accident Waiting to Happen': The Failure of HBOS*, 7 March 2013.

57 The Financial Services Authority has been abolished and replaced by three sub-units of the Bank of England: a Financial Policy Committee concerned with 'macro-prudential' risks, a Prudential Regulation Authority which will directly regulate companies, and a Financial Conduct Authority to monitor the treatment of customers and ban improper practices such as the Payment Protection scandal. Whether the culture of 'negotiation' between the regulators and the corporations that neutered the FSA will be replaced by one of serious control may be doubted, as may the probable effectiveness of the 'ring-fencing' of retail banking functions promised in the Financial Services

(Banking Reform) Bill due to be passed into law by 2014.

58   Joris Luyendijk, 'Inside the Bubble', *Guardian*, 6 April 2013. This is not quite accurate: in 2012 the FSA fined HBOS' former Head of Corporate Division Peter Cummings £500,000 for the excessive risks he took, but left his three former bosses (Sir James Crosby, Andy Hornby and Lord Stevenson) untouched. The MPs found the FSA's treatment of Cummings arbitrary and unjustifiable.

59   Tom Clark, 'UKIP Surge in Polls Unprecedented since Creation of the SDP in 1981', *Guardian*, 14 May 2013.

60   Nicholas Watt and Rajeev Syal, 'Cabinet Crisis for Cameron as Ministers Break Ranks over EU', *Guardian*, 13 May 2013, quoting Johnson's column in the *Daily Telegraph*. The former Conservative Chancellor Nigel Lawson took the same view.

61   BBC News, Business, 7 May 2013.

62   Jim Pickard, George Parker and Richard McGregor, 'Stay at the Heart of Europe, US Tells Britain', *Financial Times*, 10 January 2013.

63   *The Shadow State: A Report about Outsourcing of Public Services*, Social Enterprise UK, 2012, available at http://www.socialenterprise.org.uk.

64   Felicity Lawrence, 'Who is the Government's Health Deal with Big Business Really Good for?', *Guardian*, 12 November 2010.

65   James Ball and Henry Taylor, '"Buddy" Scheme to Give More Multinationals Access to Ministers', *Guardian*, 18 January 2013.

66   *The Context for Civil Service Reform: Data and Case Studies to Accompany the Civil Service Reform Plan*, HM Government, June 2012, p. 16, available at http://www.civilservice.gov.uk.

67   Colin Leys, 'The Dissolution of the Mandarins: The Sell-off of the British State', Our Kingdom (Open Democracy),15 June 2012, available at http://www.opendemocracy.net.

68   A brilliant sting operation by Channel 4 TV shortly after the 2010 election, which caught several Labour ex-ministers on camera offering their contacts for money, pushed the issue into the open. On previous scandals see the Wikipedia entry, '2010 cash for influence scandal'.

69   Social Investigations blogspot, http://socialinvestigations.blogspot.co.uk.

70   'Jack Grubman: The Power Broker', 14 May 2000, available at http://www.businessweek.com.

71   Response by the Department of Health to a Freedom of Information request: available at https://www.whatdotheyknow.com, under the heading 'Three Reports Commissoned by Lord Darzi'.

72   The report, consisting of 80 slides, was entitled 'Achieving World Class Productivity in the NHS 2009/10 – 2013/14: Detailing the Size of the Opportunity'; it was eventually disclosed in 2010. See http://webarchive.nationalarchives.gov.uk.

73   Jane Dudman, *Guardian Professional*, 6 March 2012.

74   According to John Harris, Labour's forward thinking comprised relentless fiscal rectitude, house-building, and 'radically pruning central government, and pushing power downwards as never before'. 'Is Labour Ready to Turn the

State Upside Down in 2015?', *Guardian*, 12 May 2013.

75   Perry Anderson, 'Homeland', *New Left Review*, 81(May-June), 2013, p. 23.

76   The breakdown was withheld by the BBC, but can be found in Mike Savage, Fiona Devine, Niall Cunningham, Mark Taylor, Yaojun Li, Johs Hjellbrekke, Brigitte Le Roux, Sam Friedman and Andrew Miles, 'A New Model of Social Class? Findings from the BBC's Great British Class Survey Experiment', *Sociology*, 47(2), 2013. See also Mike Savage and Fiona Devine's analysis available on the London School of Economics' blog at http://blogs.lse.ac.uk.

THE NEW CONFIGURATION OF THE CAPITALIST CLASS

CLAUDE SERFATI

The new configuration of the capitalist classes over the last thirty years took place in the context of two prominent changes. First, the consolidation of finance capital operated through three main channels that radically shifted the trajectory of capitalism. At the macroeconomic level, the debt trap that initially plagued the developing countries, and since 2007 the core countries, reflected the victory of lenders over debtors, and created massive and permanent flows of revenues for creditors. In terms of the firm, 'shareholder value' became the main operational objective for corporations ('shareholder value' being quite distinct from, and possibly at odds with, the creation of 'added value'). And at the level of individual social agency, international and national government policies contributed to the 'commodification' of social relations, undermining existing systems of social security and steadily replacing them with schemes that made individuals increasingly dependent upon financial markets.

Second, the continual process of the internationalization of capital since the Second World War gained momentum over the last few decades. Globalization provided capital with the opportunity to act with a maximum of freedom at the world level. Money–capital, for example, was made hyper-liquid due to the deregulation of institutions and financial innovations. This was also true for large non-financial transnational corporations (TNCs), which have, in reality, become world–scale financial groups with industrial activities.[1] They form a global web, with a mix of collusion and competition, structuring commodity chains and controlling a significant share of the world production of value and trade. The combined effects of outsourcing and offshoring, with the associated pressures on second- and lower-tier supplier firms, have aggravated the imbalance of power and distribution of value between capital and labour.[2]

This essay documents the considerable increase in the concentration of income and wealth by a tiny share of the population. The major role played by rentier incomes and the financial sector is then connected to the new configuration of the capitalist class. The political economy of the contemporary capitalist class is then analyzed demonstrating that, as social relations are territorially bounded and politically built, the realization of a transnational capitalist class (TCC) is still a long way off even in the case of the European Union (EU).

THE ONE PER CENT

If globalization was expected to work as a tide which 'raises all boats', it is more accurate to observe today that the era of finance capital driven globalization has raised mainly luxury yachts.[3] It is now widely acknowledged that income inequalities dramatically increased in the last three decades, and that most of the changes in the top decile are due to dramatic changes in the top percentile in most countries. The sharp increase in the top 1 per cent share of the national income since the 1970s led to a return to prewar levels of income inequalities, inverting the long downward reduction in income concentration between the 1920s and the early 1970s.[4] It should be recalled that the 1920-70 period of reduction in income inequalities was marked by a unique combination of a major world economic crisis, world wars and inflation, along with strong and massive popular demands, and even a threat in the initial postwar period to the maintenance of capitalist relations in major European countries.

Empirical research shows that the whole picture is not monocolour, and there are inter-country differences within both developed and developing regions. In the former, and when capital gains are excluded, the share of the top 1 per cent of income recipients in total national income ranged from 4 per cent in Sweden to 18 per cent in the United States in 2008.[5] In developing countries, the increased inequality was more pronounced in Argentina and South Africa than in India and Indonesia.

While there is little available data about the occupations of the top income earners, there is for a few representative cases. For example, in the US the share of executive, managerial and supervisory occupations in the top 1 per cent of incomes (excluding capital gains) was 42.5 per cent in 2005, with the financial professions at 18.0 per cent. Also over-represented in proportion to their weight in the active population were the occupational categories of lawyers (at 6.2 per cent), real estate (4.7), medical (4.4) and 'other entrepreneurs' (3.6). The rest of the top earners by occupation are spread across the arts, media and sports, government, professors, computer, engineering, maths and technical (non-finance) professions, management consultants and farmers (with the unknown still at 8.4 per cent).[6] In France, the available data is grouped between the salaried and the self-employed. Of the top 1 per cent earners amongst the salaried, 49.3 per cent are CEOs and managers in headquarters of companies, while 14 per cent work in the financial industry and 4 per cent are sportsmen or work in the media and entertainment sectors. Among the self-employed, medical professions and lawyers are the largest group, with a share of 43 per cent and 12 per cent, respectively.[7] Men make-up 87 per cent of the top earners in France.

Figure 1: Global Concentration of Wealth, 2011

Number (millions)	Threshold ($millions)	Total Wealth ($trillions)	Source	Comments
11.0	1	42.0	Cap Gemini & RBC Wealth management	does not include the value of personal assets and property such as primary residences, collectibles, consumables, and consumer durables
29.0	1	87.5	CSFB	real assets + financial assets − debts
12.6	1	49.2	BCG	private financial wealth
0.187	30	25.8	Wealth-X	shares in public and private companies, residential and investment properties, art collections, planes, cash and other assets
0.063	100	39.3	KnightFrank	disposable assets
0.093	100	7.1	BCG	private financial wealth

Notes: Number refers to the number of wealthy individuals rounded to the first decimal in the first three studies, and to the third decimal in the second three. Threshold is the wealth level cutoff for the individuals in the data set. Total wealth refers to the wealth of all the individuals in the data set. Source refers to the wealth management consultancy who undertook the study. The comments refer to the key basis of the wealth calculation.

The development of finance capital driven globalization has meant an explosion of new financial products and the extensive development of offshore financial centres (more than eighty such jurisdictions, with varying levels of financial secrecy, exist today). This makes much more complicated the measurement of wealth let alone the control of capital flight and tax avoidance. One study found that, as of 2010, between $21–32 trillion in global private financial wealth has been invested virtually tax-free throughout the world.[8] Available data from wealth management advisers and NGOs underline the extreme concentration of wealth within the top tier households. Figure 1 summarizes data from various wealth management funds (and also notes the significant divergences in data collection).

Within this concentration of wealth, there has been a significant rise in both the number of extremely wealthy individuals and the extent of their financial wealth. It is estimated, for example, that fewer than 100,000 people (that is, 0.001 per cent of the world's population) now control over 30 per cent of the world's financial wealth.[9] Individuals owning over $1m of investable worldwide assets were 8.2 million in 2004 and the value of their wealth managed by funds was $30.7 trillion, with the respective numbers at 11 million and $42.0 trillion in 2011.[10] This is consistent with research on world wealth that finds that its distribution is considerably more unequal than income distribution.[11] Not surprisingly, the majority of financial asset wealth is located in industrialized countries with North America at 30.9 per cent, Western Europe at 27.3 per cent and Japan at 14.4 per cent, concentrating almost three-fourths of the world financial wealth held by individuals owning over 1 $million. The group of rentiers in developing countries, however, is both growing in number (mainly within emerging countries) and in wealth rankings. One projection of the growth in financial wealth to 2016 is 1.8 per cent per year in North America and Western Europe, 0.8 per cent in Japan, and 11.1 per cent in Asia-Pacific (excluding Japan).[12]

The social reproduction of wealth within households of the capitalist class has dramatically increased as part of this phase of wealth concentration. According to recent consulting research by wealth managers in the US, never before have such a large number of young people been raised by wealthy parents and are expected to be wealthy throughout their lifetime.[13] In France, the social reproduction of wealth remains very important. All things equal (that is, not taking into account the increase in their wealth throughout their lifetime), households whose high wealth status comes from inheritance have had their wealth almost double compared to those households without wealth inheritances. In other words, the intergenerational reproduction of wealth is contributing to an increase in wealth inequalities via inheritances.[14]

The yawning gap between a tiny upper layer and the rest of the population in the distribution of income and wealth is a structural feature of the capitalist economy, but it has also been politically constructed. It has little to do with laws of markets as such, and much more with the influence of the ruling classes on government policy, not to speak of collusion between members of the ruling class and high ranking civil servants and politicians, adjusting taxation in favour of the upper classes.[15]

A tally of the massive concentration in revenues and wealth only begins to pinpoint the consolidation of the capitalist class over the neoliberal era. Such empirical measures are insufficient to address class boundaries as classes are neither reducible to a level of income (or wealth), nor to professional status. The type of distribution of revenues and concentration of wealth is historically determined by the social forms of production and the institutional backgrounds of states, which in turn depends on class relations.

If the capitalist class can be defined, in its most basic form, in terms of its ownership of means of production and control over the value created by those forced to sell their labour-power, it is a distinctive characteristic of capitalism that class boundaries are not fixed and change over time within evolving social relations of production. There is a fluidity of intra-class organization and relations, with a continual process of capitalist mergers and acquisitions, organizational alliances and oppositions, and forms of political representation and capitalist class strategies. The processes suggest an asymmetry between workers and capitalists in the political movement, to borrow a classical phrase, from a 'class-in-itself' to a 'class-for-itself'. The capitalist class is, moreover, supported by the state apparatus, specifically organized to maintain capitalist relations and continually working at forging a strategic consensus amongst the capitalist class. This remains the theoretical importance of Marx's writings on France's Second Republic of 1848-51 and Bonapartism,[16] with its detailed references to fractions of class, their intertwining and internal rivalries, to calculating the precise configuration of political power.

FINANCE CAPITAL AND THE NEW CONFIGURATION OF THE CAPITALIST CLASS

There has never been a strict correspondence between the different functions of capital in the reproduction of the circuit of capital (namely, banking, landed, industrial and commercial capital) and the fractions of the ruling class in their corporate and political organization. Already in the nineteenth century, the organizational fluidity between different fractions of capital was visible. The ascent and domination of finance capital at the turn of the twentieth century meant that, while keeping their separate existence, the different functions in the circulation of capital have tended to become more interdependent. The core role of the banking system, for example, resulted in more connections between capitalists in different industrial sectors. This prompted Rudolf Hilferding to observe: 'We have seen how industry becomes increasingly dependent upon bank capital, but this does not mean that the magnates of industry also become dependent on banking magnates. As capital itself at the highest stage of its development becomes finance capital, so the magnate of capital, the finance capitalist, increasingly concentrates his control over the whole national capital by means of his domination of bank capital. Personal connections also play an important role here'.[17] The development of stock markets gave a further boost to the circulation of ownership claims on capital, allowing money capital to move more freely and to distribute it in different companies and sectors according to their (expected) profitability.

In the contemporary period, stock markets act as a market for external corporate control, and for exerting pressures on top executives of large industrial groups to reduce the differences in the profitability of capital among industrial sectors and between the latter and other sectors such as trade and banking. This is done through specific corporate mechanisms such as mergers, acquisitions and divestures, and speculative pressures on managements to raise the rate of labour exploitation. In the last decades, large non-financial transnational corporations have developed activities that overlap different activities well beyond manufacturing, for example trading, financing, cash management, etc., which reflects their transformation into financial groups.[18] If in the process of capital valorization the different moments in the circulation process (production, trade, and, of course, finance) continue to exist, they have become less clear at the level of the firm within TNCs, organised as groups of enterprises facilitating the mobility of a massive volume of capital both internally (through the allocation of funds to different entities within the TNC) and externally (through mergers and acquisitions and stock markets).

The ascent and domination of finance capital since the end of the nineteenth century arises from both *structural* drivers – money capital as the universal form of wealth in capitalism, and *political* ones – the power of some social groups to impose their financial interests. For individual capitalists, there is always the temptation to avoid the 'detour of production' and shorten the accumulation process by having money make more money (that is financial claims producing interest, dividends, capital gains, royalties, and so on). As Marx put it: 'The process of production appears merely as an unavoidable intermediate link, as a necessary evil for the sake of money-making'.[19] This is made possible because money capital, like productive capital, is not a thing but a social relation, based on specific property rights, which gives its holders the ability to extract value and wealth from other people, even though this ability depends *in fine* on the process of production of new value. The finance capital logic of M...M' is inscribed in the nature of capitalism, because producing goods is always a means and never an end of the production process. But it also proceeds through an autonomous process, distinct from the full process of production of M...P...M'. This autonomy means that the same capital (as a social relation) exists twice: once in the form of productive (or industrial) capital; and secondly as income-bearing money-capital (financial property claims). The fictitious nature of the latter does not prevent money-capital as finance demanding an increasing share of the value created.[20]

The autonomy of money-capital has been reinforced historically by the development of specialized institutions, with the banking system being the main location for the centralization of money-capital. The duality between productive and money-capital was already noted by Marx even within a single employer or firm: 'The employer of capital, even when working with his own capital, splits into two personalities – the owner of capital and the employer of capital; with reference to the categories of profit which it yields, his capital also splits into capital-property, capital outside the production process, and yielding interest of itself, and capital in the production process which yields a profit of enterprise through its function'.[21] From the mid-nineteenth century onwards, this division was reinforced by the creation of joint-stock companies (corporations or *sociétés par actions*) and the development of stock markets as a new location for the centralization and the circulation of money-capital.

Over the last decades, the autonomous logic of finance capital (M...M') has penetrated non-financial TNCs and led to major changes in the dynamics of capitalism.[22] Two are especially relevant for studying the constellation of the capitalist class today – the drawing of new sectors into financial accumulation and the concomitant growth in the financial sector itself.

A major objective of the development of stock markets has always been to enlarge financial accumulation through the permanent entry of new investors and the drain of their savings. The ownership of financial claims was limited, and only at the end of the twentieth century reached significant sections of the middle class and, to a lesser extent, the working class. For example, one of the major objectives of the neoliberal agenda, as advocated by the World Bank, has been to privatize pension systems and increase the role of private pension funds. This forces workers' savings via pension funds into the stock market.[23] Pension funds assets are mainly concentrated in OECD countries at a level of $20.1 trillion, compared to only $1.8 trillion in Asia and $0.7 trillion in Latin America. Between 1988 and 2008, twenty-nine countries followed Chile's example and introduced neoliberal reforms that replaced a traditional pay-as-you-go public system with one based on individual accounts, market capitalization and private management.[24] It is estimated that at the end of 2011, the global fund management industry was managing $132 trillion of assets, of which $31.5 trillion came from pension funds, an amount not so far from the total volume of money coming from private wealth ($42 trillion).[25]

The individuals who invest in shares and bonds form, whether directly or via pension funds, a very heterogeneous category encompassing members of different classes. All of them cannot be called rentiers. The neoliberal notion 'that "rentiers are us"'... limits the scope for indignation and attacks on property rights'.[26] The 'rentier class' is better defined as those who hold financial assets and receive capital income in volumes that allows them to accumulate (i.e. to increase) their wealth. In that sense, most rentiers are members of the capitalist class in contrast to those who sell their own labour-power (even when their retirement income guaranteed by savings is indirectly invested in stock markets). The indirect presence of workers on stock markets does not give any more credence to the claims of 'pension fund socialism' than it does that workers have become capitalists via these holdings.[27] Rentiers do not substitute for the capitalist class, but rents constitute a significant means for wealth accumulation of that class.

That only a minority of stock and bonds holders can be labelled as capitalists is confirmed by the high concentration of financial assets holdings in a tiny fraction of the population. A staggering amount of US public debt, for example, is held by the top 1 per cent of US households. In France, private pension funds schemes are limited with a rather generous – although less and less – pay-as-you-go system; here, the proportion of shares in total financial assets held by French residents, directly or indirectly through mutual and insurance funds, is modest and declining.[28]

It is top managers who account for the bulk of the highest income households. Since A.A. Berle and Gardiner Means' classic account, *The Modern Corporation and Private Property* (1932), there has been a debate about the 'managerial class' and their social position. However, the accumulation of financial wealth by top managers through the ownership of a significant share of the capital of firms where they are employed, along with the authority they exert over the labour process, clearly identify them as members of the capitalist class.[29] The term 'working rich' is sometimes given to the upper income layer. It is similarly misleading in suggesting that these ultra-high incomes are attributable to a pay for employment tradeoff. But as confirmed by any number of studies, capital gains and revenues are the main explanation for their increase in income and wealth (although the top executives also control the decisions on their pay). In the US, the six-fold increase of CEO pay between 1980 and 2003 can be fully attributed to the six-fold increase in market capitalization of large companies during this period. In France, in 2006, capital gains income accounted for 38 per cent of the total incomes of the top 1 per cent of earners, and 55 per cent for the top 0.1 per cent.[30] They are 'rich' because they have private property claims over financial (and real estate) assets as members of the capitalist class.

A second consequence of the ascendancy of finance capital has been the extraordinary increase in the role of the financial sector (by extension the finance, insurance and real estate or FIRE sectors), and the resulting rise in its share of value-added in national output over the last two decades. Due to the growing organizational weight of finance capital, the differences among the so-called 'varieties of capitalism' (conventionally differentiated according to bank and non-bank based systems) are declining. Indeed, contradicting the traditional contrast between France and the UK, OECD data shows that the GDP share of the FIRE sector in France is now higher (at 34.1 per cent) than in the UK (at 33.7 per cent), with both countries being well above the OECD average (28.6 per cent).[31] Financial actors benefiting from the new architecture of financial markets include credit rating agencies, corporate lawyers, security analysts, and auditing firms (which are dominated by the 'Big Four' of Deloitte, Ernst & Young, KPMG and Pricewaterhouse Coopers).

These institutions and individuals form what can be called a 'financial community', the members of which have differing interests, but are all united in their pursuit of 'value capture', or what some term 'value skimming'.[32] New actors in this 'community', in particular hedge funds and private equity have become, along with – and indeed intertwined with – the traditional banks and pension and mutual funds, the central forces behind the dominance of finance capital within the contemporary capitalist class. The social power of the financial community is evidenced by the level and the rise of their remunerations. A fair share of the increase of the FIRE's 'value-added' is accounted for by the meteoric rise in the remuneration of financial executives who, in turn, account for a significant share in the top 1 per cent of income earners.[33]

THE CAPITALIST CLASS:
THE NATIONALITY OF FIRMS MATTERS

In the last decades, it has been proposed that a direct connection exists between the macro-structural processes of globalization and the configuration of the key sources of agency within the major firms.[34] A transnational capital class (TCC) now stands at the commanding heights of the world market, is conscious as a 'class-for-itself' and promotes the creation of a transnational state to advance its interests. These theses have promoted a great deal of debate, and this section of the essay contends, in contrast, that the nationality of firms and managers still matters because social relations are territorially bounded and politically built, making the realization of a TCC a long way off.

For TCC proponents, directors and top executives of the large transnational corporations are seen as the agency acting to promote the world circulation of capital. There is little doubt that firms 'match managers to strategies' in the context of the internationalization of the firms' activities. These firms also have higher levels of national diversity with a greater range of international experience within the 'top management team'.[35] The management literature is replete with strategies for the recruitment of 'global talent'. According to McKinsey Consulting, this is a 'war for talent' because of a shortage of executives for managing 'cultural diversity' and so forth.[36] But despite being in charge of 'global corporations', it is far from established that the top executives have themselves amalgamated into a new transnational class.

First, TNCs are far from becoming 'global' in the sense of being disconnected from a territorial anchor, and remain quite dependent on their 'home country'. Significant links continue to exist between TNCs and their home country through a variety of measures such as public funding of research and development, procurement, national 'security' and 'sovereignty' strictures, tax exemptions, and interpersonal and institutional links between corporations and specific branches of the state. The degree of TNC dependence varies, of course, but it remains important for sales, with an average ratio of domestic to total sales reaching 35 per cent for the top 100 TNCs in 2011, a proportion that is far from negligible, with the home market typically forming an indispensable basis for its international operations.[37] Also, the foreign activities of TNCs remain concentrated in their associated region (North America, Europe, etc.): a recent study tabulates that the world's top 500 TNCs generate 75 per cent of their sales and locate 78 per cent of their assets in their 'home' region.[38] The economic crisis from 2008 onward has reinforced the central role of public authorities in supporting TNCs in their home territory.[39]

Moreover, the persisting dependency of TNCs upon their national base also finds confirmation in the criteria adopted by rating agencies to assess the quality of corporations as borrowers and the level of their credit risk. The ratings of corporations, including the most internationalized, are linked to the economic situation of their home country; it is the exception when corporations (and even less frequently, financial institutions) are ranked above the home country assessment. Even the most internationalized corporations are not immune to their home country's rating.[40] For the corporate rating, this includes not only the risk of sovereign default, but also other macroeconomic elements such as currency depreciation, economic contraction, liquidity constraints stemming from credit shortages, restrictions on raising utility rates and other price controls, hikes in taxes and government fees amidst cutbacks in services, and delayed/partial government payments.[41] The economic crisis has led the rating agencies to make the rating of corporations more closely tied to the state of their home country. In the Eurozone, this is particularly the case for Greece, Portugal, Spain and Ireland. For some analysts, the increased ties between corporations and their home country marks a worrying reversal of the trend of globalization.[42] But for others this is recognition by rating agencies that the sovereign rating of states is still an important consideration in determining private ratings.[43]

Figure 2: Share of Foreign Directors on the Boards of Top Companies

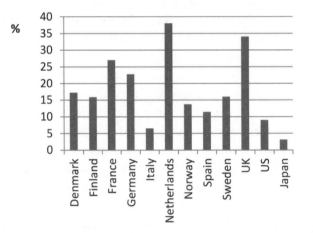

Source: Compilation by the author from various Spencer Stuart Board Indexes for 2012.
Note: Corporations surveyed: France – CAC 40; UK – 150 FTSE; Nordic countries (Denmark, Norway, Sweden, Finland) – Top 25; Japan – Top 100; Italy – Top 100; Spain – Top 106; US – S&P Top 500; Netherlands – Top 50; Germany – Top 60; Canada – Top 100.

Another way to look at the issue of TNCs superseding nationality is in terms of the contention that senior executives and the boards of directors of TNCs form the core of the transnational capitalist class. However, various studies document that these top managers remain connected to their home country. The presence of foreigners in top management, while being more widespread in 2005 than in 1993, is not yet very deep.[44] Even in Europe, the increase in national diversity within boards of TNCs, in key countries like Germany, the UK and the Netherlands, is a slow and often difficult process.[45] As Figure 2 shows, board internationalization is a development mostly confined to North America and Europe. Unsurprisingly, the TNCs of the 'smaller' European economies are more internationalized, but a majority of foreign directors still come from the region. In Japan, the ratio of foreigners on boards of the top companies is only 3.1 per cent and the ratio falls still lower for TNCs from emerging countries.[46]

There are many other obstacles to the making of a unified TCC via the presence of foreign nationals on TNC boards. This is initially evidenced at the micro-level by the simple fact that there is no clear evidence of a positive relation between the size of a TNC and the national diversity of its management.[47] This is partly a result of simple operational logistics and costs of transnational boards; and partly a consequence of the importance of national factors such as the system of higher education, the mode of selection of elites, and the dominance of national corporate governance regimes. There is also something here of the concept that some sociologists, following Bourdieu's analysis, call 'social capital', as the set of resources embodied in the structure of relationships, including group membership, social ties and networks and so forth. These allow their holders to be involved in the actual exercise of corporate decisions, strategies and powers and, as an indirect consequence, also to reproduce the hierarchies and inequalities of the capitalist system. As many key variables entering into 'social and cultural capital' carry a great deal of national specificity, differences necessarily exist in the reproduction and consolidation of ruling classes between nations as, for instance, between France and Germany,[48] or Britain and France.[49]

Another example of the limits of the making of a TCC is provided by senior managers being deployed abroad. Although the rate of 'corporate expatriates' has increased in recent years, the flow is largely in one direction. Most corporate expatriates are parent–country nationals sent from their headquarters. In contrast, the flow of corporate 'inpatriates' – employees from other countries – to company headquarters has only slowly increased.[50] The persistence of home country affiliations for the main 'agents' of globalization is also seen as a somewhat mundane management problem for TNCs: senior executives and managers are themselves not very enthusiastic about international mobility. One study, for example, finds that only 18 per cent of American, 13 per cent of European and 5 per cent of Asian senior managers move abroad at their own request.[51]

There is other evidence of how the operational practices of TNCs limit the notion of a TCC. The global 'footloose' top executive, with its corresponding 'international market for talent' heralding the making of a TCC, still remains a distant reality. Research on CEO appointments of the Fortune Global 500 reveals that an insignificant proportion of CEOs of the largest TNCs are recruited from another company in another country.[52] Ironically, the advertisers and consulting cadres that peddle the 'borderless world' mythology are some of the least internationalized of capitalist firms and maintain strong ties to their national base.[53] Even for large TNCs, then, the home country continues to play a more important role than claimed in discourses on 'global firms' and the alleged displacement of national states and national ruling classes.

SOCIAL RELATIONS: TERRITORIALLY BOUNDED, POLITICALLY BUILT

Large capitalist non-financial and financial corporations remain dependent on their home country today. Historically, capitalist development has been anchored in national territories which include the development of specific political relations and the state as a formally autonomous institution. As such, the development of modern 'nations' has been inseparable from the development of capitalism, with the national consciousness of social classes an integral aspect of the life experiences within societies shaped by the nation–state form.[54]

If the 'ultimate secret of capitalist production is a *political* one',[55] then this secret is not limited to the early stages of capitalism. It is a characteristic of contemporary capitalism as an uneven and combined process of social development.[56] Capitalist relations have to be continually reproduced and this reproduction needs state institutions as crystallizations of social relations and power structures within an evolving configuration of international relations. In no way has globalization meant de-territorialization: no space disappears in the course of growth and development. Capitalism does not – and cannot – abolish the national or the local, but makes for denser, overlapping socio-spatial networks which remain dependent on national states to help arbitrate between the different scales of the circulation of capital.[57]

In other terms, social relations are territorially bounded and politically built, and it is not possible for any individual, class or capitalist firm to escape from grounded socio-political relations. The most outward-oriented TNC, conceding the greatest latitude for capital mobility, cannot become 'apatride' (or stateless). Even in the case of the circulation process of interest-bearing capital where financial assets produce their own revenues (M…M'), financial capital still depends on the value created in a labour process located within territorially specific class relations. Indeed, money-capital (including its most fictitious components) is still a social relation based on 'drawing rights' on the new value created and crystallized in territorially bounded organizations.

To give an example, when capitalists as a class (and not only its internationalized fraction) are pursuing 'fiscal competition' and social cuts to get tax reductions, they have first to struggle in their home countries to get their national governments to accept this 'tax race to the bottom'. This requires a specific national class strategy and struggle organized against the resistance of workers, associations and political parties, even if this strategy also mobilizes international financial institutions and capitalist clubs.[58] Further, capitalist interests (including TNCs) need to mobilize allies. This implies that capitalists are politically and socially organized as a social bloc of interests to advance their strategy. Even the most advanced, liquid and internationalized layer of capital is dependent upon other segments of capital. This economic and political interdependence between the different fractions of capital is too often neglected by assertions of an internationalized capital (and their agents as a TCC) separated from national capitals and states.

The Military-Security Industrial System

That social relations are territorially bounded and politically built is especially evidenced by the enduring role played by the military and their relation to TNCs and national states. The role of military–industrial systems cannot be reduced to the functional role of defending external and internal threats to sovereignty and private property.[59] In the core capitalist countries, in particular the US, UK and France, as well as Russia and China, these military systems have linked financial and industrial interests. Since the initial postwar GATT system, 'national security' has often been invoked to escape limits imposed by international agreements, especially in the recent period under the WTO trade rules. Based on national security mandates, defence oriented research and development programmes have provided public funding that also aid industrial groups and public research institutions. This has been a central feature of US technological policy, and along with the regional dispersion of weapons procurement and military bases provided for the embeddedness of the military–industrial system in regions and communities.[60] Aeronautics and space is another sector in which defense oriented public funding remains essential for business. In the US, government research funding for the ICT sector, with its strong linkages with the military and security branches of the state, accounts for a quarter of their total R&D expenditures in 2012.[61] In France, the 'arms meso-system' continues to hold a significant place in the economy and governmental policy.[62]

Since 2001, the security agenda has opened up new horizons for public funding, particularly through the American administration's *The National Security Strategy of the United States* (2002) and the European Council's *A Secure Europe in a Better World* (2003). The new security project gained support from the high-tech aeronautics and electronics sectors of capital that were keen to receive funds from the EU and the American government for dual-use technologies.

Higher national security requirements help protect domestic markets and firms from foreign goods and investments, as do designations of 'critical infrastructure' as falling under national security concerns.[63] It is important now to speak of an emerging and deeply-rooted 'military-security industrial system' (MSIS). The turnover of the global security industry has grown rapidly, and in 2011 is estimated to be worth some $100 billion with around 2 million persons employed worldwide,[64] although this is still modest compared to the $1850 billion estimated to be spent on defence. As noted by the OECD: 'The security industry is a large and expanding area of economic activity [which] promises to have far-reaching economic and societal implications over the longer term'.[65]

MSISs are anchored in the economic, political and ideological institutions and social processes of their 'home' territory. Their reliance on powerful national constituency blocs and political social groups makes it problematic simply to define them as members of a transnational capitalist class. The weight and role of national MSISs are, however, too often ignored in analyses purporting to identify a TCC.[66] This makes for claims that are far too general that the 'beneficiaries of US military action are transnational capitalist groups',[67] as this analysis fails to take adequate account of both the general and specific interest of the US ruling class. Or, as in the case of the Iraq war, the specific interests of some of its fractions. Also, it misses the importance of lasting rivalries between internationalized fractions of capitalists. Stating that the 'the TCC thesis does not suggest that the TCC is internally unified, free of conflict'[68] begs precisely the critical question of the territorial tensions and contradictions within and between internationalizing capitals and their attendant states.[69]

The European Case

As the leading zone of economic integration, the EU has constituted fertile ground for assessment of the formation of a TCC. In the neo-Gramscian view, the postwar Bilderberg meetings in 1952 and 1954 helped lay some of the key basis for the formation of a transnational capitalist class.[70] These analyses have attempted to connect the circulation of 'capital as-a-whole' and competition over the creation of value and the distribution of profits between firms which 'incarnate' specific fractions of the capitalist class, particularly money and productive capital. The focus on who owns and controls Europe's largest TNCs has led to extensive efforts to map out the interlocking directorates between corporations to demonstrate the reality of the transnationalization process. This highlights one important linkage between large corporations and thus ties within the ruling class. But this most elementary mapping does not necessarily tell us much about the core 'elites'. Nor does it address – by definition – the relations between directors and other ruling social groups, such as senior civil servants, politicians and shareholders.[71]

If there is a broad agreement that the largest growth in transnational linkages has been within the EU where the process of transnational class formation has reached its deepest level amongst the European business elite,[72] the research on interlocking sometimes offers conflicting conclusions. There is certainly a need to take caution against making broad generalizations about a European capitalist class. Indeed, one dissenting study contends that of the European firms listed on the four main continental stock exchanges (in France, Germany, Italy and the Netherlands) for the 2006-07 period, external links decreased and in absolute terms remain quite limited.[73] The 'Europeanization' of networks (defined as the increase of bridging European interlocks relative to national bonding interlocks) by no means entails a disappearance of the strength of national links. The scope of this process is unclear and many studies stress that the rise in European interlocking directors reflects the strength and the national specificity of EU member states.[74]

It is clear, moreover, that the cooperation between national bourgeoisies in Europe through interlocking directorates cannot be separated from the national and regional political background. The Franco-German relationship, for example, stands as the backbone of this Europeanization of interlocking vis-à-vis their exchanges, leading one careful study to find that 'unsurprisingly, the majority of transnational interlocks are structured between the CAC and the DAX companies'.[75] For example, German and French business elites deploy a European network strategy that bolsters the distinctiveness on the French-German axis while still maintaining strong ties within their respective national business communities. The actual extent of incorporations between them is unclear. And it is not so clear whether it is France or Germany that is the national state leading the interlocking process in Europe: some research suggests that France is by far the most important European country within this network;[76] others claim that the transnationalization of capital is led from Europe by German corporations.[77] By way of contrast, the interlocking directors of British companies are primarily oriented to the US. Indeed, the exchange of directors between the US and UK accounts for 42 per cent of the total volume of US-Europe interlocks and this close connection between the two countries is also confirmed by the significant degree of cross-shareholdings. The British ruling class has given priority to the special geo-economic relationships with the US, and there remains a hostile attitude to further European integration by influential segments of British capital with support from successive British governments (as observed by a former Secretary General of the European Round Table of Industrialists).[78] This does not appear to be an autonomous development of a TCC, but rather a quite specific interaction between national political-economic settings and firm level strategies where the interlocking directorates are observed.[79]

The rise in interlocking directors amongst European companies has been accompanied by the efforts at institutional integration by the EU. As part of promoting capital accumulation, capitalists in Europe were able to promote the development of a structure of regional political authority.[80] But this does not mean there is a strict correspondence between economic and political processes. In assessing the formation of a European capitalist class, William Carroll and his colleagues rightly argue that 'within European integration, the process of "state formation" and corporate community building are two separate strands'.[81] Nation-states are not reducible to their governments, but are based on social relations that are territorially bounded and politically built. The construction of the European Union has always been antidemocratic, and its legitimacy always mediated through national states, which remain the central locus for the formation of capitalist classes and class struggles.

SETTLING MATTERS WITH RULING CLASSES

In the new pattern of accumulation and distribution that has taken hold over the last three decades, pre-eminence has been given to the class owning financial (and real estate) assets. The rentier features of the capitalist class as finance capital have thus been reinforced, and this has, in turn, led to the mass concentration of income and wealth in the top 1 per cent. While this has been a global trend, this does not mean that one can identify – let alone speak of – a single unified TCC ruling the world.

Globalization does not mean de-territorialization as no space disappears in the course of accumulation and internationalization. As Ellen Wood argues: 'Capital reproduces and benefits from the fragmentation of political space, so the current association of capitalism and the territorial state with all its attendant contradictions – is not just a historical relic but is reinforced by the essential dynamics of capitalism'.[82] The anchoring of capitalist relations in a 'home' country is both an economic and political necessity. Being a member of a political community creates a range of obligations from which even members of the ruling class cannot simply withdraw, even as today they struggle vigorously to re-write those obligations.

The political economy of the capitalist class underlines the continuing importance of national configurations, including in Europe. The interrelations between the leading segments of the contemporary capitalist class should not be interpreted as presaging a transnational capitalist class. The old edict from *The Communist Manifesto* still bears attention: 'Though not in substance, yet in form, the struggle of the proletariat with the bourgeoisie is at first a national struggle. The proletariat of each country must, of course, first of all settle matters with its own bourgeoisie'. [83]

NOTES

1   Claude Serfati, 'Transnational Corporations as Financial Groups', *Work, Organisation, Labour and Globalization*, 5(1), 2011, pp. 10-39.

2   Hein Eckhard, 'Finance-dominated Capitalism and Redistribution of Income: A Kaleckian Perspective', *Jerome Levy Institute*, Working Paper N. 76, January 2013.

3   Branko Milanovic, *The Haves and the Have-Nots: A Brief and Idiosyncratic History of Global Inequality*, Basic Books, 2010. In the last decades, there have been cumulative effects on income and wealth inequalities between and within nations. The latter is especially based on class divisions and not individual trajectories. The recent UNCTAD *Trade and Development Report* (2012) calls this a distinction between *functional* and *personal* income distribution.

4   Anthony B. Atkinson, Thomas Piketty and Emmanuel Saez, 'Top Incomes in the Long Run of History', *Journal of Economic Literature*, 49(1), 2011, pp. 3-71. The data collected in most studies do not give the full magnitude of inequalities, as they are based on taxpayer filings. This underestimates the tax evasion and optimization, along with the real amount of capital gains. But the picture of rising inequalities is still unequivocal.

5   Peter Hoeller, 'Less Income Inequality and More Growth – Are they Compatible? Part 4: Top Incomes', *OECD Economics Department Working Papers*, N. 927, 2012. Countries also differ in the evolution of the scope of inequalities, especially when disposable household income is taken into account, and such things as the system of redistribution via taxes and transfers.

6   Jon Bakija, Adam Cole and Bradley T. Heim, 'Jobs and Income Growth of Top Earners and the Causes of Changing Income Inequality: Evidence from US Tax Return Data', April 2012, available at http://web.williams.edu.

7   Michel Amar, 'Les très hauts salaires du secteur privé', *Insee Première*, N. 1288, avril 2010.

8   James S. Henry, 'The Price of Offshore Revisited', *Tax Justice Network*, July 2012.

9   Nicholas Shaxson, John Christensen and Nick Mathiason, 'Inequality: You Don't Know the Half of It', *Tax Justice Network*, 22 July 2012. Available figures concern only financial wealth. This data – and it is the case for most research on wealth management – do not include real estate, yachts, and so forth. These are also owned via offshore structures where it is impossible to identify the owners.

10   Cap Gemini and RBC Wealth Management, *2012 World Wealth Report*.

11   James B. Davies, et al., 'The Level and Distribution of Global Household Wealth', *The Economic Journal*, 121, March 2011, pp. 223-54.

12   BCG, *Global Wealth 2012: The Battle to Regain Strength*, 2013. Developed countries remain the main source of financial wealth accumulation. The draining of revenues from the rest of the world is confirmed by macroeconomic data. Between 1995 and 2013, aggregate net investment income has been $1974.0 bn for Japan, $1605.4 bn for the US, $527.7 bn for France, $495.2 bn for Germany and $368.4 bn for the UK. Investment income covers receipts and payments of income associated, respectively, with residents' holdings of external financial assets and with residents' liabilities to non-residents, and compensation of employees. These computations based on *OECD Factbook, 2011-12*.

13   Harrison/Amexpress, 'Annual Survey of Affluence and Wealth in America', 9 May 2012.

14   Pierre Lamarche and Laurianne Salembier, 'Les déterminants du patrimoine : facteurs personnels et conjoncturels', *Les revenus et le patrimoine des ménages*, 2012. As in France, inter-generational wealth transfers are also very concentrated in OECD countries. See Bonesmo K. Fredriksen, 'Less Income Inequality and More Growth – Are they Compatible? Part 6: The Distribution of Wealth', *OECD Economics Department Working Papers*, N. 929, 2012. See also Facundo Alvaredo, Anthony B. Atkinson, Thomas Piketty and Emmanuel Saez, 'The Top 1 Percent in International and Historical Perspective', *Journal of Economic Perspectives*, 27(3), 2013, pp. 3-20.

15   Stephen Matthews, 'Trends in Top Incomes and their Tax Policy Implications', *OECD Taxation Working Papers*, N. 4, 2011.

16   Peter Hayes, 'Marx's Analysis of the French Class Structure', *Theory and Society*, 22(1), 1993, pp. 99-123.

17   Rudolf Hilferding, *Finance Capital: A Study of the Latest Phase of Capitalist Development*, London: Routledge & Kegan Paul, 1910, Chapter 14.

18   Serfati, 'Transnational Corporations as Financial Groups'.

19   Karl Marx, *Capital: A Critique of Political Economy*, Volume 2, Chapter 1, available at http://www.marxists.org.

20   Wolfram Elsner, 'Financial Capitalism: At Odds with Democracy', *Real-World Economics Review*, N. 62, 2012, pp. 132-59.

21   Karl Marx, *Capital: A Critique of Political Economy*, Volume 3, Chapter 2, available at http://www.marxists.org. Put otherwise, the increasing 'division of labour' between shareholders and managers, so much studied by the managerialist school, is not the cause but a consequence of the 'structural' separation between money and productive capital.

22   Claude Serfati, 'Le rôle actif des groupes à dominante industrielle dans la financiarisation de l'économie', in F. Chesnais, éditeur, *La Mondialisation financière, Genêse, enjeux et coûts*, Paris: Syros, 1996.

23   The World Bank, *Averting the Old Age Crisis*, Washington, D.C.: The World Bank, 1994.

24   Robert Holzmann, 'Global Pension Systems and Their Reform Worldwide Drivers, Trends, and Challenges', *The World Bank*, May 2012.

25   TheCityUK, *Fund Management*, November 2012.

26   Ismail Erturk, Julie Froud, Johal Sukhdev, Adam Leaver and Karel Williams, 'Against Agency: A Positional Critique', *Economy and Society*, 36(1), 2007, pp. 51-7.

27   As speculated, for example, by management expert Peter Drucker in his *The Unseen Revolution: How Pension Fund Socialism Came to America*, New York: Harper & Row, 1976.

28   See Sandy Hager, 'What Happened to the Bondholding Class? Public Debt, Power and the Top One Per Cent', *New Political Economy*, April 2013, pp. 1-28; Lesechos.fr, 'Bourse: l'exode des investisseurs', 4 June 2012, available at http://www.lesechos.fr.

29   Gerard Dumenil and Dominique Levy, in what they call a 'major revisionist proviso' in an otherwise Marxist theoretical framework, suggest that managers (and not only their top segment) constitute a class. They suggest it is a hybrid one, in the full sense of the term, given the position they occupy within relations of production as a result of their function in the modern corporation. But it is unclear why top managers increasing their share ownership holdings should have transformed this fraction of the capitalist class into a hybrid class. See their study, *The Dynamics of Modes of Production and Social Orders*, Paris: EconomiX, PSE, 2012.

30   Xavier Gabaix and Augustin Landier, 'Why Has CEO Pay Increased So Much', NBER Working Paper N. 12365, 2006; Camille Landais, 'Les hauts revenus en France (1998-2006): Une explosion des inégalités?', Paris School of Economics, 2007.

31   *OECD Factbook 2011-12, Economic, Environmental and Social Statistics*, Paris: OECD, 2013.

32   Erturk, et al., 'Against Agency: A Positional Critique'.

33   Philippon Thomas and Reshef Ariell, 'Wages and Human Capital in the U.S. Financial Industry, 1909-2006', NBER Working Paper N. 14644, 2009.

34   As put by William I. Robinson and Jerry Harris: 'A transnational capitalist class (TCC) has emerged as that segment of the world bourgeoisie that represents transnational capital'. See their 'Towards a Global Ruling Class? Globalization and the Transnational Capitalist Class', *Science & Society*, 64(1), 2000, p. 11. Leslie Sklair comments: 'Capitalism is organized politically on a global scale through the transnational capitalist'. See his 'The Transnational Capitalist Class and the Discourse of Globalization', *Cambridge Review of International Affairs*, 14(1), 2000, p. 82.

35   Winfried Ruigrok, Peder Greve and Sabina Nielsen, 'Transcending Borders with International Top Management Teams: A Study of European Financial

MNCs', *SCALA Discussion Paper*, N. 6, 2007.

36   Matthew Guthridge and Asmus B. Komm, 'Why Multinationals Struggle to Manage Talent', *McKinsey Quarterly*, 2008.

37   UNCTAD, *World Investment Report: Towards a New Generation of Investment Policies*, Geneva: UNCTAD, 2012.

38   Alan Rugman and Chang Hoon Oh, 'Why the Home Region Matters: Location and Regional Multinationals', *British Journal of Management*, February 2012.

39   European Commission, 'Facts and figures on State Aid in the EU Member States', Brussels, December 2012.

40   Fitch Rating, 'Rating Corporates Above the Country Ceiling', 27 January 2012; Moody's Investor Service, 'How Sovereign Credit Quality May Affect Other Ratings', 13 February 2013.

41   Standard & Poor's, 'Methodology and Assumptions: Request for Comment: Ratings Above The Sovereign – Corporate And Government Ratings', 12 April 2013.

42   Ryan Vincent, 'Corporate, Sovereign Debt Ratings Closely Linked: S&P', *CFO.com*, 2013, available at http://www3.cfo.com.

43   Eduardo Borensztein, Patricio Valenzuela and Kevin Cowa, 'Sovereign Ceilings "Lite"? The Impact of Sovereign Ratings on Corporate Ratings in Emerging Market Economies', Wharton Financial Institutions Center, 2013, available at http://fic.wharton.upenn.edu.

44   Clifford L. Staples 'Board Globalization in the World's Largest Transnational Corporations 1993-2005', *Corporate Governance: An International Review*, 15(2), 2007, pp. 311–21.

45   Kees van Veen and Janine Elbertsen, 'Governance Regimes and Nationality Diversity in Corporate Boards: A Comparative Study of Germany, the Netherlands and the United Kingdom', *Corporate Governance*, 16(5), 2008, p. 387.

46   Spencer Stuart Board Indexes 2012. This consulting firm publishes indexes based on board reports for various countries.

47   Sirik Honing, 'Does Diversity in Executive Boards Make a Difference? Nationality Diversity and Firm Performance in German, Dutch and British Multinational Enterprises', 28 June 2012, available at http://ssrn.com or http://dx.doi.org.

48   Michael Hartmann, 'Internationalisation et spécificités nationales des élites économiques', *Actes de la recherche en sciences sociales*, N. 190, 2011, pp. 10–23.

49   Mairi Maclean, Charles Harvey and Robert Chia, 'Dominant Corporate Agents and the Power Elite in France and Britain', *Organization Studies*, 31, 2010, pp. 327-48.

50   Zsuzsanna Tungli and Maury Peiperl, 'Expatriate Practices in German, Japanese, UK, and US Multinational Companies: A Comparative Survey of Changes', *Human Resource Management*, 48(1), 2009, pp. 153-71.

51   Towers-Watson, 'Globalizing Asia Pacific Maximizing the Value of Human Capital in Outbound M&A', 2012. According to a survey of 520 top world companies, the number of international assignees returning before the end of

their contracts is not negligible and reflects the real obstacles to the international circulation of elites. See Ernst & Young, 'Driving Business Success', *Global Mobility Effectiveness Survey*, 2012.

52 High Pay Centre, 'Global CEO Appointments: A Very Domestic Issue', 2013, available at http://highpaycentre.org.

53 Jochen Zimmermann and Jan-Christoph Volckmer, 'Accounting Firms: Global Spread with Limited Transnationalization', *Zentra Working Papers In Transnational Studies*, N. 11, 2012. Even the training centres formed to develop 'trans-cultural' management is called 'globaloney' by these very same management consultants. See Pankaj Ghemawat, 'Developing Global Leaders', *McKinsey Quarterly*, June 2012.

54 Neil Davidson, 'Reimagined Communities', *International Socialism*, N. 117, 2007.

55 Ellen Meiksins Wood, *Democracy Against Capitalism,* Cambridge: Cambridge University Press, 1995, p. 21.

56 Claude Serfati, *Impérialisme et militarisme. Actualité du vingt-et-unième siècle*, Lausanne: Editions Page deux, 2004.

57 Neil Brenner, 'Global, Fragmented, Hierarchical: Henri Lefebvre's Geographies of Globalization', *Public Culture*, 10(1), 1997, pp. 137–69.

58 See Jean-Christophe Graz, 'How Powerful are Transnational Elite Clubs? The Social Myth of the World Economic Forum', *New Political Economy*, 8:3, 2003, pp. 321-340

59 Luc Mampaey and Claude Serfati, 'Galbraith and Institutionalist Analysis: An Assessment Based on Transformations of the U.S. Military-Industrial System in the 1990s', in B. Laperche, J.K. Galbraith and D. Uzunidis, eds., *Innovation, Evolution and Economic Change: New ideas in the Tradition of Galbraith*, Cheltenham: Edward Elgar, 2006.

60 Ann R. Markusen and Joel Yudken, *The Rise of the Gunbelt: The Military Remapping of Industrial America*, New York: Oxford University Press, 1991.

61 Batelle, '2013 Global R&D Funding Forecast', 2012.

62 Claude Serfati, *Production d'armes, croissance et innovation*, Paris: Economica, 1995.

63 A recent example is the decision by the US administration to forbid several government agencies from buying products from the Chinese telecom giants Huawei and ZTE.

64 European Commission, *Action Plan for an Innovative and Competitive Security Industry*, Brussels, July 2012.

65 OECD, *The Security Economy*, Paris: OECD, 2004, p. 3.

66 And as observed by one of its earlier theorists: Jerry Harris, 'The Conflict for Power in Transnational Class Theory', *Science & Society*, 67, 2003, p. 329.

67 William I. Robinson, 'Gramsci and Globalisation: From Nation-State to Transnational Hegemony', *Critical Review of International Social and Political Philosophy*, 8(4), 2005, pp. 1-16.

68 William I. Robinson, 'Beyond the Theory of Imperialism: Global Capitalism and the Transnational State', *Societies without Borders*, 2(2), 2007, p. 10.

69 See Claude Serfati, 'Militarisme et imperialisme aujourd'hui: une relation

spécifique', *Carré Rouge*, N. 25, 2003, pp. 13-17. For a view contradicting military spending as a Keynesian stimulus or 'functional' to remedy to overaccumulation, see Linda J. Bilmes, 'The Financial Legacy of Iraq and Afghanistan: How Wartime Spending Decisions Will Constrain Future National Security Budgets', *HKS Faculty Research Working Paper Series*, RWP13-006, 2013.

70   Kees van der Pijl, *Transnational Classes and International Relations*, London: Routledge, 1998.

71   On these points see François-Xavier Dudouet, Eric Grémont and Antoine Vion, 'Core Business Network in the Eurozone', *Les Analyses de l'Opesc*, N. 12, Juin 2009; John Scott, 'Networks of Corporate Power: A Comparative Assessment', *Annual Review of Sociology*, 17, 1991, pp. 181-203; Mike Savage and Karel Williams, 'Elites: Remembered in Capitalism and Forgotten by Social Sciences', in M. Savage and K. Williams, eds., *Remembering Elites*, Oxford: Blackwell, 2008, p. 7.

72   William Carroll and Meindert Fennema, 'Is There a Transnational Business Community?', *International Sociology*, 17(3), 2002, pp. 393-419; Jeffrey Kentor and Yong Suk Jang, 'Yes, There is a (Growing) Transnational Business Community: A Study of Global Interlocking Directorates, 1983–98', *International Sociology*, 19(3), 2004, pp. 355-68.

73   François-Xavier Dudouet, Eric Grémont and Antoine Vion, 'Transnational Business Networks in the Eurozone: A Focus on Four Major Stock Exchange Indices', in Georgina Murray and John Scot, eds., *Financial Elites and Transnational Business: Who Rules the World?*, Cheltenham: Edward Elgar, 2012, pp. 124-45.

74   William K. Carroll, Meindert Fennema and Eelke M. Heemskerk, 'Constituting Corporate Europe: A Study of Elite Social Organization', *Antipode*, 42(4), 2010, pp. 811-43. There is also dispute amongst these various studies over the degree to whether it is finance or industry that is propelling ahead the interlocks.

75   Dudouet, et al., 'Core Business Network', p. 21. Also see Lars Oxelheim, Aleksandra Gregorič, Trond Randøy and Steen Thomsen, 'On the Internationalization of Corporate Boards', *IFN Working Paper*, N. 951, 2013; Kees van Veen and Jan Kratzer, 'National and International Interlocking Directorates Within Europe: Corporate Networks Within and Among Fifteen European Countries', *Economy and Society*, 40(1), 2011, pp. 1-25.

76   Van Veen and Kratzer, 'National and International Interlocking Directorates', p. 17; Eelke M. Heemskerk, 'The Rise of the European Corporate Elite: Evidence from the Network of Interlocking Directorates in 2005 and 2010', N. 34, 2011, p. 17, available at http://opensiuc.lib.siu.edu.

77   Kees van der Pijl, Otto Holman and Or Raviv, 'The Resurgence of German Capital in Europe: EU Integration and the Restructuring of Atlantic Networks of Interlocking Directorates after 1991', *Review of International Political Economy*, 18(3), 2011, p. 402.

78   Keith Richardson, 'Big Business and the European Agenda', *SEI Working Paper*, N. 35, 2000; Val Burris and Clifford Staples, 'In Search of a Transnational

Capitalist Class: Alternative Methods for Comparing Director Interlocks Within and Between Nations and Regions', *International Journal of Comparative Sociology*, 53(4), 2012, pp. 323-42.

79   The proportionally higher level of European links by companies from 'smaller economies' goes together with a steep decline of national linkages, partly as a result of governmental policies in favour of the internationalization of national companies. This can be seen, for example, by comparing the Netherlands, Austria and Finland.

80   Bastiaan van Apeldoorn, *Transnational Capitalism and the Struggle over European Integration*, London: Routledge, 2000, p. 46.

81   Carroll, Fennema and Heemskerk, 'Constituting Corporate Europe', p. 835.

82   Ellen Meiksins Wood, 'A Reply to Critics', *Historical Materialism*, 15, 2007, p. 156.

83   Karl Marx and Frederick Engels, *The Communist Manifesto*, London: Verso, 1998 [1848], p. 49.

WHITHER THE TRANSNATIONAL CAPITALIST CLASS?

WILLIAM K. CARROLL

Since the 1970s, the putative formation of a transnational capitalist class (TCC), typically viewed as part and parcel of capitalist globalization, has raised substantive and strategic questions for scholars and activists alike. To what extent has such a class actually formed and what is its transnational reach? What are its sources of cohesion and its capacity to act as a class-for-itself? How is the TCC articulated with other capitalist fractions and with state apparatuses that, in the same period, have developed increasingly international capacities and orientations? Most importantly, what strategic implications might be drawn from an analysis of transnational capitalist class formation in the current era? This essay takes up these questions and attempts to provide some answers grounded in scholarship from the past four decades. Although one can reasonably speak of a transnational capitalist class, its reach, cohesion and agentic capacity should not be overestimated. Moreover, the TCC is not a freestanding entity, but is linked to and indeed embedded in national capital circuits and state-capital nexuses. Given this, the task for movements opposing capitalist rule is to construct a historic bloc that is nationally rooted yet that also builds agentic capacity transnationally, while exploiting weaknesses in the bloc in which the TCC is a leading force. In engaging the challenges posed by the transnational capitalist class, the left should not trap itself within reified conceptions of a unified transnational capitalist bloc, nor should it withdraw into a self-defeating anarchism that minimizes the need for both cross-movement solidarity and state-centred politics.

CHANGING CLASS CONCEPTIONS AND REALITIES

Images of the capitalist class's internationalization go back to the *Communist Manifesto*'s description of the bourgeoisie's globalizing mission: 'The need of a constantly expanding market for its products chases the bourgeoisie over the entire surface of the globe. It must nestle everywhere, settle everywhere, establish connexions everywhere'.[1] For Marx and Engels, the objective need for self-expansion obliges capitalists to globalize, but there is no implication that national affinities, identities and forms of capitalist organization fall away in the process. Indeed, capitalists have long been active in transnational circuits of capital, but not necessarily as members of a transnational capitalist class. This is so because capital is not a unified macro subject but is divided microeconomically into competing units, positioned within and across national boundaries in an international political system, rendering tendencies towards global capitalist unity always tenuous. Thus, the question of the transnational capitalist class cannot be reduced to the globalization of capitalism per se. What matters is how capitalists and their advisers are embedded in a panoply of socio-political relations.

If the relationship between accumulation and capitalist class formation is complex, so is the articulation of states and internationalizing capitalist classes, which figures directly in the question of a TCC. A century ago, in an early phase of nationally centred imperialism, capitalist globalization followed a segmented logic. International circuits of capital developed in the tracks of colonial power – leading Lenin (who hewed to Bukharin in this) to prognosticate inter-imperialist rivalry and war as an expression of the competition between great-power national capitals exceeding their territorial boundaries. Bukharin's and Lenin's reading may have been apposite for the first few decades of the twentieth century, but since the end of the Second World War Kautsky's opposing notion of ultra-imperialism has conveyed the dominant tendency. In the midst of the First World War, Kautsky speculated that 'the striving of every great capitalist State to extend its own colonial empire in opposition to all the other empires of the same kind … represents only one among various modes of expansion of capitalism'.[2] For Kautsky, ultra-imperialism could arise as 'a bourgeois effort supported by "every capitalist able to look beyond the immediate moment", to resolve problems of output and market not through mutually destructive conflicts but *through an appeal to general class interests*',[3] effecting a 'shift from conflict between imperialist powers to maintenance of a world system of exploitation'.[4] The WTO, World Bank, IMF, G7 and the like are precisely vehicles for the sort of collective imperialism that Kautsky envisaged, which has entailed an 'internationalizing of the state' that now runs under the banner of 'global governance'.[5]

The postwar era from 1945 until the 1970s marked a new phase in the making of global capitalism, in which transnational corporations (TNCs) became the key vehicle for accumulating industrial capital across national borders. The unrivaled, superordinate position that the United States of America held in the world system, with Europe and Japan in ruins, Fordist mass production already well developed in corporate America and Bretton Woods institutions setting the dollar as global currency, ensured that this new phase of globalization would play out under the aegis of American hegemony, whose open-door policy and neo-colonialism helped engender an informal empire.[6] From the late 1940s to early 1970s the volume of foreign direct investment worldwide burgeoned, and as of the late 1960s the lion's share of that investment was controlled by capitalists based in the USA. At the high tide of American power, US-based TNCs were so dominant that it was not uncommon to predict that by 2000 three quarters or more of the capitalist world's economic output would be controlled by US-based corporations and their foreign subsidiaries, as former US Assistant Secretary of Commerce J.N. Behrman did in 1968.[7] In the era of unmitigated US hegemony, the dominant image of international corporate power was not that of a transnational capitalist class, but of an American behemoth. Yet by the 1970s the rapid expansion of TNCs based in Western Europe and Japan disclosed a tendency away from unilateral American capitalist dominance and toward the cross-penetration of capital among the advanced capitalist countries, evoking a rather different image of capitalist internationalization.

THE EMERGENCE OF THE TCC, THEORY AND PRACTICE

In an influential 1974 paper, Canadian economist Stephen Hymer was apparently the first to note the implications of these developments for the capitalist class:

> Due to the internationalization of capital, competition between national capitalists is becoming less and less a source of rivalry between nations. Using the instrument of direct investment, large corporations are able to penetrate foreign markets and detach their interests from their home markets. Given these tendencies an international capitalist class is emerging whose interests lie in the world economy as a whole and a system of international private property which allows free movement of capital between countries.[8]

Two years earlier, Hymer had pointed to 'the great pull' of the multinational corporate system 'toward international class consciousness on the part of capital', facilitated by the corporate form of business which enabled 'the 1 percent of the population that owns the vast majority of corporate stock' to maintain control of key investments of increasingly international scope while delegating operational power to hired managers.[9]

Much of the sociological research on transnational capitalist class formation, which began in earnest in the 1980s, has been inspired not only by Hymer's imagery but by an understanding of how the corporate form entails a specific structure of class power. Since corporate directors are elected by shareowners on the principle of one share one vote, the corporation serves as a device for concentrating the control of capital in the hands of major shareholders (who may themselves be other corporations), enabling them also to control the funds supplied by the many passive investors whose fragmented shareholdings confer no substantive property rights. In practice, the directorates of large corporations are comprised of 'constellations of interests' wielding power and influence in the strategic direction of firms.[10] These may include major shareholders as well as creditors, top managers and advisors (such as lawyers and consultants), with the last category amounting to a stratum of organic intellectuals who do not control capital but help direct its accumulation.[11]

The directors of the largest companies in a given country make up its corporate elite, which, while distinct from the capitalist class, can be thought of as its leading edge or 'top tier'. Research on interlocking directorates, beginning with Jeidels's[12] study of banks and industry in early twentieth century Germany, had by the late 1970s discerned the basic architecture of corporate networks: within each advanced capitalist country, financial institutions occupied central positions in a national network connecting most major firms, directly or indirectly.[13] As corporate boards linked up with each other in processes of capital accumulation, a raft of studies under the rubric of 'power structure research'[14] documented the intricate social relations through which leading corporate directors fostered their own class hegemony as the 'dominant segment' of the bourgeoisie.[15]

The exposure of the actual structure of economic and political power provided ideological ammunition to progressive politics. Power structure research brought together new-left radicals and Marxists of the *Insurgent Sociologist* and related venues, who were committed to anti-capitalist politics, with critical liberals and social democrats concerned about corporate concentration as a threat to democracy. Through systematic mappings of interlocking directorates and other non-market relations, power structure research depicted corporate networks as 'traces' of two forms of power – the 'expressive' capacity of corporate elites to cultivate and promulgate within their ranks a shared world view and political strategy, and the 'instrumental' capacity of capitalists and their advisors to use networks as means of controlling capital across firms, reinforcing creditor-debtor relations, etc.[16]

Meindert Fennema was the first to apply the methods and reasoning of power structure research beyond the level of individual countries. Mapping the international corporate network before and after the generalized international recession of 1973-74, he documented the consolidation of a Euro-North American configuration of corporate interlocks but found very few ties extending beyond that heartland of postwar capitalism. Capitalist class formation was accelerating in Europe, but this did not mean the disarticulation of national corporate networks. In fact, national networks in most countries became more cohesive. Moreover, the interlocks spanning national borders were mostly carried by single directors, suggesting more of an expressive role of elite integration than an instrumental role of capital control.[17]

Fennema's study was soon followed by Kees van der Pijl's *The Making of an Atlantic Ruling Class*, whose historical narrative tracked a complex process of class formation, reaching back to the post–US Civil War railway boom. At that time an Atlantic circuit of money capital grew up, whose epicentre shifted from London to New York during the First World War. Van der Pijl conceptualized capitalist class formation in the North Atlantic region as 'a continuous process of redefining the coordinates of bourgeois rule in response and anticipation to the dynamic of the internationalization of capital', and introduced a fractional perspective on the capitalist class, informed by the Gramscian turn in political economy.[18] For Van der Pijl, the structural divide between production and circulation offers two distinctive standpoints from which class hegemony could be constructed – those of productive capital and of money capital. Intrinsic to production are technical issues surrounding the creation of use value, in a word, *planning*. Intrinsic to circulation is the free movement of goods and capital, especially in money form, and thus the convertibility of currencies.[19] The money-capital perspective posits 'a system of harmony and progress as long as through the price mechanism, the rate of profit remains the exclusive regulatory device'. The productive-capital perspective constructs an interest from the position of the industrialist, who is willing 'to subordinate the orthodoxy of the market mechanism to a strategy better suited to the real socialization of the productive forces'.[20]

These fractional perspectives underpin political projects developed and promoted by organic intellectuals in universities, government commissions and policy-planning groups, but they are not mutually exclusive. During the post-Second World War era they became fused in the transatlantic project of corporate liberalism. Under American control of the Atlantic circuit of money capital and as Fordism became generalized as a productivist class compromise, a strategic synthesis was extrapolated to Western Europe where it served as the standpoint from which successive concepts of Atlantic unity were developed, and to which the entire Atlantic ruling class would in due course adhere.[21]

Van der Pijl agreed with Fennema that the crisis of the early 1970s had major implications for capitalist class formation: the hypertrophy of de-nationalized financial capital (after the dollar was severed from gold in 1971) facilitated transfer of parts of the productive apparatus of the North Atlantic heartland to new semi-peripheral zones – thereby 'breaking the territorial coincidence of mass production and mass consumption' and destroying 'the very structure of Atlantic integration'.[22] Capitalist internationalization in the 1970s thereby widened the scope of the crisis, strengthened the fractional position of money-capital and provoked the search for a new hegemonic strategy. By the end of the decade corporate liberalism had been eclipsed by a neoliberal strategy. Neoliberalism, in championing free labour, 'sound money' and unimpeded international circulation, presents the perspective of money-capital as a general interest around which the interests of different capital fractions can be assembled.[23]

Later work on transnational class formation, also in a neo-Gramscian vein, helped specify the new strategy and its class underpinnings. Robert Cox's *Production, Power and World Order* provided the first sustained analysis that identified the formation of a 'transnational managerial class', including active capitalists and their organic intellectuals. In contrast to the prognostication given in the *Communist Manifesto*, tendencies in late twentieth century global class formation showed 'a movement toward the unification of capital on a world scale, while industrial workers and other subordinate groups have become fragmented and divided'. Cox's key contribution to the analysis of transnational class formation turned upon his innovative use of the concept of historic bloc. In a hegemonic world order

production in particular countries becomes connected through the mechanisms of a world economy and linked into world systems of production. The social classes of the dominant country find allies in classes within other countries. The historic blocs underpinning particular states become connected through the mutual interests and ideological perspectives of social classes in different countries, and global classes begin to form. An incipient world society grows up around the interstate system, and states themselves become internationalized in that their mechanisms and policies become adjusted to the rhythms of the world order.[24]

In Cox's formulation, the transnational managerial class had three components: top managers and directors of TNCs, those controlling major national enterprises and locally-based smaller capitalists hooked into the transnational capitalist circuitry. However, as a hegemonic bloc, the class extended to a raft of organic intellectuals providing indispensable support – officials in agencies of economic management, technical experts such as business educators and corporate lawyers, etc.

The first full-fledged analysis purporting to show the emergence of a transnational capitalist class, and the first explicit use of that term, appeared in Leslie Sklair's *Sociology of the Global System*, a work that criticized overly state-centric formulations and questioned the claims of dependency theory about the debilitating impact of TNCs in holding back development on capitalism's periphery. Sklair's conception of the TCC posited four fractions which functioned together in directing the transnational practices of global capitalism: (i) owners and controllers of TNCs and their local affiliates, (ii) globalizing bureaucrats and politicians, (iii) globalizing professionals and (iv) consumerist elites (merchants and media). Sklair was clear on the hegemonic project pursued by this variegated group:

> This class sees its mission as organizing the conditions under which the interests of its various fractions and the interests of the system as a whole (which do not always coincide) can be furthered within the context of particular countries and communities. This implies that there is one central *transnational* capitalist class that makes system-wide decisions, and that it connects with the TCC in each community, region, country, etc.[25]

In this formulation, which was further fleshed out through interviews with leading corporate executives in Sklair's 2001 book, *The Transnational Capitalist Class*, the TCC amounts to an historic bloc of class, state and civil-society actors who are principal protagonists in constructing global capitalism. Executives, both of TNCs and of subsidiary corporations, provide the TCC's 'backbone'. This executive faction leads within the economic sphere, socialized by the corporation into 'a global worldview' that mandates global business strategy as a necessity. However, Sklair's account emphasized the political and cultural agency of the other fractions, including agents of what Cox earlier termed internationalizing states. Globalizing state bureaucrats provide the politico-legal framework (including foreign investment promotion) within which TNCs are encouraged to operate while 'capitalist-inspired politicians' toe the line on economic policy. Similarly inspired professionals offer their legal, journalistic, academic and other skills to TNCs and thus 'find for themselves places in the transnational capitalist class'. Consumerist elites, promoting commodity consumption through the media or retail sales, play important roles beyond the economic, producing and disseminating a 'culture-ideology' that addresses capitalism's endemic crisis of underconsumption by institutionalizing the commodification of culture.[26] Although Sklair acknowledged the possibility of frictions across the four fractions, his general thesis was that 'leading personnel in these groups constitute a global power elite, dominant class or inner circle in the sense that these terms have been used to characterize the dominant class structures of specific countries'; placing the transnational capitalist class in opposition to anti-capitalists and also to localized, domestically-oriented capitalists who reject globalization.[27] However, the global shift underway in the 1980s and 1990s would in Sklair's estimation weaken the latter, as its base in accumulation became marginalized.

Sklair was the first to construct a grand narrative with the TCC at its centre, but problems in the formulation did not go undetected. Abdul Embong critiqued both Cox's and Sklair's concepts as unwieldy and overworked due to too many fractions forced into the same class category. Although globalizing bureaucrats, politicians and professionals perform governance and technical functions for transnational business, they should not be confused with a TCC, whose economic base includes corporate salaries and perks and 'shares in the various corporations they own or control, or in which they work or serve as board members'. Embong's alternative differentiated a transnational capitalist class – owners/controllers and executives of TNCs – from a transnational managerial class – the 'lower fractions within the dominant groups', including managers of subsidiary firms and 'the capitalist-inspired politicians, bureaucrats, consultants, lawyers and other professionals who operate transnationally to service the TNCS in various ways'. Embong also questioned the assumption in Cox and Sklair that members of the TCC share a common class consciousness, an outward-oriented, global rather than inward-oriented, national perspective. Although Sklair's interviews with *Fortune* 500 executives provided evidence of a common world view imbued with the culture-ideology of consumerism, this does not rule out fractional differences based in nation, region and other interests, which was evident, for instance, in the 1997-98 financial crisis. Members of the TCC and transnational managerial class may support and help reproduce the global capitalist system, but their own particular interests and actions should not be covered over in an assumption of class unity.[28]

WILLIAM ROBINSON AND HIS CRITICS

Enter William Robinson, who with colleagues has presented the most forceful case for the transnational capitalist class as a fait accompli. Compared to Sklair, Robinson offers a narrower definition of the TCC as 'the owners of transnational capital [...] the group that owns the leading worldwide means of production as embodied principally in the TNCs and private financial institutions'.[29] The TCC is transnational because it is tied to 'globalised circuits of production, marketing, and finances unbound from particular national territories and identities', endowing it with interests that prioritize global over local or national accumulation.[30] Robinson asserts that the transnational capitalist class is in the process of constructing a new globalist historic bloc whose policies and politics are conditioned by the logic of global rather than national accumulation. Surrounding the owners and top managers of transnational corporations, who form the core of the bloc, are the elites and the bureaucratic staffs of the supranational state agencies such as the World Bank, and the dominant political parties, media conglomerates, technocratic elites and state managers – both North and South.[31] Robinson's concept of the globalist bloc roughly matches Sklair's more expansive concept of the TCC. But Robinson advocates a stronger thesis of transnational capitalist class formation, claiming with Harris that the TCC 'is increasingly a class-in-itself and for-itself'; that it has 'become conscious of its transnationality and has been pursuing a class project of capitalist globalization, as reflected in a transnational state under its auspices'.[32]

Indeed, if Sklair's analysis gestures toward a reading of the TCC consistent with Kautskyan ultra-imperialism (but with a broadening of its locus beyond a few European great powers), Robinson embraces a full-blooded Kautskyan perspective that minimizes the dynamic of inter-state rivalry within TCC formation: *'the old nation-state phase of capitalism has been superseded by the transnational phase of capitalism'*, as the 'commanding heights' of state power shift to supra-national institutions. Meanwhile, beneath the global level, national states, 'captured' by transnational capitalist forces, internalize authority structures of global capitalism, shifting real policymaking power within national states to the global capitalist bloc, which is represented by local groups tied to the global economy. This formulation locates the prime *agency* for economic globalization within a transnational capitalist class that remakes the world, if not in its own image then according to its needs.[33]

Robinson's work is notable not only for its clarity but for the spirited responses it has inspired. Analysts like Walden Bello sharply disagreed with Robinson's ultra-imperialist prognosis. Pointing to the turn in 2002-03 to national imperialism by the George W. Bush administration – with the attendant disciplining of peripheral states – Bello argued that globalization has actually been going into reverse. Radhika Desai also questioned the cumulative character of globalization but allowed for the possibility of global governance superseding a declining US hegemony.[34] Beyond the question whether the globalization driving TCC formation is an entirely cumulative process, there is the issue of how the TCC is articulated to the still nationally defined spaces into which world capitalism is structured. For Robinson, the TCC is ascendant in an era of global deterritorialization: 'spatial relations have been territorially-defined relations. But this territorialization is in no way immanent to social relations and may well be fading in significance as globalization advances'. More recently, he has claimed that 'global production and service chains or networks are *global* in character, in that accumulation is embedded in *global* markets, involves *global* enterprise organization and sets of *global* capital–labor relations'.[35] Missing from this kind of analysis is a more nuanced view of spatial divisions within global capitalism, as in distinctions among the global, the transnational, the national, the local. As I have suggested elsewhere, 'labeling all this as global does not actually *make* it "global", in the sense of having transcended locality. It is not clear what is gained in such labeling, but what seems lost is a sense of specificity and place'.[36]

Similarly, Kees van der Pijl observed that in Robinson's claims about the TCC and the transnational state 'a formal unity between concepts leads us astray': terms like globalization, the transnational state and TCC 'remain *abstract* whereas they claim to denote concrete realities'.[37] Jason Moore also noted the abstract placelessness at the heart of Robinson's characterization of the late twentieth century as a new, global era of stateless, mobile, transnational capital and pointed to new forms of territorialization and regionalization that suggest capital's 'global' moment 'depends upon very particular *places*'. What appear, abstractly, as formative aspects of a single TCC may actually be macro-regional processes – as in the rise of South and East Asia or the economic integration of Europe.[38]

Robinson's responses to his critics demonstrate the pitfalls of taking too maximalist a stance on TCC formation. Replying to concerns about his thesis's evidential base, he claimed that, 'by definition', the transnationalization of capitalism means the transnationalization of its classes – a position at odds with our starting point in this essay and with the continuing lack of transnational collective organization and action by workers.[39] In this, Robinson elided the important distinction between class-in-itself and for-itself, which he and Harris drew elsewhere.[40] The increasingly transnational circuitry of capital may create conditions for a TCC-in-itself, presiding over accumulation processes that transect borders (and also for a transnational proletariat-in-itself), but this says very little about the TCC's political capacity to define and act in its own interests. The latter implies TCC organizations of interest formation at a global level, and TCC influence over state projects and policies.

Indeed, the issue of the state is central to appraising TCC collective agency. Robinson responded to charges of underplaying the continuing importance of national states by emphasizing, in addition to his notion of TCC state 'capture', the 'function' that national states now perform for transnational capital.[41] At its heart, and despite the instrumentalist image of 'capture', the case Robinson makes for the role of national states as agencies of the TCC is a largely functional one (and suffers, as one critic noted from its immunity to possible empirical falsification).[42] A good example of how this reasoning operates can be seen in Robinson's critique of what he sees as the 'reification of the state' in David Harvey's and also Ellen Wood's analyses of contemporary imperialism:

> As the most powerful component of the TNS [transnational state], the US state apparatus defends the interests of transnational investors and of the system as a whole. Military expansion is in the interests of the TNCs. The only military apparatus in the world capable of exercising global coercive authority is the US military. The beneficiaries of US military action around the world are not 'US' but transnational capitalist groups.[43]

In this formulation, the US state is assimilated into the TNS and the specific, 'national' interests of the American capitalist class disappear as all transnational capitalists share in the bounty of what only appears, in each particular instance, to be US imperial aggression. Among the problematic assumptions in this functional analysis is that transnational capital is itself unified. A more nuanced view which draws directly on Panitch and Gindin's essay in the Socialist Register a decade ago is offered by Stokes, who sees Robinson as putting the cart before the horse.[44] In Stokes's formulation, 'the US state acts to secure the generic global conditions for transnational capital accumulation less at the behest of a TCC, but rather because, in so doing, the US state is, by default, acting in the generic interests of its national capital *because of its high level of internationalization*'.[45]

A recent study of the US state-capital nexus indicates most clearly the problems with Robinson's formulation of the TCC and TNS. Van Apeldoorn and De Graaf explore how the US corporate elite has been embedded within the 30 top positions in successive post-Cold War administrations (1992-

2011). They see the US Open Door policy as a specific project of American imperialism, in which the US state has acted less on behalf of global capital as a whole than

> on behalf of US transnational capital *in particular*. Here we should note that what we call transnational capital still is *also* nationally based economically – for many US TNCs the home market is still by far the largest single national market – as well as nationally embedded politically. The latter must inter alia be seen in terms of the close (personal) ties that exist between US transnational capital and the US state that in itself makes it implausible to view the latter as merely an agent of all global capitalists.[46]

The specific, territorialized project of Open Door imperialism is not to construct a global order for the TCC; rather, 'Open Door imperialism is about serving *the general and long-term interests of US transnational capital*, that is, opening and keeping open the door not just for today's US corporations but also for the future'. When these authors examine the corporate affiliations of key cabinet-ranking and senior advisors in the Clinton, Bush and Obama administrations they find not only a remarkable number of connections into the American corporate community, but a strong presence of US-based transnational capital. The overwhelming predominance of this fraction, *at once national and transnational*, at the heart of the US capital-state nexus 'helps to explain the fact that US grand strategy-making reflects the interests of US transnational capital'.[47]

Here, the category 'US-based transnational capital' offers a depiction that is more sensitive than the schematic division of capital along a national/transnational binary. But even within it, there may be divisions between capital that accumulates transnationally (in circuits that transect borders without the commercial involvement of states) and capital that accumulates 'internationally' (in international circuits that involve states commercially). In an intriguing study Jerry Harris has made this distinction, identifying a military-industrial fraction of the American bourgeoisie, whose interests he takes to be quite distinct from the TCC. The former is strongly (co) dependent upon the US state, but is also involved in the arms trade and in foreign investment. TNCs like Boeing, General Electric, General Dynamics and United Technologies accumulate capital *inter*nationally rather than *trans*nationally, leading Harris to suggest that contradictions within the military-industrial fraction could raise 'a significant challenge to globalization'.[48] These studies demonstrate that as our analysis becomes more concrete, the TCC appears less as a coherent, homogeneous actor that has transcended national states.

THE TURN TO POWER STRUCTURE ANALYSIS
ON A GLOBAL SCALE

To go beyond the interventions of Sklair and Robinson, several sociologists in the first decade of the twenty-first century picked up the thread of power structure analysis as a way of illuminating the social organization of transnational capital. If there has been a recent surge in transnational capitalist class formation, it should be evident in a tendency for the directorates of the world's largest corporations to interlock across national borders, forming a global corporate elite. Fennema and I compared his 1976 transnational network with the network circa 1996, and found only a modest increase in transnational interlocking alongside the persistence of national networks, suggesting strong path dependencies that reproduce the patterns of national corporate-elite organization.[49]

Figure 1. Regional corporate affiliations of G500 interlockers

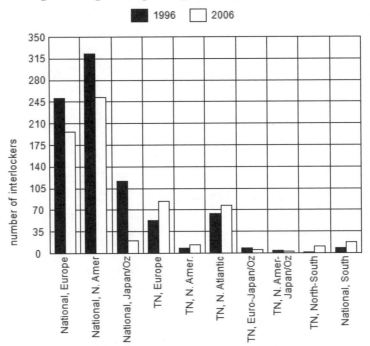

Similarly, my 10-year study (concluding in 2007) of the world's 500 leading corporations (G500) and their interlocking directorates offered support for only a qualified version of the thesis that a TCC has actually formed, as opposed to its being in the making. Over the decade there was some decline in national corporate communities, and a shift to transnational corporate affiliations with the formation of a cohesive stratum of capitalists directing firms based in multiple countries. As of 2007, the transnational elite segment, comprising 29 per cent of all interlocking G500 directors, was internally integrated, but not as a group unto itself. It appeared more as a *bridge*, with growing internal cohesion, across persistent national networks.[50] Moreover, most corporate networkers remained national in their directorships, and most networkers with directorships in multiple countries participated primarily in one national network.[51] In Figure 1, it is clear that the vast majority of G500 interlockers connected corporations based in western Europe or North America, although the number of interlockers serving simultaneously on North-based and South-based directorates did increase from only one in 1996 to twelve a decade later.[52]

Indeed, the global corporate elite is very specifically regionalized: the vast majority of firms that engage in transnational interlocking are headquartered in Europe and North America, underlining the enduring influence of a North Atlantic ruling class. The transnational elite configuration is a networked hierarchy constituted through the selective participation of corporations and directors, and of the cities and countries they call home. A relatively small inner circle of mainly European and North American men constitutes the network; a relatively small number of countries host most of the interlocked corporations, and within those countries a few cities predominate as command centres for global corporate power. The transnational network is most integrated in Europe and spans across the Atlantic, connecting corporations based in the cities of North-Western Europe with those of North-Eastern North America.

Corporate capital based in the global South has made inroads into this North-dominated class configuration, but the increasing numbers of South-based giant corporations were by 2007 only very tentatively linked into the elite network of corporate interlocks, as is evident in Figure 2.[53] Despite a surge in the number of large China-based corporations (from zero to sixteen), only three G500 directors (all based in the global North) sat on Chinese corporate boards in 2007.[54] These findings underline a certain *disjuncture* between class formation as a sociocultural process and the economic process of capital accumulation. World financial markets are highly integrated, and giant corporations have achieved unprecedented global reach, but the governance of corporations, and the life of the *haute bourgeoisie,* remain in important ways embedded in national and regional (including transatlantic) structures and cultures. Owing to this cultural and organizational inertia, most transnational elite relations bridge across the countries and cities of world capitalism's centre, replicating the long-standing structure of North-South imperialism.

Figure 2. The international network of transnational interlocks, 2007

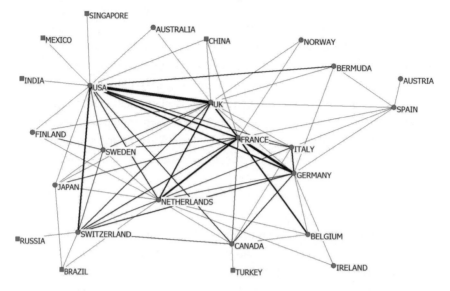

Perhaps the strongest evidence from my 2010 study for TCC formation lies in the further elaboration of an elite corporate-policy network, part of a transnational bloc of capitalists and organic intellectuals that builds consensus and exercises business leadership in the global arena. As leading capitalists serve on such transnational policy boards as the Trilateral Commission, TransAtlantic Business Dialogue and World Business Council for Sustainable Development, they help shape a transnational business agenda and create an additional layer of social organization, underwriting the elite cohesion behind what has been a hegemonic project of transnational neoliberalism. But despite this ideological solidarity (and the reach into policy formation), the TCC exists neither as a freestanding entity (it is deeply embedded in national business communities) nor as a homogeneous collectivity.[55]

My conclusion from this empirical work – that 'as a class-for-itself, the transnational capitalist class is in the making, but not (yet) made' – gained further credibility via Burris and Staples's comparison of the global corporate-elite network in 1998 and 2006.[56] They found European corporate boards to be highly multinational, with directors from a variety of European countries as well as North Americans. At the level of individuals, what stood out was the profuse exchange of directors resident in the US and UK, accounting for 42 per cent of the total volume of US-Europe interlocks, and highlighting 'the historic tie between the US and British capitalist classes as an essential bridge upon which the formation of a broader North Atlantic capitalist class crucially depends'.[57] Their painstaking analysis of elite relations leads them to conclude that the emergence of a transnational capitalist class as a truly global phenomenon is a very long way from realization and probably unlikely for the foreseeable future. On the other hand, there are regions in the global economy where the evidence is much stronger for the emergence of a supra-national capitalist class that has gone a considerable way toward transcending national divisions. Whereas skeptics of the TCC thesis might argue that most of the evidence for transnationalism is confined to Europe and largely an artifact of the formation of the European Union and associated processes of European economic integration, our research suggests that the regional locus of transnational class formation is more accurately described as the North Atlantic region rather than Europe alone.[58]

If global corporate-elite networks offer valuable insights on TCC formation, several studies have depicted the process from the vantage point of capitalists' *accumulation base* in the ownership of corporate shares. In a 1976 study of 2000 European and 250 US corporations, Fennema and Schijf found a sharp asymmetry in the pattern of transnational ownership, underlining the unilateral dominance of US-based capital in the 1970s. American companies had 116 majority financial participations in the eight European countries, but European firms had only two in the US, with the other 134 transnational ownership relations distributed among the European countries. Only one fifth of the European subsidiaries of US corporations had board interlocks with their parents, but within Europe half of foreign subsidiaries shared one or more directors with the parent firm, suggesting a stronger tendency to class formation across the borders of Western Europe than across the Atlantic.[59]

Three decades later, my exploration of financial-industrial and intercorporate ownership relations within the global network of giant companies (circa 2007) showed a pattern of capital integration on a transnational basis, as a few large financial institutions came to own small stakes (less than 5 per cent of voting shares) in various industrials (and in each other), and as financial-industrial interlocking increased among firms based in Germany, Italy and France, pointing to pan-European finance capital. However, the relations were very specifically regionalized: financial-industrial interlocks spanning national borders were restricted to Europe, and the extensive investments of the world's largest companies in each other were largely held within the North Atlantic region.[60]

Moreover, most of the conjoint shareholding/directorial relations, and most financial-industrial interlocks, were confined *within* national boundaries, pointing to the persistence of national business communities. This research confirmed that, with very few exceptions, transnational board interlocks are *not* vehicles of strategic control – they occur independently of transnational intercorporate ownership. The situation presents a 'new form of finance capitalism' in which share ownership is both concentrated and liquid, and 'active control is largely avoided'.[61] In place of interlocking directorates, the symbiosis of industrial and financial capital is expressed in informal and more ephemeral ways such as one-on-one meetings between institutional investors and CEOs.[62] By 2007, with global capitalism on the threshold of a massive accumulation crisis, an extensive network of intercorporate ownership knit many of the world's major corporations into a loose configuration, with investment management companies and a few key financial institutions playing key integrative roles. Within this new transnational finance capitalism, investments are rarely matched by the directoral ties that might give investors voice in the direction of companies. Rather, power resides in the exit option – the capacity of institutions to invest and divest in any of a wide range of companies.[63]

This interpretation gains further plausibility in light of an extensive study of nearly 25,000 firms listed on any of the world's major stock exchanges in early 2007 which identified the 'backbone' of the global corporate ownership network by extracting the subnetwork of the most powerful shareholders (whether persons, other firms or institutional investors) in each of 48 countries. Interpreting these as 'the seat of power in national stock markets', Glattfelder and Battiston identified ten shareholders positioned to exert the most allocative power in the world's stock markets – seven based in the US, three in Europe, and all of them large financial institutions or fund managers of institutional investments.[64] Neither people nor industrial corporations appeared as major multinational shareholders, underlining the importance of financial institutions as central organizations in the allocation and control of corporate capital.

Most recently, Murray and Peetz have examined the financialization of global corporate ownership in the 299 largest corporations worldwide, a year after the 2008 financial crisis. They report that, of over 2100 entities owning significant shares of the 299 leading firms, the top 30 (21 of them financial institutions and nine of them states) hold or control 51.4 per cent of total assets, an enormous concentration of finance capital. These global asset managers include banks, life insurers, pension funds, hedge funds, investment management companies and sovereign funds (particularly those of the UK and China), and their holdings are spread among great numbers of corporations. Murray and Peetz infer that 'a true transnational *class*' has formed: 'a group that, sometimes directly, sometimes indirectly, sometimes consciously and sometimes unconsciously, controls the exercise of economic power across and within national boundaries. Their power is exercised in part through individual agency but even more so through the collective structures of ownership of very large corporations'.[65] However, we might add that compared to the modest accretion of elite connections across borders, it is collective ownership structures among the world's largest corporations that show a remarkable degree of transnationalization in the early twenty-first century.

Tax havens also play a role in transnationalizing capitalists' accumulation base. The many offshore financial centres studied by Van Fossen now form part of the circuit of capital for individuals and corporations intent on avoiding taxes and often laundering profits. Like the TCC, 'the tax haven is identified with global capitalism, maximizing profit by minimizing loyalty to any specific country and reassigning property claims and income away from their sources'. Sixty per cent of global trade now occurs within TNCs, 'with tax havens as frequent intermediaries – overinvoicing, underinvoicing, collecting royalties, dividends and interest to increase consolidated profits'. And although the 2008 crisis provoked a movement of investments back to home bases, the general trend is for the world's wealthy to hold ever larger proportions of their fortunes outside their own domiciles, typically in tax havens. Indeed, 'capitalist personal wealth has transnationalized far more than corporate elite networks have transnationalized', pointing again to a contrast between the far-reaching global investments of the TCC and the more modest extent to which processes of transnational socio-cultural consolidation and community building have constructed a class–for–itself.[66]

STRATEGIC IMPLICATIONS: CHALLENGING THE TCC

As a prelude to drawing out some strategic implications, let us summarize what recent studies of the TCC tell us. Clearly, the tendency toward TCC formation has occurred amid persistent national business communities. The TCC exists more as a superstructure of social, economic and political relations that bridge across but do not supplant national capitalist classes. Although the financialization of global corporate ownership has produced an unprecedented concentration of capital, there is a continuing disjuncture between class formation as a sociocultural process and the economic process of capital accumulation. The reach of today's TNCs and the increasingly integrated financial markets are global, and transnational capital relations have fostered a new form of finance capital; but the governance of corporations and the life of the *haute bourgeoisie* have remained significantly embedded in national and regional structures and cultures.

Indeed, the regional factor is critical to any discussion of the TCC. The post-Second World War era begat an Atlantic ruling class, under the aegis of American hegemony, and the period since the mid-1970s has seen further elaboration of that formation. Much of the recent transnationalization of corporate-elite relations has accompanied European economic integration. However, the formation of corporate Europe does not break from the territorial logic of states, 'it reproduces it on a larger scale, even as it provides firmer conditions for the international investment flows that ultimately integrate the world economy'.[67] Meanwhile, capitalists from beyond the heartland are arrayed on the margins of the global corporate elite: there is scant participation from the South or, for that matter, from Japan.

A significant source of TCC unity resides in the elaboration of a transnational policy-planning network, extensively interlocked with the boards of the world's largest corporations and reaching across the North Atlantic and indeed, the Triad. Proliferating since the 1970s, transnational policy groups have been agents of business activism, mobilizing corporate capitalists and various strata of intellectuals around visions and policies that enunciate the common interests of Northern-based transnational capital, and which persuade state managers, journalists and others to see those interests as universal in scope.[68] However, although the last 30 years have witnessed an internationalization of states within a neoliberal policy consensus, this does not mean that national states and state-capital nexuses have been seamlessly integrated into a transnational state that serves the interests of the TCC.

Although the confluence of economic, political and cultural power in which the TCC is a leading force may be conceptualized as an historic bloc conducting a war of position within what has been termed global civil society, it is not detached from national states. Nor has it eliminated rivalries based in the objective necessity of capitalist states to influence capital flows to their own territorial advantage; it only mutes and manages them. The state-capital nexus, most evident and powerful in the US, takes in capitalist interests that may be rooted in the national economy but that extend well beyond it, through foreign investments and trade. We can acknowledge, with Robinson and other TCC theorists, that growing interdependencies across states preclude a return to sharp territorial conflicts of the sort that provoked two world wars in the last century. Yet the territorial logic of the state form means that competitive tensions persist. These, along with the continuing rootedness of corporations in national domiciles, limit the extent to which the TCC can become a class-for-itself. Indeed, as crises in the world system deepen, interstate rivalries may intensify, and the putative unity of the TCC may itself be severely tested.

In taking up some of the strategic issues that flow from this analysis, it may be helpful at the outset to replace the antinomic reasoning that has tended to predominate in some TCC analyses – the positing of a fully transnationalized capitalist class that supplants national capitals, and of a transnational state that replaces national states – with more nuanced thinking 'that makes clear the immanence of TCC formation as a tendency without the implication of dominance by this emergent class'.[69] An adequate strategic response to the TCC requires a clear political-economic analysis. The danger in 'maximalist' readings of TCC formation is that a 'structurally deterministic teleology' provides little strategic guidance as to 'what is to be done now, concretely, in the places working people live and do politics'.[70] An abstract analysis that overestimates TCC unity creates a totalizing discourse that can disempower workers and their allies, casting them as victims of a supra-national force rather than as protagonists.[71]

If, as we have seen, the TCC is not a freestanding entity, but is linked to and indeed embedded in national capital circuits and state-capital nexuses, the task for movements opposing capitalist rule is to construct a historic bloc that is nationally rooted, and capable of action in national political fields, yet that also builds agentic capacity transnationally. Indeed, it is prudent to resist the tendency, implicit in some TCC formulations, to see transnational activism as the default mode of challenging TCC power. Given that the transnational is embedded in the national, 'the resources and institutional backing of state power' are crucial to transnational activism; hence a global left must be rooted in strong movements at the national level. As Sam Gindin has put it: 'As we develop the capacity to struggle more effectively within our own countries, the safe and flexible havens available to corporations become more limited and we help to open the space for struggles elsewhere. In this sense, national struggles are internationalized'.[72]

TCC formation does compel the left, more than ever, to develop capacities to act transnationally, but these must gain sustenance from national and local movements. Unsurprisingly, the most effective transnational activist formations in the era of global capitalism, such as Our World Is Not for Sale, La Via Campesina and Friends of the Earth International, display this combination of national and transnational organization. Importantly, such potential exists in the global labour movement, and recent years have seen increased interest by unions in mounting 'comprehensive cross-border campaigns', rooted nationally but coordinated transnationally, against the world's largest transnational firms.[73]

It is by now a commonplace that capitalist globalization makes go-it-alone projects of social transformation ever more dubious. But just as the TCC is a far more regionalized formation than has sometimes been claimed, the formation of a global left will often take a regional shape, with Latin America's 'pink tide' offering the key example to date. Initiatives like the Bolivarian Alliance for the Americas (ALBA) and the Bank of the South build regional capacity for an alternative paradigm of human development and ecological sustainability. Alternative, people-centred regionalisms[74] can also provide focal points for counter-hegemonic struggle in the global North, notably in Europe – where, amidst the crisis of the eurozone, 'a process of construction' may be underway, associating unions, movements, networks of intellectuals and representatives of the Party of the European Left, to 'refound' Europe around an alternative social logic.[75]

Finally, in rising to the challenge posed by the transnational capitalist class, the left needs to think in terms not simply of constructing an opposition but of *disorganizing and disassembling the hegemonic bloc*. Here again, it is helpful to conceptualize the TCC and the larger bloc in which it is a leading force as an assemblage in the process of formation rather than a fait accompli of globalization. If the TCC represents only a tendency, its bloc may be subject to possible defection and deconstruction. Importantly, as Van der Pijl argues, the strata of intellectuals who organize and subtend the institutional practices of contemporary capitalism may in varying degrees be less invested in its survival than the image of a solid, fully-formed historic bloc suggests. A virtue of Van der Pijl's analysis of 'the modern cadre', as a class of 'knowledge workers' who subtend socialization of labour in the broadest sense, lies in the element of contingency that issues from cadres' ambiguous class position. Entrusted by capital with tasks of conception and direction in production, and with normative unification in the wider society, cadre are enmeshed not only within transnational capitalist class networks such as the World Economic Forum but also within the non-governmental organization sector.[76] Evoking the classical contradiction between developing forces of production (socialized labour) and the limited property relations afforded by capitalism, Van der Pijl portrays the transnational cadre as fluid in political perspective, and open to left initiatives:

> The commitment to a private property-owning mode of production, for the cadre is ideological rather than material, and capitalism in crisis erodes this commitment more easily…. As the socialization of labour and the flow economy develop, capital increasingly turns into the private appropriation of the fruits of a vast, collaborative and ultimately global process of socialized labour…. [Hence] the growing cadre stratum

in contemporary capitalist globalization … may become receptive to arguments and forces emerging from the grassroots resistance to capitalist development.[77]

The strategic implication is that the left should not trap itself within reified conceptions of a transnational capitalist historic bloc, nor should it withdraw into a self-defeating 'autistic anarchism'. Instead, the forces of resistance that might be placed under the rubric of a global left 'can realistically aim to force an increasingly adrift middle class of cadre into new arenas of negotiation and democratization'.[78] Indeed, such a stance may be indispensable to a radically transformative politics in this era of global capitalism.

NOTES

1   Karl Marx and Frederick Engels, 'Manifesto of the Communist Party', in K. Marx and F. Engels, *Selected Works*, New York: International Publishers, 1968 [1848], p. 38.

2   Karl Kautsky, 'Ultra-Imperialism', *New Left Review*, 59(January/February), 1970, p. 45.

3   Massimo Salvadori, *Karl Kautsky and the Socialist Revolution*, London: New Left Books, 1979, p. 188, emphasis added.

4   Anthony Brewer, *Marxist Theories of Imperialism*, London: Routledge, 1980, p. 124.

5   Robert Cox sees the internationalizing of the state as arising in 'a process of interstate consensus formation regarding the needs or requirements of the world economy that takes place within a common ideological framework'. It is hierarchically structured and involves the adjustment of national state policy and practice to the global consensus. See his *Production, Power and World Order*, New York: Columbia University Press, 1987, p. 254. For an introduction to more recent work see Markus Wissen and Ulrich Brand, 'Approaching the Internationalization of the State: An Introduction', *Antipode*, 43, 2011. For a critical analysis of global governance see Suzanne Soederberg, *Global Governance in Question*, Winnipeg: Arbeiter Ring Publishing, 2006.

6   Leo Panitch and Sam Gindin, *The Making of Global Capitalism*, London: Verso, 2012.

7   Kari Levitt, *Silent Surrender: The Multinational Corporation in Canada*, Toronto: Macmillan, 1970, pp. 37, 45.

8   Stephen Hymer, 'International Politics and International Economics: A Radical Approach' (mimeographed), 1974, published posthumously in *Monthly Review*, 29(1), 1978.

9   Stephen Hymer, 'The Internationalization of Capital', *Journal of Economic Issues*, 6, 1972, pp. 101, 100.

10   John Scott, *Corporate Business and Capitalist Class*, New York: Oxford University Press, 1997.

11   Jorge Niosi, *The Economy of Canada*, Montreal: Black Rose Books, 1978.

12   O. Jeidels, 'Das Verhältnis der deutschen Grossbanken zur Industrie mit besonder Berücksichtigung der Eisenindustrie' [Relation of German big banks to industry with special reference to the iron industry], *Staats- und sozialwissenschaftliche Forschungen*, 24(2), 1905, pp. 1-271.

13   Meindert Fennema and Huibert Schijf, 'Analysing Interlocking Directorates: Theory and Method', *Social Networks*, 1, 1978, p. 327.

14   G. William Domhoff, ed., *Power Structure Research*, Beverly Hills, CA: Sage, 1980.

15   Michael Useem, 'The Inner Group of the American Capitalist Class', *Social Problems*, 25(3), 1978, pp. 225-40.

16   Gideon Sonquist and Thomas Koenig, 'Interlocking Directorates in the Top U.S. Corporations: A Graph Theory Approach', *Insurgent Sociologist*, 5(3), 1975, pp. 196–229; W.K. Carroll, *Corporate Power in a Globalizing World*, Toronto: Oxford University Press, 2004.

17   Meindert Fennema, *International Networks of Banks and Industry*, The Hague: Martinus Nijhoff Publishers, 1982.

18   Kees van der Pijl, *The Making of an Atlantic Ruling Class*, London: Verso, 1984, p. 1.

19   Kees van der Pijl, 'The International Level', in Tom Bottomore and Robert J. Brym, eds., *The Capitalist Class: An International Study*, New York: New York University Press, 1989, pp. 237-66.

20   Kees van der Pijl, *Imperialism and Class Formation in the North Atlantic Area*, Doctoral Dissertation, University of Amsterdam, 1983, pp. 22, 28.

21   Van der Pijl, *Imperialism*, pp. 14, 20.

22   Van der Pijl, *The Making*, p. xviii.

23   Van der Pijl, 'Neoliberalism vs. Planned Interdependence. Concepts of Control in the Struggle for Hegemony'. paper presented at the conference on Interdependence and Conflict in the International System, Polemologisch Instituut, Groningen, 19-21November 1986, p. 3.

24   Cox, *Production, Power and World Order*, pp. 358, 7.

25   Leslie Sklair, 'Capitalism and Development in Global Perspective', in Leslie Sklair, ed., *Capitalism and Development*, London: Routledge, 1994, pp. 174-5; Leslie Sklair, *Sociology of the Global System*, London: Harvester, 1991.

26   Sklair, 'Capitalism and Development', pp. 176, 177.

27   Leslie Sklair, 'The Transnational Capitalist Class and the Discourse of Globalization', *Cambridge Review of International Affairs*, 14(1), 2000, pp. 67-70. See also Leslie Sklair, *The Transnational Capitalist Class*, Oxford: Blackwell, 2001.

28   Abdul Rahman Embong, 'Globalization and Transnational Class Relations: Some Problems of Conceptualization', *Third World Quarterly*, 21, 2000, pp. 994, 995, 997.

29   William I. Robinson, *A Theory of Global Capitalism*, Baltimore: Johns Hopkins University Press, 2004, p. 47.

30   W.I. Robinson, 'The Pitfalls of Realist Analysis of Global Capitalism: A Critique of Ellen Meiksins Wood's *Empire of Capital*', *Historical Materialism*, 15,

2007, p. 78.

31 Robinson, *A Theory*, p. 75.

32 William I. Robinson and Jerry Harris, 'Towards a Global Ruling Class? Globalization and the Transnational Capitalist Class', *Science & Society*, 64, 2000, pp. 22-3.

33 William I. Robinson, 'Globalisation: Nine Theses on our Epoch', *Race & Class*, 38, 1996, p. 18; Robinson, *A Theory*, p. 50.

34 Walden Bello, 'The Capitalist Conjuncture: Over-accumulation, Financial Crises, and the Retreat from Globalisation', *Third World Quarterly*, 27(8), 2006, pp. 1345–67; Radhika Desai, 'The Last Empire? From Nation-Building Compulsion to Nationwrecking Futility and Beyond', *Third World Quarterly*, 28(2), 2007, pp. 435–56.

35 W.I. Robinson, 'Beyond the Theory of Imperialism: Global Capitalism and the Transnational State', *Societies without Borders*, 2(2), 2007, p. 14; Robinson, 'Global Capitalism and the Emergence of Transnational Elites', *Critical Sociology*, 38, 2012, p. 354.

36 W.K. Carroll, 'Global, Transnational, Regional, National: The Need for Nuance in Theorizing Global Capitalism', *Critical Sociology*, 38, 2012, p. 366.

37 Kees Van der Pijl, 'A Theory of Global Capitalism', *New Political Economy*, 10(2), 2005, pp. 275, 274.

38 Jason W. Moore, 'Capital, Territory, and Hegemony over the Longue Duree'. *Science & Society*, 65, 2002, p. 481.

39 W.I. Robinson, 'Response to McMichael, Block, and Goldfrank', *Theory and Society*, 30, 2001, p. 501.

40 Robinson and Harris, 'Towards a Global Ruling Class?'

41 Robinson, 'The Pitfalls', pp. 83-4.

42 Michael R. Smith, 'Review of *A Theory of Global Capitalism*', *Canadian Journal of Sociology*, 30, 2005, pp. 382-4.

43 Robinson, 'The Pitfalls', p. 89; cf. Robinson, 'Beyond the Theory of Imperialism'.

44 Leo Panitch and Sam Gindin, 'Global Capitalism and American Empire', *Socialist Register 2004*, London: Merlin, 2003, pp. 1-42.

45 Doug Stokes, 'The Heart of Empire? Theorising US Empire in an Era of Transnational Capitalism', *Third World Quarterly*, 26, 2005, p. 228, emphasis added.

46 Bastiaan Van Apeldoorn and Nana de Graaf, 'The Limits of Open Door Imperialism and the State-Capital Nexus'. *Globalizations*, 9, 2012, p. 597.

47 Van Apeldoorn and de Graaf, 'The Limits', pp. 597, 600.

48 Jerry Harris, 'The Conflict for Power in Transnational Class Theory', *Science & Society*, 67, 2003, p. 330.

49 W.K. Carroll and Meindert Fennema, 'Is there a Transnational Business Community?', *International Sociology*, 17, 2002, pp. 393-419; Scott, *Corporate Business*.

50 W.K. Carroll, *The Making of a Transnational Capitalist Class*, London: Zed Books, 2010, pp. 111-15.

51 Case studies of national corporate-elite networks clarify the relationship between

the national and transnational in corporate communities. For instance, research on the transnationalization of large Canada-based companies after the mid-1970s has shown that by the century's end the national corporate-elite network had not decomposed but had been re-centred around a core of transnational banks and corporations, extensively interlocked with sub-transnational enterprises. See Carroll, *Corporate Power*, pp. 81-6. Subsequent study in the early years of the twenty-first century showed both the reproduction of a national corporate network and '*a process of regional elite reproduction in the North Atlantic zone*' (Carroll and Klassen, 2010: 22), as 'Canadian TNCs ... reinforced a national network of corporate power and simultaneously interlocked with foreign-based TNCs both inside and outside of Canada, in the grooves formed by transnational investment'. See, respectively, W.K. Carroll and Jerome Klassen, 'Hollowing out corporate Canada? Changes in the corporate network since the 1990s', *Canadian Journal of Sociology*, 35 2010, p. 22; Jerome Klassen and W.K. Carroll, 'Transnational class Formation? Globalization and the Canadian Corporate Network', *Journal of World-Systems Research*, 17 2011, p. 400. See also Georgina Murray's research on the Australian case, in 'Australia has a Transnational Capitalist Class?' *Perspectives on Global Development and Technology*, 8(2-3) 2009, pp.164-88.

52   Carroll, *The Making*, pp. 116-18. The bar chart categorizes G500 interlockers according to head office locations of the firms they direct. For instance, the 'National, Europe' category includes interlockers whose G500 directorships were all contained within single European countries, whereas the 'TN, N Atlantic' category includes interlockers whose G500 directorships spanned the North Atlantic (that is, at least one directorship in a North American corporation and at least one in a European corporation).

53   See Carroll, *The Making*, pp. 105-7. In this international network, which shows core countries as circles and semi-peripheral countries as squares, the thickness of lines connecting two countries indicates the *number* of interlocking directorates between the G500 firms of one country and the other. Comparing this network to its equivalent in 1996, the number of semi-peripheral states hosting corporations that participate in the global network has increased from one (Kuwait) to seven, but the semi-peripheral states inhabit the network's margins while the main states of Europe and North America make up its core.

54   Carroll, *The Making*, pp. 128, 242. The absence of an East Asian component in the transnational corporate-elite network, despite considerable regional economic integration via investment and trade relations, underlines the extent to which it remains a Euro-North American configuration. Most of the research literature on East Asian business organization has been conducted from within a comparative, 'varieties of capitalism' perspective, which emphasizes national specificities in business systems. See for instance Andrew Walter and Xiaoke Zhang, eds., *East Asian Capitalism: Diversity, Continuity and Change*, Oxford: Oxford University Press, 2012, which contrasts Japan's 'networked capitalist system' with more family-controlled systems in Indonesia, Taiwan, the Philippines and Malaysia, and both of these with the statist form that continues to structure capitalism in China, despite the resurgence of a Chinese

bourgeoisie.

55   Carroll, *The Making*, p. 228.

56   Carroll, *The Making*, p. 233.

57   Val Burris and Clifford L. Staples, 'In Search of a Transnational Capitalist Class: Alternative Methods for Comparing Director Interlocks Within and Between Nations and Regions', *International Journal of Comparative Sociology*, 53, 2012, p. 336.

58   Burris and Staples, 'In Search', p. 339.

59   Meindert Fennema and Huibert Schijf, 'The Transnational Network', in F.N. Stokman, R. Ziegler and J. Scott, eds., *Networks of Corporate Power: A Comparative Analysis of Ten Countries*, Cambridge: Polity Press, 1985, pp. 250-66.

60   W.K. Carroll, 'Capital Relations and Directorate Interlocking: The Global Network in 2007', in G. Murray and J. Scott, eds., *Financial Elites and Transnational Business: Who Rules the World?*, Northampton, MA: Elgar, 2012, pp. 54-75.

61   G.F. Davis, 'A New Finance Capitalism? Mutual Funds and Ownership Re-concentration in the United States', *European Management Review*, 5, 2008, p. 20.

62   See W.K. Carroll, 'The Corporate Elite and the Transformation of Finance Capital: A View from Canada', *Sociological Review*, 56(S1), 2008, p. 59; Martin Beckmann, 'Institutional Investors and the Transformation of the European Economy', presented at *Finance, Industry and Power: The Capitalist Corporation in the twenty-first century*, Toronto: Department of Political Science, York University, April 2006.

63   Carroll, 'Capital Relations', p. 70.

64   J.B. Glattfelder and S. Battiston, 'Backbone of Complex Networks of Corporations: The Flow of Control', *Physical Review E*, 80, 2009, p. 7, available at http //www.realtid.se.

65   Georgina Murray and David Peetz, 'The Financialization of Global Corporate Ownership', in Murray and Scott, eds., *Financial Elites and Transnational Business*, p. 50.

66   Anthony Van Fossen, 'The Transnational Capitalist Class and Tax Havens', in Murray and Scott, eds., *Financial Elites and Transnational Business*, pp. 88, 89, 84.

67   Carroll, *The Making*, p. 232.

68   One can, and should, take note of other transnational practices which contribute to TCC formation, including philanthropic engagements, fueled by the burgeoning incomes of the world's super-wealthy, which increasingly substitute for the diminishing flow of foreign aid from North to South. Recent research shows that assets of the world's 78,000 ultra-high net worth individuals (each with financial assets exceeding $30 million) total fifteen trillion dollars – equivalent to more than a quarter of World Gross Domestic Product ($58 trillion in 2009). In addition to tax havens, philanthropy offers a significant tax shelter to the very wealthy and enables them to direct funds toward causes they deem worthy, in lieu of democratic decision-making (Hay and Muller

2012: 76, 82). The prominent media profile of Bill Gates and other top philanthropists burnish the prestige of transnational capitalists, and reinforce the hegemonic notion that the world's problems are technical matters that can be addressed through charity. However, the idea that the transnational super-rich are 'deterritorialized' by virtue of their extreme global mobility is probably an exaggeration. Rather, the dominant tendency is toward 'super-gentrification' in elite enclaves where plutocrats can enjoy wealth that issues from many places without the disruption of ordinary city-dwellers. See Iain Hay and Samantha Muller, '"That Tiny, Stratospheric Apex that Owns Most of the World" – Exploring Geographies of the Super-rich', *Geographical Research*, 50(1), 2012, pp. 76,82, 79.

69 William Tabb, 'Globalization Today: At the Borders of Class and State Theory', *Science & Society*, 73, 2009, p. 48.

70 Tabb, 'Globalization Today', p. 51.

71 See the provocative analysis in J.K. Gibson-Graham, *The End of Capitalism (as we knew it)*, second edition, Minneapolis: University of Minnesota Press, 2006.

72 Sam Gindin, 'The Fight Against Globalization Must Begin at Home', *Canadian Dimension*, (November/December), 2004, available at http://canadiandimension.com.

73 See Kate Bronfenbrenner, ed., *Global Unions*, Ithaca: Cornell University Press, 2007, p. 1. The International Trade Union Confederation has shown signs of trading its longstanding 'diplomatic' function within the machinery of international institutions (see Richard Hyman, 'Shifting Dynamics in International Trade Unionism: Agitation, Organisation, Bureaucracy, Diplomacy', *Labour History*, 46(2), 2005, pp. 135-54) for political ventures that challenge transnational capitalist dominance, such as the Decent Work, Decent Life Initiative and the Labour and Globalisation Network, both launched at the 2007 World Social Forum (Andreas Bieler, '"Workers of the World Unite"? Globalisation and the Quest for Transnational Solidarity', *Globalizations*, 9(3), 2012, pp. 365-78).

74 For extensive discussion of alternative regionalisms see the project initiated by the Transnational Institute, available at http://www.tni.org.

75 Elisabeth Gauthier, 'Europe: Existential Danger: New Political Challenges'. *The Bullet*, 769, 4 February 2013, available at http://www.socialistproject.ca.

76 Kees van der Pijl, 'Two Faces of the Transnational Cadre under Neo-liberalism', *Journal of International Relations and Development*, 7, 2004, pp. 199-200.

77 Van der Pijl, 'Two Faces', pp. 201-2.

78 Van der Pijl, 'Two Faces', p. 202.

THE EUROPEAN CAPITALIST CLASS AND THE CRISIS OF ITS HEGEMONIC PROJECT

BASTIAAN VAN APELDOORN

More than any other area in the world Europe has over the past three decades witnessed a process of transnational capitalist class formation, representing the most transnationally oriented sections of European capital and overlaying national capitalist classes. Transnationalization here does not imply the withering away of national states and national social formations but rather the rise of relations across national borders and the constitution of actors that operate not 'above' the national state, but in different national contexts simultaneously.[1] It is from this perspective that we can understand how transnational class agency has helped to transform the project of European integration into an ever more undiluted neoliberal project. The essence of this hegemonic class project has been the creation of a transnational space for capital in which the latter's rule is established precisely by preserving the formal sovereignty of the member states while subordinating their democratic governance to the dictates of the single market. The inherent contradictions of this project have been exposed and exacerbated by the current Eurozone crisis, which is endangering more than the single currency but threatens to derail the neoliberal project that has been spearheaded by the European capitalist class over the past three decades. While its steadfast adherence to the current austerity drive may be seen as shortsighted, there are no attractive alternatives for the European capitalist class.

THE MAKING OF THE EUROPEAN CAPITALIST CLASS

Transnational class formation is a historically contingent and geographically uneven phenomenon the contours and extent of which can only be examined empirically. Rather than simply positing the existence of a homogenous and *global* transnational capitalist class (TCC), we need to investigate to what extent processes of transnational class formation actually crystallize in the construction of class-conscious collective social and political actors. From this empirical perspective the notion of a single global TCC becomes hard to sustain.[2] The process of transnational class formation has reached a much deeper level, however, within Western Europe, engendering a transnational capitalist class – consisting of those who own and control Europe's largest transnational corporations (TNCs) – that takes the European region as its primary frame of reference and organizes itself to influence the (socio-economic) governance of that region, in particular through the institutions of the European Union (EU).[3]

The origins of this class can be traced back to the previous world economic crisis of the 1970s and early 1980s, and further back to the early stages of the European integration process that had started under the aegis of American hegemony in the 1950s. This laid the basis for a subsequent transnationalization of European capital. Until the 1980s European integration had remained largely limited to the trade in goods, and even there, liberalization had been largely restricted to the removal of tariffs, preventing a deeper economic integration. In the wake of the 1970s economic crisis and intensifying global competition, sections of European capital, hoping to use the European market as a launching pad to the world market, began to champion precisely such a deeper integration. This is what came to be dubbed 'the completion of the internal market', centred around the four freedoms of goods, capital, services and people.

Corporations clustered around the car and electronics sectors took the lead in this, as they confronted the limits of the Fordist growth model and of a European integration process restricted to trade. To reach their potential as MNCs, they came to see that a new political project was required that would transform European statehood in order to create a single European market through which they could realize such economies of scale as would allow them to compete more successfully with American and Japanese multinationals.

It was in fact with this purpose in mind that the European Round Table (ERT) of Industrialists was organized in 1983. It has since that time come to function as the premier policy-planning body of the European transnational capitalist class. The ERT consists today of some 45 CEOs and chairmen of the boards of Europe's largest MNCs from across all major industrial sectors (though still concentrated in the old core of the original six plus the UK, Switzerland and Scandinavia).[4] It is important to stress that the members of the ERT lead Europe's most *transnationally* oriented corporations and that these have become more transnational over time, having both Europeanized but also increasingly globalized their production.[5] Moreover, notwithstanding its name, the ERT must not be seen as a mere club of industrialists by virtue of their many interlocks with banks and other financial firms. The ERT thus must be seen as broadly representing European transnational capital, and its role in this respect has been increasingly sustained by networks of interlocking corporate directorships which, as recent research has shown, has increased among Europe's leading corporations even as national and global networks have thinned.[6]

Even if still to some extent embedded within national capitalist classes as well (which certainly can be identified in the bigger member states) ERT members arguably have more in common (in terms of interests and outlook) with each other than with their fellow capitalists at home that are not the apex of European transnational capital. As such, the ERT must not be viewed as a body that coordinates the views and interests of national capitalist classes, or affirms a pre-existing cross-national consensus and relays it to the institutions of the EU. Rather, the ERT has played a key role in mobilizing European corporate capital politically in order to construct a common strategy. And it has often played an agenda-setting role for the institutions of the EU, as well as generally contributed to developing the key ideas behind European integration (such as regarding the internal market), and inserting them into the EU's policy discourse.[7]

Although Brussels is awash with all kinds of business groups and lobbies, the ERT can be seen as a privileged institutional node in the organization of Europe's corporate elite. It is, in fact, in the vanguard of the European capitalist class, providing it with internal cohesion, arbitrating rival outlooks and welding them into a coherent project and long-term strategy to advance the general interests of European transnational capital. In pursuing this strategy within the European polity, the activities of the ERT transcend both lobbying and corporatist interest intermediation, which is more the role of BusinessEurope, the formal association of national business and employers' associations. Indeed, the ERT has an unmatched degree of political access to EU institutions – especially the Commission – as well as national governments. As the prominent former European Commissioner Peter Sutherland (who was an ERT member as chair of British Petroleum) explained:

I think that the importance of the ERT is not merely in the fact that it co-ordinates and creates a cohesive approach amongst major industries in Europe but because the persons who are member of it have to be at the highest level of companies and virtually all of them have unimpeded access to government leaders because of the position of their companies … That is exactly what makes it different [from other organizations]. The fact that it is at head of company level, and only the biggest companies in each country of the European Union are members of it. So, by definition each member of the ERT has access at the highest level to government.[8]

THE MAKING OF NEOLIBERAL EUROPE

While the internal market was initially conceived to shield European industry within its new home market against global competition, the subsequent globalization of European industrial capital shifted ERT's strategic orientation to a neoliberalism that embraced the breakdown of barriers to trade and investment at both the European and the global level. This involved not only the successful incorporation and neutralization of the (former) Euro-protectionists, but also the defeat of a pan-European social democratic project that, while accepting much of the internal market discourse, also sought a more explicit 'embeddedness'. The defeat of this notion was indicative of a persistent weakness, in particular, of transnationally organized labour within the EU.

Beginning with the 'Europe 1992' programme (for which the ERT played a key role in setting the agenda), the content of European governance in the 1990s became increasingly neoliberal, establishing the primacy of supranational marketization. The Economic and Monetary Union (EMU), agreed to as part of the 1992 Maastricht Treaty, was conceived as both completing the internal market by eliminating the currency risk and as a cornerstone of European financial market integration. As the ERT put it at the time, what was required to meet its members' need for 'huge capital resources' to realize its globalizing strategies was 'open access on competitive terms to the capital Europe can generate'.[9] The convergence criteria in the years leading up to the introduction of the single currency, and the Stability and Growth Pact (SGP) in the years since, were designed as instruments of neoliberal discipline, putting pressures on European welfare states and making the labour market the primary macro-economic adjustment mechanism.[10]

It was also with these purposes in mind that the project of monetary union was actively promoted from 1987 onwards (that is before it was on the intergovernmental agenda) by many Roundtable industrialists organized in the Association for Monetary Union of Europe.[11] The ERT itself, in the months before Maastricht, called for a 'single currency before the end of the decade', presenting it as essential for the creation of a 'single financial market' without which the benefits of the internal market could not be fully realized, and formulating as an absolute precondition governments' acceptance of 'binding disciplines' (sic) and a 'total ban on the monetary financing of budget deficits'.[12]

In so far as organized labour still needed to be kept on board, lip-service was paid by tying the notion of a 'European social model' to 'competitiveness and social cohesion', which indeed became the slogan of the Lisbon strategy launched in 2000.[13] In fact, this was the framework for reorienting labour market and employment policies towards supply-side flexibilization strategies in order to enhance 'national competitiveness'. The ERT was instrumental in the 'push for the implementation of the Lisbon "reforms"'.[14] The national reform programmes required of Member States in the Lisbon 'benchmarking' and surveillance process have been entirely in line with the neoliberal competitiveness discourse promoted throughout the 1990s by the transnational capitalists of the ERT, including the emphasis on labour market deregulation, welfare state retrenchment and reorientation of training and education to the exigencies of Europe's TNCs.

As part and parcel of the Lisbon strategy, the financialization of European capitalism – and of the European capitalist class – also accelerated in the 2000s. The concrete formulation of a more comprehensive class strategy was mainly left to the representatives of 'industrial' capital in the ERT even as the European financial sector also came to organize itself more directly at the EU level in order to shape European governance in the relevant policy realms. When the ERT's founding chairman, Pehr Gyllenhammar, oversaw the founding of European Financial Services Round Table (EFR), in 2001, this did not imply a marginalization of the ERT, which continues to be the primary body articulating and propagating the general interests of the European transnational capitalist class. As Carroll et al argue, while 'the ERT ... has defined and pursued a hegemonic project for European corporate capital; in comparison, the EFR represents little more than a sectional interest in improving conditions for the circulation of money capital in and beyond the EU'.[15]

Although there is a potential divergence of ideological outlook and interests between 'industrial capital' and 'financial capital', which might become manifest under particular conditions, it must be emphasized how much the perspectives of these 'fractions' have really fused. Industrial capital has come to adopt in many respects a 'money capital' perspective, even if there are still elements in its outlook that are specific to the needs of production.[16] European industrial capitalists have increasingly come to adopt the 'financial' shareholder value discourse (with top management also materially bound to it through stock options, etc.), while access to deep global financial markets has increasingly become essential to the globalizing strategies of industrial TNCs (funding global expansion through acquisitions; insuring currency and other risks through derivatives; facilitating tax evasion or other profit-optimalization tactics).[17] Moreover, the discipline inherent in financialization for workers and governments alike has proved very appealing to industrial capital.

THE MAKING OF THE EUROPEAN CRISIS

As the project of market liberalization and its attendant (re-)commodification of social relations advanced, its contradictions became more manifest. Indeed, although Lisbon and its hegemonic formula of competitiveness with social cohesion, as we have seen, initially had succeeded in bringing together both European transnational capital and organized labour, it was never a real class compromise. As an elite hegemonic project, Lisbon came to unravel inasmuch as it became clear that the European ruling class was not willing to make any substantive concessions to European working classes, exposing the increasingly hollow talk about the European social model. And even if mere ideological interpellation could work for a while, given the political weakness of European labour, the hegemony of neoliberalism was severely challenged when it proved incapable of generating sufficient growth to maintain the prospect of social and economic advancement for European workers. Throughout the 1990s unemployment had remained persistently high, and the recession that hit most of the EU in the early 2000s further deteriorated economic prospects for the working classes. In this context, the European trade union movement became increasingly disillusioned about Lisbon and European socio-economic governance more broadly. Thus, already by the mid-2000s the European labour movement as a whole grew increasingly critical of Lisbon and of the whole of neoliberal European governance.[18]

Growing disillusionment with neoliberal Europe on the part of labour reflected broader alienation from European institutions and policies. Even if the transnational mobilisation of labour remained relatively underdeveloped and uneven, class conflict across Europe did intensify. Popular rejection of neoliberal European integration reached a highpoint in 2005 with a majority voting 'no' in France and the Netherlands in the referenda on the proposed European Constitution.[19] As I have argued elsewhere, this was part and parcel of a more general Euro-scepticism that was indicative of an unfolding multi-legitimacy crisis growing out of the contradictions and limits of neoliberal European governance and calling into question the integration process as a project driven by and serving the interests of a European transnational capitalist class.[20]

These developments did lead to a growing anxiety within the ranks of the European ruling elite, raising worries that the pace of the 'necessary reforms' (i.e. of neoliberalization) might be slowed down or even derailed altogether. Yet rather than leading to any policy change it only led to a minor discursive shift, if not to say a public relations offensive, in order to try to better sell the same message.[21] This became clear in 2010 when the new 'Europe 2020' strategy was launched as a successor to the Lisbon strategy. The new narrative of 'a new sustainable social market economy' and 'a smarter, greener economy' repackaged the old message about the necessity of labour market flexiblization and the 'modernisation of social protection' in the context of advancing the institutional upgrades needed to heighten surveillance of the implementation of neoliberal reforms. From 2011 onwards the Europe 2020 strategy was integrated into the new *European Semester*, referring to the period in which member state governments have to report to the Commission and the Council on their progress with regard to 'structural reforms' as well as 'budgetary discipline'.[22]

Notably, this new neoliberal reform agenda laid out by the Commission followed very closely that of a key report published by the ERT just a month *before* the Commission document came out.[23] The ERT's 'vision for a competitive Europe' contained much of the same wording that ended up in the Commission document, including the emphasis on 'sustainability' to restore hegemonic appeal after Lisbon's erosion of legitimacy. Importantly, the ERT clarified that sustainability should be viewed as a 'multi-faceted concept', applying to public finances, pensions, health care and social security in order to 'reinforce competitiveness', while still insisting on the deepening and broadening of the single market and yet more labour market flexibility based upon 'a new understanding of job security'. Europe 2020 was presented as Europe's 'exit strategy' out of the financial and economic crisis that had started in 2007 (though strikingly lacking any analysis whatsoever of its causes).[24] This was foreboding for how Europe's political elite would respond to the euro crisis, which hit in 2010, just months after Europe 2020 was launched.

While the European sovereign debt crisis must be seen as part and parcel of the global crisis unfolding from 2007 onwards, it was mediated and refracted by the particular institutional architecture of neoliberal monetary union and by the imbalances within the Eurozone caused by monetary union itself in conjunction with a particular accumulation strategy enabled by the financialization of European capitalism and pursued by transnational capital in the European core.[25] Moreover, the vulnerability of the southern periphery must be seen as the result of an uneven development that the neoliberal European integration process (not just monetary union) has been deepening rather than seeking to correct. The creation of even more open space for transnational capital (and the further commodification of labour masquerading as social policy, combined with the most minimalistic interstate and interregional redistributive mechanisms) might be seen as a huge success from the perspective of the elites of the European core and above all from the perspective of the European capitalist class that has played such a pivotal role in its making. Now, however, its inner contradictions have been brought fully into the open by the current crisis.

This was a strategy that combined an aggressive neoliberalism with what some have identified as a new mercantilism vis-à-vis the periphery – based on a consistent policy of wage repression in the northern core. Even if led by the German capitalist class, it must be emphasized that as an *accumulation strategy* this has been much more widely followed by capital, not only across the northern part of the Eurozone but to a significant extent as well by transnationally oriented capital from the South.[26] Although a beggar-thy-neighbour strategy from the perspective of national economies and national labour, it worked for transnational capital inasmuch as workers in different member states were played off against each other, with the resulting overall suppression of wage levels leading to higher corporate profits.

The dominant perception – emanating from Europe's political elite but successfully spread via an uncritical media – amongst large sections of the population in the creditor countries remains that the crisis is borne out of a lack of fiscal discipline on the part of profligate peripheral Eurozone countries. It is on this myth of fiscal indiscipline that the European crisis management, led by the Merkel government and ostensibly aimed at 'saving the euro', has been premised. And it has resulted in a draconian and long-term austerity policy whereby the affected countries have only one choice, either accepting the neoliberal diktat of the Troika, or default and exit. The latter would allow them to maintain some democratic sovereignty but also involve huge economic and political risks.[27]

Costas Lapavitsas has argued that from the perspective of Germany and 'its' capitalists class, the current 'rescue strategy' followed by the European Council in seeking to 'save the euro' is rational inasmuch as the 'German ruling class' seeks to preserve the single currency which has accorded it such great financial and trade benefits while not wanting to foot the bill for it.[28] Moreover, arguably the *überausterity* imposed as a condition to any bail-outs ostensibly serves the purpose of protecting the value of the euro (as a world currency). But notwithstanding the geopolitical and geo-economic weight of Germany within the current EU, it would be a mistake to view the management of the euro crisis and the apparent efforts to save the single currency purely in national, and intergovernmental, terms and as such primarily a *German* strategy. This would miss the important transnational dimension, that is to say it would fail to understand how not only EMU and the broader neoliberal project in which it is embedded has been the outcome of struggles between transnational social forces and shaped by the agency of a transnational capitalist class, but how in responding to the crisis governmental leaders, including Chancellor Merkel, are pursuing policies cast in the same neoliberal mould, and as such are closely following the recommendations that representatives of the European capitalist class have for so long been advocating, and still are today.

More generally, then, for not only German capital but also for transnational European capital as a whole – which still has its geographical stronghold in the core countries of the Eurozone – the following logic applies. On the one hand, transnational capital is fully committed to the single currency, a project it promoted in the first place. On the other hand, saving the monetary union by breaking with the logic of neoliberal European governance would defeat the purpose. Therefore, it is important to stay the course and maintain neoliberal discipline of European welfare states and of European labour – which increasingly has, as we have seen, come to 'carry the burden' of 'adjustment' with the loss of other (macroeconomic) policy instruments. In fact, the crisis is perceived by the European ruling class and much of its political elite as an opportunity to accelerate so-called structural reforms and thus deepen neoliberal discipline. Here the 'fiscal myth' serves as a stick to beat the welfare state with and to entrench and deepen the so-called reforms, that is, the neoliberal restructuring which the EU institutions, implementing an agenda set by Europe's capitalist class elite, have been pursuing since the early 1990s.

This logic is also reflected in how the European capitalist class, led by the ERT, has thus far responded to the crisis and in the solutions it has offered. It has called for restoring 'Euro area credibility' and to 'reinforce EMU' in line with the current orthodoxy, and consistent with their own message over the years, only immediately adding that this means creating a 'blueprint for a return to fiscal sustainability' and implementing 'structural reforms'.[29] In fact, both the ERT and BusinessEurope have not only expressed their support for the conditionality attached to the so-called rescue packages for countries such as Ireland, Greece and Portugal, but have also been staunch advocates for institutionalizing this kind of discipline for the whole Eurozone, including the so-called Euro Plus Pact and the intergovernmental Fiscal Compact designed to make the current austerity regime permanent and legally binding.[30]

In line with this, the European capitalist class also fully supports the process being led by Council president Van Rompuy under the heading of 'towards a genuine economic and monetary union'.[31] Although presented as mending the defects in the institutional design of the original EMU and thus to put the euro on a more secure footing, the proposals represent above all an attempt to further institutionalize – most notably through a new instrument of 'economic contracts' to be concluded with member states – the neoliberal agenda of 'structural reforms'. This will amount to the further retrenchment of European welfare states, the erosion of workers' rights and overall the deepening of liberalization and commodification under the flag of competitiveness. While there is much talk about fiscal union, a true fiscal federalism – that could redistribute resources between core and periphery in case of asymmetric shocks – is of course out of the question.

Not only do the representatives of the European capitalist class support these measures and initiatives, it has been the transnational class strategy as pursued by actors like the ERT for many years that has created the political and ideological conditions of their emergence. That in spite of the crisis, and in spite of the erosion of legitimacy of the neoliberal European project that was going on for some years, the attempts to solve the crisis still follow the neoliberal script should not surprise us to the extent that the script for this was written by the organic intellectuals of the European capitalist class, within the ERT as well as other organizations (going back to the origins of EMU itself).

Although we may understand the rationality of all of this from the perspective of the ruling class, this does not mean that there is any guarantee that this strategy will secure the long-term interests of this class. On the contrary, insofar as the current crisis management is based on a misdiagnosis (whatever useful purposes that misdiagnosis may also serve) of the causes of the crisis – i.e. as a problem of fiscal policy – and as there is no strategy to address any of the structural imbalances underlying the centrifugal forces currently threatening the Eurozone, it is very questionable whether this high risk gamble can be pulled off.[32] In Greece, and increasingly in Spain and Italy as well, the austerity is self-defeating inasmuch as the subsequent shrinking of the economy makes the targets of debt reduction relative to GDP ever more elusive (leading to calls for even more spending cuts, etc.). As *Financial Times* commentator Wolfgang Münchau insists: 'We have reached a point where the policies adopted to resolve the Eurozone debt crisis are causing more damage than whatever may have caused the problems in the first place'. [33]

THE UNMAKING OF THE EUROPEAN CAPITALIST CLASS?

Despite the depth of the crisis, and the fact that is still far from resolved, as the periphery is kept in depression and the core is stuck either in low growth or even has slid back into recession, the neoliberal power bloc within the European arena – which includes both financial capital and 'industrial' TNCs oriented to the world market – still seems to be in place. However, its rule appears to be far from hegemonic. It is striking, for instance, how the ETUC – the official voice of labour within the EU (and which always has, in a corporatist fashion, been quite pro-European and implicitly accepting of much of the European project's market-liberal content) – has been from the start much more critical of Europe 2020 than it was for many years of the earlier Lisbon agenda.[34] More worrying from the perspective of Europe's elites are the ongoing protests against austerity in Greece, in Spain and increasingly elsewhere, the declining support for the EU and the euro and generally the growing (often nationalist and xenophobic) resentments among the populations of both the North and the South.[35] In an increasingly Eurosceptic Eurozone there seems to be little popular appetite for any further integrative moves of whatever kind. As a result, neoliberal hegemony is increasingly giving way to a new authoritarian neoliberalism in which democracy is hollowed out. Yet the time that such public discontent could simply be ignored appears to be over.

Maybe then, what we are witnessing today, rather than a successful deepening of neoliberal governance – completing the class project launched from within Europe's transnational corporate capitalist class around two decades ago – is a *fuite-en-avant* that will prove to be a cul-de-sac. In this context, the unity of the European transnational capitalist class may yet come under pressure. Here it must be underlined that such a unity can never be taken as given but has to be carefully constructed and maintained through capitalist class agency. Even though transnational capitalists have more in common with each other than with their more domestically oriented compatriots, they do not form a fully homogenous group either; the capitalist class generally remains potentially divided along structural lines, and these may be the fault lines that give way under pressure.[36]

In the current conjuncture the European transnational capitalist class is confronted with several dilemmas, which will have to be resolved if the European capitalist class is to successfully confront not only the ongoing Eurozone crisis but indeed the more existential crisis threatening the European project from which European transnational capital has benefited so much. This is not to suggest that the European capitalist class as such has the capacity to in and of itself solve this multi-faceted crisis. Any successful reconstitution and deepening of the neoliberal European project will have to take place through Europe's multi-level state formation, which includes both national states and quasi-state supranational institutions.

A first set of dilemmas stems from the fact that the neoliberal finance-led accumulation strategy has run aground, which confronts the European capitalist class ultimately with a looming problem of effective demand. Although the instability that financialization has now so evidently led to must surely be worrisome for all capitalists but in particular those who are more directly involved in accumulation through production, it has not yet led to a split (as one might have expected) between the 'industrial' and 'financial' fractions within the European capitalist class. This is partly due to the structural reasons mentioned above that make the lines between these two fractions increasingly blurred. Although the ongoing banking crisis in Europe hampers especially the financing capacities of the small and medium sized firms, large TNCs have suffered much less from any credit squeeze and are still able to access large pools of finance at low costs.[37] This is not to say, however, that there are no meaningful difference left between for instance a carmaker and a bank, and that these differences may yet lead to new divisions within transnational capital – especially if either a successful restoration of the neoliberal accumulation regime or its replacement by an effective alternative will remain elusive for a long time.

The fact that industrial capital is more immediately dependent than finance on sufficient aggregate demand for their products makes them sensitive to the flipside of austerity, which tends to lower (social) wages to the benefit of corporate profits but in a way that may come to block a return to successful capital accumulation. Although this of course explains the persistently low or negative economic growth in much of the Eurozone, European transnational corporations (inside and outside the ERT) thus far seem to have suffered much less than the economy as a whole from the depressed demand as in many cases this has been compensated for by rising demand from so-called emerging markets, China in particular. More generally, it may be said that for transnational industrial capital neoliberal accumulation has in part been premised on both increasing exports (towards the periphery of the Eurozone and increasingly outside it since the euro crisis has reduced imports from the South) as well as on outsourcing of production on a global scale. Although such a strategy implies lower growth levels at the national level (keeping wages, and hence domestic demand low to enhance international competitiveness) it has allowed for steady profits for TNCs, also in the years since the crisis.[38] Unilever, for instance, last year reported growing revenues despite weak Eurozone demand as it now makes more than 50 per cent of its sales in emerging markets.[39] Repressing wage growth at home while continue to expand in non-European markets may thus still be a rational corporate growth strategy for many of these firms. Yet, it is also a fragile one given its dependence on a continuing rising demand from other (extra-European) markets which is indeed far from assured – especially inasmuch as these markets need to compensate for falling demand from within the Eurozone's periphery.

There are, moreover, increasing signs that the protracted crisis in Europe is taking its toll on the profit outlook of even the most transnationalized and globally operating corporations. Furthermore, growth prospects are uneven. Thus the aforementioned sales and profits growth of Anglo–Dutch Unilever goes against the trend for the European consumer goods sector as a whole.[40] And while BMW from Germany is continuing to show vigorous growth, the European car sector as a whole (and above all in Italy and France) is suffering from a serious overaccumulation crisis.[41] While it is true that transnational capital as a whole has profited from wage repression and austerity, it is also true that in the current crisis not only is the German economy doing much better than most others but also its large corporations tend to outperform TNCs headquartered in other member states, even if at the same time business confidence recently has been sagging further in Germany too. [42] In sum, the demand loss due to the crisis is starting to reduce or threaten to reduce corporate profits across the board (including among German TNCs), even if the impact remains uneven. If this situation persists, the first cracks in the united transnational capitalist front in favour of Brussels-imposed austerity just might begin to appear.

There is a growing conviction among mainstream economists that any sustained recovery will be impossible without a Keynesian stimulus. But for reasons that long ago were compellingly explained by Michael Kalecki, the class instincts of most capitalists tend to set them against Keynesianism.[43] Therefore a Keynesian solution – which of course will of necessity be temporary and not resolve any of the deeper contradictions of global capitalism (even if welcome from the perspective of many Europeans workers, both employed and especially unemployed) – will only be viable politically if there is sufficient mobilisation from below. The problem here of course is the already noted structural weakness of (organized) labour, especially at the transnational level.

The deeper, underlying dilemma, however, is that the European capitalist class has much of its fate bound up with the European integration project. To avoid the collapse of that project – that is, not just of the euro but of the whole integration project – Europe's deeply running legitimacy crisis will have to be solved. But that may only be possible if Europe comes to serve a different social purpose than maximizing the freedom of capital – with or without a single currency. This would, of course, threaten to defeat the purpose from the perspective of Europe's capitalist class. As such what we are witnessing instead, in the well-worn Gramscian phrase, is the appearance of a 'great variety of morbid symptoms' – from Islamophobia shifting into EUphobia, as an increasingly authoritarian austerity politics appeals to popular notions about the virtues of thrift and discipline. Such discipline, however, may yet turn out to be counterproductive even from the perspective of the European capitalist class itself. Even if corporate profit levels are maintained, the social costs of permanent austerity in the context of a prolonged recession without any prospects for a real recovery are setting loose centrifugal forces that may ultimately lead to the unmaking of the European project, or at least in its neoliberal form. This would not necessarily (or even be likely to) spell the end of capitalist class rule in Europe, but it might promote a return to the *primacy* of national capitalist class strategies, which would threaten to severely undermine the cohesiveness of the European transnational capitalist class and cause long-term damage to its capacity to effectively shape the socio-economic content of European governance.

NOTES

1   See B. van Apeldoorn, 'Theorizing the Transnational: A Historical Materialist Approach', *Journal of International Relations and Development*, 7(2), 2004.

2   For this notion see W. Robinson, *A Theory of Global Capitalism: Production, Class, and State in a Transnational World*, Baltimore and London: The John Hopkins University Press, 2004. Offering a far more nuanced view, empirical evidence on interlocking directorates presented by Carroll shows that while at the global level we do find emerging transnational class networks, these are superimposed on persisting national layers within which networks are generally still a lot denser; see W. K. Carroll, *The Making of a Transnational Capitalist Class: Corporate Power in the 21st Century*, London: Zed Books, 2010; also W.K. Carroll, 'Whither the Transnational Capitalist Class?', in this volume. See also Kees van der Pijl, *Transnational Classes and International Relations*, London and New York: Routledge, 1998.

3   See B. van Apeldoorn, *Transnational Capitalism and the Struggle over European Integration*, London and New York: Routledge, 2002. Inasmuch as (transnational) class formation can be read off patterns of interlocking directorates, research also confirms that capitalist class integration is much more advanced within Europe than elsewhere: '*corporate Europe forms the most integrated segment of the global corporate network*', in fact accounting for over half of all worldwide interlocks among the Global 500. See W.K. Carroll, M. Fennema, E.M. Heemskerk, 'Constituting Corporate Europe: A Study of Elite

Social Organization', *Antipode*, 42(4), 2010, p. 833 (their emphasis).

4   The membership of the ERT has always been dominated by transnational capitalists from the northwestern core of the EU (including France and some Italian companies, located in Northern Italy) with only a few 'token' members from the periphery (see van Apeldoorn, *Transnational Capitalism*, p. 94). While in the current membership roster the representation of Spanish transnational capital is numerically quite large with four, from Greece, Portugal and Ireland there is only one member each while from Central and Eastern Europe there are only two members (with the Germans forming the largest national grouping of seven), see the list available at http://www.ert.eu. This geographical unevenness, heavily biased towards the northwestern core of European capital accumulation, is also reflected in patterns of transnational corporate interlocks. See Carroll et al, 'Constituting Corporate Europe', pp. 820–23.

5   Van Apeldoorn, *Transnational Capitalism*, pp. 136–41.

6   Van Apeldoorn, *Transnational Capitalism*, p. 100. This is affirmed even more strongly by Carroll et al, 'Constituting Corporate Europe', p. 832, who argue that 'it is industrialists with financial connections that form the core of the European corporate community'.

7   See for example van Apeldoorn, *Transnational Capitalism*; and B. van Apeldoorn and S.B. Hager, 'The Social Purpose of New Governance: Lisbon and the Limits of Legitimacy', *Journal of International Relations and Development*, 13(3), 2010.

8   Telephone interview by author, 27 January 1998. For more on the nature of the ERT as a forum of and platform for Europe's transnational capitalist class and its close partnership with the EU's institutions, in particular the Commission, see van Apeldoorn, *Transnational Capitalism*.

9   ERT, *Reshaping Europe*, Brussels: European Round Table of Industrialists, 1991, p. 47.

10   On EMU and welfare states (before the crisis!) see e.g. A. W. Cafruny and M. Ryner, *Europe at Bay: In the Shadow of US Hegemony*, Boulder, CO.: Lynne Rienner, 2007.

11   Van Apeldoorn, *Transnational Capitalism*, pp. 155–6.

12   ERT, *Reshaping Europe*, pp. 41, 47.

13   European Council, *Presidency Conclusions Lisbon European Council, Lisbon Extraordinary European Council*, Lisbon, 23-24 March 2000, available at http://www.consilium.europa.eu/.

14   Van Apeldoorn and Hager, 'The Social Purpose of New Governance' , p. 219.

15   Carroll et al, 'Constituting Corporate Europe', p. 836.

16   On the potential divergence between industrial and financial capital see van Apeldoorn, *Transnational Capital*, pp. 27–9; on the possibility of these differences reappearing in the European context see B. van Apeldoorn, 'The Contradictions of "Embedded Neoliberalism" and Europe's Multilevel Legitimacy Crisis: the European Project and its Limits', in B. van Apeldoorn, J. Drahokoupil and L. Horn, eds., *Contradictions and Limits of Neoliberal European Governance – From Lisbon to Lisbon*, London: Palgrave, 2009.

17   On the marketization of corporate control in the EU see B. van Apeldoorn

and L. Horn, 'The Marketisation of European Corporate Control: A Critical Political Economy Perspective', *New Political Economy*, 12(2), 2007.

18   European Trade Union Confederation, 'ETUC and the Lisbon Mid-Term Review: A Discussion and Background Document', Executive Committee, Brussels: ETUC, 13-14 October 2004, available at http://www.etuc.org. See also A. Bieler 'Globalization and Regional Integration: The Possibilities and Problems for Trade Unions to Resist Neoliberal Restructuring in Europe', in van Apeldoorn et al, 'Contradictions and Limits'.

19   On the Dutch referendum see B. van Apeldoorn, 'A National Case-study of Embedded Neoliberalism and its Limits: The Dutch Political Economy and the "No" to the European Constitution', in van Apeldoorn et al, 'Contradictions and Limits'.

20   Van Apeldoorn, 'Contradictions of "Embedded Neoliberalism"'. See also L. Hooghe and G. Marks, eds., *Understanding Euroscepticism*, Special Issue of *Acta Politica*, 42(2/3), 2007.

21   Van Apeldoorn and Hager, 'The Social Purpose of New Governance', pp. 228-9.

22   Van Apeldoorn and Hager, 'The Social Purpose of New Governance'. On the 2020 strategy see European Commission, *Europe 2020: A European Strategy for Smart, Sustainable and Inclusive Growth*, COM(2010) 2020, Brussels: European Commission, 3 March 2010.

23   ERT, *ERT's Vision for a Competitive Europe in 2025*, Brussels: European Round Table of Industrialists, February, 2010. Given the similarities of the two documents it seems quite likely that the Commission had also received drafts of the ERT document, as well as vice versa with the ERT being able to comment upon the Commission's work in progress, a procedure that has been followed with some key Commission publications in the past. See van Apeldoorn, *Transnational Capitalism*, p. 174.

24   European Commission, 'Commission Working Document – Consultation on the Future "EU 2020" Strategy', Brussels, COM (2009) 647 final, 24 November 2009.

25   See e.g. C. Lapavitsas, 'Default and Exit from the Eurozone', *Socialist Register 2012*, Pontypool: Merlin, 2011; Lapavitsas et al, *Crisis in the Eurozone*, London: Verso, 2012; E. Altvater, 'From Subprime Farce to Greek Tragedy: The Crisis Dynamics of Financially Driven Capitalism', *Socialist Register 2012*; H. Overbeek, 'Sovereign Debt Crisis in Euroland: Implications for European Integration', *The International Spectator*, 47(1), 2012; B. van Apeldoorn, 'The Eurocrisis and the Crisis of Neoliberal Europe: Dilemmas for Europe's Transnational Corporate Elite', *Corporate Europe Observatory*, 23 April 2012, available at http://corporateeurope.org; M. Ryner, 'Financial Crisis, Orthodoxy and Heterodoxy in the Production of Knowledge about the EU', *Millennium*, 4, 2012.

26   The notion that especially German capital has pursued an essentially mercantilist strategy – at the expense of the Eurozone periphery *and* of its own workers – can be found in Overbeek, 'Sovereign Debt Crisis in Euroland'; Lapavitsas et al, *Crisis in the Eurozone*; R. Bellofiore, F. Garibaldo and J. Halevi, 'The Global

Crisis and the Crisis of European Neomercantilism', *Socialist Register 2011*, Pontypool: Merlin, 2010.

27   On this choice see F. Scharpf, 'Monetary Union, Fiscal Crisis and the Preemption of Democracy', Max Plank Institute for the Study of Societies Discussion Paper 11/11, 2011. For a much stronger and radical version of this argument see Lapavitsas et al, *Crisis in the Eurozone*.

28   Lapavitsas, 'Default and Exit from the Eurozone'.

29   ERT, *Euro Crisis: European Industry Leaders Call for Coordinated Actions to Reinforce EMU*, Press Release, Brussels: European Round Table of Industrialists, October 2011, available at http://www.ert.eu. The aforementioned 'vision' report had already laid it out very clearly. At the top of the report's list of 'policy recommendations' was the goal of securing a 'quick return to sustainable public finances', which entailed first of all to '[r]espect of the Stability and Growth Pact' and to 'encourage public budget surpluses over a sustained period of time as soon as the economic situation allows this', which 'should be financed by cutting public expenditure on policies that are not sustainable', such as public pensions and social security. See ERT, *ERT's Vision*. The same austerity programme has been promoted from the start by Europe's 'official voice' of business, the European federation of national employers' federations, BusinessEurope. See BusinessEurope, *Combining Fiscal Sustainability and Growth: A European Action Plan*, Brussels, March 2010.

30   Thus the ERT welcomed what came to be called the Euro Plus Pact, praising it for containing 'many elements that will bring the attainment of ERT's Vision for a competitive Europe in 2025 closer'. ERT, *Industry Leaders Welcome 'Pact for the Euro'*, Press Release, Brussels: European Round Table of Industrialists, March 2011, available at http://www.ert.eu.

31   H. van Rompuy (President of the European Council), 'Towards a genuine Economic and Monetary Union', 5 December 2012, available at http://www.consilium.europa.eu.

32   Cf. Lapavitsas, 'Default and Exit'.

33   See W. Münchau, 'Relentless Austerity Will Only Deepen Greek Woes', *Financial Times*, 7 October 2012.

34   See R. Hyman, 'Trade Unions, Lisbon and Europe 2020: From Dream to Nightmare', *LSE 'Europe in Question' Discussion Paper Series*, LEQS Paper No. 45/2011, London: London School of Economics, December 2011. For the growing critical attitude by organized labour at the EU-level see L. Horn, 'Anatomy of a "Critical Friendship" – Organized Labour and the European State Formation', *Globalizations*, 9(4), 2012.

35   For some public opinion trends showing generally growing negative attitudes vis-à-vis the EU see European Commission, Standard Eurobarometer 78, August 2011, available at http://ec.europa.eu.

36   On the fractional divisions of capital and the capitalist class see Van der Pijl, *Transnational Classes and International Relations*; Van Apeldoorn, *Transnational Capitalism*, Chapter 1.

37   M. Steen, 'Business Gloom Adds to ECB Pressure on Rates', *Financial Times*, 25 April 2013.

38   This has been interpreted by some as constituting a neo-mercantilist strategy.
     See Bellofiore et al, 'The Global Crisis'. In Bellofiore et al's account, this
     neo-mercantilist strategy positions the core of the Eurozone – Germany, the
     Netherlands, Finland, and to a lesser extent Italy (with France occupying a
     somewhat more contradictory position) – against the periphery, especially
     Greece, Portugal and Spain (note here that most of Europe's large TNCs
     are located in the core, and this is also reflected in e.g. ERT membership).
     However, inasmuch as this interpretation of mercantilism takes national states
     as the unit-of-analysis it refers to a different dimension than what is my focus
     here (focusing on the strategies of transnational capital and of a transnational
     capitalist class rather than of states). Furthermore, this analysis tends to focus
     too much on intra-European dynamics and imbalances and tends to downplay
     the importance of markets outside Europe for European transnational capital.
     This is not say that the imbalances within Europe caused by this strategy may
     not constitute a problem for the European capitalist class.

39   L. Lucas, 'Unilever Turnover Rises 10% Despite European Weakness',
     Financial Times, 24 January 2013.

40   A. Jones and L. Lucas, 'Unilever Bucks Sectoral Trend for Profit Warnings',
     Financial Times, 27 July 2012.

41   J. Reed, 'In the Slow Lane; Carmaking: A Sector Long Seen as an Engine
     of European Industry Looks Increasingly Shaky', *Financial Times*, 2 February
     2012. Although the French and Italian car industry is particularly hit, German-
     based Daimler and Volkswagen also recently saw their profits fall: see J. Reed
     and E. Sylvers, 'All Eyes on Fiat as Crisis Deepens in Car Industry', *Financial
     Times*, 30 October 2012; Steen, 'Business Gloom Adds to ECB Pressure on
     Rates'.

42   See Steen, 'Business Gloom Adds to ECB Pressure on Rates'; and Wilson and
     R. Atkins, 'German Strength Propels Dax to Near Record Highs', *Financial
     Times*, 21 March 2013.

43   M. Kalecki, 'Political Aspects of Full Employment', *Collected Works of Michal
     Kalecki, Volume 1: Capitalism: Business Cycles and Full Employment*, Oxford:
     Clarendon Press, 1990 [1943].

BRAZIL'S NEW IMPERIAL CAPITALISM

VIRGINIA FONTES AND ANA GARCIA

A close relation between the public sector and the private sector. Close in the good sense, that is, a relation of partnership, cooperation, support of the government to its private companies, whether national or foreign. We have to do this. We will enter a period of internationalization of part of our major companies and this is an advantage for the country. All countries that had a solid development succeeded in establishing an alliance, a partnership ... we also do not want to reinvent the wheel. We need the capitalist. Dilma Rousseff[1]

Brazil has entered a new phase of capitalist development, with an active role of the state in the economy, favouring capital, but also some strata of the working class, with an increase of formal employment, social policies against extreme poverty, and price stability. For organic intellectuals in the government, Brazil has reached 'maturity' with the concentration and internationalization of capital, and now figures as an emerging power capable of intervening in world economic politics. For others, tensions and contradictions are deepening more than ever, with inescapable consequences for class struggles.

This essay seeks to make two contributions, one pertaining to the analysis of Brazil specifically, the other more general and theoretical, which challenges what have become almost common-sense assumptions concerning capitalism, imperialism and core-periphery relations in light of significant changes in capital, states and, not least, labour on a world scale today. The first part analyzes the relation between Brazilian multinationals and the state. Despite Brazil being behind China and India in the leading rankings of 'emerging multinational companies', Brazilian multinationals are shown as 'engines' of economic development of the country affecting Brazilian foreign policy. A new consensus has been created on the need for policies aimed at supporting Brazilian foreign direct investment. Social, environmental and labour aspects of life, that are essential for the working class, have been systematically excluded from the main analyses and reflections on the role of the state in supporting Brazilian investments abroad. Conflicts involving communities, environment and workers point to contractions within an apparent over-all consensus on the need for the international expansion of Brazilian capital.

Taking into account these new features, the second part of the essay analyzes their broader and deeper implications. Insofar as capitalist expansion needs to be understood differently than political forms of territorial expansion, the current dynamics of capital formation and accumulation which lead an expansive Brazilian bourgeoisie to compete and accumulate beyond its own borders may be captured by the concept of *imperial capitalism*.[2] This is a concept specifically formulated to allow us to grapple with the conditions that led to the dissemination and development of capitalism in peripheral countries, such as Brazil, India and others, which are now developing their own significant transnational capitalist dynamics. However, insofar as Brazil's imperial capitalism is one which retains strong traces of dependency, and even stems from the contradictions of dependency, this means that any proper understanding of Brazil today needs to start with an awareness of the contradictions that still attend the emergence of this new type of imperial capitalism.

That said, we suggest that Brazil's position within global capitalism needs to be understood in terms of the complex interactions of imperialism and class struggles, and not in terms of core-periphery dislocations and conflicts. In terms of the strategic implications of our analysis, two issues are central. First, today's imperial capitalism confronts a new configuration of labour organizations and workers' movements, reflecting the emergence of an internationally larger working class, which remains, however, nationally divided and faces a strong trend towards a reduction of national rights, with further implications for the fragmentation of the working class and its instruments for struggle. Secondly, imperial capitalism involves active participation of states, operating in parallel with extensive international networks of persuasion, as well as managerial training, engaged in what amounts to a permanently preventive bourgeois counter-revolutionary strategy on a world scale in defence of the internationalization of capital.

BRAZILIAN MULTINATIONALS

The UNCTAD World Investment Report 2006 highlighted, for the first time, the volume of foreign direct investment (FDI) originating from 'developing' economies. These had reached US$133 billion, representing 17 per cent of worldwide flows, a record never seen before. Furthermore, the flow of South-South investment went from four billion spent in 1985 to 61 billion in 2004.[3] The increase of 115 per cent of investment of Latin American companies in their own region (though not limited to it) by the middle of the last decade, which momentarily exceeded the growth of investment from the North, was portrayed, with considerable understatement, as 'a significant change'.[4]

The economic crisis, which began in 2007-08, accelerated the new role performed by the 'emerging' economies in investment flows. The 2013 UNCTAD World Investment Report showed that, in 2012, developing and transition economies absorbed, for the first time ever, more FDI than developed countries, accounting for 52 per cent of global FDI inflows.[5] Concerning global outflows, the Report affirms a continuing 'steady upward trend' of developing economies, which reached in the same year $426 billion, a record 31 per cent of the world total FDI outflows. Multinationals from these countries continued to expand abroad despite the global downturn, especially those from the BRICS countries, which accounted for 10 per cent of total world flows, growing from $7 billion in 2000 to $145 billion in 2012.[6] Among the 20 largest world investors there are eight developing and transition economies.[7]

According to the Boston Consulting Group,[8] Brazil – only behind China (with 33 companies) and India (with 20 companies) – has 13 companies in the 'global challengers' list – companies capable of facing off globally with other international giants: Camargo Correa, Coteminas, Embraer, Gerdau, JBS-Friboi, Marcopolo, Natura, Odebrecht, Brazil Foods, Petrobras, Magnesita, Votorantim and WEG, with, the largest, Vale, already considered an established multinational, not a 'challenger' anymore.

The internationalization of Brazilian companies started in the late 1960s (during the corporate-military dictatorship, with Petrobras and construction companies leading the way), fluctuating between periods of increase and decline over the next three decades. A new burst of expansion, with supportive public policies and direct credit playing a decisive role, began in 2003, pushing Brazilian investments abroad from an average of approximately $1 billion to $14 billion per year between 2004 and 2007.[9] By 2007, the twenty largest Brazilian multinationals were investing a total of $56 billion abroad. The purchase of the Canadian mining company Inco by Vale especially signaled Brazil's shift from receiver of investments to international investor: from $3 billion in 2005, the flow of Brazilian investment abroad jumps to $28 billion in 2006.[10]

These numbers initially receded with the onset of crisis, but as evidence of the long-term trend, the Central Bank of Brazil[11] reported that the total stock of foreign assets in Brazil reached of $274.6 billion in 2010 (23 per cent more than in 2009), and the total of Brazilian direct investment abroad increased from $49.7 billion 2001 to $189.2 billion in 2010, with a growing concentration in financial services and mining (38.2 per cent and 27.4 per cent respectively of the total by 2010).[12] The Central Bank proudly concluded that this demonstrated 'the strong and accelerated internationalization of Brazilian-capital companies'.

In 2010, the 20 most transnationalized Brazilian companies had for-eign holdings of $209 billion, which secured $130 billion in revenues.[13] Companies in the meat sector stand out from all others by the measure of revenues obtained abroad; indeed, two Brazilian slaughterhouses, JBS-Friboi and Marfrig, now dominate the meat industry in the US. Construction and engineering companies (led by Odebrecht and Andrade Gutierrez) are most internationalized in terms of the relative weight of foreign and domestic projects in which they are engaged. But in terms of geographical spread, Vale is the company with the widest presence abroad (37 countries), followed by Andrade Gutierrez (33 countries) and Votorantim (28 countries). The number of workers employed abroad by Brazilian companies is growing every year, from approximately 169,000 in 2008 to 198,000 in 2009 and 216,000 in 2010.[14]

South America remains what is often called the 'natural path' for this expansion of Brazilian companies, with Petrobras taking the main part in gas production in Bolivia, construction conglomerates building roads and hydroelectric dams in Peru, and Brazilian agricultural companies heavily involved in soy bean production in Paraguay. In Argentina alone, Brazilian investments went from $164 million in 2003 to $1.1 billion in 2008, led by Ambev buying up the beer company Quilmes, and JBS taking over the American meat company Swift Armor.[15]

However, there is also increasing investments elsewhere. A recent survey conducted by the Dom Cabral Foundation indicates that, in 2011, Latin America was the destination of 38.3 per cent of Brazilian companies operating abroad, followed by Europe (21.1 per cent), Asia (16.8 per cent), North America (12.6 per cent), Africa (9.6 per cent) and Oceania (1.9 per cent).[16] In terms of capital flows, no less than 30 per cent of total Brazilian investments are in North America (steel, meat, food and more recently mining) which has especially raised eyebrows. In the mining and steel sectors, besides Vale's acquisition of Inco in Canada, Gerdau acquired Ameristeel; while in the food sector (with takeovers clearly aimed at jumping US protectionist tariff barriers), JBS acquired Swift Foods and Pilgrim's Pride, and most recently the Brazilian investor Jorge Lemann acquired Heinz.[17] Increasingly, the most action seems to be taking place in Africa. Brazilian multinationals started operating there in the 1970s, with Petrobras and Odebrecht in Angola, as part of President Geisel's 'third world foreign policy' under the military regime. Today it is concentrated in oil and gas, mining and infrastructure, mostly (but not only) in Portuguese-speaking countries.[18]

THE ROLE OF THE BRAZILIAN STATE

Why would the state in a 'developing' country (i.e. which by definition presumably lacks sufficient domestic investment) articulate strategies to support, with public policies and resources, its companies investing in other countries? To sceptics, this amounts to investments that are needed at home being 'diverted' abroad, and encouraging companies to move their production abroad in order to escape negative domestic conditions.[19] But the prevailing view is that to avoid being 'swallowed' by foreign multinationals, Brazilian companies had no choice but to internationalize, as *'the only alternative* for companies which compete in a globalized world and face the changes in the technological and productive fields'.[20]

The case for this was put by economists with the Brazilian National Social and Development Bank (BNDES): 'In a globalized economy, the competitiveness of national companies in foreign markets becomes increasingly important to the performance of the country as a whole. ... Without internationally competitive companies, a country cannot improve its economic performance'.[21] This would result in positive effects in the medium and long term: increased intra-firm trade, reduced external vulnerability of the country, technological forecasting and R&D cost reduction, input of profits and dividends in foreign currency, import of equipment and raw materials by the subsidiaries abroad encouraging the development of suppliers, etc. In short, investments abroad would 'spill back', taking along other service companies. According to this argument, public and private interests become one: the need for state support for business is justified by the earnings generated for the country as a whole. Private interests are presented as public ones.

A consensus is thus formed on the need for public policies and resources to promote international (and domestic) expansion of Brazilian multinationals, stressing 'the importance of internationalization to increase the international competitiveness of countries – with consequent increased ability to generate income and employment in the country of origin – and to reduce external vulnerability ... [with] a public sector proactive role in supporting investments abroad'.[22] Such typically neoclassical economic arguments are silent about the social, labour or environmental contradictions involving operations of Brazilian multinationals, and its various impacts on the working class. And state policies which are elaborated on the basis of such arguments have systematically ignored how they contradict the needs of communities, workers and nature as key elements of Brazilian 'development' and the 'development model' that is brought to other peoples.

Notably, Brazil is not yet a signatory to any bilateral investment treaty. Even though it did sign 15 protection agreements in the 1990s, the Brazilian Congress did not ratify them.[23] But given the volume of Brazilian investment in South America, and specific conflicts that firms have had with governments in the region, business associations have increasingly called for protection against 'arbitrary interventions' such as those 'experienced in Bolivia and Argentina',[24] and the Lula government's initiation of negotiations within Mercosur on this.[25] In response to an ECLAC survey, companies affirmed the necessity of a flexible and stable legislation to support their internationalization; the participation of Brazil in bilateral trade agreements with the USA, Europe and other countries of the South; and taking advantage of market access in countries that already have free trade agreements with the major markets.[26]

But an affirmative credit policy has been the most important demand. And this has most generously been provided through direct credit given by BNDES, where using state credit to foster the concentration of capital is presented as part of a national development strategy, aimed at creating 'national champions', capable of competing globally. According to BNDES's vice president, 'there is no case of any country that wants to occupy a space in the international arena that does not have powerful companies', being part of the capitalist process and the evolution of the country itself.[27] In the words of the Bank's president, Luciano Coutinho, 'if the BNDES does not support national companies, who will?'[28]

In terms of the amount of resources at its disposal, BNDES is nowadays bigger than the World Bank, having increased its loans since 2005 by 391 per cent. In 2010 it provided $96.32 billion in loans, 3.3 times more than that granted by the World Bank that year.[29] Under the Lula administration, the Bank oversaw two fundamental moments of internationalization: in 2003, the creation of a specific credit line for foreign investment of Brazilian companies; this was soon followed by the internationalization of the Bank itself, opening a subsidiary in London (for the purpose of equity interests in other companies and to lend to Brazilian companies directly abroad), and an office in Montevideo, with the goal of injecting resources in regional integration projects. There is no access to information about the overall volumes lent by the Bank for projects of Brazilian companies abroad. But according to press reports, from 2005 until July 2011, BNDES had provided

$12.7 billion to support acquisitions, joint ventures, greenfield projects and expansions for 18 companies which were involved in 23 operations that matched the Bank's criteria.[30]

Moreover, the Bank became a key actor of Brazilian foreign policy, above all as the main financier of infrastructure integration in South America. Brazil approved, between 2003 and 2010, more than $10 billion in funding for regional construction works, with the major engineering and construction conglomerates and their suppliers the main beneficiaries of loans for these projects.[31] Some of the construction projects are: in Argentina, the construction and expansion of a pipeline network with approximately $1.9 billion (Odebrecht and Confab); in Bolivia, the controversial San Ignacio de Moxos–Villa Tunari highway, passing through the TIPNIS park, with $332 million (OAS); in Venezuela, the construction and expansion the Caracas Subway, with approximately $943 million (Odebrecht); in Cuba, the works of the Mariel Harbor, with $680 million (Odebrecht). In addition to this, there is the construction of large hydroelectric dams in Peru, Venezuela, Ecuador, Colombia and the Dominican Republic by Odebrecht, Camargo Correa, OAS and also Eletrobras. This kind of credit has also been provided for similar projects in Africa: in Angola, a credit of $3.5 billion for the national reconstruction project, performed by major Brazilian contractors; in Mozambique, Nacala Airport with $80 million (Odebrecht); and in Ghana, the Road Corridor with $200 million by Andrade Gutierrez.[32]

Aside from the provision of public loans, the Bank created, during the Lula government's term in office, a financial holding company, the BNDESPar, which became a sophisticated state instrument of capital accumulation, by participating directly as a main shareholder within firms. In 2009, it had shares in 22 Brazilian multinationals, and investments amounted to R$92.8 billion, corresponding to 4 per cent of the total capitalization of the Brazilian stock market.[33] By 2012, the number of companies in which BNDESPar held shares had jumped to more than 40, in some cases exchanging debts and debentures for shares.[34]

Since the onset of the economic crisis, there has been a significant increase of capital concentration and centralization in Brazil, with a record of over 700 mergers in 2010 alone.[35] BNDES was an important engine of this process, becoming, in some cases, a joint member of new conglomerates. With the support of BNDES, these conglomerates not only increased their exports, and leaped forward in corporate internationalization rankings, but also secured a larger share of the domestic market.[36] However, the dispensation of such large amounts of public resources in this process results in tensions among the major economic groups involved, as they themselves compete, under a logic of accumulation on the market, for the advantages of the distribution of BNDES resources.

Those who have criticized such 'excessive' state intervention in the economy, and characterize Brazil as a 'tangled capitalism',[37] with a maze of promiscuous and clientelistic public-private relations, forget that the greater role of the state, in fact, strengthens major businesses groups, especially by allowing them to leverage their capital. Yet while participating directly in the capital accumulation process, as in the case of BNDES, the state still acts strategically in the economy as a whole, more or less autonomously from particular corporations, economic sectors or bourgeois fractions, while remaining dependent on the accumulation of capital for its overall legitimization and reproduction.[38]

Brazil's foreign policy under Lula also combined the traditional goals of 'autonomy' and 'development' with 'credibility' in global markets. The country has presented itself as a 'friend' and generous partner to poorer neighbours, and aligned itself with other 'emerging' countries such as China, India and Russia. Through this it sought to establish a common identity to participate in international organizations such as the UN, WTO and G20, at the same level as 'developed' countries. Regional integration and new South-South political and economic articulations have provided the basis for a broader intervention on the world stage and an alternative centre to negotiate with traditional global powers. The global financial crisis has accelerated the process of articulation between the BRICS, while Brazil also has a new status as the tenth largest shareholder of the IMF.

Indeed, the very image of 'twenty-first century Brazil' is embedded in a context of reorganization of the world order. The country has functioned as a 'stabilizer',[39] mediating conflicts and political crises at the regional level, as in Venezuela, Bolivia, Ecuador, Haiti, and finally, Honduras as well as beyond its region, as in the case of Iran. The greater 'responsibility' of Brazil was especially expressed in what was called the 'principle of non-indifference'[40] in the face of the poorest countries. But Brazilian 'soft power' is accompanied by its economic 'hard power'. Latin America, Africa and the Middle East appear as regions for resources and new markets for Brazilian investments and exports. According to the Ministry of Foreign Affairs (MRE or *Itamaraty*, in Portuguese),[41] one of the effects of the prioritization of regional integration is the greater presence of Brazilian companies on the continent. While Brazilian exports to the world are primarily commodities, Brazil exports mainly manufactured goods to South America. In relations with Central America and the Caribbean, a region that has lighter tariffs via free trade agreements with the United States and Europe, energy was the key focus for Brazil, especially the promotion of ethanol and hydropower. With African countries, the *Itamaraty* states that, alongside humanitarianism and solidarity, there are 'concrete gains earned by Brazil', such as 'access to markets, favourable economic opportunities and greater influence in multilateral forums'. In relations with the Middle East, presidential trips accompanied by delegations of businessmen, organization of trade missions and trade fairs demonstrate the mix of political and corporate interests.

This mix is also seen in technical cooperation and international aid. Under the Lula government, Brazil became a new donor, providing US$33 million in aid in 2010 (in contrast with only $1.5 million in 2003). Public institutions such as the Brazilian Cooperation Agency, the Brazilian Agricultural Research Corporation (Embrapa) and the Oswaldo Cruz Heath Foundation (Fiocruz) have become especially important state actors in foreign affairs through the so-called 'aid for development' to other Southern countries (often working in concert with USAID and other agencies from the advanced capitalist states). An anti-retroviral drug factory of Fiocruz in Mozambique, considered one of the main measures of cooperation for Africa, had 80 per cent of its construction funded by the mining company Vale.[42] Embrapa's project for the introduction of soy-exporting agriculture in northern Mozambique (known as ProSavana), in conjunction with the Japanese International Cooperation Agency (JICA), has combined various corporate interests with aid measures, articulating the introduction of agribusiness (which includes the land donation for Brazilian soy producers) with infrastructure transportation projects designed by Brazilian construction companies (Odebrecht and Andrade Gutierrez) with partial funding from BNDES.[43]

Another relevant player has been the Brazilian Trade and Investment Promotion Agency (APEX), which has offices in eight countries, with a mission to identify business opportunities to expand Brazilian trade and investment in different regions. As part of the Ministry of Industry and Trade, APEX organizes trade fairs and business missions for government members. Such foreign policy strategy for advancing South-South relations is consistent with the logic of fostering corporate investment abroad. This includes the opening of new embassies where there are business interests, as was the case with Tanzania, Equatorial Guinea and the Sultanate of Oman, greasing the wheels for Petrobras and Vale to gain concessions in those countries.[44] Indeed, a range of diverse state and other public sector contacts work as efficient 'catalysts' for new businesses for Brazilian multinational companies. The various actors now operating for Brazil in international affairs, going beyond the classic competence of the *Itamaraty*, entails a reordering of state bureaucracies in a way that expresses the close connection between political and corporate interests.

CONTRADICTIONS AND CONFLICTS

The international rise of Brazilian companies not only reflects a consensus about the need to increase Brazil's global competitiveness among fractions of the bourgeoisie and various state apparatuses, but also extends to privileged sectors of the working class (especially among the leading elements of the trade unions and the left parties in government). But it gives rise to contradictions and conflicts, within and outside of the country, reflecting the fact that the close relationship between capital and the state has not been translated into any greater *public control* of the economy.[45]

The strategy of creating 'national champions' has at least two weaknesses. Whether it is really Brazilians who benefit is open to question insofar as the majority of corporations who are supported with public credit have at least foreign capitalist participation in their ownership, to an extent that varies with the global transactions of these companies. The second weakness is the social and environmental vulnerability of the funded sectors (cross-country roads, huge hydroelectric dams, oil, gas, mining, ethanol, cellulose and others). The potential benefits of large infrastructure projects in the context of South American integration (such as improving energy and transportation, promoting a productive integration) also generate high social costs, such as mobilization of migrant labour with poor working conditions, enormous number of work accidents in the plants, creation of great poverty areas with all sorts of social impacts (drugs, prostitution), environmental and health problems, as well as cooptation of social leaders in the territories of mega-projects. New forms of regulation are created, setting some 'allowable level' for rights claims for people directly affected by those projects.[46] Integration processes that sustain the circuits of capital lead to the *disintegration* of previous conditions of life, work and wealth production, expropriating whole populations, which lived so far from their labour in the territories.

Brazilian companies in extraction and construction sectors have also become enveloped in conflicts that may create diplomatic tensions. One important dispute involved Odebrecht's building of the San Francisco hydroelectric plant in Ecuador, which had a US$242.9 million financing from BNDES. Equipment and operation failures of the plant caused President Rafael Correa to expel Odebrecht from the country.[47] The case is emblematic of how the representation of a private company's interests as advancing the 'national interest' of Brazil can fuel a diplomatic conflict between Brazil and Ecuador. Recently, the financing of $332 million from BNDES to the construction company OAS to build the San Ignacio de Moxos–Villa Tunari highway in Bolivia, passing through the TIPNIS aboriginal reserve, created one of the most serious conflicts between the communities and the Evo Morales administration. With the violent escalation of the conflict and the tension between social sectors, and between these and the Bolivian government, the works had to be redesigned and BNDES suspended the loan.[48]

In Brazil, Petrobras is strongly tied, in people's minds, to the country's 'national interest' and the struggle for sovereign control over Brazil's natural resources. Yet Petrobras's activities abroad often clash with other people's interests. In Bolivia, where Petrobras operates the main gas plants, the company was at the centre of disputes over the Bolivian government's attempt to restore sovereignty over natural resources by nationalizing hydrocarbons.[49] A resolution of the conflict between Petrobras and the new elected Evo Morales government, in 2006, was strategically negotiated by the Lula government with discourses of recognition of inequalities between Brazil and Bolivia, producing a notable reactionary retaliation from various sectors of the Brazilian bourgeoisie.[50]

Lula's strategy here could be understood as an attempt to build a regional hegemony, recognizing that this required certain concessions to smaller countries, while also providing regional leadership in advancing these countries' interests, against the US for example. But the accommodations and concessions to the interests of smaller countries are always made in ways that do not touch, or at least undermine, the interests of strong economic sectors in Brazil, as demonstrated by the positive outcome for Petrobras in the conflict in Bolivia.

The mining company Vale has especially faced conflicts of many kinds – social, environmental and labour – inside and outside Brazil.[51] At home, its privatization, in 1997, is still the subject of protests and legal disputes. And abroad, its truculence provoked the longest strike in Vale's history in its dispute with the United Steel Workers (USW) in Canada.[52] Notably, shortly before the confrontation with Canadian workers, Vale had massive lay offs of workers in Brazil.[53] In fact, contradicting the argument of those who assume that the 'national interest' is at play in the internationalization of Brazilian companies, the disruption of rights of Canadian workers did not benefit Brazilian workers.

IMPERIAL CAPITALISM AND CLASS STRUGGLES TODAY

All this indicates that the economic expansion project of Brazilian multinational corporations, which reflects a political project with strong internal backing, is giving rise to new tensions and contradictions, conflicts and adjustments within historically dependent social formations. The comprehension of this cannot be secured by analyses that focus only on the economic power of those bourgeoisies with long historical associations with the internationalization of capital. One must reflect upon this process in the light of new and broader transformations in the internationalization of capital, resulting from uneven and combined expansions of capitalism's interconnecting yet unequal bourgeoisies.

As demonstrated here, the Brazilian state's role in supporting multinationals has elevated private interests of companies to *raison d'état*. But the extensive network of popular persuasion which presents this under the label of neo-developmentalism contributes to obscuring the imperial capitalist nature of this, and marginalizing it in public debate. This is sustained by a range of other state practices, including the subordinate participation of trade union leaders on administrative councils to the establishment of programmes of poverty alleviation which promote popular political passivity.

This poses a huge difficulty. Where there is minimal politicization, the trend persists to denounce imperialism as only what comes from the core countries, in particular the United States. Without a doubt, there is no diminution of capitalist imperialism, but anti-capitalist struggles need to get more complex: alongside the imperial capitalist performance of the core countries, we must face up to the Brazilian bourgeoisie's actions not only in its subordinate aspects but also, nowadays, in its own imperial capitalist expansive aspects. Is it possible today to denounce imperialism and be silent about the multiple forms of imperial capitalism?

To be sure, awareness of the results and the contradictions of uneven and combined development are still relevant for our analysis and struggles today. But the contemporary universalization of capitalist social relations in all their economic, political, cultural and ideological dimensions requires that we incorporate multiple levels of analysis. More than before, we must seize and understand the contradictions generated by the overall movement of the expansion of capital and its state-political forms. Unilateral accentuation of conditions of domination, whether at the national or international level, leads us to consider the history and conditions of certain countries – whether emerging or developed capitalist countries – not only as having more impact on the whole, which is true, but as their prefigured or desirable future. The risk therefore is to create a sort of history – albeit critical – of the victors, without understanding all the contradictions involved.

The reversed, but equally unilateral, image is based on the recognition – and denunciation – of the undeniable arrogance of some countries, their bourgeoisies and their state apparatuses, and their domination at once economic, technological, cultural, ideological, institutional and military. Some interpretations firmly set on the side of the most vulnerable people suggest that the existence of domination, to the extent that it imposes constraints, freezes subjugated countries in an unalterable position of structural dependence whose outcome is an untenable independence under capitalism. From a theory that described not paralysis but capitalist expansion at the periphery we moved to a theory of stable centre-periphery relationships with rigid parameters. The *historical* impacts of capitalist expansion – including feedback effects on core capitalist countries and the desperate defense of traditional ways of life – and its uncontrollable aspects and contradictions, are sometimes criticized, although apprehended in a fixed manner.

Old oppositions such as nation *versus* imperialism or development *versus* regression are misleading, and this is particularly visible in the Brazilian case. The concept of development (whether characterized as 'sustainable', 'green' or 'social') is completely pervaded by the expansion of the social bases of capital, hence reinforcing the concentration of property. In this sense, 'national' development serves as the launching pad of a certain bourgeoisie ready to jump to the international market, not by claiming any autonomy, but rather by brandishing the full acceptance of the rules of the game. New determinations and contradictions are therefore added to the classic forms of the national question. Unilateral perspectives, whether Eurocentric or third-worldist, have their limits. The first reinforces the role of 'driving force' performed by the capitalist centre (in countries where the bourgeoisie is predominant), while the second emphasizes resistance, as the reversed image of domination.

The Marxist theory of dependency, in particular that elaborated by Ruy Mauro Marini,[54] focused on the penetration of imperialism in dependent social formations, with simultaneous expansion of capitalist relations. This was, however, usually understood as being mainly skin-deep in terms of domestic social relations. According to Marini, imperialist penetration resulted in the over-exploitation of workers at the periphery, who were thereby integrated into the *capitalist whole*, for they served *both* the interests of the national and foreign bourgeoisies. From this followed an intimate connection between a theoretical analysis and a political strategy resolutely turned towards socialism and anti-capitalism. However, if this dialectical interplay is neglected, the strategic focus falls on opposition between subjected and imperialist countries, between the national and the imperial. This has resurfaced today in the name of sovereignty and economic development, ignoring how far national bourgeoisies are integrated, albeit unevenly, into the international market. There are no 'proletarian nations' aligned against imperialist nations, but only an increasing contradiction between labour and capital, situated in political contexts circumscribed by nation states. This requires us to assess the new configuration of capitalist power structures in relation to the organizational and alliance strategies of working-class organizations.

In this respect, one key observation stands out above all others about today's capitalist expansion: the working class is significantly expanding worldwide. The social ground which allows the existence of capitalism is the permanent production of new workers, that is to say, social beings who objectively need the market to which they get subjectively attached. The market becomes a condition of their existence; it projects their lives and well-being onto them. For at least three centuries, primary accumulation has expropriated peasants from their land in an endless movement. By 2006, the urban population globally had finally exceeded the rural population through a process of primary accumulation which is still accelerating.[55] The number of workers thrown onto the market is expanding exponentially and massive expropriations are still ongoing. In addition, new forms of secondary expropriations curtail social rights, subordinating to property all human relationships to nature, such as access to water, patents on human biology, and GMOs, for example. All these expropriations seek to make workers available for the market. Conditions of vulnerability therefore become similar between urban workers and landless peasants. This process is not only characteristic of the beginning of capitalism: it is, at this moment, showing its worst face.

The movement toward the concentration of capitalist property is also accelerating and has reached a new level, not only for businesses, banks and non-banking financial sectors, but also in terms of becoming the concentrated control of the *social conditions of production*. Given the mass of capital that must be valorized, direct means of production lose relative (but not absolute) importance. The extraction of surplus value must be done as soon as possible and by all means. If this process does not announce the end of competition among bourgeois class fractions, we must nevertheless seriously consider the new divisions that overlap the old ones.

The international breakthrough and movement of capital, fostered by states, is coupled with a corporate capture of democracies from the popular conquests that hinder market growth. Snatched by capitalism, democracies are limited to national territories whose governments aim to reassure markets and property. Yet electoral representation remains the space where broad political projects are currently put forward. Given these conditions, the struggles of workers are trapped. On the one hand, the real need to struggle tends to be reduced to sub-national conditions as well as to defending immediate and urgent necessities, all contributing to disruption of their organizations. On the other hand, the struggle to preserve democratic gains is exhausting, and confines workers further into the national-electoral trap. Fighting neoliberalism in such a limited way is a defensive retreat, at once theoretical and practical. It is sometimes undertaken with nostalgia for the 'good' old capitalism that did exist for a very small portion of the globe, but imposed harsh conditions on the rest.

The conservation and multiplication of an increasingly concentrated mass of capital is firmly anchored in national states and cannot eliminate the question of democracy. We are witnessing the state's strong grip on the combative energy of workers, which contributes to converting their *claims* into requests. This is played out on a double register: workers' 'requests' legitimize the very productive logics (production of value) built on the ruins of expropriated social rights. Meanwhile internationally-oriented management training, with Masters of Business Administration 'degrees' dispensed all over the globe, increasingly focus on managing social problems. This is often even cast in a certain progressive tenor, which sounds appealing to the left but remains obedient to the dictates of capitalism, becoming even more essential in reproducing imperial capitalism. In this context, democracy has become a malleable project of conflict management, culminating in an electoral market subject to concentration of property in its pure form, while, just in case, capital's fundamental ties to the state are, of course, defended by all legal and military means.

All this is essential to reproducing imperial capitalism on a global scale. At the level of today's imperial-capitalist connections, development and regression are not opposites, but signs of a dramatic future where social forms and ever-evolving technologies are inextricably linked to the most backward and reactionary modalities. Consensus and coercion are more closely intertwined than ever by the incessant call for democratic participation and accountability, all happening beside the direct violence of primary and secondary expropriations.

The totality is not a reflection of experiences at the capitalist core, but the result of a greater extension of contradictions. Many interpretations of the contemporary crisis simply generalize the idea of a deadlock or impasse as the crisis continues to hit countries of the core. Yet the crisis has been the outcome of a strong impetus on part of imperial capitalism whose forces continue to deepen it. We live the contradictions yielded by the expansion of imperial capitalism fostered as much by a development-oriented left as by the right wing. Our period is one of social crisis in the countries of classical capitalism, of concentration of pure capital ownership in countries under the auspices of the United States, and of an expansion of the working class.

The history of capitalism is characterized by the expansion of recognizable and identifiable markers. It seems therefore reasonable to think that the experience in advanced capitalist countries would tend to be repeated elsewhere – albeit within forms peculiar to local circumstances. This is both true and false. On the one hand, it is true that there is a strong trend to spread similar types of social relations, capable of broadening surplus-value extraction, allowing constant capital to expand to the detriment of variable capital, concentrating property in increasing expropriation, and divorcing the economic from the political sphere in democracies emptied of their real content. It is also true that these trends do not occur in a vacuum, but in very specific and uneven social contexts. On the other hand, it is erroneous to endow the bourgeoisie and their respective states with an almost teleological power of 'making' history. The more imperial capitalism spreads, the more national histories intersect. In both processes, whether through different capitalist fractions and state actors, or different sections of the working class (wage-workers, peasants, immigrants, precarious, unemployed), there is agency, with actors capable of learning from prior experiences elsewhere and thus lead their struggles in a global context. Moreover, although explicitly committed to produce and reproduce results at the global scale, imperial capitalism can lead to new and unexpected features. The large-scale, complex and contradictory processes that this entails can frustrate the intentions of today's most powerful actors.

How best to contribute to class struggles from below to this end is the challenge we face. Humanity as a whole is currently going through a period where the creation of new workers does not necessarily correspond to either jobs on the market or common rights, even though they participate in the production of surplus value. The experience and consciousness of this expanded working class are built in struggles to keep previous gains. But this class will inevitably need to produce new syntheses and a much stronger consciousness, beyond those of old struggles.

NOTES

1   Interviewed in her former role as Chief of Staff. 'Governo quer companhias fortes e globais, diz Dilma'. *Valor Econômico*, 24 September 2007.

2   See *O Brasil e o capital-imperialismo*, 3rd ed., Rio de Janeiro, Ed. UFRJ/EPSJV-Fiocruz, 2012, available at http://www.epsjv.fiocruz.br. In this book, the category of *capital-imperialismo* seeks to address the contemporary expansionist capitalist dynamic, its economic and social elements, pointing to the current

challenge to understand a system whose results are beyond the control of its main powerful decision makers.

3   UNCTAD, 'World Investiment Report 2006. FDI from developing and transition economies: implications for development', available at http://www.unctad.org.

4   Andre Almeida and Sherban Cretoiu, 'Internacionalização de empresas: a experiência brasileira e o contexto latino-americano', *Revista Dom*, ano II, nr. 5. março/junho 2008.

5   UNCTAD, 'World Investment Report 2013. Global value chains: investment and trade for development'.

6   UNCTAD, 'World Investment Report 2013', p. 2.

7   Those are China, Hong Kong, Russia, Virgin Islands, Republic of Korea, Mexico, Singapore and Chile. See UNCTAD, 'World Inventment Report 2013', p. 5.

8   Boston Consulting Group, 'Global Challengers 2011. Companies on the move. Rising stars from rapidly developing economies are reshaping global industries', available at http://www.bcg.com.

9   'Revista Multinacionais Brasileiras', *Valor Econômico*, October 2009.

10 Fundacao Dom Cabral, 'A decolagem das multinacionais brasileiras', Press Release, 3 December 2007.

11 Banco Central do Brasil, 'Capitais brasileiros no exterior (CBE), ano-base 2010', available at http://www4.bcb.gov.br.

12 The total assets go beyond the direct investments of Brazilian companies, since loans, portfolio investments, as well as all types of deposits of individuals and corporations are taken in account. It is important to note the role of tax havens as the main destination of Brazilian capital sent abroad, which are 'black holes', not allowing the identification of investment.

13 Fundacao Dom Cabral, 'Ranking das Transnacionais Brasileiras 2011. Crescimento e gestão sustentável no exterior', available at http://www.fdc.org.br.

14 'Revista Multinacionais Brasileiras', *Valor Econômico*, September 2010.

15 'Revista Multinacionais Brasileiras', *Valor Econômico*, October 2009.

16 Fundacao Dom Cabral, 'Ranking das Transnacionais Brasileiras 2010. Repensando as estratégias globais', available at http://www.fdc.org.br.

17 'Revista Multinacionais Brasileiras', *Valor Econômico*, October 2009.

18 IPEA and World Bank, 'Bridging the Atlantic: Brazil and Sub-Saharan Africa. South-South Partnering for Grow', 2011, available at http://siteresources.worldbank.org; see also Ana Garcia, Karina Kato and Camila Fontes, 'A história contada pela caça ou pelo caçador? Perspectivas sobre o Brasil em Angola e Moçambique', 2012, available at http://www.pacs.org.br.

19 Marcia Tavares, 'Investimentos brasileiros no exterior: panoramas e considerações sobre políticas públicas', *CEPAL, Serie Desarollo Productivo* 172, 2006.

20 Roberto Iglesias and Pedro Motta Veiga, 'Promoção de exportações via internacionalização de firmas com capital brasileiro', available at http://www.bndes.gov.br.

21   Ana Claudia Alem and Carlos Eduardo Cavalcanti, 'O BNDES e o apoio à internacionalização das empresas brasileiras', *Revista do BNDES*, 12(24), dezembro 2005, p. 56.

22   Ana Claudia Alem and Rodrigo Madeira, 'Internacionalização e competividade. A importância da criação de empresas multinacionais brasileiras', in Alem Giambiagi, ed., *O BNDES em um Brasil em transição*, Rio de Janeiro: BNDES, 2010, p. 50.

23   Ricardo Sennes and Ricardo Mendes, 'Políticas públicas e multinacionais brasileiras', in Almeida and Ramsey, eds., *A ascensão das multinacionais brasileiras*, Rio de Janeiro: Elsevier; Belo Horizonte: Fundação Dom Cabral, 2009.

24   Confederação Nacional da Indústria (CNI), *Os interesses empresariais brasileiros na América do Sul*: Sumário Executivo, Brasília: CNI, 2007.

25   See 'Bloco quer acordo para proteger empresas', *Valor Econômico*, 17 December 2010.

26   Marcia Tavares, 'Investimentos brasileiros no exterior: panoramas e considerações sobre políticas públicas', *CEPAL, Serie Desarollo Productivo* 172, 2006.

27   Interview with João Carlos Ferraz held at PUC-Rio on 10 November 2011.

28   'Coutinho defende a criação de grandes grupos nacionais', *Folha online*, 29 April 2008.

29   'BNDES já empresta três vezes mais que o Banco Mundial', *Estado de São Paulo*, 10 March 2011.

30   'Revista Multinacionais Brasileiras', *Valor Econômico*, September 2011.

31   Ministerio das Relacoes Exteriores (MRE), 'Balanço da Política Externa 2003-2010', available at http://www.itamaraty.gov.br.

32   Ministerio das Relacoes Exteriores (MRE), 'Balanço da Política Externa 2003-2010'. See also 'Brasil faz obras nos vizinhos temendo a China', *Folha de São Paulo*, 27 September 2009.

33   Carlos Tautz, Joao Roberto L. Pinto, Felipe Siston and Luciana Badin, 'O BNDES e a reorganização do capitalismo brasileiro: um debate necessário', in *Os anos Lula: contribuições para um balanço crítico: 2003-2010*, Rio de Janeiro: Garamond, 2010. See also Sergio Lazzarini, *Capitalismo de laços: os donos do Brasil e suas conexões*, Rio de Janeiro: Elsevier, 2011.

34   The 'Ranking of the Owners of Brazil', conducted by the Instituto Mais Democracia and the group EITA, shows the network and chains of conglomerates, holding companies, financial institutions, individuals and families, as well as government institutions, with the interconnections between them. Information about the network that involves BNDESPar is available at http://www.proprietariosdobrasil.org.br.

35   'Fusões batem recorde, diz KPMG', *Valor Econômico*, 23 December 2010; 'Brasil deve bater recorde em fusões e aquisições', *Valor Econômico*, 6 October 2011.

36   Important examples are: Fibria (formed by the merge of Votorantim and Aracruz), the fastest growing company in the internationalization index from 2007 to 2009 (88.2 per cent); Brazil Foods, (formed by a merger of Sadia and Perdigão), listed in the Sobeet foundation's ranking of major multinationals

in 2009; JBS-Friboi, the most internationalized company of Brazil in the Sobeet Foundation's list; Itaú Unibanco (formed through the merger of two internationalized banks), with the largest volume of overseas assets, totaling over R$100 billion (Fundacao Dom Cabral 2010; 2009, *Valor Econômico*, 2010).

37 Sergio Lazzarini, *Capitalismo de laços: os donos do Brasil e suas conexões*, Rio de Janeiro: Elsevier, 2011.

38 Leo Panitch and Sam Gindin, 'Superintending global capital', *New Left Review* 35(September/October), 2005.

39 Maria Regina Lima and Monica Hirst, 'Brasil como país intermediário e poder regional', in Hurrel et al., eds., *BRICS e a ordem global*, Rio de Janeiro: Editora FGV, 2009.

40 Celso Amorim, 'Política externa é uma política pública como as demais. Está sujeita à expressão das urnas', *Desafios do Desenvolvimento*, Edição 61, 13 de agosto de 2010.

41 Ministerio das Relacoes Exteriores (MRE), 'Balanço da Política Externa 2003-2010', available at http://www.itamaraty.gov.br.

42 Available at http://www.mozambique.org.br.

43 Ana Garcia, Karina Kato and Camila Fontes, 'A história contada pela caça ou pelo caçador? Perspectivas sobre o Brasil em Angola e Moçambique', 2012, available at http://www.pacs.org.br.

44 Ricardo Sennes and Ricardo Mendes, 'Políticas públicas e multinacionais brasileiras', in Almeida and Ramsey, eds., *A ascensão das multinacionais brasileiras*, Rio de Janeiro: Elsevier; Belo Horizonte: Fundação Dom Cabral, 2009. See also Ministerio das Relacoes Exteriores (MRE), 'Balanço da Política Externa 2003-2010', available at http://www.itamaraty.gov.br.

45 Carlos Tautz, Joao Roberto L. Pinto, Felipe Siston and Luciana Badin, 'O BNDES e a reorganização do capitalismo brasileiro: um debate necessário', in *Os anos Lula: contribuições para um balanço crítico: 2003-2010*, Rio de Janeiro: Garamond, 2010.

46 Luis Fernando Novoa, 'O Brasil e seu desbordamento': o papel central do BNDES na expansão das empresas transnacionais brasileiras na América do Sul', in IRLS et al., eds., *Empresas transnacionais brasileiras: um debate necessário*, São Paulo: Editora Expressão Popular, 2009.

47 'Equador questiona dívida de US$ 243 mi com o Brasil', *Valor Econômico*, 21 November 2008.

48 'Bolívia suspende obra de estrada em meio a grave crise no governo', *Valor Econômico*, 28 September 2011.

49 'Bolívia nacionaliza gás, ocupa instalacões e eleva crise com Brasil', *Valor Econômico*, 2 May 2006.

50 According to the former foreign minister, Celco Amorim, 'many people wanted us to dialogue with Bolívia as if we were Ted Roosevelt. Our policy has always been, and will always be of good neighbor, and not of force. We do not have Marines, and even if we had, we would not send them to displace Bolivian administrators'. See the interview in 'O Brasil não usa marines', *Carta Capital*, 17 May 2006.

51   Several cases are reported in 'Vale Unsustainability Report 2012', available at http://atingidospelavale.files.wordpress.com.

52   'Greve da Inco vira ícone para sindicalistas', *Valor Econômico*, 1 July 2010.

53   'Vale demite 1.300 funcionários e 5.500 têm férias coletivas; mais afetados estão em MG', *Folha online*, 3 December 2008.

54   A good selection of Marini's works is available at http://www.marini-escritos.unam.mx.

55   United Nations, '2012. World Urbanization Prospects. 2011 Revision', available at http://esa.un.org.

MASS PROTESTS: BRAZILIAN SPRING OR BRAZILIAN MALAISE?

ALFREDO SAAD-FILHO AND LECIO MORAIS

Vast demonstrations erupted in Brazil in early June 2013, seemingly from nowhere, demanding free transport, improvements in public services, the reform of a dysfunctional and corrupt political system, and much more. The federal government, led since 2003 by the left-wing Workers' Party (*Partido dos Trabalhadores*, PT), was stunned. The right-wing opposition vanished in the *mêlée*, while the TV showed, night after night, masses of young people pouring into the streets, most of them marching for the first time. For a few days, it seemed that a revolutionary situation might emerge, leaderless, perhaps, but fully formed in the womb of the masses. Then strange things began to happen.

The right-wing TV and most newspapers stopped attacking the demonstrations and, effectively, started supporting them. Popular approval for the government tumbled. White, articulate and economically privileged demonstrators seemed to be everywhere. The demonstrations became displays of individual creativity, including hundreds of carefully drawn home-made placards with original slogans. And each 'demonstration' was found to include several independent marches, which may or may not meet at some point.

Then the movement took a slightly sinister turn. At the margins of large concentrations, small groups of people regularly went on the rampage. The police sometimes attacked the demonstrations, and sometimes disappeared from view. Bands of muscular men with cropped hair, wrapped in the national flag, beat up people with a red T-shirt or waving a red flag. There were calls for the impeachment of President Dilma Rousssef, and for a military coup. Finally, unknown persons launched, on Facebook and Youtube, a call for a general strike on 1 July, but they did not think it useful to issue specific demands.

The left parties, trade unions and social movements rapidly realized that something was amiss. Seventy-six organizations met in São Paulo on 21 June, issued a list of demands, drafted a letter to President Dilma Rousseff, and agreed on a national day of mobilizations on 11 July around issues of immediate interest to the working class. The federal government called a political meeting in Brasília to propose a 'national pact', and the left withdrew from the streets. The demonstrations deflated in a matter of days, except for a small number of trade union movements and marginal events which rarely involved more than a few dozen people. There was no more talk of coups, and nothing happened on 1 July. In the meantime, the media continued to harass the government.

This essay offers a political economy interpretation of the context, origins, implications and challenges posed by the 'Events of June' to the Brazilian left, in the light of the achievements and limitations of the federal administrations led by Luiz Inácio Lula da Silva (2003-10) and Dilma Rousseff (2011-present). The argument is developed in six substantive sections. The first three review the Lula and Dilma administrations. The fourth describes the Events of June, and the fifth examines the lessons for the left. The sixth section draws the relevant conclusions.

THE FIRST LULA ADMINISTRATION

Lula was elected president in 2002 by an 'alliance of losers': a coalition of heterogeneous social groups that had in common only the experience of losses under neoliberalism.[1] These groups included the organized working class, the domestic bourgeoisie, large sections of the traditional oligarchy and sections of the middle class and the informal proletariat.[2] This collection of disparate supporters had few objectives in common beyond more expansionary macroeconomic policies and some redistribution of income, and it could not be relied upon to support radical policies leading, for example, to a break with neoliberalism. In this sense, the common complaint among the left that Lula 'betrayed' his supporters is misplaced: in 2002, Lula neither sought nor received a mandate to introduce radical policy changes. In order to bring together the 'losers' and avoid a fourth consecutive defeat in the presidential elections, Lula's discourse emphasized a diffuse spirit of 'change', but he studiously avoided making any specific commitments. The only exception is Lula's 'Letter to the Brazilian People', issued under duress, in June, in the midst of a severe currency crisis. In this document, Lula declared that his government would respect contracts (i.e., service the domestic and foreign debts on schedule) and implement the agreement recently signed with the IMF.

Lula's administration maintained the macroeconomic policy 'tripod' introduced in 1999 by his predecessor, the Marxist sociologist turned neoliberal Fernando Henrique Cardoso: inflation targeting, floating exchange rates and fiscal restraint. In order to secure his credibility with 'the markets', Lula appointed a prominent member of Cardoso's right-wing social democratic party (*Partido da Social Democracia Brasileira,* PSDB) president of the country's independent Central Bank, with *carte blanche* to raise interest rates to the level required to secure low inflation. The Executive also raised the primary fiscal surplus target from 3.75 per cent of GDP to 4.25 per cent, and cut fiscal spending by almost 1 per cent of GDP. The minimum wage was virtually frozen for two years, and the government pushed through Congress a harsh reform of social security that had eluded Cardoso for years, partly because of the opposition from the PT and and its allies.[3]

The conservative credentials of Lula's economic policies were tempered, first, by a significant expansion of the federal programmes of social assistance. In late 2003, the government consolidated four existing programmes into the *Bolsa Família* which, initially, reached 3.6 million households. The programme was scaled up rapidly, reaching 11 million families in 2006 and 13 million today, with 50 million beneficiaries (one-quarter of the country's population). Federal social spending (health, social security and income transfers) was equivalent to 13 per cent of GDP in the 1990s; in the late 2000s, it reached 23 per cent of GDP.

Second, the Lula administration appointed a large number of progressive political, trade union and NGO cadres to the federal administration, not always from the trade union arm of the PT:[4] the president, a former metalworker, appointed five working-class cadres to ministerial-level posts; more than 100 trade unionists took other high-level posts in the public administration and in state-owned enterprises (SOEs); in turn, they appointed hundreds of lower-level colleagues.[5] Their elevation opened the floodgates to the election of an unprecedented number of poor candidates by parties across the political spectrum to all manner of posts since 2004. While these changes aligned the material interests of the leaders of many social movements (with the exception of the landless peasants' movement, *Movimento dos Trabalhadores Rurais Sem Terra,* MST) with the government's agenda and the interests of the state bureaucracy and effectively 'nationalized' them, they also changed the social composition of the Brazilian state. For the first time, poor citizens could recognize themselves in the bureaucracy and relate to friends and comrades who had become 'important' in Brasília. This change in the social composition greatly increased the legitimacy of the state, and it supported from inside the government's distributive policy agenda.

In mid-2005, Lula's first administration was paralysed by a furious right-wing and media offensive triggered by the *mensalão* corruption scandal, involving allegations that government officials paid deputies and senators a monthly stipend in exchange for votes. The *mensalão* led to the resignation of the President's Chief of Staff, the president of the PT, and several high-ranking federal officials.[6]

The scandal triggered a catastrophic loss of support for the PT. After 25 years of growth, the PT had reached 25 per cent of voter preferences in early 2005; after the *mensalão*, these rates fell by half, and Lula's bid for re-election seemed close to collapse.[7] Yet, Lula's share of first-round votes reached 49 per cent in October 2006 (up from 46 per cent, in 2002), and he maintained his second-round share at 61 per cent.

This surprising feat was due to the dissolution of the 'loser's alliance' and the transformation of Lula's base of support: he lost the middle class after the *mensalão*, but conquered the unorganized poor because of the distributive programmes introduced in his first administration: *Bolsa Família*, university admissions quotas, the formalization of the labour market, mass connections to the electricity grid (the Light for All programme, or *Luz Para Todos*), and a 48 per cent real increase in minimum wages since mid-2005, which triggered automatic increases to most pensions and benefits.

For the first time, support for the PT became inversely correlated with income.[8] In households earning more than 10 times the minimum wage (roughly, the 'middle class'), PT support fell from 32 per cent in 2002, to 17 per cent in 2006. Lula's rejection among voters with university education jumped from 24 per cent to 40 per cent between August and October 2005; 65 per cent of these voters chose the opposition candidate in 2006. In 1997, the PT had 5.5 million 'high income' and 3.1 million 'low income' supporters, and only 17 per cent of PT supporters earned less than 2 times the minimum wage. In 2006, the PT had only 3.3 million 'high income' supporters but 17.6 million 'low income' ones, and 47 per cent of its supporters earned less than twice the minimum wage.[9]

Lula won in 2006 because of his massive majority among first time voters, beneficiaries of transfer programmes, poor women (the main recipients of *Bolsa Família*) and low earners. Correspondingly, Lula lost in most rich states, but he received more than three-quarters of the votes in several poor states. In contrast, the PT elected only 83 Federal Deputies in 2006 (down from 91 in 2002), showing that the support of the poor was tightly focused on the President.[10] Voting patterns between 1982 (just after the PT was founded) and 2006 suggest that the Brazilian poor traditionally voted for the right, and they shifted to Lula only *after* he had been elected by other social groups, and had delivered to the poor higher incomes, benefits and considerable improvements to their living conditions.

The transformation in Lula's base of support was part of a structural realignment of Brazilian politics. On the side of the government, we now find the domestic bourgeoisie, the organized working class and the informal proletariat.[11] The opposition is based on the alliance between the neoliberal bourgeoisie and the middle class, bound together by a rabid mainstream media.

THE SECOND LULA ADMINISTRATION

In Lula's second administration, a number of elements of neo-developmentalist economic heterodoxy diluted the neoliberal policy 'tripod'.[12] This policy inflection, and the favourable global economic environment in the mid-2000s, led to a marked uplift in macroeconomic performance and in employment creation, and supported an unprecedented reduction of inequality in the country.

Brazil's growth surge was driven by consumption and state-led investment. Let us start from the latter. The fiscal and financial stresses experienced after the international debt crisis, in the early 1980s, and during the neoliberal transition, in the 1990s, followed by successive rounds of public spending cuts in order to stabilize the debt/GDP ratio led to a severe degradation of the country's infrastructure. In order to release funds for investment without overtly confronting the neoliberal lobby, the second Lula administration changed the form of calculation of the primary surplus in order to exclude the state-owned enterprises (SOEs, especially the oil and electricity companies, Petrobras and Eletrobrás). This allowed SOE investment to quadruple in nominal terms, rising from 1.8 per cent of GDP in the mid-2000s, to 2.2 per cent of GDP in 2010.

This investment spree was supplemented by private investment, mostly directly funded or, at least, guaranteed by the state-owned banks (especially BNDES, which became the largest development bank in the world). The government also launched a 'growth acceleration programme' (PAC) in early 2007, focusing on energy, transport and infrastructure. This was followed by a large housing programme ('My Home My Life', or *Minha Casa Minha Vida*), increased funding for education, health and other public services, and the expansion of the civil service, together with significant pay increases, in order to recover policy-making capacity and reduce the number of subcontracted workers in the state sector. The government also supported diplomatically and through BNDES the transnationalization of selected domestic firms ('national champions'). They include Itaú and Bradesco (banking), Embraer (aviation), Odebrecht (construction), Vale (mining), Inbev (beverages), Gerdau (steel) and Friboi and Brazil Foods (processed foods).[13]

In turn, consumption rose because of the rapid rise in the minimum wage, the increase in federal transfers to pensioners, the unemployed and the disabled from R$135 billion to R$305 billion between 2002 and 2009, and the quadrupling of personal credit, which rose from 24 per cent of GDP to 45 per cent, while mortgage lending expanded from R$26 billion in 2004 to R$80 billion in 2009.[14]

Despite these aggressive spending initiatives, the fiscal deficit remained stable and the domestic public debt declined from 55 per cent of GDP, in mid-2002, to 40 per cent in 2010, because of the rapid growth of GDP, the increase in fiscal revenues due to economic growth and the programme of formalization of the labour market, which brought in new social security contributions. The average rate of growth of real per capita GDP rose from 0.75 per cent per annum between 1995-2002, in the Cardoso administration, to 2.4 per cent between 2003-06, and to 3.5 per cent between 2007-10, in Lula's second administration, despite the adverse impact of the global crisis.

The pattern of growth under Lula was unquestionably pro-poor.[15] First, the economic expansion in the 2000s created 21 million jobs (in contrast with 11 million during the 1990s; see Tables 1 and 2). Around 80 per cent of them were in the formal sector.[16] Significantly, around 90 per cent of jobs created in the 2000s paid less than 1.5 times the minimum wage (51 per cent in the 1990s). Unemployment fell sharply, especially in the lower segments of the labour markets, reaching less than 10 per cent of the workforce for the first time in decades.

Table 1: Brazil: Net new employment creation (thousands)[17]

	1970s	1980s	1990s	2000s
> 5 minimum wages	2,856	5,980	953	-4,279
3 - 5 minimum wages	3,100	3,377	482	311
1.5 - 3 minimum wages	5,437	4,084	4,002	6,122
< 1.5 minimum wages	5,892	4,586	-295	19,941
Unwaged	-62	126	5,905	-1,080
Total	17,223	18,153	11,047	21,015

Table 2: Brazil: Distribution of wages (%)[18]

	1970	1980	1990	2000	2009
> 5 minimum wages	4.7	9.6	14.5	16.7	7.5
3 - 5 minimum wages	4.3	10.0	11.4	12.0	8.9
1.5 - 3 minimum wages	13.8	21.1	21.3	25.5	24.9
< 1.5 minimum wages	64.3	51.9	45.3	34.3	47.8
Unwaged	12.8	7.4	7.5	11.5	10.9

Second, inequality declined across a broad spectrum of measures.[19] The Gini coefficient fell from 0.57 in 1995 to 0.52 in 2008. The incomes of the bottom decile rose by 91 per cent between 2001 and 2009, while the incomes of the top decile increased by a more modest 16 per cent. Incomes rose by 42 per cent in the poorer northeast of the country against 16 per cent in the southeast; more in the periphery than in the centre of São Paulo, and more in rural than in urban areas. Female income rose by 38 per cent against 16 per cent for men (60 per cent of the jobs created in the 2000s employed women), and the income of blacks rose 43 per cent against 20 per cent for whites. Finally, the population below the poverty line fell from 36 per cent in 2003 to 23 per cent in 2008, benefitting 20 million people.

Unsurprisingly, Lula's approval rate touched on 90 per cent towards the end of his second term.[20] He hand-picked and secured the election of his successor, former Chief of Staff Dilma Rousseff, who won 56 per cent of the ballots in the second round.[21] Despite these considerable achievements, a closer examination of Lula's administration reveals limitations at four levels.

First, the labour markets remain weak. Subcontracting is still rising in SOEs, large private companies and in the services sector, and these workers earn 40-60 per cent less than their peers performing similar tasks. This might help to explain the extremely high proportion of very low-paid jobs created during the 2000s and the slow recovery of the wage share of national income, which rose only from 38 per cent in 2000 to less than 50 per cent today (the same level it had 30 years ago, at the end of import-substituting industrialization, and still under the military dictatorship).[22] Conversely, 4.3 million jobs paying more than 5 times the minimum wage were lost in the 2000s (while 950,000 were created in the 1990s). This may be partly due to the rise of the minimum wage and to the (largely involuntary) exit of relatively high earners from the labour markets, as many were compelled to become small entrepreneurs through a severe lack of alternatives. It does, however, shed some light on the employment difficulties faced by the middle class.

Second, the balance of payments constraint has been relaxed, but not hugely. Brazil has become a net creditor for the first time in history, and it now holds US$370 billion in international reserves. Although this can provide a cushion against fluctuations in the global economic environment, the country continues to run a current account deficit; therefore, its currency reserves are 'borrowed' rather than 'earned': they are due to capital inflows, which are volatile and give rise to corresponding foreign currency liabilities.

Third, the exchange rate has been overvalued throughout Lula's administration, because of the high interest rate policy of the Central Bank, the commodity boom and the capital inflows due to foreign investment and quantitative easing programmes in the US, UK and the eurozone.

Fourth, at a political level the PT is large but weak, and riven by contradictions.[23] The party defends both economic stability and structural reforms; it supports large capital while postulating the socialization of the means of production; and it advocates a new political culture while making alliances with deeply unsavoury characters. Beyond its inability to choose a programme which it can actually support, the PT has neglected its most committed supporters in the trade unions and the MST, and shied away from reforming the media even though the press has repeatedly attempted to destroy the PT, its leaders and their administrations. The PT has also been increasingly shunned by a noisy middle class, but it continues to receive the support of the poor.

DILMA ROUSSEFF'S ADMINISTRATION

Dilma Rousseff was a technocrat; she had never fought an election before, and had no support base. Having been anointed by Lula, she inherited both his voters and his detractors. The voting pattern in 2010 closely mirrored that of the 2006 elections: Dilma won in the poorer states of the north and northeast and in most of the southeast, except São Paulo state. In each state, her vote was concentrated in the poorer areas and among the least educated voters. Her main rival, from PSDB, won in São Paulo and in the richer states in the 'arch of agribusiness' across the south and the centre-west and, nationally, among higher income and more educated voters.

After Dilma's inauguration, in January 2011, the government expanded further its social programmes in order to eliminate absolute poverty, which still impinges on 17 million people, and tilted economic policy a bit more towards neo-developmentalism, but without formally abandoning the neoliberal 'tripod'. Monetary and exchange rate policies were aligned more closely with the government's industrial policy, in order to limit the current account deficit and support the internalization of strategic production chains. Real interest rates fell to their lowest levels in 20 years (from an average of 22 per cent in Cardoso's first administration, to less than 3 per cent under Dilma), and the Central Bank started extending the maturity and lowering the costs of the domestic public debt. The government introduced successive rounds of tax rebates in order to incentivize production and control inflation (in a significant departure from the single-minded focus on the manipulation of interest rates, under neoliberalism), and strong-armed the private operators into reducing the price of electricity. Finally, the government sought to attract private investment into infrastructure and transport through concessions, public-private partnerships and regulatory changes, in order to bypass budgetary constraints and legal limitations to state funding, and to commit the domestic bourgeoisie to the government's investment programme.

Despite these policy changes, the Brazilian economy has slowed down significantly. First, because the government has failed to kick-start a virtuous circle of growth driven by private investment, despite the increase in fiscal spending, SOE investment, loans by state-owned banks and the profusion of incentives and tax rebates.

Second, because of a deteriorating balance of payments due to the slowdown in Brazil's main markets (China, the EU and the US), sluggish commodity prices and the aggressive devaluations and export-led recovery strategies in several large economies. Moreover, low interest rates and quantitative easing in the advanced economies have triggered capital flows to Brazil, leading to the appreciation of the *real* and worsening the country's competitive position. These adverse outcomes were compounded by the high income-elasticity of Brazil's imports (every 1 per cent growth in Brazil raises imports by 3.4 per cent), in contrast with the country's low income elasticity of exports (every 1 per cent growth in the rest of the world raises Brazil's exports by 1.3 per cent).[24] The country's current account deficit rose from 2.1 per cent of GDP in 2011 to 2.7 per cent in 2012 and 3.8 per cent in the first two quarters of 2013.

This worrying trend was tempered by the reversal of capitals flows, anticipating the unwinding of quantitative easing. This outflow sucked the life out of the São Paulo stock exchange, which tumbled from 62,000 points in January 2013 to 46,000 in July, and triggered a rapid devaluation of the *real* between May and June. For this reason, and because of poor food crops, inflation edged up in early 2013.

Under severe pressure from the media, the financial markets, its parliamentary base, the middle class and most economists, the government reaffirmed its commitment to the inflation targets and signalled to the Central Bank that it was time to start raising interest rates; at the same time, the Ministry of Finance announced cuts in public spending. Wage income and the level of employment have remained stable, but they now tend to decline slowly. These policy adjustments do not necessarily signal the return of naked neoliberalism, but they do illustrate the limits of government power in a globally integrated middle-income capitalist economy, and the political fragility of Dilma's administration.

In the first months of 2013, the media was trumpeting the 'failure' of every aspect of government policy, and the 'imminent threat' of runaway inflation. Their negative campaign shifted the popular mood, and Dilma's popularity fell by 8-10 percentage points, although starting from an extraordinary level of 70 per cent, which had never been achieved by any Brazilian president in their third year in office.

The government's economic difficulties were compounded by political limitations. Lula was a charismatic leader, and he excelled at the conciliation of differences. Dilma lacks these virtues. Although she is an accomplished manager, she is said to be abrasive and intimidating, and her government has deliberately turned away the trade unions, left-wing NGOs and the MST in order to pursue a progressive technocratic agenda, which has created a sense of despondency among her strongest supporters.[25] On top of it all, the entire – badly divided – left controls less than one-third of the seats in Congress, of which only half (around 15 per cent of the seats in the Chamber of Deputies and in the Senate) are held by the PT. This makes it impossible to govern without volatile alliances with undisciplined parties and grubby individuals, which have to be managed under the gaze of a hostile press and the scrutiny of a right-wing judicial system. After ten years in federal office, the PT seems to have political hegemony without the substance of power; at the same time, it seems to engage in the same dirty political games as everyone else, belying its historical claim to hold the moral high ground.

An economic recovery in 2014 remains plausible, depending on the productivity gains due to better infrastructure provision (half of PAC projects are nearing completion), improvements in the balance of payments and the recovery of private investment, which has declined from 16.4 per cent of GDP in 2010, to 14.7 per cent in 2012.[26] The government can also pump up personal credit and mortgage loans, which remain small by global standards. Around 40 per cent of the workforce remains in the informal sector, and does not contribute to the coffers of the social security system. Finally, the government can also loosen fiscal policy further, or engineer another round of devaluation of the *real*. Unfortunately these options are limited: the global crisis is likely to drag on, productivity gains from specific projects are notoriously uncertain, and the accumulation of personal debt may not fuel a sustained process of growth. It will be difficult to continue increasing the formalization of the workforce in a slowing economy, further fiscal loosening risks a political backlash, and the devaluation of the currency is inflationary in the short-term. The scenario in mid-2013 pointed towards the gradual deterioration of the main macroeconomic variables, the build-up of social and political tensions, and the continuing reduction of the degrees of freedom available to the state.

THE EVENTS OF JUNE

On 6 June, the radical left Free Fare Movement (*Movimento Passe Livre*, MPL), an autonomist organization, led a small demonstration demanding the reversal of a recent increase in public transport fares in the city of São Paulo, from R$3 to R$3.20 (a similar fare increase had also been introduced in Rio de Janeiro).[27] The movement was criticized by the press for obstructing the roads and making unrealistic demands, and their demonstration was attacked by the police. The MPL returned in larger numbers in the following days, and the police responded with increasing brutality, beating up scores of people and shooting demonstrators and journalists with rubber bullets.

Suddenly, the main press and TV networks changed sides and started supporting the movement. The media provided abundant coverage of the demonstrations, effectively calling people to the streets, and it sponsored the multiplication and de-radicalization of demands, towards a cacophony focusing on citizenship issues, state inefficiency and corruption. The demonstrations exploded in size and spread across the country; they also became much more white and middle class in composition.[28] In less than two weeks they involved well over one million people in hundreds of cities, mostly young workers, students and the middle class, categories of workers with corporative demands (bus drivers, lorry drivers, health sector workers, and so on), and working-class neighbourhoods seeking local improvements.

In common with recent mass movements elsewhere, for example in Turkey, the Brazilian demonstrations were highly heterogeneous, including a multiplicity of groups and movements with unrelated demands, and organized primarily through social media and TV. Interestingly, the Brazilian demonstrations often had no clear leaders and no speeches. Groups of people would often get organized on Facebook and Twitter, meet somewhere, and then march in directions that were frequently unclear, depending on decisions made by unknown persons more or less on the spot.

Anyone could come up with their own demand or call their own demonstration, and if they were anti-political and humorous this would increase their chances of appearing on TV. The demonstrations included banners about a whole range of issues, among them public services (for); FIFA, the 2013 Confederations Cup and the 2014 World Cup (against); gay rights and the legalization of drugs (mainly for, but most churches are against); compulsory voting (mostly against); abortion and religious issues (all over the place); public spending, privatizations and the state monopolies (unclear); Dilma Rousseff and the PT (strongly against); the return of military rule (a far-right pipe-dream); and, strongly highlighted by the media, corruption (against which everyone could happily march together). It was especially paradoxical to see middle-class people expressing indignation over public services that they neither use, nor intend to use any time soon.

Police repression was sometimes accompanied by riots, and then the police pulled back, partly because of concerns for their public image; at other times, the police would attack the demonstrators while leaving the rioters alone. Infiltration by the police and the far right was both evident and widespread. Some marches were, somehow, declared 'party-free', and left-wing militants and trade unionists were harassed and beaten up by thugs shouting 'my party is my country'. During this period, the mobilizations continued to grow; as they did so, they became both more radicalized and more fragmented. When the federal government finally pushed São Paulo and Rio de Janeiro to reverse the transport fare increases by offering them tax breaks, accompanied by the threat of leaving them alone to sort out the mess otherwise, the mobilizations were already out of control.

In late June, the left made a coordinated effort to regain the leadership of the movement, while the federal government, after considerable hesitation, sought left support for the first time. In a meeting with state governors and mayors of the major cities on 24 June, Dilma Rousseff proposed a 'national pact' to reduce corruption, introduce political reforms and expand public service provision, especially in health, education and public transport, to be funded in part by the revenues flowing from the country's new deep water oilfields (which were originally going into a sovereign wealth fund).

Dilma's two key initiatives were, first, to call a plebiscite to reform the electoral and party political legislation. The current system is highly complex, and it creates incentives for career politicians to take large private donations or steal public funds in order to fund their campaigns. Since Congress is unlikely to agree a significant change in the rules, much less a progressive one (including, for example, the right of recall of elected officials and the prohibition of private campaign funding), a plebiscite offers the best way forward for the left. The media, the right-wing opposition and part of the government's notional supporters in Congress immediately decided to obstruct this initiative, which risks floundering. Second, the government proposed a significant expansion of basic health provision through additional funding and the hiring of foreign doctors to work in three thousand deprived municipalities. This initiative was strongly opposed by the medical lobby, and its future remains uncertain.

In the meantime, eight national trade union confederations, including CUT, joined together with the MST and a broad range of popular organizations to organize a 'day of action' on 11 July, attempting to shift the focus of the wave of protests back towards immediate working-class demands. These include the reduction of the working week from 44 to 40 hours, higher state pensions and the restriction of subcontracting. The demonstrations and strikes taking place on that day included several hundred thousand workers; unsurprisingly, media coverage was very modest.

The demonstrations dwindled rapidly at the end of June. They were succeeded by scattered mobilizations of a few dozen or (rarely) a few hundred people, often with a heavy presence of 'Black Bloc' anarchists and right-wing hooligans intent on attacking shops and banks. Rio de Janeiro is the only exception, because there the demonstrations morphed into a left political offensive (including the PT) against the state governor, a member of the centre-right PMDB and, nominally, an ally of Dilma Rousseff. The tendency, however, points to the continuing fragmentation and decline of the demonstrations, although new flare-ups remain possible in the run-up to the 2014 Football World Cup and the start of the electoral campaign.

CHALLENGES FOR THE LEFT

The Events of June have posed difficult challenges for the Brazilian left. Most radical left parties, trade unions and mass organizations were disabled long ago by the neoliberal reforms; the mass base of the left has been extensively decomposed, collective action has become harder, and the left has been both supported and tainted by association with the PT federal administrations. The cultural identifiers and political expectations of the formal and informal working class and the middle class have been transformed, and the internet has changed radically the modalities of social interaction among the youth. For many workers and students, the military dictatorship is ancient history, and the PT is the only party they have ever seen in office in Brasília. The demands and expectations of the formal and informal working class have shot up in the last decade, while the middle class, stuck in opposition for years, has become embittered. The press devalues the political system and harasses the left relentlessly, and the economy has been slowing down for three years. Suddenly, the streets seem to explode: every social group parades its own frustrations, unprecedented rioting takes place, and the government – already disconnected from the organized left and the middle classes – is clearly bewildered. What now?

The first challenge for the Brazilian left is to appreciate what has been achieved in the last decade. The second challenge, inseparable from the first, is to recognize the shortcomings of the PT administrations and identify where progress is most urgent.

The economic, social and political achievements of the administrations led by Lula and Dilma are in no way revolutionary, but they are real enough, both for the workers and for the national economy. The fragilities of Dilma's administration are due, in part, to her personal style, the frailty of her parliamentary base, her simultaneous isolation from the organized workers and the middle class, the dysfunctionalities of the political system, widely-held perceptions that politics is inherently corrupt, the legal straitjacket that makes it painfully difficult to spend public money, the growing activism of a conservative judiciary, media hostility, and the depth and extent of the remaining inequalities in the country. Dilma's fragilities are also due to the *achievements* of the PT administrations, which have raised the expectations of the workers and the poor much faster than their income or the state's capacity to deliver public goods. The economic slowdown has also created the impression that the cycle of prosperity which started with Lula has become exhausted, adding to the sense of dissatisfaction that fuelled the recent explosion.

It follows that the demonstrations are the outcome of three distinct processes. First, they result from a confluence of dissatisfactions. The middle class has lost much through the recent improvements in income distribution and the democratization of the state, and finance has lost because of the policy inflection towards neo-developmentalism. Finance is clear about its own losses, and it seeks to rebalance the books through the perpetuation of a 'fear of inflation' leading to higher real interest rates and better returns on its assets. In contrast, the middle class has no clear understanding of its predicament, and it has projected its discontent on to the state and the political system ('corruption', 'inefficiency') and – guess what – the threat posed by inflation to its standard of living. These are purely negative platforms. In contrast, the formal and informal workers want to protect what they have achieved, and they also demand more – *right now*. This confluence of frustrations is a recipe for social and political volatility.

Second, the PT has been unable to manage the demands emerging through the success of its own policies, and it is, in this sense, a victim of its own success. For example, economic growth, income distribution and the wider availability of credit and tax breaks to domestic industry have led to an explosion in automobile sales, while woefully insufficient investment in infrastructure and in public transport has created traffic gridlock in many large cities.[29] Rapid urbanization has overwhelmed the electricity, water and sanitation systems, leading to power cuts and repeated disasters in the rainy season. Public health and education have expanded, but they are widely perceived to offer poor quality services. There has been virtually no progress on land reform, condemning millions to a life of marginality while agribusiness prospers. The press remains heavily concentrated, and it attacks the government insistently. In this sense, the Events of June were *not* primarily due to perceptions of losses, except by the middle class (which poured into the streets *en masse*, but only in the second phase of the movement). Instead, the protests were sparked by popular demands for the improvement of services that are already available, but that have become completely unsatisfactory in the light of the growing expectations of the workers and the poor. As the economy has stagnated and social and distributive conflicts have picked up, the government has found it increasingly difficult to juggle these contradictory pressures, and it shows signs of running out of steam.

It is impossible to address these challenges purely institutionally, without the aggressive deployment of public resources for strategic ends and the mobilization of the working class to confront the traditional elites. However, these destabilizing options were never considered by the PT administrations. Instead, they have systematically chosen a gradualist strategy including minimal legislative and regulatory changes and, until recently, as little involvement by the popular organizations as possible. The Events of June suggest that this strategy may be exhausted, and it may even help to paralyze the government, potentially sealing its defeat in the 2014 elections.

Third, the protests have revealed a deep disconnect between most social classes and fractions and their political structures of representation. The demonstrations were, generally, against politics *as a whole*, rather than focusing on specific administrations or political leaders. Many demonstrated against Dilma and the PT, and Dilma's approval in the opinion polls halved in the month of June to 30 per cent, but no one demonstrated for neoliberalism, the return of Cardoso's policies, or the PSDB. It is also sobering to realize that there were no mass demands for socialism: discontent is high, but revolution remains off the working-class agenda.[30] No party has gained from the demonstrations, except, perhaps, the new 'Rede de Sustentabilidade' (Sustainability Network) led by former Minister Marina Silva, who has 20 per cent of the preferences for the 2014 presidential elections. This overtly 'green' organization is a potentially useful front for the right, as it searches far and wide for viable candidates; however the Rede's growth has been limited by its inability, so far, to obtain the 500,000 signatures required to register a new party.[31]

CONCLUSION

In the wake of the largest mass movements in a generation, it has become essential for the left to support Dilma Rousseff's administration. This has been recognized by most working-class organizations, including the MST.[32] The Brazilian experience demonstrates the feasibility of policy alternatives to neoliberalism, and it supports more ambitious political experiences in Latin America and elsewhere. If the current government became incoherent or paralysed, this is unlikely to facilitate a socialist revolution in Brazil, because there are no ideological, organizational, social, material or international conditions for that to happen. It would, instead, facilitate a right-wing victory in the 2014 presidential elections, demoralize and disorganize the Brazilian left, and halt the painfully slow progress towards democratic policies in the country.

A new policy agenda for the left can be based on the government's recognition that it has failed to improve living conditions in urban areas sufficiently rapidly, and that further improvements in these areas, and in growth and distribution more generally, require not only technocratic solutions with a progressive character, but the integration of left social movements into the policy-making process. This could help to strengthen and radicalize the political agenda, increase the legitimacy of administration's policies, and expand the mass base of the government. This would also incorporate the most significant lesson of the Events of June for the left: that the careful choice of targets, organization, dedication to the struggle and persistence can bring important successes. The reduction of transport fares has put public services at the top of the political agenda. This is a massively popular area of struggle, directly affecting tens of millions of people. However, even beyond reducing bus ticket prices, the demonstrations have been a political school for a new generation of workers, with potentially far-reaching consequences.

Left initiatives in the current circumstances can seek to bring together the workers and the poor, marginalize and fragment the middle class and the right and put pressure on the state apparatus, while allowing a radical working-class movement to work together with some state institutions in order to raise, from below, their influence on policy formulation and implementation. The left should, then, engage in a dialogue with the government, while insisting that a predominantly parliamentary strategy to introduce democratic Constitutional and policy reforms will fail.

Feasible reforms include the decommodification of public goods and services, starting with education, health, transport, water and sanitation, and improvements in the quantity and quality of provision; legal changes in fiscal and budgetary policy to facilitate a counter-cyclical and growth-accommodating policy stance; the break-up of media monopolies; the limitation of working hours; the reform of the political system; police reform; and the full implementation of the country's environmental laws.

This strategy is not risk-free. Indeed, it is likely to trigger another finance, media and middle-class backlash, backed up by the judiciary and a large part of Congress. But the left is running out of options. The risk of inaction is that – given the economic slowdown – media pressures, financial sector plotting, middle-class hostility and far-right provocations could pin down the administration and deliver the 2014 elections to the right. Even if this does not lead to a complete reversal of the distributive gains achieved under Lula and Dilma, it would have a lasting and profoundly negative impact upon the organized working class and the left in Brazil.

NOTES

We are grateful to Al Campbell and Ben Fine for their generous comments on this essay. The usual disclaimers apply.

1   See Lecio Morais and Alfredo Saad-Filho, 'Snatching Defeat from the Jaws of Victory? Lula, the Workers' Party and the Prospects for Change in Brazil', *Capital & Class*, 81, 2003, pp. 17-23; and 'Lula and the Continuity of Neoliberalism in Brazil: Strategic Choice, Economic Imperative or Political Schizophrenia?, *Historical Materialism*, 13(1), 2005, pp. 3-32.

2   For a description of the Brazilian class structure, see Armando Boito Jr., 'Governos Lula: a Nova Burguesia Nacional no Poder', in Armando Boito Jr. e Andréia Galvão, eds., *Política e Classes Sociais no Brasil dos Anos 2000*, São Paulo: Alameda, 2012, pp. 67-104.

3   The implementation of the economic policies associated with Cardoso under Lula and the *mensalão* scandal led radical left groups within the PT and religious leaders concerned with ethics in political life to set up the Party of Socialism and Freedom (*Partido Socialismo e Liberdade*, PSOL) in 2005. The most prominent member of PSOL was an evangelical leader, Senator Heloísa Helena, known as 'The Little Saint' (*Santinha*) by the poor in her home state of Alagoas. Her bid for the presidency in 2006 was welcomed by the middle classes in metropolitan areas in the south and the southeast, and she received 6.8 per cent of the ballots, but the party only elected three federal deputies. In

the 2010 presidential elections, the PSOL obtained 0.9 per cent of the votes and, again, elected three deputies. Since then, despite its socialist discourse, the party has worked mainly among the radicalized middle classes; it focuses its attention on corruption.

4   Two trade union confederations were founded in final years of the military dictatorship (1964-85). The United Labour Congress (*Central Única dos Trabalhadores*, CUT) was the largest by far, and it operated as the trade union arm of the PT; the General Confederation of Labour (*Confederação Geral dos Trabalhadores*, CGT) included trade unions aligned with the right as well as the far left, but united in their opposition to CUT. Today, there are eight trade union confederations in Brazil, of which five are closely aligned with rival political parties. The largest are CUT and Trade Union Power (*Força Sindical*, FS), which is connected with the Democratic Labour Party (*Partido Democrático Trabalhista*, PDT), founded by the left nationalist and populist leader, Leonel Brizola. Most confederations work together with the PT administrations, but CUT and FS have managed to appoint a large number of cadres for the Ministry of Labour, which has considerable power over the structure and the operations of the trade unions.

5   Armando Boito, 'A Hegemonia Neoliberal no Governo Lula', *Crítica Marxista*, 17, 2003, p. 6; André Singer, 'A Segunda Alma do Partido dos Trabalhadores', *Novos Estudos Cebrap*, 88, 2010, p. 109.

6   Most of the accused were found guilty by the Supreme Court in 2012, and several were given prison sentences. The President of the Supreme Court is now touted as a potential right-wing candidate in the 2014 presidential elections.

7   Singer, 'A Segunda Alma', p. 94.

8   André Singer, 'Raízes Sociais e Ideológicas do Lulismo', *Novos Estudos Cebrap*, 85, 2009, pp. 83-102.

9   Singer, 'A Segunda Alma', pp. 96-7.

10   Singer, 'Raízes do Lulismo'; see also Singer 'A Segunda Alma', p. 98; and Jean Tible, 'O Fenômeno Político do Lulismo e a Construção de Uma Nova Classe Social', in *Classes Sociais no Brasil de Hoje*, available at http://novo.fpabramo. org.br.

11   The terms 'organized working class' and 'informal proletariat' concern the type of capitalist relationship in which these workers are included. The organized sector refers to formally registered enterprises operating according to typically capitalist principles and hiring workers through legally enforceable contracts. This sector includes the civil service, all state-owned enterprises (SOEs) and the largest private firms. The informal proletariat has heterogeneous occupations, performs non-standardized work and does not produce standardized commodities for sale; they often depend on transfers for survival, which may be legal (state benefits), voluntary (charity) or involuntary (crime). They are normally employed in households or in unregistered firms, do not sign legally enforceable contracts and, often, do not have fixed wages. They include most domestic servants, unregistered street sellers, irregular (unskilled) workers, prostitutes, vagrants and petty criminals. In Brazil, only the organized sector

workers are legally allowed to set up or join trade unions. Under neoliberalism, the informal proletariat has had an increasingly close relationship with the working class, with whom they intermingle at the margins of the 'liberalized' labour markets.

12   Lecio Morais and Alfredo Saad-Filho, 'Brazil beyond Lula: Forging Ahead or Pausing for Breath?', *Latin American Perspectives*, 38(2), 2011, pp. 31-44; 'Neo-Developmentalism and the Challenges of Economic Policy-Making under Dilma Rousseff', *Critical Sociology*, 38(6), 2012, pp. 789-98.

13   Boito, 'A Hegemonia Neoliberal'.

14   Marcio Pochmann, 'Políticas Sociais e Padrão de Mudanças no Brasil Durante o Governo Lula', SER Social, 13(28), pp. 25-7.

15   Alfredo Saad-Filho, 'There is Life beyond the Washington Consensus: An Introduction to Pro-Poor Macroeconomic Policies', *Review of Political Economy*, 19(4), 2007, pp. 513-37.

16   Wladimir Pomar, 'Debatendo Classes e Luta de Classes no Brasil', in *Classes Sociais no Brasil de Hoje*, p. 42.

17   Marcio Pochmann, *Nova Classe Média?*, São Paulo: Boitempo, 2012, p. 27.

18   Pochmann, *Nova Classe Média?*, p. 28.

19   Estêvão K.X. Bastos, *Distribuição Funcional da Renda no Brasil: Estimativas Anuais e Construção de Uma Série Trimestral*, Texto para Discussão IPEA, No. 1702, 2012; Marcio Pochmann, 'Estrutura Social no Brasil: Mudanças Recentes', *Serviço Social & Sociedade*, 104, 2010, pp. 640, 648; Pochmann, 'Políticas Sociais', p. 38; Pochmann, *Nova Classe Média*, p. 32; André Singer, 'Realinhamento, Ciclo Longo e Coalizões de Classe', available at http://www.reded.net.br; and Tible, 'O Fenômeno Político do Lulismo', p. 68.

20   Brazilian presidents can be re-elected only once, but they can run again after a break. There are persistent rumours that Lula may yet try his luck.

21   For a detailed account, see Morais and Saad-Filho, 'Brazil beyond Lula'.

22   Pomar, 'Debatendo Classes', p. 42. Using a different dataset, starting in the mid-90s, Bastos, '*Distribuição Funcional da Renda*', pp. 29-31, shows that the wage share declined steadily until 2003, when it had lost around 6 percentage points of GDP; it then turned around and recovered most of the lost ground by 2008.

23   Singer, 'A Segunda Alma', pp. 110-1.

24   André Nassif, 'Estagnação: Reflexões e Sugestões', available at http://www.valor.com.br.

25   Josué Medeiros, 'O PT e as Classes Sociais no Brasil: Reflexões após Dez Anos de "Lulismo"', available at http://novo.fpabramo.org.br, p. 59.

26   Data available from http://www.planejamento.gov.br and http://www.ibge.gov.br.

27   For a more detailed review of the protests, see Alfredo Saad-Filho 'Mass Protests under "Left Neoliberalism": Brazil, June-July 2013', *Critical Sociology*, 2013 (forthcoming). The history of the MPL is outlined in Euan Gibb, 'Brazil: Private Transit, Public Protests', available at http://www.socialistproject.ca.

28   For an anecdotal account of the demonstrations, see http://www.rededemocratica.org. An opinion poll in eight state capitals on 20 June (a day

of large demonstrations) suggested that 63 per cent of the demonstrators were aged 14-29, 92 per cent had completed at least secondary school, 52 per cent were students, 76 per cent were in paid employment, and only 45 per cent earned less than 5 minimum wages. In other words, they had attended school for much longer and had much higher incomes than the population average; see http://g1.globo.com and http://thesmokefilledroomblog.com.

29   Marilena Chauí, 'As Manifestações de Junho de 2013 na Cidade de São Paulo', available at http://www.teoriaedebate.org.br.

30   The radical left has found it difficult to prosper under the twin pressures of neoliberalism and PT political hegemony. The recomposition of the working class in the last 30 years has increased social heterogeneity and reduced the workers' organizational and political capacities, while the dissolution of socialist alternatives worldwide and Brazil's integration into 'global' culture have deprived the proletariat of alternative political references (with the partial exception of Chavez's Venezuela, which is demonized by the right and remains contested among the left). Since the early 1980s, no party has grown to the left of the PT, and debates about the desirability and feasibility of revolutionary alternatives to capitalism have largely died down.

31   Marina Silva is an ascetic popular leader from the Amazon, and a strict adventist. She rose in the PT as an environmentalist with extensive connections with international NGOs, and acquired a good reputation among the urban middle class. She served as Minister of the Environment in Lula's first administration, where she had no measurable impact. She subsequently left the government and the PT, and ran as the Green Party candidate against Dilma in 2010. Marina obtained 20 per cent of the ballots in the first round, against the PSDB's José Serra's 32 per cent. In the second round of the elections, against Dilma Rousseff, both Serra's and Dilma's shares of the votes increased by 10 per cent, suggesting that Marina's voters split evenly among the two camps. Marina has thrived in the environmental movement and through her extensive use of social networks; however, her economic and social policies remain vague, except for her opposition to abortion and gay rights.

32   The MST is the most important radical left-wing mass organization in Brazil. In contrast, the far left parties are relatively small, and they have been largely ineffective in terms of their own programmatic ambitions. The Communist Party of Brazil (*Partido Comunista do Brasil*, PCdoB) has reiterated its support for Dilma's administration, where it heads the Ministry of Sport. PSOL was initially critical of Dilma and the PT, but joined the mainstream left when it became clear that the protests were being kidnapped by the middle class and the far right; the party is now contributing to the debate about the Constitutional reform (http://www.psol50.org.br; document issued on 16 July 2013). The Unified Socialist Workers' Party (*Partido Socialista dos Trabalhadores Unificado*, PSTU) has called for a decisive break with the PT in order to prepare the launch of a revolutionary left alternative (http://www.pstu.org.br; document issued on 30 July 2013).

BEYOND THE LABOUR OF SISYPHUS: UNIONS AND THE CITY

IAN MACDONALD

The dominant perspective of trade unionism in the United States has for decades been to lead an orderly retreat, giving ground on this and that issue, while defending the union as a 'precious thing', an end–in–itself. For much of the left, the hope is that spirited local defensive battles may be generalized to the class as a whole, thereby transforming economic into political struggles. But as a strategy for labour renewal this confronts a series of dilemmas, especially as rates of union representation have declined to 6.9 per cent of private sector employment in the US (12 per cent when public sector workers are included). This important measure of how far American class society has been transformed by neoliberalism demonstrates clearly that defensives struggles that have occurred have largely remained isolated, and have been defeated as such. Moreover, they have usually involved defending an institutional form of trade unionism that was built on the ruins of a labour left. Insofar as a left strategy for labour must begin with the practices of the existing institutions, it is because no new form of working-class organization exists to take their place.

There is a more important dilemma at issue. A great many of the social struggles we see today – and are sure to see more of in the future – do not arise from the workplace or from the wage relation narrowly conceived. They are sparked by the destruction of a park, a rise in transit fares, racist policing strategies, and the dismantling of public education. No one familiar with labour history could deny that the fate of the labour movement is linked to these struggles. Yet in too many instances we find union apparatuses on the other side, deeply implicated in the very neoliberal urban accumulation strategies and governing regimes that are at the root of the problems.

In 1906, Rosa Luxemburg identified the purely trade union struggle with a labour of Sisyphus – 'the proletarian of the gods' – while criticizing trade union leaders who 'refer with the greatest satisfaction to the achievements of the last fifteen years', instead of mobilizing against

> the simultaneous and immense reduction of the proletarian standard of life by land usury, by the whole tax and customs policy, by landlord rapacity which has increased house rents to such an exorbitant extent, in short, by all the objective tendencies of bourgeois policy which have largely neutralised the advantages of the fifteen years of trade-union struggle.[1]

How much more pertinent this charge is today, when instead of fifteen years of past achievements we have thirty years of eroding standards.

It is not at all surprising, then, to find that many activists today have simply abandoned strategic engagement with labour, and with it any class-based project for social transformation. Even young staffers going into the unions expect that any revival of the US labour movement will arise only out of the rubble of the existing business-unionist institutions. But this only begs the question: if the existing institutions are inadequate, what organizational forms and strategies for labour would be adequate? The privilege of our time is to act in a moment of widening realization that both capitalism, and the labour unions that would ameliorate capitalism, have failed to meet the needs and expectations of the vast majority. To move on, it will be necessary, first, to show how dominant labour strategies are hopelessly entangled in class contradictions as a result of their being embedded in neoliberal capitalism; and second, to outline a strategy for labour that develops anew in working-class struggles what Luxemburg called 'the power of seeing the larger connections and of taking a survey of the whole position'.[2]

THE URBANIZATION OF TRADE UNIONISM

A quick survey of US union membership shows that the majority are located in branches of the economy at one or more remove from what Marxist political economy has traditionally considered the primary circuit of the production of surplus value. In the private sector, the highest union density rates are not in manufacturing (10 per cent), but in transportation (20 per cent), utilities (25 per cent), and construction (14 per cent).[3] Furthermore, the labour movement is overwhelmingly composed of members in service sector occupations rather than materials extraction and processing. Education, health care, sales and office, transportation and even private security occupations are each more important sources of union employment than production occupations. As of 2009, half of all union members were located in the public sector, with two thirds working for local governments providing front-line services necessary to the reproduction of class society.

We are left with a kind of social and physical infrastructural trade unionism.

When Colin Clark and other Keynesian economists devised the standard industrial classification system in the immediate postwar period, the point was to classify labour by its geographical location to better coordinate national economic development. Primary industries were located close to raw materials while manufacturing was thought to exhibit a more dispersed locational pattern. Services were urban, the delivery of services being increasingly the 'principal function of cities'.[4] The residual concentration of union members today in the broad service sector is owing to ongoing transformations in global capitalism, not least technological displacement of labour in material production, the perennial union avoidance in plant siting and suppression of new industrial organizing, the increasing economic weight of private consumption, and shifts to various rentier-type accumulation strategies. Describing residual US trade unionism as 'post-industrial' or 'service-based' suggests an urban concentration: because it is service-based, organized labour is in the city.

But it is inadequate to merely think of unions as in the city. Unions are active producers of capitalist urban spaces. This production involves not only the built environment that we commonly associate with an urban landscape, but more generally a production of the socio-spatial relationships – spaces of luxury consumption, social reproduction in working-class neighbourhoods, the separation between production and social reproduction and the commodification of space itself – which enlist urban space in the reproduction of capitalism.[5]

This has significant implications for the role of unions in elaborating class consciousness because urban strategies articulate key sites of working-class formation. Even a narrow trade unionist politics cannot, if it is to have any purchase, avoid addressing everyday life beyond the workplace. In order to shift the struggle from the economic to the political level – and to be effective at the political level – unions must mobilize their members and the broader working class around issues that link demands from the workplace to the nature of what is being produced and to social reproduction. One of the key elements of Andre Gorz's *Strategy for Labor* (published exactly 50 years ago) was its insistence on

> the possibility of designing a strategy which links the condition of the workers at the place of work with their condition in society, thus shifting the struggle away from the purely economic level ... toward the level of class struggle – this possibility is inherent in the close connection which exists in the life of every worker between the three essential dimensions

of labor power: 1) The work situation: that is to say, the formation, evaluation, and utilization of labour power in the enterprise. 2) The purpose of work: i.e., the ends (or productions) for which labor power is used in society. 3) The reproduction of labor power: i.e. the life style and milieu of the worker, the manner in which he (sic) can satisfy his material, professional and human needs.[6]

The politics of linking the dimensions of labour power across an urban terrain can be very complex, of course; and it may be ambiguously related to the dominant accumulation strategies. We can see this in the ways in which the current trade unionism is increasing reliant on the political mobilization of members and allies around 'pro-labour' public policy. The left has long argued that trade unions should be more political. But the politicization of the unions should be recognized for what it is: a compensatory shift in the context of labour's long retreat from organizing working-class agency at the workplace, and a much weakened bargaining relationship with employers. Operating as urban electoral machines, policy entrepreneurs and insider lobbyists, the union apparatus increasingly relies on ways of sustaining bargaining relationships and organizing leverage through the promotion and re-regulation of its sector. To go beyond this, a labour left would need to envision the possibility of breaking out of a narrow trade unionist representation of class that has failed to confront neoliberalism and confined class agency to the economic level by subordinating the 'right to the city' to the neo-corporatist demands of a dying business unionism.

ACCUMULATION STRATEGIES AND CLASS CONTRADICTIONS

Neoliberal accumulation strategies remain dominant all the way down the urban hierarchy, where the mantra that successful cities must provide a friendly environment to business as the fount of all job growth and innovation is repeated with numbing regularity.[7] This urbanization of trickle-down economics is nevertheless far removed from the classical prescriptions of laissez-faire, as we shall see. And we shall also see that the anodyne language in which the mantra is couched masks not only a variety of dispossessions but also sharp contradictions.

As Bob Jessop has defined the term, an accumulation strategy seeks to unite capitalist class fractions around a plan for growth, inclusive of the extra-economic preconditions of capital accumulation.[8] Urban accumulation strategies are typically led by the real estate industry, which anticipates the needs of the most profitable sectors of the local economy and can be relied upon to represent these sectors' interests through the city building agendas of local states. High skill/high wage sectors like finance, information technology, biotechnology and the creative industries are especially prized because their positive effects on local consumption, the tax base and property values reinforce real estate's economic hegemony. Profitable low wage sectors that are export-oriented, such as tourism and hospitality, are promoted for the same reasons.

These neoliberal urban accumulation strategies rely as much as ever on public subsidies to corporate tenants, developers and inward investment. Property, payroll and corporate income tax incentive programmes that were devised in the 1970s to retain industrial employment in rustbelt cities have been generalized across different sectors to include highly profitable firms and industries, including banking, high tech and entertainment. A 2012 *New York Times* investigative report tallied $80 billion in annual business incentives doled out by local and state governments across the US.[9] This is apart from the common use of tax abatement urban development strategies across North America. These may offer initial 'first-mover' advantages to a city, but as these tools become generalized across jurisdictions and incorporated within firm investment decision making, locational advantages fall back on stronger forms of competition such as deep labour markets, infrastructure and quality services – all of which require high levels of public investment.

At the top of the urban hierarchy, there are choices to be made between low cost/low quality and high cost/high quality strategies; cities further down the hierarchy may face contradictions rather than choices. In New York, the Bloomberg administration evinced Rudolph Giuliani's regime, particularly its law and order campaign, but has expressed disenchantment with the business retention tax incentives, which were considered to be too generous and ineffective. Developer incentives, on the other hand, would be retained and even expanded. The new strategy, dubbed 'luxury city' in a speech given to members of the city's growth regime (with union leadership in attendance), envisions a city with a high cost structure, especially with respect to real estate prices and taxation, that offers a platform for high value-added production.[10]

Regardless of which strategy is selected, public resources in the form of tax credits, developer incentives or strategic public investments are directed towards high skill/high wage sectors in cities where the fastest employment growth is in low wage sectors, including retail, accommodation, food service and home health care. The economic crisis and municipal austerity budgets which came on its heels have accelerated a restructuring of labour markets away from middle wage to low wage employment in large cities across the

US. In Chicago, 31.2 per cent of all payroll employees earn \$12/hour or less, up from 23 per cent ten years ago.[11] In New York, 35 per cent of all workers – and up to half in the Bronx – now earn \$12/hour or less, up from 31 per cent before the crisis.[12] The urban services on which these workers depend – childcare, special education programmes, inner suburban transit service – do nothing to promote dominant accumulation strategies and are being retrenched.

It does not follow that low wage workers are therefore to be allowed to be left alone. The fact that an immiserated and racialized working class occupies potentially valuable urban space figures in the containment and displacement orientation of prevailing urban development, education and policing policy. Attracting the holders of human capital by attending to their quality of life concerns – prior to the crisis, New York City's official plan hoped to attract a million in this class by 2030 – rationalizes the transformation of whole neighbourhoods to suit their imputed tastes, fears and prejudices. Land use planning is a key tool, used to extend gentrification and commercial development into manufacturing, working-class and waterfront areas of the city. Over the past decade, one third of New York City's total territory has been rezoned in over a hundred amendments to the zoning map. The majority of amendments involve increased density restrictions to preserve neighbourhood character and are located largely in white and upper-income areas of the city. Raised density limits and shifts in use restrictions from manufacturing to commercial and residential are predominantly located in poorer and more racially diverse areas of the city, channelling development pressures to these areas.[13]

The cultures and institutions of poor and working-class populations – the highly segregated public housing and public schools in particular – are so many barriers to be overcome. Of major US cities, Chicago has moved most aggressively to demolish its public housing stock in favour of a more selective and market-oriented 'mixed-income' model. The education reforms which followed mayoral control of schools in 1995 – closing down majority black schools in poor areas and establishing charters and more selective magnet schools – complements housing reform as a strategy of attracting and retaining higher income families in the city. Schools in which 99 per cent of the student body are African American represent 80 per cent of all public school closings and consolidations in the city to date.[14]

These are the objective tendencies of bourgeois urban policy. In the luxury city, a policy of wealth accumulation through increasing land values makes it impossible for all but the wealthiest to accumulate property of any description. State-led gentrification constantly redistributes wealth upwards and expels workers outwards, only to then selectively reintegrate them 'depending on the needs of production and consumption'.[15] This is the across-the-board policy orientation which generates anger at displacement, containment and disrespect that is so palpable whenever working-class people gather to discuss city politics and everyday life. This is also where the real movement is: the anti-gentrification 'site fights', Stop Stop and Frisk, Stop School Closings. Occupy Wall Street grew from the July 2011 'Bloombergville' encampments staged outside City Hall to protest cuts to daycare, homeless housing, libraries and education programmes, and to demand an end to local tax giveaways to banks and corporations.

URBAN LABOUR STRATEGIES

Successful accumulation strategies must provide the framework for mediating divisions between dominant class fractions as well as allow for the incorporation of non-dominant classes and non-economic elites.[16] The sharpest contradictions pit development capital against working-class communities, and these must be softened to some extent in order to secure a modicum of democratic legitimacy. Urban capitalist fractions may be united on the big questions, but compete at a more discrete level to secure the conditions of accumulation in their respective sectors or to gain narrower firm advantages. The decisions they make in the process are sometimes highly visible and publicly contested, precisely because urban accumulation strategies seek to extract land rents and thus involves the social relational nature of land value. In this context, public decisions are crucially important in determining both the aggregate level of rent as well as which plots of land will command the highest rents.[17] This often leads to conflicts which play out over the regulation of land and labour and the direction of public investment, and this in turn often leads to major political contestations as a result of the broader alliances that form to push policy through the legislative or regulatory process.

This is the terrain on which existing labour strategies in the city are enacted. Private sector unions with large urban memberships have sought new sources of organizing and bargaining leverage in the regulatory functions of the local state, especially land use regulation, and the importance of tax abatements and productive state investments in local economic development strategies. In the public sector, unions seek to build competitive-corporatist coalitions by promoting 'high road' practices that overlap with the shared concerns of the local state and locally-dependent firms in workforce development and increased inward investment. These are viable strategies because state regulation remains pervasive, and because this regulation is still subject to the ways in which liberal democracy elicits consent from the governed – especially, as is often the case, when the regulation in question does not contradict the interests of dominant class fractions. Unions are able to push these strategies forward politically by turning their highly disciplined organizational capacities towards electoral mobilization in get-out-the-vote campaigns. These are particularly effective in areas of the city where union memberships may form voting blocs with the broader working class. These strategies may be critiqued in their own terms – how successful are they in sustaining bargaining relationships and standards? – as well as from a broader perspective that considers the implications for advancing social struggles and labour renewal.

Consider the strategic use of tax abatements to sustain union employment levels. The payroll tax incentives that have been generalized across the North American film industry were pioneered in Vancouver, British Columbia, as part of a larger sector development strategy of drawing 'run-away' productions from Los Angeles. Union lobbying for provincial film production tax abatements was paired with concessions on continental wage schedules and work-rules to reinforce other locational advantages.[18] The strategy was initially successful in raising the local level of inward investment and employment. But of course the Californian unions retaliated with their own tax inducement strategy in Sacramento, pitched in chauvinistic terms against the Canadians even as California's tax credits side-swiped unions in Chicago and New York.[19] In 2001, film unions in New York began lobbying at both the state and city levels of government for their own tax credits, escalating from a 10 to 30 per cent rebate on payroll taxes. (New York has since recouped all the employment decline in the sector, but at a cost of $359 million a year in foregone revenues.) The national leaderships of each of the local unions involved in this see-saw battle saw no scalar contradiction to their strategy because competitive local tax cuts lower social production costs (as opposed to wages) across the domestic market, reaffirming the US's global competitive position. Nationally, the very profitable film industry receives $1.5 billion annually through 86 tax credit programmes across 45 states, including those with no hope of developing the infrastructure and labour pool required to foster a local industry.[20] The studio owners sit back and receive.

Consider also the use of developer tax abatements to further union organizing goals. In New York, the building services workers union, SEIU 32BJ, is mounting an organizing campaign in buildings which receive tax exemptions from the city under a programme (421-a) which values buildings for tax purposes on the property's land value prior to construction, extending over a 25 year period. Originally intended to spur residential development in the 1970s and 1980s, the programme has since become a giveaway to the real estate industry with dubious benefit to affordable housing.[21] In 2007, 32BJ succeeded in adding a provision to the legislation requiring building owners receiving abatements under the programme to pay building service workers the prevailing industry wage, set at $22/hr. The union estimates that half of tax rebated building owners are in non-compliance with its amendment and is attempting to leverage this failure to comply towards securing union organizing rights. This could result in the unionization of 380 workers in non-compliant buildings, with the possibility of an additional 250 in buildings under construction. 421-a tax exemptions cost the city $1.1 billion a year in foregone revenue.[22]

State-led gentrification creates opportunities for unions of embedding union goals in sector regulation through land use planning. This can be done through land use review processes either in aligning with developers facing public opposition, or in aligning with communities opposed to developers. Following a model developed on the US west coast, unions in New York have developed a practice of forming project-specific labour-community coalitions to extract community benefit agreements and organizing rights in neighbourhoods the Bloomberg administration and real estate industry have targeted for development. In these cases, unions must be able to form a common platform across a 'temporary workers/permanent workers' divide: the building trades are concerned with securing the use of union contractors for the duration of construction and are indifferent to the uses to which that construction is intended. The retail, building services and hotel workers unions are concerned with securing more complex restrictions on the business models and labour relations practices of firms that will eventually occupy the space. This often requires that private agreements be concluded with developers that they will include such restrictions in their commercial leases. In working-class residential neighbourhoods assigned for up-zoning, labour must furthermore broaden the coalition to include the affected community if the support of the local councilperson and community boards is to be secured. In poorer and working-class areas community concerns relate primarily to gentrification pressures and employment opportunities. This model was successfully applied to the rezoning of Willets Point in Queens in 2008 and has been replicated in a number of rezonings since – Atlantic Yards, Coney Island and Kingsbridge Armory in South Bronx.[23]

The range of concessions available to labour and community groups is shaped by how much land value is likely to be unlocked by the rezoning process. The amount of value released is determined by the rent gap, the difference between existing and prospective rents.[24] The wider the rent gap, the greater the leverage labour-community coalitions bring to bear against developers, and the higher value of concessions they are likely to extract. The union's leverage is higher if its members are residentially located along the advancing edge of the development frontier. These members will have to weigh their workplace interests against their interests as working-class residents. The rent gap is widest when neighborhoods that have undergone long periods of disinvestment are transformed into luxury-oriented spaces. While the value of concessions extracted from developers can vary according to the political leverage of the coalition, and the distribution of this value can be shifted among coalition partners, any strategy that seeks to maximize developer concessions cannot at the same time seek to prevent gentrification. The land use strategies pursued by labour-community coalitions in working-class neighbourhoods therefore result in a negotiated gentrification. Furthermore, any conflicts within the coalition over distribution of the surplus will tend to be resolved according to the political weight of the affiliates, defined by financial resources and by the ability to exert political power at both the local and, especially, the city scale. In the Kingsbridge Armory case, the developer decided that there was not enough profit in the project to warrant the retail workers' demands that commercial tenants be bound by their leases to pay wages of at least $10/hr. The union decided to have the project defeated on city council.[25]

In the broad public sector, earlier waves of neoliberal fiscal retrenchments, labour market and welfare reforms have put pressure on local growth interests to assume responsibility for managing the social conditions of accumulation. In seeking out new partnerships with large employers and chambers of commerce, social service unions and allied advocates have pivoted towards reframing social rights of citizenship as 'social infrastructure for economic growth'.[26] In the child care sector, unions in US cities have sought to build high road employer partnerships with the proposition that increased access to better quality child care reduces workplace absenteeism and conflicts, with longer term productivity benefits resulting in increased investment in the city and the region. This strategy has been modestly successful in rolling out tax credit programmes for privately delivered care, and partly successful in defending these programmes in austerity budgets. But this strategy has not addressed the continuing decline of the municipally funded childcare centres and it only reinforces welfare systems designed to tighten labour market dependency. Drawing state governments into subsidizing the sector builds employer/employee type relationships between state and county agencies and home-based care providers, opening a political route to the recognition of bargaining units. Some of the largest organizing wins in recent years have come through union-backed legislation and executive orders, including the recognition of a 70,000 homecare workers bargaining unit in Los Angeles in 1999 and of 60,000 homecare workers in city and upstate bargaining units in New York in 2007.[27]

The existing labour strategies have a number of features in common. They begin with the need to defend bargaining relationships and sector-wide standards and proceed from there to identify the points of leverage found within the limits and contradictions of the dominant accumulation strategies. They follow the logic, 'if gentrification, then organizing rights' and, 'if developer tax cuts, then prevailing wages'. The zero-sum nature of these bargains at the social level means that they do not alter the distribution of the surplus or class power. Many of these strategies are of course highly constrained by the failure of labour law to enforce associational rights and relentless competitive pressures. At best, they are effective in defending the existing institutions and union employment levels but with diminishing returns due to the ways in which they ramp up inter-urban competition. At worst, they normalize competitiveness as the end of public policy and labour agency, further fracturing an already divided and unorganized working class.

Class contradictions appear at both the economic and political levels. The labour-dominated coalitions formed to contest the terms under which real estate capital flows back into urban spaces that have undergone long periods of disinvestment fail to challenge the nature of the spaces being produced, which are nearly always spaces of private consumption favouring consumers and residents with high disposable incomes. There are spatial contradictions to unions negotiating neighbourhood transitions when union structures are being reproduced through the dismantling of working-class neighbourhoods. As Kevin Cox and Andrew Mair have argued, 'whether or not working-class people will possess a working–class consciousness, engage in class practices and form labour unions, their own political parties, (depends on) enabling social structures in which people find a sense of community that can sustain them'.[28]

To the extent that labour is in a position to bargain distributional shares out of land rents and the tax base, unions develop the political profile of 'place entrepreneurs' and become active, if subordinate, members of urban growth machines. Here, tensions arise between organized workers whose interests relate to urbanization or who are employed in industries or firms favoured by local economic development policy, and those who are called on to subsidize private investment in industries from which they are excluded, often along racial and gender lines. When city councillors in New

York asked film unions why the beneficiaries of the tax incentives looked nothing like their constituents, an answer of sorts came in the form of an equity job placement programme for 'professional assistants'. City tracking of the racial and ethnic composition of the screen-based workforce since the provisions were enacted show next to no progress on equity goals.[29] Nor have the difficult questions of what all this means for competing public demands for health care and education spending been answered. In any case, the success of these strategies hinges on unions winning political influence within the local state and the growth regime. Unions that have avoided political endorsements since McCarthyism, such as the film unions, are now endorsing municipal candidates.

Unions which have allowed their urban political operations to wither under late Fordism are rebuilding sophisticated get-out-the vote operations. Even relatively small unions, such as the New York Hotel Trades Council, are able to summon mayoral candidates to their offices to field urban policy questions. The union is able to do this because it has built a political action network, based in the workplace alongside but separate from the shop steward system, which is capable of mobilizing 3,000 members for street actions or electoral mobilization on short notice. When electoral participation rates fall to historic lows – only 22 per cent of the electorate bothered to vote in the 2009 New York City municipal elections – electoral campaigns turn on the ability to get out the vote. The decline of the old ward-based machines, electoral finance reform and term limits have all increased the political value of union support to local candidates.

The rebuilding programme Bloomberg has overseen in New York City has not only had the intention of 'turning Manhattan into one vast gated community for the rich'.[30] It has also allowed him to build a strong electoral coalition of private sector labour unions on the basis of a series of political deals struck around the development process. In the final weeks of the 2009 municipal election, trade unionists leafleted at subway entrances, called every residence and knocked on hundreds of thousands of doors for the 'billionaire mayor' in a field operation of unprecedented scale directed by a former political affairs director at Unite Here.[31] For the next mayoral election, Bloomberg's union backers are now closing ranks behind Christine Quinn, the closest of the Democratic candidates to the growth regime and the most faithful to Bloomberg's record in office. It is thus very clear that the 'luxury city' accumulation strategy does not solely represent the spatial agency of Wall Street, transnational capitalist class fractions and upper-income professionals and managers. It also represents the political agency of a sector of the labour movement that relates to the city as a capitalist product rather than as a habitat.

The political incorporation of organized labour through capitalist urbanization is not an especially new phenomenon. In his critique of the 'Hausmannization' of Paris during the Second Empire, Engels argued that the goal of the rebuilding programme was not simply to turn the city into 'a pure luxury city', but also 'to develop a specifically Bonapartist building trades' proletariat dependent on the government'.[32] Engels thus anticipated a now familiar critique of the political incorporation of the building trades into urban growth regimes and their support for 'value-free development' to the end of increasing jobs in their sector.[33] This kind of union incorporation can be, and indeed has been, extended to other urban workers, including those in retail and hospitality industries.

A LEFT URBAN STRATEGY FOR LABOUR

There can be an optimistic reading of all of this, insofar as it shows that trade unions are not totally incapacitated. Indeed, there is evidence of a great deal of creativity and effective agency being expressed in existing labour urban strategies. These strategies do articulate workplace interests with class interests in the nature of what is being produced and social reproduction, and this is why major North American urban centres are often seen as laboratories of union renewal.

The dilemma for labour renewal is that these strategies start in the wrong place and end up promoting the interests of the wrong class. It should not surprise us that union renewal would take neoliberal accumulation strategies as a point of departure when unions are being renewed in the absence of a labour left. A left strategy for renewal is in fact available should such a labour left once again emerge as a significant force. It will then be a matter of running their logic the right way around: identify the class contradictions of the dominant accumulation strategies, use workplace organization to build the social struggles around these contradictions, and through these struggles renew and transform union structures.

The great merit of this orientation is that it has been shown to work in practice. This is how a union reform caucus in the Chicago Teachers Union won elected office, transformed the internal life of their union, and won a strike against a neoliberal government – a rare occurrence. CORE, the union reform caucus that won leadership of the union in 2010 and led the union to a successful conclusion of the 2012 city-wide strike, was built by a cadre of left and social justice activists within the union through a series of teacher-parent actions against school closings. During the strike, the new union leadership explained that the education reforms

... being pushed by the mayor and his Board of Education had more to do with maintaining a racist system of educational apartheid in which resources were denied neighborhood schools of predominately African-American and Latino students and shifted to elite magnet schools, while charters were proposed to replace the low-performing neighborhood schools. This willingness openly to state the reality that many black and Latino parents face in underfunded and overcrowded schools, and ally with those same communities to advocate for real educational reform, ultimately was decisive in bringing the overwhelming support of the parents to the side of the union.[34]

Public sector unions would have to figure centrally in left labour strategy. By virtue of their location in the state sector providing (in most cases) socially reproductive services, public sector workers are pushed by the nature of what they produce to oppose austerity and neoliberal restructuring of the public sector. Whether or not public sector unions serve as organizing centres of resistance or scapegoats of crisis resolution depends on how public sector trade unionists conceive of this relationship, and how they follow through on the practical implications of this conception.[35] The producerist, business unionist ideology that holds sway within many public sector unions is a major barrier to a more successful strategy.

Public sector workers are engaged in the production of society itself.[36] Several practical implications for labour strategy follow from this. First, it follows that social conditions are workplace conditions; they impinge on the quality of worklife and enter into the bargaining context even if restrictive labour laws declare them beyond the scope of bargaining. The limits of public sector bargaining do not impinge, however, on the political agency of the union, which is at its most formidable when it assumes the mantle of popular tribune. Second, the public sector is not just about delivering useful services. Tasked with reproducing class society, public sector work also involves disciplining people as effective wage labourers. All public services have this contradictory character, and neoliberal public sector restructuring is shifting the emphasis towards discipline. A left strategy for public sector labour would perform a social audit at work, separating the use-value from the disciplining and exchange-value oriented nature of what is being produced. There are ways of withdrawing consent at work that highlight this contradiction and deliver services the way they should be delivered: teachers refusing to teach to the test while still overseeing extra-curricular activities, for example; or a campaign for free public transit, including no fare strikes, by transit workers unions. [37] The public sector struggles that are needed must be more than defensive: what is required to mobilize people are struggles to improve and expand the level of public services.

Even with these more social unionist strategies, it is unlikely that public sector unions will survive without a large-scale reorganization of the private sector workforce. The recent campaigns to organize low-wage food and retail service workers on a city-wide basis, involving community organizing techniques and short, carefully strategized workplace actions, are a hopeful initiative. These campaigns have to be paired with local labour market reforms, including minimum wage and benefit legislation, if workers in the sector are to exercise any bargaining leverage over individual employers. These city-wide initiatives, often promoted as sector regulation strategies by municipal and retail workers, are also being won in a growing number of cities. There is a tendency for these efforts to be crafted so narrowly as to target specific competitive threats and outsourcing of municipal services. These initiatives have the potential to be much more transformative if they can be extended to sectors targeted for organizing, such as the chain restaurants and retail outlets. The strongest such measures have been secured in San Francisco, where, notably, they were pushed forward by a workers centre and won through a ballot initiative. It will take reformed public and private sector service unions to see to it that the necessary political and financial resources are used to win labour market reforms to sustain the organizing drives. Raising wages and standards in private sector services and increasing employment levels in the public sector presume a break with the dominant neoliberal accumulation strategies in favour of a demand- and public sector investment-led economic recovery.

Rebuilding a labour left is crucial to generalizing these strategies because only a left can place workplace organization within a survey of the whole position. Only a left can re-articulate critique, struggles and strategy which cut across separations between the workplace and the broader society. These separations are given in the structure of wage labour and are reinforced by union ideologies, practices and their regulation by the state. They can therefore be overcome to a degree by trade unionists acting and thinking differently. The memberships of urban-based unions do not respect a separation between workplace and social needs when they look to union staff for help with landlords, accessing public assistance or any number of personal and family crises. The most active and conscious layers of the union membership do not respect these separations when they choose to direct their political activism as workers towards community struggles, rather than union politics. A labour left can be rebuilt by drawing these elements behind a clear strategic vision.

NOTES

1   I would like to thank my fellow SR contributors and Stefan Kipfer for their comments on an earlier draft.
     Rosa Luxemburg, 'The Mass Strike', in *Rosa Luxemburg Speaks*, New York: Pathfinder Press, 1970, p. 215.
2   Luxemburg, 'Mass Strike', p. 215.
3   2012 figures from the US Bureau of Labor Statistics, available at http://www.bls.gov.
4   Colin Clark, 'The Economic Functions of a City in Relations to its Size', *Econometrica*, 13(2), 1945, p. 97.
5   Henri Lefebvre, *The Production of Space*, Oxford: Oxford University Press, 1991. Thus the 'urbanization of labour' extends beyond an urban rescaling of union strategies seen in living wage activism, for example, to involve labour's agency in the reproduction of capitalist urbanization. For Andy Merrifield's use of the concept, see Andy Merrifield, *Dialectical Urbanism: Social Struggles in the Capitalist City*, New York: Monthly Review Press, 2002.
6   Andre Gorz, *Strategy for Labor: A Radical Proposal*, Boston: Beacon Press, 1964, p. 32.
7   Edward Glaeser, *Triumph of the City*, New York: Penguin Press, 2011.
8   Bob Jessop, 'Accumulation Strategies, State Forms and Hegemonic Projects', *Kapitalistate*, 10/11, pp. 89-112.
9   Louise Story, Tiff Fehr and Derek Watkins, 'United States of Subsidies', *New York Times*, 1 December 2012. Counted among the largest year-on-year recipients in New York City were J.P. Morgan Chase ($157 million), Yankee Stadium ($102 million), Morgan Stanley ($55 million), A.I.G. ($51.6 million) and Bank of America ($49 million).
10   Diane Cardwell, 'Mayor Says New York Worth the Cost', *New York Times*, 3 December 2003. See also Julian Brash, *Bloomberg's New York: Class and Governance in the Luxury City*, Athens: University of Georgia Press, 2011. In Canada, as part of a general reorientation towards reducing business tax rates so as to spur commercial and industrial development, the city of Toronto established a tax credit policy in 2008 that refunds back to the developer an average of 60 per cent of the increased tax assessment on new development over a period of ten years. In a similar fashion to New York City under Bloomberg, it presented this policy as the cornerstone of a strategy of promoting high skill/high wage sectors, including manufacturing, creative industries, biotech and finance and corporate headquarters.
11   Marc Doussard, 'Chicago's Growing Low-Wage Workforce: A Profile of Falling Labor Market Fortunes', *Women Employed Policy Brief*, 2012, available at www.womenemployed.org.
12   Christian González-Rivera, 'Low Wage Jobs, 2012', *Center for an Urban Future*, 2012, available at www.nycfuture.org.
13   Brad Lander and Laura Wolf-Powers, 'Remaking New York City: Can Prosperity Be Shared and Sustainable?', Pratt Institute Center for Community and Environmental Development, 2004.

14   Pauline Lipman, 'Mixed-Income Schools and Housing: Advancing the Neoliberal Urban Agenda', *Journal of Education Policy*, 23(2), 2008, pp. 119-34. Figures on school closures in Chicago from Carol Caref et. al., 'The Black and White of Education in Chicago's Public Schools', *Chicago Teachers Union*, 30 November 2012.

15   Guy Debord, 'Society of the Spectacle', 1968, available at http://www.marxists.org.

16   Jessop, 'Accumulation Strategies'.

17   John R. Logan and Harvey L. Molotch, *Urban Fortunes: The Political Economy of Place*, 20th Anniversary edition, Berkeley, CA: University of California Press, 2007.

18   Neil M. Coe, 'A Hybrid Agglomeration? The Development of a Satellite-Marshallian Industrial District in Vancouver's Film Industry', *Urban Studies*, 38(10), 2001, pp. 1754-75.

19   Andrew Dawson, '"Bring Hollywood Home!" Studio Labour, Nationalism and Internationalism, and Opposition to "Runaway Production", 1948-2003', *Revue belge de philologie et d'histoire*, 84(4), 2006, p. 1114.

20   Story, Fehr and Watkins, 'United States of Subsidies'.

21   Pratt Center for Community Development, 'Reforming New York City's 421-a Property Tax Exemption Program: Subsidize Affordable Homes, Not Luxury Development', 2007, available at http://prattcenter.net.

22   Michael Powell, 'Luxe Builders Chase Dreams of Property Tax Exemptions', *New York Times*, 24 June 2013. A similar property tax grant programme introduced in Toronto in 2008 emerged in close collaboration between the City, Labour Council and the Toronto Board of Trade. Labour's concern to protect employment in high wage new economy sectors was considerably broadened in the process to include finance and commercial real estate in the corporate headquarters sector. The Board of Trade objected to the sector focus but saw an opportunity to expedite ongoing across-the-board reductions in local business taxes. The sector focus was further broadened to include large-scale retail and entertainment in order to accommodate a $120 million tax grant request by the developer of a big-box retail and gaming project in an economically distressed area of the city. Unite Here Local 75, the main union representing hotel and gaming workers in the city, deputed in favour of the necessary amendment to the grant programme in the hope – vain, in the end – of securing a card check agreement from the developer in exchange. When the sector-based tax incentives were introduced in Toronto, concerns over an erosion of the city's tax base did not come from where they should have, the public sector municipal unions, but rather from the office of the city treasurer. For a discussion of this case, see Steven Tufts, 'Labour and (Post)Industrial Policy in Toronto', *Relay*, 23, 2008, pp. 30-4.

23   For a discussion of labour's role in the rezoning of Coney Island, see Ian Thomas MacDonald, 'Bargaining for Rights in Luxury City: The Dilemmas of Organized Labor's Urban Turn', *Labor Studies Journal*, 36(2), 2011, pp. 197-222.

24   Neil Smith, *The New Urban Frontier: Gentrification and the Revanchist City*, New

York: Routledge, 1996.

25 Sam Dolnick, 'Voting 45-1, Council Rejects $310 Million Plan for Mall at Bronx Armory', *New York Times*, 14 December 2009.

26 Mildred Warner and Susan Prentice, 'Regional Economic Development and Child Care: Toward Social Rights', *Journal of Urban Affairs*, 35(2), p. 195.

27 David L. Gregory, 'Labor Organizing by Executive Order: Governor Spitzer and the Unionization of Home-Based Child Day-Care Providers', *Fordham Urban Law Journal*, 35(2), 2007, pp. 277-305.

28 Kevin R. Cox and Andrew Mair, 'Locality and Community in The Politics of Local Economic Development', *Annals, Association of American Geographers*, 78(2), 1988, p. 313.

29 Lois S. Gray, 'Film–TV Production Unions in New York's Policy Arena', paper presented to the *Labor and Employment Relations Association* Annual Conference, St. Louis, MO, 8 June 2013.

30 David Harvey, *Rebel Cities: From the Right to the City to Urban Revolutions*, London, Verso, 2012, p. 23.

31 Serge F. Kovaleski, 'Union Ties Raise Ethics Questions for a Bloomberg Aide', *New York Times*, 12 October 2009.

32 Friedrich Engels, *The Housing Question*, Moscow: Progress Publishers, 1970, p. 69.

33 Logan and Molotch, *Urban Fortunes*, p. 81.

34 Robert Bartlett, 'Creating a New Model of a Social Union: CORE and the Chicago Teachers Union', *Monthly Review*, 65(2), June 2013.

35 Michael Hurley and Sam Gindin, 'The Assault on Public Services: Will Unions Lament the Attack or Lead a Fightback?', *The Bullet*, 515, 2011, available at www.socialistproject.ca.

36 Paul Johnston, *Success While Others Fail: Social Movement Unionism and the Public Workplace*, Ithaca: Cornell University Press, 1994, p. 12.

37 When the New York transit workers union dropped its longstanding opposition to fare increases in 1948, it was done in exchange for a significant wage increase in the following round of collective bargaining and to marginalize the left within the union. The political shift towards business unionism and the rise in wages were seen as mutually reinforcing and was supported by the membership. But today, the link between fare and wage does not work this way. On the contrary, it is used to ratchet down wages and discipline workers. See Joshua B. Freeman, *In Transit: The Transport Workers in New York City, 1933-1966*, Philadelphia: Temple University Press, 2001, pp. 288-93. To take another highly relevant example in this sector, the Toronto transit workers union has long prided itself on running the system on a cost recovery basis, and does not support reducing or eliminating the fare, which is seen as the source of the wage fund. At the same time, the union argues and mobilizes publicly for increased public funding to the operations budget, complains that management times fare increases to coincide with wage increases in order to reinforce the relationship between the two in the public mind. Violence directed at drivers is one of the biggest concerns of the membership, some of whom want the union to move beyond its support for increased surveillance and legal penalties

to promote the right of bus drivers to bear arms. In fact, much of the workplace violence issues from fare disputes. For a discussion of how free transit would undercut these negative dynamics see: Ian Thomas MacDonald, 'Public Transit Strikes in New York and Toronto: Towards an Urbanization of Trade Union Power and Strategy', *Canadian Journal of Urban Research*, 21(1), 2012, pp. 24-51; and Stefan Kipfer, 'Free Transit and Beyond', *The Bullet*, 738, December 2012.

LEFT UNITY OR CLASS UNITY?
WORKING-CLASS POLITICS IN BRITAIN

ANDREW MURRAY

There is a saying on the British left that the only thing more futile than trying to transform the Labour Party into an instrument of radical change is trying to set up a viable party to the left of it. The joke works just as well the other way around. The difficulty of either project is attested to by a large body of evidence accumulated over generations of Sisyphean exertions by socialists, not to mention a large body of articles in the *Socialist Register* dating back to the 1960s.[1]

The 13 years of the bewitched-by-bankers and imperialist 'New Labour' governments of Tony Blair and Gordon Brown, allied to the demonstrable failure of the British left to make much political impact over the last five years of economic crisis, both before and after Labour's loss of governmental office, have given the old dilemma an acute edge.

On the one hand, the post-Blair/Brown Labour Party is taking only the most timorous steps away from its luridly neoliberal past. Ed Miliband has, in conference speeches, pointed a direction different from New Labour in economic thinking, but when it has come to practical policy follow-through, the priorities of the City and international capital markets have still been ascendant – reflected in a commitment to stick to Tory austerity budgets if/when in office. It is uncertain that Labour will succeed in defeating the reviled Tory-Liberal Democrat coalition at the next time of asking, in 2015, and further uncertain that, even if it did, a Miliband government would be able or willing to lead a sustained shift away from austerity politics. The example of Francois Hollande across the Channel is unpromising.

On the other hand, the left-of-Labour scene is a wilderness of wrecked or aborted initiatives – Arthur Scargill's SLP, the Socialist Alliance, Respect, the Trade Unionist and Socialist Coalition and the Scottish Socialist Party, to name just those left electoral projects which have taken the field since the 'New Labour' coup of 1994-95. Some of these retain an existence but only

Respect, with George Galloway as MP for Bradford West, is more than vestigial, and even Respect now lacks any serious base outside of Bradford itself or any apparent capacity to win parliamentary elections except where Galloway himself is candidate. Their political failure can be attributed to a vast variety of contingent factors, but it can scarcely be disputed.

The most recent attempt to establish a new electoral party of the left in Britain, in summer 2013, was styled 'left unity', the Rubik's Cube of progressive political initiatives – crack this and anything is possible. This proposal emanated from Ken Loach, an eminent (and Trotskyist) film director currently celebrated for his nostalgic look at the postwar Labour government, *Spirit of 45*, and from Kate Hudson, the general secretary of the Campaign for Nuclear Disarmament, amongst others.[2]

The idea that the time is now ripe for socialists to prioritise another unity project, leading to the creation of a new party to the left of Labour, rests on three connected propositions. First, that the experience of New Labour has vacated a considerable political space on the left which no one is filling and many voters feel deprived of any party expressing their views and values, on election day in particular. There is an argument that Labour no longer represents the broad progressive coalition that it once at least to a limited extent did, having become both less democratic and more bourgeois over the last generation.

Second, there is a European-wide revival of such a left, which Britain is missing out on – we should not, in the words of the Left Unity Draft Statement, 'remain outside … the political developments in Europe and beyond'. Finally, the continuing economic crisis demands a fresh, and united, left response since existing political responses have been inadequate. None of these arguments should be dismissed, but all need scrutiny.

Here it will be argued that this initiative, like others before it, is based on a flawed assessment as to how worthwhile socialist parties can be created. It misreads European experience and its applicability to Britain; fails to seriously address the issue of the Labour Party and working-class support for it; ignores the failure of previous new left parties and indeed the real state of the contemporary left; prioritises a chimerical 'left unity' over class unity; and draws a causal connection between economic crisis and socialist politics which is at best questionable. As such it risks being an impediment to socialists actually making the most of present opportunities for working-class reconstruction and advance.

POLITICAL SPACE

It is beyond dispute that the main working-class political parties internationally have moved well to the right over the last generation. The mass social democratic parties have mostly embraced neoliberalism, and none more extravagantly than the Labour Party in Britain, to the extent that classical social democracy could be said to scarcely exist as a major political force. Communist parties have disappeared or been reduced to the political margins with a few exceptions. In the case of many of the former ruling parties they have openly converted to social democracy and, hence, to variants of the global elite consensus.

All this is true, but it only of itself creates 'political space' if one takes an entirely mechanical view of politics, in which opinion is ranged on a left-to-right spectrum in more or less non-variable quantities and in which, therefore, a shift to the right by a large party must automatically leave a compensating space to the left unrepresented. Clearly, this is a perspective which could only hold true if nothing else were changing in the world, if classes were not rising, falling, recomposing and decomposing; if ideological propositions were not being tested, adopted and discarded in the light of experience; if capitalist society were an endless assembly line which might break down but never develop or mutate.

In Britain, the first to dive into the empty 'political space' swimming pool was the Socialist Labour Party, which assumed that Tony Blair's abandonment of Clause Four would mean masses of socialists, their Party snatched from them, would flock to the old standard. All the SLP proved was that even the greatest working-class leaders, in whose number Arthur Scargill should surely be counted, can mistake their own views for being the mood of the masses. At the time the latter regarded *any* Labour government as a relief, and were living, in any case, through the brief period when history was declared 'ended'.

Nearly twenty years later, the same show is being played, to an even thinner audience, by the Trade Unionist and Socialist Coalition, which fails to attract more than the smallest number of either to its standard. Its existence is predicated on the belief that such is the disgust with New Labour, even in opposition, that the working class will rally to stentorian champions of a sort of Old Labour-Plus. No amount of raspberries blown by the voters have shaken this belief so far, and perhaps they never will, since those who argue the case for an electoral alternative have adequately immured themselves behind arguments through which reality cannot penetrate. Essentially, the masses are being offered what they need, and if they are rejecting it, it can only be for some contingent reason or other – if an outstanding election campaign under a Labour government fails to break through, it is because the otherwise ready-to-rock workers *want to keep the Tories out*, if under a

Conservative administration, it is because their priority is to *keep the Tories out*. And so it goes on, election after election. It all sounds plausible until someone joins the dots.

Previous left electoral ventures may have had good policies, well-known leaders and enthusiastic cadre. But they have all lacked the social weight that could only be imparted by support in working-class organisations. Political space is ultimately secured by the strength that comes from the adhesion of mass organisations or movements rooted in important social classes. It is brought into being by factors quite other than the subjective wishes of potential occupiers of it. It is determined above all by the emergence, development or disappearance of classes and other social formations as political actors, and by what Harold Macmillan would have termed 'events' (like, briefly, the Iraq war for example). Its scope and duration can be shaped by purposeful intervention, but it cannot be invented by propaganda. Social weight does not step into a declared political space by kind invitation from its self-anointed gatekeepers.

Electorally, the space to the left of Labour is presently filled by … the Labour Party. That is, many people whose views are to the left of the Labour leadership still vote for the Labour Party. That was true when the Labour leader was Tony Blair, and it is all the more true when it is Ed Miliband, about whom people on the left generally feel more comfortable, his having apologised for the Iraq war and talked of 'New Labour' now being of the past. The obvious question is: if that 'space' could not be filled by a left alternative under the most ideal circumstances imaginable – a widely reviled war-mongering Labour government under a discredited leader – why on earth should an electoral intervention be expected to do any better today when most people on the left see the enemy as the Tory-led government, and most working-class voters view the possibility of a Miliband-led Labour government with at least a tepid optimism?

Naturally, that does not exhaust a discussion about the Labour Party today – but *that* is the discussion that is needed. It would encompass a realistic assessment as to the roots sunk by the 'New Labour' clique in the Party, the extent to which the changes wrought by Blair and Brown are irreversible, or to what extent they were contingent on the neoliberal 'Edwardian summer' which ended in 2008; the direction of the Miliband leadership; the possibility of unions playing a more dynamic and less passive role than in the Blair years; and so on. These are not just questions for debate, they are questions of the class struggle today. One can easily argue a view that the Labour Party on its own will never secure a socialist society; likewise one can certainly argue that the Blair-Brown governments *governed for* imperialism and the City of

London (at least in part as a consequence of the weakness of the movement in the 1990s and beyond). In my view, both opinions are incontestable. It is another thing to simply seek to bypass or ignore a party which is evidently the only alternative government to the Con-Dems at present, which retains the affiliation of the main working-class organisations in Britain, which includes more socialists than all those grouped in the parties further to the left aggregated, which controls (with variable results) many local authorities, and whose level of electoral support runs at perhaps forty times that of the further-left.

To in effect dismiss all that with the observation that 'its achievements are in the past', to quote the article on the *Guardian* website promoting the initiative, is scarcely serious. *All* achievements of which we can be certain are in the past, and no achievements in the future will be secured by ruminating on electoral fantasies as opposed to addressing the difficult tasks of the present.[3]

THE EUROPEAN DIMENSION

As already noted, much of the case being made for a new left party rests on the observation that we are in the midst of a continent-wide economic crisis allowing similar parties to exist and prosper elsewhere. Clearly, an international perspective is not an add-on but a starting point for socialist politics. However, the envious gaze cast at the left in other European countries needs to be tempered with realism.

First of all, there is the generic nature of these parties, acknowledging that there are differences between them. The Euro-left parties stand to the left of contemporary social democracy in advocating more radical measures, in varying degrees, to tackle the economic crisis. They are constitutional and electoral parties – their measure of success is electoral support, which they seek to secure through advocating pro-welfare and egalitarian policies aimed at broadly mitigating the effects of the slump on the working class. Their ultimate aim may be a socialist society (although this is not always explicit), but it is to be attained primarily by parliamentary means, and within the framework of the European Union, a construct shaped by the dominant fractions of capital. To some extent, they could be described as 'two-and-a-half parties' in the manner of the left parties which positioned themselves between the second and third internationals, between revolution and counter-revolution within the workers' movement after the First World War, before they retreated to the social democratic mainstream.

The present day two-and-a-half parties make no claim, as the centrists of 1919-21 did, to stand for revolution and the dictatorship of the proletariat.

They are explicitly reformist. Their attraction as a new left model derives, at least in part, from the absence of a revolutionary international, and of major revolutionary parties in almost all European countries. Two-and-a-half looks sweet when there is no Three. But that does not make it necessarily the answer to the crisis of working-class political representation. In practice (with the exception of the Greek situation, which will be considered shortly) the summit of the ambitions of the left parties Europe-wide at present is to secure enough parliamentary seats to be considered a coalition partner in a government which would be dominated by the 'old' social democratic parties, perhaps with the addition of Greens, or of centre-ground bourgeois parties. As the Left Unity Draft Statement accurately notes, these parties challenge 'the capitulation of social democracy to neo-liberalism'. Implicit in this formulation is the demand – make social democracy social democratic again! The spirit of 2013 is to be the 'spirit of 45'. But if returning social democracy to its social democratic roots is indeed a sensible first step, then surely it is an argument better made within the mass social democratic parties, at least where they are the main electoral vehicles of the working-class movement, than it is outside them? That is not a point which applies with equal force under all circumstances – it would be unrealistic and for that matter undesirable, for example, to expect the French Left Front, including the PCF, to merge with the Socialist Party. However, the goal of working-class political unity must remain a central consideration everywhere – restoring it where it does not exist makes a lot more sense than new splits where it (more or less) does.

A further consideration is the great difference in national circumstances across Europe, never mind beyond. It would be wrong for the left to internalise the Brussels assumptions regarding the homogenisation of the political scene across the continent. All the left parties which carry some electoral weight in the EU stand on the basis of either the influence of a pre-existing mass Communist Party (the most common foundation), or a serious split to the left in social democracy, or a prolonged regroupment of far left organisations, or some combination of all three. This is true of the Left Front in France, Die Linke in Germany, the now marginalised Rifondazione in Italy and so on. Certainly, none have arisen as a consequence of a Facebook appeal, so if 'Left Unity' succeeds it will represent a sociological first.

In Britain, building on the heritage of a mass Communist Party is not an available option, a mass split in social democracy shows little sign of happening, and far left unity would still aggregate to a very minor organisation in the improbable event of its occurrence. Even in countries better favoured by political history and development (at least from this perspective), the left parties are electoral shadows of the mass Communist Parties of living memory, and in some cases even of their own performance much more recently. There is no obvious European-wide 'silver bullet' for popularity at the polls to be found.

The obvious exception is Syriza in Greece, working in the country where the decomposition of capitalism and its conventional methods of rule are most advanced. Syriza, originally an amalgam of left factions of varying ideological provenance (Eurocommunism being the most important), has effectively displaced PASOK as the main party of the left (also securing votes from the communist KKE). The scale of the economic calamity in Greece, of a different order (so far) to almost anywhere else, and the fact of PASOK's deep and corrupt implication in the management of it, have conditioned this development. However, even before the crisis hit, Syriza had built up a significant electoral base and had developed links to a range of mass movements in Greek society, leaving it well positioned to profit from the mounting exposure of PASOK's corruption and evident solidarity with the Greek elite.

Syriza has not merely won over many voters from mainstream social democracy, it has also acquired chunks of the erstwhile PASOK apparatus, as the latter party crumbles. It secured a huge increase in its votes in the two general elections of 2012, but in neither did it secure anything like the support won by PASOK in its prime (more than 40 per cent), and in neither did it secure enough parliamentary seats, even if those won by Democratic Left and the KKE were added, to form a government. Nor does it begin to match the influence of the KKE (or even PASOK for that matter) in the trade union movement in Greece.

It is possible that Syriza could do better next time the opinion of Greek voters is sought. Indeed, under Greek electoral procedures, if Syriza were to secure the greatest share of the vote in a future election it would possibly be able to govern in its own right. Then the essential contradiction in its politics – opposition to austerity while supporting Greece's continued membership of the EU and the single currency will move centre-stage. There is limited value in speculating as to what may happen then, beyond noting the studied ambiguity of Tsipras, the Syriza leader, as to whether he stands for socialism or a 'non-austerity' capitalism, an ambiguity only deepened by Syriza's equivocal role in, for example, the teachers' dispute of spring 2013. The moment when a Syriza-led government *might* have constituted the start of a systemic rupture with capitalism in Greece may have passed. If Tsipras does come to power it could now prove to be within the range of 'normal' social democratic governance – his insistence on sticking with the Euro and the

EU would make such an outcome nearly unavoidable.

That is of course speculative. For now, some will be enthused at the prospect of British Eurocommunists, Trotskyists and Maoists joining together in a similar common electoral front. Others would rather spend a week at the dentist. Whatever, the British working class will support a 'British Syriza' when they regard the British Labour Party in the same way as the Greek working class regards PASOK. That is not where we are at present.

Beyond Greece, an even more severe reality check is in order. It seems that the parties most often immediately profiting from the economic crisis, even with votes that would have once gone to the left, are either of the far right (let's not forget Marine Le Pen's parliamentary defeat of the Left Front's Melenchon and the sudden rise of UKIP in Britain) or are expressions of a generic anti-political outlook like Beppe Grillo's MS5 movement in Italy or the Pirate Party in Germany. Of course, this is not to denigrate the efforts made to offer a real fighting alternative by, for example, the Left Front in France, which stands in the better traditions of the working-class movement there, but to indicate that in circumstances of a relatively decomposed working class across Europe, even the most promising initiatives are finding it hard to get much wind in their sails. They are all to some extent or other facing the same crisis of 'agency'.

In summary then, the Euro-left is presently hardly politically decisive outside Greece, lacks revolutionary perspectives, polls less in general than when it was explicitly Communist in times gone by, and in some countries at least risks being outflanked both by the far right and by a gallimaufry of clowns and 'pirates' whose advance signifies the contemporary decay of both bourgeois politics and of the labour movement.

If this all seems a bit postmodern, it is because it is, and it strikes to the consideration at the heart of the contemporary situation and, indeed, the speculations about 'political space'. That is the decline of the working-class movement in Europe along almost every axis over the last generation, to the point where its constitution on a new basis is the *only* question which need really detain anyone serious about breaking from capitalism. This issue is both at the core of a critique of the existing left, unity initiatives included, and at the heart of a positive programme of work for socialists.

IMPACT OF THE CRISIS

However, it could well be argued that the economic crisis changes the calculations and has, or will shortly, create the elusive 'political space' for a new party of the left. In a sense the answer to this has already been supplied.

The strength of the left in all countries in Europe is less than it was in easier times a generation ago, as measured by election results. If there is new 'space' at all it is, outside Greece, small and only slowly expanding. Indisputably, class consciousness was higher in the relatively prosperous 1960s than it is in conditions of twenty-first century austerity. Furthermore, the old saw that economic crisis favours the right before the left appears to have some merit still. Certainly it is the right-wing populist UKIP which is benefiting from disenchantment with the 'mainstream' parties in Britain (or England to be precise) at present, cutting with the grain of prevailing ideological assumptions as it does. The idea that a resurgent far right can best be countered by a new 'UKIP of the left', rather than by labour movement unity, contradicts all historic international experience on the subject.

In fact, the assumption that economic slump equals a boom for socialism has little historical evidence to support it. Crises impact variably on politics, depending on the prevailing balance of class power at the time. The movement defeated in the General Strike was in no position to determine the political outcome of the Great Depression, at least until the Second World War had created the conditions for its social reassertion. The slump of the early 1970s was met by a united and fairly self-confident labour movement, which was able to defend its own organisations and working-class living standards and, politically, secure the re-election of a Labour government. This ended, however, with capitulation before the demands of the International Monetary Fund. That unity and confidence was already crumbling (as a result) by the time the Thatcher offensive opened up, coinciding with the big economic slump of the early 1980s. The left, within the Labour Party and without, believed the space was opening up for a radical left programme; but the main political consequence of the crisis was the breakaway of a considerable chunk of the Labour right to form the Social Democratic Party. This split had the support of more than 30 sitting Labour MPs, the covert backing of some trade union leaders and the overt support of significant sections of a panicky establishment, of course. That is worth remembering as constituting the sort of 'weight' required to get a new party off the ground as a serious force. By contrast, not a single Labour MP left over the Iraq War, despite 142 voting against it (George Galloway was expelled); and no MP is known to be contemplating such a departure now.

But the 'crisis' argument also reflects more profound political weaknesses, a sort of bastardisation of the view that politics is nothing but concentrated economics. This leads much of the left to be almost overcome with excitement when a crisis hits, at the same moment that most working-class people (and even their organisations) risk being overcome with anxiety.

It is a close relation to the view that strikes and mobilisations against poverty are 'real' class struggle, while anti-war or other 'democratic' campaigning is all very well for filling in time until a slump bites but not the real work of socialists; and to the view that revolution emerges from economic misery.

Other opinions have been advanced, of course. 'We cannot tell … how soon a real proletarian revolution will flare up [in Great Britain] and what immediate cause will most serve to rouse, kindle and impel into the struggle the very wide masses who are at present dormant. …It is possible that the "breach" will be forced, "the ice broken" by a parliamentary crisis, or by a crisis arising out of the colonial and imperialist contradictions'.[4]

Thus Lenin in 1920. Not a word about slumps or strikes, but in a time when the two political issues which have gripped the very wide British masses over the last ten years have indeed been a 'parliamentary crisis' (MPs expenses) and an 'imperialist crisis' (the Iraq War) he may not have been so far off the mark in identifying the issues that can galvanise a deep and angry response (if not a 'real proletarian revolution' yet).

What *is* right is Left Unity's critique of the feeble nature of the Labour response to the crisis to date, and the requirement for it to stand far more clearly and unequivocally on the side of the poor in the face of this onslaught. *Guardian* commentator Simon Jenkins was spot on in his observation, as of summer 2013, that Labour is 'as mesmerised by the bankers as [Tory Chancellor George] Osborne'. Shadow Chancellor Ed Balls, long a close confidante of Gordon Brown, has yet to make the break with the City-first ideology of the boom years which would be the prerequisite for even a mildly reformist Labour government post-2015.[5]

If a break is to be made, even to a limited extent, it will not be the consequence of a left electoral initiative, but of a rising level of anti-austerity struggle, of the sort which the People's Assembly movement, uniting unions and community campaigns against poverty and welfare cuts, is aiming to generate, alongside trade unions willing to fight back in the workplace. Indeed, introducing a new party into that mix is more likely to provide a fresh point of division when that is least needed (this is indeed what occurred when the Assembly convened, with Ken Loach taking the opportunity to make a notably sectarian intervention). There is no requirement − indeed, no possibility − to make the People's Assembly movement a pro-Labour vehicle, but to turn it into an anti-Labour one is a route to undermining its potential as an instrument of the necessary class reconstruction which can be the only underpinning of any advance.

WHAT SORT OF LEFT UNITY?

So what sort of party would Left Unity be? Different, presumably, to all the other existing electoral formations on the left. Most of Left Unity's promoters have been in one or the other fairly recently and some have been in all of them. A view has been expressed that previous initiatives failed either because they were dominated by a charismatic leader (Scargill, Sheridan, Galloway) or because they hosted too many far-left factions. Certainly, Left Unity does not have a charismatic leader, but it could be argued that such figures are essential to make any breakthrough in the public imagination, and that the problem hitherto has been that each initiative has only had *one* such (always a democratically challenging scenario) rather than several. As for factions, the major far left groups, (to the extent that that is not an oxymoron) have stayed aloof, but that has not prevented Left Unity engaging the interest of the British affiliates of the Fourth and Fifth (!) Internationals, as well as a breakaway group from the latter.

On policy, the common denominator is going to be set pretty low. For example, opposition to US-UK international aggression is by some measure the most important political issue of this century to date, so the Left Unity Draft Statement's rejection of imperialism and war is essential. However, this can only be vitiated by the fact that the project's most significant public statement thus far (the *Guardian* article already mentioned) does not refer to the issue, possibly because it wishes to reach out to those on the left who have supported the more recent NATO interventions in Libya and Mali. Other supporters of Left Unity have argued that the Party should avoid describing itself as 'socialist', lest potential supporters be repelled.[6]

It will also be non- or even anti-Leninist. This is most likely designed to make it easier for the new party to scoop up those refugees from the Socialist Workers Party who believe that their party's problems have been due to a 'Leninist' regime. The 'brutality and distortions of traditional left structures' are rejected without qualification as, more justifiably, is the 'reproduction of … gender domination' within the left. Presumably this is a nod towards the drama within the SWP over the handling of an allegation of rape against one of its leading members.

This is absurd. The experience of Leninism is the story of the world's first successful socialist revolution, of working-class state power, of the construction, defence and ultimate disintegration of world socialism in the twentieth century, of parties which led masses in the struggle against capitalism, fascism and imperialism, and of millions who died on the battlefields and in the dungeons of the bourgeoisie as partisans of a world movement for a communist future, all with its historic achievements and imposing crimes and errors. To imagine that anything can be added to the analysis of this experience (essential for any serious socialist organisation) by studying the goings-on in small and marginal groups almost entirely external to the working class is merely testimony to the capacity of some of the left to dwell in their own Truman Show. *Pace* Alex Callinicos, there is absolutely *nothing* that can be adduced for or against Leninism from the crisis eroding the SWP, any more than the results obtained by the experiments of the Large Hadron Collider need verifying by observing the Duracell Bunny.[7]

In fact, while there is a renewed and welcome interest in Marxism post-2008, the ruling classes of Europe would only tremble at a fresh mass engagement with Lenin's focus on the politics of revolution – certainly they would be more worried by that than they are by a new left social democracy of the type described.

Can either actually be woven out of the existing left-of-Labour left in Britain? That left is an agglomeration of organised groups, some of which style themselves 'parties' and which range from the small through the very small to the miniscule and a number of individual 'independent socialists' who have mostly passed through one or several of the aforementioned organisations and have suffered thereby. This left exhibits several pathologies which have in part conditioned not only its failure to make much of the economic crisis but also its effective abstention from serious political intervention (with some significant exceptions) for the last generation or more. Since the more or less simultaneous defeat of the 'Benn left' in the Labour Party and of the miners in the great strike in the mid 1980s, rapidly followed by the collapse of the USSR, the left has struggled to get a purchase on British politics. It has been deprived both of an obvious vehicle to realise its project, as well as any clear sense as to what that project might now be, or at least capacity to communicate it. Two exceptions of note have been the Stop the War Coalition, which, certainly from 2002-05, represented a breakthrough in as much as the main groups on the left stopped shouting at each other long enough to instead talk to the mass of people on the Iraq issue, allowing it to hegemonise a vast movement overwhelmingly composed of people well to the right of its leadership (full disclosure – the author was Chair of StWC from 2001-11). Similarly, Ken Livingstone secured election as Mayor of London in 2000 as an independent running against the official Labour candidate (he was re-elected as Labour candidate in 2004) by building a broad coalition of support for policies which, despite too much unnecessary pandering to the City, were probably as radical as the times and the limited powers of the Mayoralty allowed.

One of the most obvious problems for the left in trying to move forward is the obsessive identification with the symbols, structures and strategies of the past (be it 1917, 1945, 1968, 1971-74 or all of them); to the point where the Jacobins of the Paris Commune appear as futuristic speculators by comparison. We know that 'the tradition of the dead generations weighs like a nightmare on the minds of the living', but even Marx could not have envisaged the mind of the British left of 2013, with those not waiting for a Winter Palace or at least a St Germain-de-Pres 'moment' chewing on the cud of a highly romanticised 'spirit of 1945'.

Cohabiting in a contradictory connection with this fascination for dwelling in (as opposed to critically analysing) bygone decades is the treatment of the experience of socialism. As an alternative form of society, rather than a broad indication of outlook, socialism is not unproblematic for most people today. Experience and opinion polling does indeed indicate considerable support for what might be termed socialist values and sometimes policies, but the systemic socialism advocated by the left does not properly account for the widely-held belief that it has been tried and – in both the main variants understood as socialism by most people (Soviet socialism and Labourite social democracy) – failed. The left generally does not defend its past. Instead, it addresses the problem by disassociating itself from its own collective record even as it perseveringly seeks to replicate that same legacy in its present proceedings. 'That wasn't really socialism' it is argued in relation to the USSR and Harold Wilson alike by the main trends on the left, which then seek to build organisations effectively identical to those which created and presided over this 'non-socialism', whether it is to be a new revolutionary party or a new trade union party.

The result is an 'offer' to the working people of the twenty-first century which amounts to 'we want to re-run the twentieth century but this time get it right'. The appeal of this pitch is unsurprisingly negligible. Apart from any other reason, no one can take seriously the proposition that if the Soviet Union and/or the Labour governments of 1945-51, 1964-70 and 1974-79 were indeed merely disasters to be moved on from as fast as possible (not my own view), it was only because Ken Loach or 'comrade Delta' were not in charge. Nostalgia has its part in political life, but a self-negating nostalgia which finds almost nothing but one defeat after another in the same past as it wallows in is no serious basis for a twenty-first century political intervention. Neither is a view that the working class always screws things up by choosing the wrong leaders, for that matter.

In fact, the contemporary left is almost entirely isolated from the working class it seeks to speak for. More prosaically, it has limited engagement with 'ordinary people' in general. The left and the working class have never been the same thing of course, but the divergence has only widened over the last generation as the working class has seen its institutions and organisations reduced to near-rubble, and the political left has retreated into a self-referential subculture from which it only emerges to address the class through propaganda, rather than as a living part of the whole. Every failure sends it not deeper into society but back into the garage to further fine-tune its ideological principles and proposals. Next time we will get it right! As the Arabs say, the dogs may bark, but the caravan has moved on ...

Any left project has to address these problems. The list of them could be extended. Left organisations tend to be heavily male-dominated and to have only barely absorbed the insights of feminism. They can be uncomfortable in working across cultural differences in an increasing diverse working class. They obsess about maintaining the 'tradition' appropriate to their own group, apparently oblivious to the historic irrelevance of most of them and their very slight impact on the course of events over the last fifty years. And so on.

Making something straight of this crooked timber is challenging. However, the negatives point towards a positive. What left politics today lacks is that union of socialism with the mass movement which can be the only real foundation of a social transformation. As Sam Gindin rightly notes 'workers may or may not provide the spark for new possibilities, but *if* socialism is possible, it is only so if the working class comes to be at the centre of the struggle'.[8] That is the central issue on the table – if we believe that socialism is no longer possible, or can be introduced without working-class involvement, then the whole discussion can of course be left to the professional politicians and their media/think-tank retinue.

The estrangement of the left from the 'agency' it has historically prioritised cannot be overcome by creating yet another external organisation substituting itself as a solution to their problems – at least not if the aim is to politically organise and mobilise the working class as the leading force for general human emancipation.

Today's left is ambivalent on the question of social agency. Some sections speak of the 'working class' as an undifferentiated abstraction, incarnate and unchanging once, now and forever. Others may acknowledge the changes and crises of the last thirty years, but still assume that someone else (usually trade unions) will recreate the agency in a more or less serviceable form, whereupon their own particular group, or the left as a whole, can reassume its historically mandated role of leadership. It ain't going to happen. Socialists can lead to the extent that their work is intimately interwoven with the development and fresh constitution of the working class, often in combat, or they can, in the time-honoured manner of the Socialist Party of Great

Britain (Clapham) sit it out and do their own thing instead. In spite of honourable intentions, Left Unity will likely be drawn down the latter path. Socialists should consider a better use of their resources.

WORKING-CLASS POLITICS

The centre of any strategy for socialism has to be the working class – not an abstract working class assigned a particular political role because that is what sub-Marxist teleology requires, but the actual working class of today, in Britain and internationally. Only the working class can emancipate itself, and thereby open up better prospects for the world. The reality, already briefly argued above, is that the labour movement in Britain, and to varying degrees in other countries, has been reduced over the last generation to the point where it scarcely articulates an independent political project, let alone one so far-reaching. It is now perceived as simply one interest group among many in a sociologically spliced-and-diced society that is unquestionably capitalist but where the class struggle has been at a very low level for a fairly long time. The movement has to a certain extent internalised that perception as self-perception. A class *for* itself? Not so much right now. The whole of society has suffered as a consequence, perhaps above all in the increasingly evident fact that democracy itself requires class struggle – the absence of it leads to the atrophying of even limited representative democracy and the passage of power into the hands of a narrow plutocracy which, while far from being fascist, has moved beyond any form of popular control. So most of society has need of a newly confident and empowered working class, even for the attainment of social goods that fall short of socialism itself. We are all too aware of the consequences post-1991 of a unipolar, 'sole superpower' world – the results of a socially unipolar society are no more attractive.

It is trite to observe that the working class in Britain has changed. Women have always constituted half the working class, but no longer can they be treated as a sort of auxiliary detachment in the struggle, backing up the main industrial army. Likewise, heavy manual work, with the elemental solidarity such work engenders, or employment in manufacturing of any sort, are now fairly small minority occupations. Globalisation has given further impetus to the migration of labour and the consequent transnationalisation of the working class, a historically progressive but politically challenging development. In a nutshell, surplus value is created by a greater diversity of people working in a wider range of situations. These changes make it all the more essential that socialists engage with the actual organisations of the working class, rather than simply invoking the class as a fetish.

Reconstituting the labour movement so that it becomes a powerful expression of the working-class interest, and thereby a means of the working class giving a lead to everyone interested in a new and better society, needs to be seen as the main task for socialists to address. This is Sam Gindin's 'modest project' of making unions once more 'effective reformist organisations' and re-establishing the socialist idea as part of serious political debate.[9] This may not sound sufficiently millennial, but without it there is no prospect for advancing beyond specific and limited single-issue interventions, with at best local/partial successes that cannot change the fundamentals of the prevailing system.

What does this reconstitution mean? Not going back to the labour movement of the past, obviously, because that is neither possible nor, since that movement never established a socialist society, necessarily desirable either. But some of the objectives that have to be set include the strengthening of trade union organisation numerically, in the workplace and ideologically; the reconnection of organised workers with the wider working-class community, where the links of work-union-community have atrophied or disappeared; the elaboration of campaign goals and policies which prioritise the capacity for the working class to stabilise and strengthen itself (in the fields of employment, housing etc.); the fighting and winning of strikes which build collective confidence; the creation of unity between British-born workers of various ethnicities and immigrant workers; special attention to reaching out to the young and connecting with campaigns which already mobilise youth (anti-war, students, UK Uncut etc.); and the reassertion of socialism as the only way to break the 'groundhog day' cycle of capitalist crises.

Socialists have the responsibility to raise not just the anti-austerity commonplaces necessary to fire up a renewed sense of struggle, but also the question of class power. It is a fact that the ruling elite in Britain is more discredited than it has been since 1940, and there is a growing sense of the unfitness of the ruling class to rule – yet there is no (or little) confidence in the capacity of ordinary people to take over the running of society themselves. Only a revived labour movement can give the leadership to fill *that* political space as it expands.

And it expands in novel ways. My own union, Unite (Britain's largest) has launched an ambitious community membership initiative, opening its doors to those not in work, on benefit, students etc. As part of this programme, it has established a centre in Cable Street in London's East End, site of the celebrated and victorious confrontation with the fascists in 1936. The opening was attended by representatives of the local community, mainly Bengali in origin. More than anything else they wanted to discuss union support for the Dhaka textile workers just after more than 1,000 had died in the factory collapse of May 2013. Here is a new circuit of struggle linking past and present, unions and the community, Britain and Bangladesh, which must be in embryo the twenty-first century working class emerging.

Likewise, as already indicated, several major unions joined with a range of community and campaigning organisations to organise the People's Assembly Against Austerity, which brought more than 4,000 workplace and local activists together to build a united front against the Tory-Liberal Coalition's policies of social misery, leading to a mounting catastrophe for the poorest and weakest in society. The People's Assembly movement is now rolling out across the country and has the potential to mobilise the united response to the crisis which previous left-led campaigns tied to a particular sect failed to do.

The success of these initiatives, and other moves like intensive efforts to extend trade unionism to the huge unorganised areas of the low-wage private sector, is in the balance. No more than parties of the left do trade unions have a God-given right to a future. The legacies of more than a generation of defeat, decline and disorientation need to be overcome in the trade unions. The overdue development of purposeful leadership is an essential part of the answer, but it will need more if the limited progress to date is to be sustained, above all the re-emergence of something the trade unions have not been developing in a mass way since the 1970s – self-reliant, politically oriented activists at all levels. Today, they need to be nurtured in a far more unfavourable economic and legal environment than forty years ago, but the task seems far from impossible.

The argument is not that trade unions can be the sole focus of socialists' work. Unions cannot be the agency for establishing socialism, but they are the essential arena for reconstituting the working class, which *is* the only such agency. Scepticism about trade union politics is understandable, and can be buttressed by recent observation as well as theory, given the practical acquiescence of most of their leaders in the Blair-Brown agenda for 13 years, a consequence of what has been aptly described as 'their ingrained reluctance to act as political not just industrial leaders'.[10]

Sam Gindin's question – 'are unions now exhausted as an effective historical form through which working people organise themselves' – is therefore reasonable.[11] Nevertheless, it is indisputable that they remain far deeper-rooted in society, and the working class in particular, than the socialist left or any single-issue movements (except for a time the anti-war movement), and that they alone have the heft to start rebuilding the labour movement as a plausible alternative to capitalist class rule.

The role of socialists in the work of rebuilding is vital. It can be done.

Neither the anti-war movement nor Ken Livingstone's leadership in London are necessarily a model but lessons can be learned from both as to how to intervene in a purposeful and effective way, as well as from their shortcomings. The main limiting factor, which affected both in different ways, it could plausibly be argued, was the very absence of a strong labour movement able to take the fight to a higher level. Socialists who intervene in the movement with a view to raising its political capacity are playing a central role in developing the only force able to challenge and overturn capitalism. In different ways, and with their common and different limitations, the Communist Party, Counterfire, Socialist Action (all from different twentieth-century left 'traditions' it should be noted) and of course individuals in other groups can be found presently playing that sort of role – building the movement, seeking to shape it politically, setting new challenges for the organisations of the class and then working to meet them. Greater unity among such forces would really be a 'left unity' worth having.

Here it is worth considering what the idea of a 'vanguard', encrusted as it is with an effusion of ideological barnacles, might mean today. The monolithic, ideologically 'pure' and exclusive model of the past seems to have very limited purchase on the future. But neither should the concept itself be discarded. Socialists who work to set out the 'line of march' and then take that strategy into the existing mass movements (not discounting the need to sometimes develop new collectives) can get results. The same forces which united in the leadership of Stop the War – mainly Marxists of one sort or another and largely, although not entirely, from the groups mentioned above (the Labour left being additionally central, in particular) – are now coming together in the People's Assembly, in both cases bringing much of the rest of the left and *tens of thousands of 'ordinary' people* behind them. One could call this a 'vanguard of a new type' – one not presupposing total ideological homogeneity – or even the 'party' in the sense which Marx and Engels used the term in 1848. These socialists do not agree, or even attempt to agree, about everything, have discrete organisational affiliations and do not subject themselves to a discipline more severe than respect for commonly arrived at decisions and comradely loyalty. The objective is unity for purposeful intervention on the key issues of the time – anti-imperialism, opposing the social calamity of austerity economics – and for building rooted movements for change, re-establishing the basis for mass socialist politics, while tolerating diversity of opinion about the nature of the USSR, the long-term prospects for the Labour Party and much else; issues which have provided the ostensible rationale for endless splits among the many fag-end 'vanguards' of the last forty-fifty years. It seems to work.

Contrast this with, say, the Socialist Party (the erstwhile Militant Tendency) which has many fine and self-sacrificing activists in its ranks, yet which insists on trying to create a shadow labour movement around itself, with its own electoral front, its own shop stewards network etc. Such groups are reproducing the mistake Paul Buhle identifies US socialists as making a century ago – 'substitut[ing] themselves for a political working class that did not exist but might be successfully constituted'.[12] The first approach strives to lift socialists to the level of leading the movement; the second in effect works to shrink the movement to a size amenable for a small group to dominate. Being a 'vanguard' is no guarantee of making the correct tactical decisions, of course, but at least one gets to find out if they are right or not, because the decisions are tested in the real world.

There will also doubtless be scope for the creation, not of new competing socialist or 'left' groups, but of new campaigning organisations, reflecting the diversity of the contemporary class which need to be mobilised, which can strengthen the movement politically and ideologically. The key element, however, is the orientation towards the labour movement, towards the working class and its organisations. This may be slightly unfashionable, in a world of Occupy, UK Uncut and similar movements but the latter, for all their undoubted successes in highlighting anti-capitalist issues, have not yet supplied a programmatic or organisational model sufficiently robust to make discarding (as opposed to supplementing) the existing institutions seem like a sensible option.

It is in this context that we return to the question of the Labour Party. Under circumstances of a stronger and developing working-class movement, can it be turned into an instrument of deeper social advance – not a revolutionary party but one which can contribute towards opening up the way to socialism? The only honest answer is – who can say for sure? The main working-class organisations have set it as their task to try to accomplish that transformation after the disastrous New Labour episode – the first, and successful, step, being to work for the election of the best of the possible (and plausible) leaders on offer in 2010, Ed Miliband. Since then, some progress has been made away from the worst positions of New Labour but it has undeniably been uneven and incomplete – pretending New Labour is dead is as wrong as pretending nothing has changed since 2010 (the latter being the Left Unity position in effect). This underlines the sober reality that neoliberalism is an exercise in class power by the global capitalist elite as much or more than it is a specific set of economic policy prescriptions. If it was only the latter, it would be shipwrecked beyond redemption by now; as the former it survives until there is a force which will no longer allow the elite to rule in the old way. Absent that force, social democratic opposition parties will be drawn towards the maintenance of the prevailing consensus defined above all by the interests of the international financial markets, of which the City of London is perhaps the most powerful centre, at least in terms of its relationship to its host political environment. All roads forward lead through working-class unity, confidence and mobilising capacity.

No one, therefore, can confidently assert that it is likely that a 2015 Labour government will master the economic crisis in the interests of ordinary people, although such a government could certainly generate – even in spite of itself – an arena of struggle over its direction which could bring benefits in itself in terms of strengthening the movement, and could create circumstances for the working class to recover a measure of confidence. That is the task that the major organisations of the class have set themselves. That can only be held as inconsequential if one regards the working class and its organisations as mere fingerbowls at the great left buffet.

It is certainly possible that the working-class movement will learn through experience, over the next few years (and probably not much longer either way), that the struggle to 'reclaim Labour' is not going to work. If it fails then that will be because of one of two factors – the working class itself lacks the 'social weight' in the here and now to sustain its own political project, at least on that scale, in which case the necessity for socialists to redouble their efforts to rebuild the strength of the class is obvious (and a new mass socialist party, resting on a serious and durable foundation, may eventually come out of such an endeavour) but we would be in for a definite period of unchallenged bourgeois political domination at the parliamentary level at any event. Or, the effort will be thwarted by establishment manoeuvres, with what has been termed the 'Blairite undead', supported by a frightened elite, obstructing democratic and constitutional efforts to transform Labour which might have otherwise succeeded. The assault on union involvement in the Party in the Summer of 2013 was a clear sign of this 'New Labour' fightback. Under those circumstances, the creation of a new class party might be higher up the agenda, because the class is already fighting for it, but it would be hard to see it much resembling Left Unity or any of the others presently on offer. In the meantime, to stand outside the general objective of electing a Labour government as the only alternative to the Coalition by engaging in separate and marginal electoral interventions is self-defeating.

Any left political intervention which does not partake of the strength of the organised working class can only achieve very limited objectives. So socialists and the unions need to reach out (and not in an exclusive relationship!) and elaborate common projects. If it does indeed fall to socialists to set out the 'line of march', they can only do so if they are themselves among the body of the troops, in the workplaces, communities and organisations of working people. This may not be as exciting as setting up another new party hoping to elect a local councillor here or there, but it is the real agenda today. Today's rulers should feel themselves to be on the edge of a precipice, after the disasters they have sponsored. What would shake them up more – a resurgent working class rebuilding and transforming its established political and social institutions, or left parties getting, to be very generous, 5 per cent of the vote? Not a tough call really.

NOTES

1   This essay has evolved out of a polemic written against the 'Left Unity' project in Britain in spring 2013. The original text was published at http://21centurymanifesto.wordpress.com and it was republished, to its credit, by Left Unity itself at www.leftunity.org. The original was published pseudonymously in order to avoid the union, Unite, which I serve as Chief of Staff, being dragged into any public controversy on the issue at the time. At time of writing (July 2013) the plan appeared to be to convert Left Unity into a new Left Party as of November 2013.
    See among others, Ken Coates, 'Socialists and the Labour Party', *Socialist Register 1973*, London: Merlin, 1973; Ralph Miliband, 'Moving On', *Socialist Register 1976*, London: Merlin, 1976; Duncan Hallas, 'How Can We Move On?', *Socialist Register 1977*, London: Merlin, 1977; and Leo Panitch, 'Socialists and the Labour Party: A Reappraisal', *Socialist Register 1979*, London: Merlin, 1979.
2   Documents can be found at www.leftunity.org.
3   Ken Loach, Kate Hudson and Gilbert Achcar, 'The Labour Party has Failed Us. We Need a New Party of the Left', *Guardian*, 25 March 2013.
4   Lenin, *Left-Wing Communism*, Beijing: Foreign Languages Press, 1970, p. 102.
5   Simon Jenkins, 'Ed Balls is as Mesmorised by the Bankers as George Osborne', *Guardian*, 4 June 2013.
6   Joe Lo, 'Let's Explain What Socialism is Before We Call Ourselves Socialists', available at http://leftunity.org.
7   Alex Callinicos's article, 'Is Leninism Finished?', conflating the need to uphold the SWP leadership's handling of the rape allegation with the defence of Leninism can be found at http://www.socialistreview.org.uk.
8   Sam Gindin, 'Rethinking Unions, Registering Socialism', *Socialist Register 2013*, Pontypool: Merlin, 2012, p. 46.
9   Gindin, 'Rethinking Unions', p. 27.
10 Leo Panitch and Colin Leys, *The End of Parliamentary Socialism*, London: Verso, 1997, p. 148.
11 Gindin, 'Rethinking Unions', p. 26.
12 Paul Buhle, *Marxism in the United States*, London: Verso, 2013 [1987], p. 90.

RETHINKING CLASS:
THE LINEAGE OF THE *SOCIALIST REGISTER*

MADELEINE DAVIS

In 1960, the American sociologist C. Wright Mills wrote to a letter to his friends in the British New Left, published in its recently founded house journal *New Left Review*, in which he urged them to abandon what he dubbed the 'labour metaphysic' – a belief in the working class of the advanced capitalist societies as *the* historic agency of change – as 'a legacy from Victorian Marxism that is now quite unrealistic'. This labour metaphysic, Mills said, 'is an historically specific idea that has been turned into an a-historical and unspecific hope'. His phrase quickly became a classic. Much quoted, it may be seen as presaging later debates in the US New Left as well as the broader displacement of class as the major analytic of the left. Convinced that working-class agency in the advanced capitalist countries 'has either collapsed or become most ambiguous', Mills was especially interested in the potential of the radical intelligentsia as an agent for change, an interest often taken to be a distinguishing feature of New Left movements.[1] Yet the early British New Left was by no means ready to follow his advice. Among the friends on the editorial board of *NLR* to whom Mills addressed himself were Ralph Miliband and John Saville, who three years later, following the organisational and political crisis that engulfed the early British New Left, would found the *Socialist Register*. Miliband, in fact, was a close personal friend as well as political ally of Mills', but he thought his views on the question of working-class agency mistaken. Others in the early New Left took a different view: if few were ready to make the leap that Mills suggested, they were certainly convinced of the need to address questions of class composition and structure, class relations and class consciousness. As the *Register* revisits similar questions some fifty years later, the purpose of this essay is to reappraise the early New Left's class analysis, to provide the reflection on the origins of the *Register* that such a significant anniversary warrants, and to see whether these past debates can help orient our present perspectives.

THE EMERGENCE OF THE BRITISH NEW LEFT

The term New Left describes a wide array of left activist and intellectual currents arising from the late 1950s in different national contexts. Sometimes regarded as synonymous with the student and broad-based radical movements of the 1960s that culminated in the uprisings of 1968, its claim to novelty vis-a-vis the 'old left' is most often seen to lie in characteristic emphases including a strongly libertarian and democratic impulse; a commitment to cultural as well as political transformation; experimentation with novel forms of political organisation such as direct action and participatory democracy, and a readiness to consider non-class or cross-class forces as agencies for radical change. In comparison with this broader activist and international milieu the New Left in its British incarnation was somewhat distinct, in its nature as a primarily intellectual formation and in its relatively stronger connection to established traditions including Marxism, Communism and the British labour movement.

A vibrant and intellectually fertile expression of the conjuncture of 1956, the British New Left emerged from the convergence of a group of disillusioned Communists who published a dissident journal, *The Reasoner* (later *New Reasoner*, 1956-59), to debate the implications for Communism of the Khrushchev revelations, and who subsequently resigned over the Soviet invasion of Hungary, with a group of younger, independent socialist students around the Oxford-edited journal *Universities and Left Review* (1957-59). This broader grouping adopted the label 'New Left' in 1958 to denote their aspiration to create an activist and participatory, but theoretically-informed, socialist 'movement of ideas' through channels such as the Campaign for Nuclear Disarmament (CND) and the network of left clubs begun by ULR. *New Left Review* (*NLR*), produced from a merger of the two original journals, was originally intended as voice and pivot for this novel formation. Its early editorial board comprised many who were or would become leading lights of the British intellectual scene, including its first editor Stuart Hall, who along with Raphael Samuel and Charles Taylor had founded ULR, founders of the *Reasoner* Edward Thompson and John Saville, and Raymond Williams, who was closer in age to the Reasoners but in some of his preoccupations to the ULR group. Closer in age to the ULR founders but based at the London School of Economics rather than Oxford, Ralph Miliband, who had joined the *New Reasoner* board in 1958, also joined the *NLR* editorial board. A little later, a third group was co-opted that included Perry Anderson, Tom Nairn and Robin Blackburn, some of whom had been involved with the Oxford magazine *New University*.[2]

Internationally, the key political contexts for the New Left endeavour comprised the crisis in world Communism touched off by Khrushchev's 1956 'secret speech', the Cold War, nuclearism and anti-nuclearism, decolonisation and the rise of third world national-liberation movements. Domestically, it was a political scene dominated by the discourse of postwar 'affluence' and, on the mainstream left, by Labour Party 'revisionism', to which Anthony Crosland's recasting of socialism to emphasise (as he saw it) its ethical ends of welfare and equality over economic means such as nationalisation made the single most important intellectual contribution.[3] Crosland's thesis relied on a widely shared perception that the character of postwar British capitalism had been qualitatively altered via a separation of the functions of ownership and control and the rise of the 'welfare state'. In similar vein, developments such as rising working-class incomes; changing patterns of production and consumption; rapid social, technological and cultural change; suburbanisation and the rise of a 'mass society' – all contributed to a loss of confidence in the continued relevance of socialism and its claim on working-class support, aptly encapsulated by Richard Crossman when he asked 'If welfare capitalism can provide the majority with security, how can we ever persuade them to prefer socialism?'[4]

The New Left responded to its conjuncture by positioning itself outside ideological orthodoxies as an independent formation whose avowed commitment to 'a socialist and humanist transformation of our society' involved an explicit recognition that socialism and Marxism must be opened to critical scrutiny, both in terms of their theoretical basis and political practice.[5] The *NLR*'s first editorial at the beginning of 1960 put it this way:

> The humanist strengths of socialism – which are the foundations for a genuinely popular socialist movement – must be developed in cultural and social terms as well as economic and political ... the task of socialism is to meet people where they are, where they are touched, bitten, moved, frustrated, nauseated – to develop discontent and, at the same time, to give the socialist movement some direct sense of the times and ways in which we live.[6]

Conceiving itself as a forum for discussion and fresh thinking, the diversity of this early New Left (before the differences that led to reorientation of *NLR* and the launching of the Socialist Register by 1964, of which more later) makes efforts to categorise its political and theoretical positions difficult. On any given issue, including its relationship to Marxism, there was no New Left 'line' but rather a range of contending perspectives. Nevertheless, its location 'between Stalinism and social democracy' implied certain orientations. Opposing bureaucratism and authoritarianism of whatever stamp, New Leftists saw socialist strategy as necessarily grassroots and democratic. In a notable contribution, E.P. Thompson attempted to rethink the reform/revolution dichotomy for British conditions, effectively arguing that cumulative reforms could acquire a radicalizing and mobilizing potential that could have transformative implications.[7] Although this view was by no means universally shared, the early New Left pursued a strategy of 'making socialists' which aimed to bridge the gap between intellectual and political work in a genuinely novel way, by offering a theoretical reworking of socialism as communitarian, democratic, and humanist, while at the same time seeking to discover, model and popularise this vision through practical efforts to create a distinctive grassroots New Left movement.

THE NEW LEFT'S CLASS ANALYSIS

New Left thinkers made highly original, in some areas groundbreaking, interventions around class consciousness, agency, the significance of culture and the dynamics of class struggle. However, while their class analysis both drew on and challenged Marxist sources and ideas, it did not always do so explicitly. There was disagreement – though it was not always fully explored – on some fundamental issues, and the milieu as a whole achieved no synthesis of its various perspectives. Thus, as with many of the issues it addressed, it is in the range and prescience of its discussions of class, rather than in any single insight or resolution, that the New Left contribution lies.

As the early New Left cohered, the nature of contemporary British working-class culture and consciousness became one of its distinct preoccupations, shared, though with different emphases, by the Reasoner and ULR groups. Interest here was stimulated in particular by Richard Hoggart's *Uses of Literacy* (1957), a pioneering text of cultural studies which combined personal reminiscence with a nuanced study of the ways in which newer forms of mass publishing were received by working-class audiences. Hoggart's central thesis – that working-class culture and ways of life were threatened by an encroaching 'mass culture' – was keenly debated within the New Left. Williams, writing as part of a ULR symposium on the book, rejected the pessimism implicit in Hoggart's approach and argued that it was the 'collective democratic institution, formed to achieve a general social benefit' that represented the most distinctive expression of working-class culture, rather than the everyday practices romanticised by Hoggart.[8] Williams' critique reflected his own developing project at this time, pursued through *Culture and Society* (1958), his essays within the New Left, and *The Long Revolution* (1961) to articulate a new theoretical and strategic centrality for culture in socialist thought, a project the ULRers found particularly inspiring. His discussion of Hoggart also took in the broader debates of the period, rejecting a creeping tendency to equate low, or mass commercial culture with working-class culture, insisting that 'there are in fact no masses, there are only ways of seeing people as masses'[9] and arguing that working-class adoption of new consumer goods in no way signified 'embourgeoisement': 'these changes are changes in the use of personal things, and have nothing to do with becoming bourgeois in any real sense'.[10]

The reception of Hoggart's text touched off a broader debate within the New Left in which its thinkers responded to the challenges 'affluent capitalism' was thought to pose for socialism. In general, New Leftists were highly sceptical of the Labour Party's revisionist claims regarding a supposed transformation of capitalism and the presumed effects in terms of altering class structures, identities and political preferences. They disputed the extent and significance of phenomena such as the 'incomes revolution', separation of the functions of ownership and control in the capitalist economy, and rising social mobility, and found little evidence to support arguments for a reorientation of Labour and socialist objectives.[11] Roused in particular by the arguments of *Industry and Society*, a 1957 Labour policy paper that proposed a shift of the party's goals from the full nationalisation implied by the party's founding commitment to 'the common ownership of the means of production, distribution and exchange' to a more limited policy of greater state control of capitalist enterprises, the New Left published a series of pieces that rebutted revisionist claims and renewed arguments for traditional socialist objectives.[12] The centrality of common ownership to socialism was restated, but the New Left tried to shift the grounds of the debate: far from being a mere means among many, as Crosland argued, common ownership was the sole route to secure human and democratic control over productive life, an end to alienation and the achievement of socialism as a classless community.[13] Saville and Miliband also developed a strand of work that disputed the revisionist presentation of the welfare state as a 'halfway house' to socialism, instead seeing it as functional for the maintenance of capitalism. In perhaps his most significant essay for the *New Reasoner*, Miliband coined the term 'marginal collectivism' to describe the role of the welfare state and nationalised sector of the economy; this marginal collectivism, which left the central interests of property untouched, was simply the price capitalism had learned to pay for political security.[14]

Overall, then, there was little sense within the New Left that the objective structures of the capitalist economy and class system were changing. However, a 1958 piece by Stuart Hall, 'A sense of classlessness', which detected a growing disjunction or disconnect between these objective structures and the subjective consciousness and identity of class, was more controversial. Though Hall, in common with other New Leftists, rejected any notion that higher living standards and consumption in themselves would necessarily alter class attitudes, he nevertheless saw the shift from production to consumption within capitalism 'as a social system' as a key change. Consumerism, he suggested, tied the working class into the market in new and insidious ways:

> the 'new things' in themselves suggest and imply a way of life which has become objectified through them, and may even become desirable because of their social value. In those places in welfare Britain where the working class has been put directly in touch with 'the new opportunities', the 'whole way of life' is breaking down into several styles of living ... each imperceptibly but ... exquisitely, differentiated from one another.[15]

This, he suggested, was engendering a sense of confusion and disorientation around perceptions of class identity – the 'sense of classlessness' of the title – which even though it was a false consciousness (since objective class relations remained the same), inasmuch as it rendered 'the real problems not only more difficult to solve but more difficult to see', was indeed a critical strategic problem for socialists, demanding the development of a new kind of left cultural politics.[16] As theoretical justification, Hall's piece challenged traditional Marxist distinctions between economic, cultural and political spheres, arguing against any 'simplistic economic determinist-reading' of base-superstructure in favour of a reconceptualisation that allowed for mutual interpenetration.[17]

Such a critique of Marxist economism, and more specifically, of the base-superstructure metaphor, was common ground within the New Left, underpinning both Thompson's eloquently articulated 'socialist humanism' and Williams' as yet only embryonic project to articulate a position he would later describe as 'cultural materialism'. Not surprisingly, given the differing political formations of the two groupings, the attitude of the ULR group to Marxism was more deeply revisionist that that of the Reasoner cohort. As former Communists, the Reasoners identified far more easily with Marxism, which (with some notable exceptions, most obviously Thompson, whose work was somewhat unique among this group) they tended to see as a more or less self-sufficient body of theory, albeit distorted in the application. The ULR group, formed by postwar conditions and student politics, though they made in some areas a deeper appropriation of Marxist themes (particularly alienation), were more likely to see Marxism as a tradition itself requiring reworking and scrutiny.[18]

More immediately controversial than these underlying theoretical divergences, however, was the practical question of the differing extent of the two groups' orientations to a politics based within the working class. The theme of 'classlessness' brought this to the surface. Hall's piece was the most important statement of a more general openness amongst the ULR grouping to consider non-class or cross-class forces as potential agencies for change. This, it should be said, remained rather implicit than explicit, conveyed mainly through the characteristic, youthful style and eclectic preoccupations of the journal, which included some attention to an emergent politics of race, as well as in its involvement in an array of spin-off and outreach activities. But it was enough to provoke a response from Thompson, who penned a robust defence of working-class self-activity and an uncompromising critique of the 'anti-working-class attitudes' he detected among some of his younger New Left colleagues. Published as 'Commitment in Politics' in ULR, his essay opened by rehearsing the 'jibes' he said he had heard being directed at ULR's politics by 'the active rank and file socialist', stalwarts of the 'old' left, amongst whom, though he did not say it directly, he might have included himself:

> These ULR types (the jibe runs) are passionate advocates of commitment in the arts, but they evade commitment on the central issues of class power and political allegiance. They are angrier about ugly architecture than they are about the ugly poverty of old-age pensioners, angrier about the 'materialism' of the Labour Movement than about the rapacity of financiers. They wear upon their sleeves a tender sensibility; but probe that tenderness, and one finds a complex of responses which the veteran recognises as 'anti-working class'. They are more at ease discussing alienation than exploitation. ... They see the authentic expression of the younger generation in a squalid streetfight in Notting Hill, but the thousands of young men and women who flock every night into the technical colleges ... do not come into the picture at all.[19]

Though his immediate target was an impressionistic article that saw in sections of working-class life 'a population jaded almost beyond redemption', Thompson was also addressing the wider arguments of his ULR colleagues, whom he criticised for over generalising from the present period of relative working-class quiescence, and of lacking a sense of history.[20] Taking up Stuart Hall's assertion that contemporary capitalism was based upon consumption rather than production, for instance, Thompson argued that the working class had always been 'built into the market' – the change was one of degree rather than of quality. And he found in a tendency to bemoan the 'materialism' of working-class culture (though this was in fact less typical of ULR than of the wider mainstream discourse around affluence) a patronising and ahistorical denial of the right of each new generation to make 'fuller and more complex claims on life' than their predecessors: 'What do we want the present generation of working people to fight for? We do not want to push them back into the old, cramped claustrophobic community which was based on the grim equality of hardship. The aspiration toward community, if it arises in the present generation, will be far richer and more complex, with far more insistence on variety, freedom of movement, and freedom of choice, than in the old-style community'.[21]

In recognising the justice of these new claims, Thompson's position in fact had much in common with ULR's own aspirations for 'socialism at full stretch'. But in contrast to ULR's (at this point) somewhat vague 'culturalist' emphasis, he insisted that socialism must be rooted in the actual experience and history of the working class as political agents. Thompson emphasised a continuous radical lineage, best seen in the self-organisation of a minority of politically conscious working-class activists. Ignorance of this history could make 'the record of our working class look like an instinctual, almost vegetable evolution, in which the active role of the minority, as the agent of social change, is belittled'. Against these attitudes, Thompson presented working-class history as a continuous 'way of struggle' between 'competing moralities' within the working class as well as against class rule above.[22]

Thompson's arguments in 'Commitment' clearly anticipated those he would pursue in The Making of the English Working Class, on which he was working at the time. Yet they did not fully address some of the concerns that animated ULR's exploration of 'classlessness'. As Stuart Hall pointed out in an exasperated reply to his critics, his own concern was with the potential of the media, advertising and consumerism to engender a 'sense of confusion about what class is and how much it matters, and where class allegiances lie' – in other words, to change the perception of class identity in ways that were depoliticising.[23] Thompson, insisting on working-class agency as a fundamental of socialism but also admitting a 'dulled' political consciousness on the part of the contemporary working class, saw the problem as essentially one of political organisation, perhaps brushing aside too easily those questions of ideology and hegemony that would continue to preoccupy Hall. The 'classlessness' debate then gave an early but very incomplete indication of some serious theoretical and political divergences that would come to the fore later in the oppositions between humanism and structuralism and later still, the various post-Marxisms of the last two decades of the twentieth century.

In the meantime, Thompson published in 1963 what was undoubtedly the most important single contribution to class analysis to emerge from this early New Left milieu, his *The Making of the English Working Class*.[24] Its key emphases – in theoretical terms, on class as a historical phenomenon, as process, and as relationship, and in political terms, on the importance of working-class agency in its own 'making' – are well enough known and have been often enough debated not to require restatement here. Yet one of the reasons that Thompson's book proved such a rich resource for subsequent discussion is precisely the relative absence from the text of sustained conceptual analysis. At the centre of Thompson's endeavour was an imaginative and subtle exploration of the interaction between social being and social consciousness, between agency and necessity (or structure) in class formation, drawing on but not limited to the Marxist tradition. But this was only made partially explicit.[25] As Bryan Palmer has argued, while the precise detail of this interaction provides fertile ground for theoretical appropriations and reappropriations, the real significance of *The Making* lay not in the detail of its specific arguments but rather in 'that the book opened interpretative eyes to a new way of seeing class. ... Its meaning ... and its consequent great achievement, lies in the unmistakable rupture it forced in the historical literature ... where class formation could no longer be posed, by radicals and reactionaries alike, as a mechanical reflection of economic change'.[26]

FROM *REASONER* TO *REGISTER*

As well as a work of history, *The Making* was a further, and definitive, intervention in New Left discussions of working-class consciousness, identity, agency and experience, as well as a powerful expression of Thompson's 'socialist humanism'. But its completion actually coincided with the disintegration of the early New Left.

Pulled apart by internal contradictions and unable to sustain the momentum that had briefly propelled it, by late 1961 the early New Left was already in the process of disintegrating. Political differences and financial difficulties combined to exacerbate the critical tension at the heart of the early *NLR* enterprise: was it primarily a journal of ideas or a movement of people? A transfer of editorship and subsequently ownership of *NLR* in 1962-63 to Perry Anderson secured the journal's future whilst also inaugurating a shift in its perspectives. The well-known controversies and animosities attending this transition have sometimes been overplayed, masking underlying continuities that render the commonly accepted 'generational' periodization of these 'two New Lefts' somewhat suspect. It is nonetheless true that Anderson's *NLR* became a more self-consciously and narrowly intellectual project than the earlier version, renouncing organising and activist ambitions in favour of a project of gradual transformation of the British intellectual scene, envisaged as being achieved in the main via a sustained programme of translation and exposition of continental Marxist theory.[27]

Thompson's arguments in *The Making*, coinciding as they did with the final stages of the collapse of the early New Left, were not really taken up by his early New Left peers. Anderson and (especially) Tom Nairn, now beginning to define a different direction for *NLR* in a series of essays that began with 'Origins of the Present Crisis' in early 1964, did respond to the book, but they did so in a somewhat selective and incomplete way that exaggerated theoretical and methodological differences and was over-determined by an uncompromising judgment of the political failures of their New Left predecessors.[28] Nairn and Anderson presented their analysis of British historical development as a reversal of the Thompsonian class optic. Against his stress on agency, on the possibility and promise of native radical traditions in a creative encounter with Marxism, and on a history of working-class resistance, they emphasised what they saw as the structural subjugation of the working class, the result of a historic class compromise between agrarian and mercantile capitalism. Arguing that 'a supine bourgeoisie produced a subordinate proletariat', they saw in English working-class consciousness no more than a reactive and defensive impulse, such that its struggles were 'the very opposite of coherent, aggressive self-assertion. It was an experience of being driven into revolt, and finding every means of expression cut away, every channel blocked'.[29]

The achievements of working-class culture that early New Leftists such as Williams and Thompson most valued, their collective democratic institutions, became in this schema expressions of withdrawal, corporateness and defeat. The ensuing, and famous, polemic between Anderson and Thompson only partially explored the theoretical differences at stake.[30] In the meantime the fragmentation of the project of the early New Left ended a phase characterised by an exploratory treatment of class that anticipated future controversies but was ultimately inconclusive.

It was in the wake of an acrimonious meeting of the *NLR* editorial board that the idea for a new 'socialist annual' was first mooted among a small group of former *New Reasoner* editors in April 1963. Miliband was the main originator of the idea, and he invited Saville and Thompson – the latter of whom was at that time also considering suggestions from other former 'Reasoners' to reconvene their group and perhaps revive the *New Reasoner* – to join him in the enterprise.[31] In the event, the *New Reasoner* was not refounded, and Thompson eventually declined to serve on the board of what became the *Socialist Register*. The *Register*, then, while in some ways a clear successor of the *New Reasoner*, had its own orientation which perhaps more than anything else reflected Miliband's distinctive perspective. The only member of the *New Reasoner* editorial board never to have been in the Communist Party, he was also the only member of either editorial team to vote against the merger of ULR and NR, which he correctly regarded as possessing somewhat different perspectives, particularly on the question of political organisation. As, essentially, party-oriented Marxists, the Reasoners' rejection of the discipline and orthodoxy of the CPGB left them without a party, but still with a strong sense, as Miliband put it 'of political agencies', and a close orientation to working-class politics, and it was these elements that attracted him to their project. Miliband saw the ULR group, by contrast, as part of a 'more or less anti-organisation current', which, though vibrant and energetic, was not capable of providing the sharp political orientation he believed was required for the left to regroup.[32] Having seen the early New Left primarily as preparatory work for 'something a good deal more oriented', he did not, therefore, fully share Thompson's enthusiasm for the more nebulous possibilities of a New Left 'movement', and as his biographer Michael Newman has shown, remained consistent in his basic belief that party organisation was what the left ultimately required.[33]

There were also further differences, between Miliband (and increasingly also Saville) and Thompson in the nature and degree of their orientation to Marxism. Although these were neither explicitly aired in the early New Left's journals nor fully explored in private correspondence, they were significant enough to be a factor that weighed in Thompson's decision not to join the SR editorial board.[34] In an exchange of letters in 1963, Miliband responded exasperatedly to Thompson's mention of such differences – declaring, in reply to the latter's admission that he could not identify himself as a Marxist 'without important qualifications on essential matters' – 'My God, isn't that exactly my own position?'.[35] Yet Miliband, though he greatly respected Thompson and admired his work, was relatively unsympathetic to some aspects of his thought, particularly, perhaps, the moral emphasis that so shaped his 'socialist humanism'. When Saville mooted the idea of soliciting a piece (from Alasdair MacIntyre) for the *Register* on 'The Moral Basis of Socialism', his co-editor rejected this as 'an utterly lousy idea ... it is exactly the kind of waffle which this sort of piece always produces that I should like to see avoided'.[36] While his objection was less to a humanist reading of Marx per se than to what he saw as the imprecise and rhetorical style in which such humanist readings were too often couched, it was nevertheless noticeable that his own contributions to the *New Reasoner*, like Saville's, drew mainly on Marxism as social theory rather than as a source of ethical inspiration. According less prominence to questions of culture and consciousness than did some of his colleagues, his position on Labour revisionism and 'affluence' was also more uncompromising. 'I <u>hate</u> people speaking of working-class affluence, it is such a shameful mockery', wrote Miliband in a letter in 1963.[37] And when Labour leader Hugh Gaitskell attempted to revise Clause IV of the party constitution to de-emphasise common ownership, Miliband wrote a parody for the *New Statesman* – casting Gaitskell as a priest delivering a sermon entitled 'Should we drop Christ?' – that could hardly have been more to the point.[38]

What Saville and Miliband most sought, then, to carry over from the *New Reasoner* was not its socialist humanist commitment nor its pronounced literary flavour. These had been Thompson's distinct contribution, and though neither theme would be entirely absent from the new annual, they were peripheral concerns. Rather, they wanted to recover the former journal's accessibility of style and directness of tone, its sense of appeal to a readership within the labour movement and its adoption of an idiom of internationalism that was solidaristic and politically responsible, in sharp contrast to the variety developing within *NLR*, whose uncritical Third Worldist tendencies Miliband, like Thompson, deplored, (though he objected far less to its orientation to continental traditions of Marxism). Above all – and for Miliband particularly – it was the urgent need to a 'recreate a journal of the autonomous left', with the sharp political orientation that the new model *NLR* now signally lacked, that motivated him to found a new publication.[39] By May 1963, plans were crystallising for the annual, spurred on by Miliband's view that *NLR* was now doing 'NO political work' and was even 'a positive discredit to intellectuals in the Labour movement'. 'And the whole journal', he added, 'is now written in a barbarous, Fringlish sort of way'.[40]

By November, the title *Socialist Register* was settled upon. It was suggested by Martin Eve (the close friend of Thompson's who ran the Merlin Press) in a reference to Willliam Cobbett's *Political Register*, the radical weekly which had run from 1802 to 1835, and strongly advocated the extension of the suffrage. This title was enthusiastically received by the editors – 'I kick myself for not having thought of it first' wrote Miliband to Saville, 'I think it's got everything we want, it's sober, sharp, distinct'.[41] With the subtitle 'a survey of movements and ideas', the first issue appeared in April 1964. Reflecting the closeness of Saville and Miliband's collaboration, in which, as Miliband later recalled, there had been a 'largely unspoken agreement between us that we would mainly publish work that would fall within the broad Marxist tradition … to which we both belonged',[42] its first, brief editorial set out a clear agenda: to the journal's purpose of 'socialist analysis and discussion' its editors brought 'a definite and committed point of view, and this bears a direct relationship, not only to what we write ourselves, but to our choice of contributors. At the same time, we have no wish to imprison discussion within a narrow framework.'[43] This distinct position, later characterised by Miliband as 'unsectarian left', and as 'somewhere between ultra leftism and left Labourism' was intended to have political as well as simply intellectual significance.[44]

With its coordinates clearly established, the *Register*'s treatment of class and agency has been basically consistent, though by no means static. In regards to the British context, its early volumes developed the strand of work Miliband and Saville had begun within the *New Reasoner*, which focused in the main on the problem of political organisation. Miliband's *Parliamentary Socialism* had expounded in 1961 his basic position at this time, which was that notwithstanding its major shortcomings (chief among which was a dogmatic attachment to parliamentarism that made it essentially a party of social reform rather than of socialism), the Labour Party, as the dominant expression of working-class politics, remained the only realistic party political vehicle for socialists in the UK to be involved in. 'Get in and push', was the nub of his advice to socialists, and to this end essays in the *Register* in its first two years considered 'Labour Policy and the Labour Left', nationalisation, trades unionism and the limits of the welfare state.[45] By 1966, Miliband would himself leave the Labour Party in disgust at the Wilson government's policies, but the basic orientation to a class-based politics and party organisation would remain. The *Register* also published, in its second volume, Thompson's excoriating critique of the Nairn-Anderson analysis of British class and capitalist development.[46] Miliband fought hard to persuade Thompson to moderate his tone, and particularly the imputation, at the end of the essay, of Stalinism to Nairn and Anderson. This was mainly due to an unwillingness to allow any hint of sectarianism within the journal, but it was also true that the *Register* editors, Miliband particularly, were coming to admire the intellectual seriousness of the new *NLR*. Nairn's analysis of the Labour Party, in fact, had much in common with Miliband's own, indeed in 1961 Nairn had written a long letter to Miliband in which he set out many of the arguments and premises that underpinned his *NLR* essays, and sought the other's opinion.[47] Miliband was also much impressed with the *NLR* edited volume, *Towards Socialism*, of 1965. In a letter to Saville, he criticised Thompson for not seeing 'how genuinely important some of that stuff of Perry's and Tom Nairn is. Particularly Perry … he is absolutely brilliant'.[48] Though the projects of the two journals were quite distinct, Miliband and Anderson shared key orientations, and particularly following the latter's reassessment of *NLR*'s priorities in the early 1980s, the *Register* and *NLR* would make common cause to articulate a 'resolute left' position against 'post-Marxism' and the 'new revisionism' associated with *Marxism Today*.[49]

A basic consistency may also be seen in regards to the journal's coverage of ideas and movements internationally, where new departures and developments were subjected to careful analysis uninfluenced by intellectual faddism. Thus *SR* maintained a critical distance from the radical eruptions of 1968, warning of the insufficiency of students and intellectuals as agencies of change.[50] It is also worth noting that in its discussions of the US New Left, the *Register* was at least as interested in the black civil rights movement as in the white student movement: though the first published evidence of this was a piece on Black Power in 1968, Miliband had in fact wanted to commission something on this earlier but had proved unable to find anyone to write the kind of socialist analysis of the black movement he sought.[51] There were also considered treatments of class politics and guerrilla struggle in Latin America, a sustained interest in Third World radical movements, especially in Africa, and analysis of the possibilities of peasant movements, in addition to a developing strand of theoretical work that developed and illuminated Marxist analysis of class, party and state.

CONCLUSION

As C. Wright Mills so clearly saw, the New Left emerged, and to some extent defined itself against, an intellectual and political climate already in the 1950s characterised by a gathering sense of anxiety on the left about the role and relevance of class analysis. What resources then can this New Left, from which the *Register* traces its lineage, offer for a renewal of class analysis today?

Among the general emphases most worthy of restatement might be its willingness to interrogate the theoretical, empirical and sociological bases for those phenomena – 'affluent' capitalism (or in today's context 'globalization'), the 'end of ideology', or 'crisis of Marxism' – so often adduced in support of arguments that declare class analysis redundant; and equally as important, to recognize that the effects of social and economic change, at the level of class consciousness and political allegiance, are never pre-determined, but rather sites of struggle and resistance. A general sense of refusal, too, of the more patronising and simplistic manifestations of a leftist 'loss of faith' in the agency of the working class; and an alertness to the complexities of working-class culture and history, an attention to the lived experience of class, is also surely as necessary as ever. More specifically, in regard to such fundamental theoretical questions as how class is to be defined; how class formation occurs; what class consciousness is, the New Left also produced a rich and suggestive body of work, though one which does not point in any single direction. Some of the issues at stake in its discussions (class as relationship versus class as objective structure, for instance) were only clarified rather later, while others, such as ULR's exploration of classlessness, which began to consider the significance of ideology and the workings of hegemony, might be seen as themselves anticipating some aspects of the 'discourse-theoretical' and 'post-Marxist' challenges to class analysis. In terms of orienting the *Register*'s perspectives today, we might end with Miliband's rejoinder to Mills, some years later, which can also serve as a characterisation of the *Register*'s distinctive contribution. If 'metaphysic' in Mills' formulation may be taken to denote that which is above matter, a first principle, an abstraction, then Miliband was surely right to insist that there is nothing 'metaphysical' about the centrality of class struggle to Marxism: for it is not, and has never been, an attachment that rests on groundless faith nor an 'a-historical and unspecific hope', and nor does it preclude a recognition that the capacity of working-class agencies to realize their transformative potentials is far from inevitable.[52] In this sense, he certainly had no trouble at all with Mills' conclusion: 'we can't "write off the working class." But we must *study* all that, and freshly'.[53]

NOTES

1   C. Wright Mills, 'Letter to the New Left', *New Left Review* (*NLR*), I/5(September/October), 1960, pp. 21-2.

2   On the origins and nature of the British New Left, see Michael Kenny, *The First New Left: British Intellectuals after Stalin,* London: Lawrence and Wishart, 1995; Lin Chun, *The British New Left,* Edinburgh: Edinburgh University Press, 1993; Madeleine Davis, 'The origins of the British New Left', in Martin Klimke and Joaquin Scharloth, eds., *1968 in Europe,* London: Palgrave, 2008. On Miliband's role in the early New Left, see the excellent political biography by Michael Newman, *Ralph Miliband and the Politics of the New Left,* London: Merlin, 2002, esp. pp. 63-71.

3   Anthony Crosland, *The Future of Socialism,* London: Jonathan Cape, 1956. For a recent reconsideration of Labour revisionism see Ben Jackson, *Equality and the British Left,* Manchester: MUP, 2007.

4   R. H. S. Crossman, *Socialism and the New Despotism*, Fabian Tract No. 298, 1956, p. 3.

5   Editorial, *Universities and Left Review (ULR)*, 4, 1957.

6   Stuart Hall, 'Introducing New Left Review', *NLR*, I/1(January/February), 1960.

7   Edward Thompson, 'Revolution', in *Out of Apathy*, London: Stevens and Sons, 1960; and 'Revolution Again!', *NLR*, I/6(November/December), 1960.

8   Richard Hoggart, *The Uses of Literacy: Aspects of working class life, with special reference to publications and entertainments*, London: Chatto and Windus, 1957; Raymond Williams, 'Working class culture', *ULR*, 1(2), Summer, 1957, p. 31.

9   Raymond Williams, *Culture and Society 1780-1950*, London: Chatto and Windus, 1958, p. 289.

10   Williams, 'Working class culture', p. 30.

11   In this section I draw on arguments made at greater length in Madeleine Davis, 'Arguing affluence: New Left contributions to the socialist debate 1957-1963', *Twentieth Century British History*, 23(4), 2012.

12   *Industry and Society: Labour's Policy on Future Public Ownership*, 1957. For the New Left response see especially the joint ULR/NR pamphlet 'The Insiders', *ULR*, 3, 1957; and Michael Barratt Brown, 'The Controllers' I, *ULR*, 5, 1958, pp. 53-61; II, *ULR*, 6, 1959, pp. 38-41; III, *ULR*, 7, 1959, pp. 43-9.

13   'The Insiders', p. 61; Thompson, 'Revolution', p. 289; R. Miliband, 'The Transition to the Transition', *New Reasoner*, 6, 1958, p. 36.

14   John Saville, 'The Welfare State: An Historical Approach', *New Reasoner*, 3, 1957-58; Ralph Miliband, 'The Politics of Contemporary Capitalism', *NR*, 5, 1958; and 'Transition to the Transition', p. 36.

15   Stuart Hall, 'A Sense of Classlessness', *ULR*, 5, 1958, p, 29.

16   Hall, 'Classlessness', p. 40.

17   Hall, 'Classlessness', p. 43.

18   'Marx's work itself', Hall argued, 'is a body of analytic concepts and not a sealed house of theory', 'Classlessness', p. 37. Writing in response to Thompson's keynote essay 'Socialist Humanism', *NR*, 1, 1957, Charles Taylor questioned the compatibility of Marxism and humanism in 'Marxism and humanism', *NR*, 2, 1957.

19   Edward Thompson 'Commitment in Politics', *ULR*, 6, Spring 1959, pp. 50-1.

20   Thompson, 'Commitment', pp. 51-3. The offending ULR article was Gordon Redfern, 'The Real Outrage', *ULR*, 5, 1958, quote from p. 10.

21   Thompson, 'Commitment', p. 53.

22   Thompson, 'Commitment', pp. 52, 54.

23   Stuart Hall, 'The Big Swipe', *ULR*, 7, 1959, p. 50.

24   Edward Thompson, *The Making of the English Working Class*, London: Victor Gollancz, 1963.

25   For an excellent and sympathetic reconstruction of Thompson's argument see Ellen Meiksins Wood, *Democracy against Capitalism*, Cambridge: CUP, 1995, Chapter 3, 'Class as process and relationship'.

26   Bryan Palmer, *E.P. Thompson: Objections and oppositions*, London: Verso, 1994, p. 94.

27 On the two 'generations' see Peter Sedgwick, 'The Two New Lefts', in David Widgery, ed., *The Left in Britain*, Harmondsworth: Penguin, 1976, pp. 147-50; Ellen Meiksins Wood, 'A chronology of the New Left and its successors: or, who's old fashioned now?', *Socialist Register*, London: Merlin, 1995; Michael Rustin, 'The New Left and the present crisis', *NLR*, I/121(May/June), 1981, pp. 7-9. Those involved in the early New Left went on to found new initiatives: organisations and publications with a direct New Left lineage, aside from the *Register*, included the Birmingham Centre for Contemporary Cultural Studies established by Richard Hoggart and Stuart Hall in 1964 and History Workshop founded by Raphael Samuel at Ruskin College, Oxford, in 1966. In addition to these, New Leftists were active in a plethora of radical organisations and initiatives including the Centres for Socialist Education, the Institute for Workers' Control, and the May Day Manifesto project; the short-lived newspapers *Black Dwarf* and *Seven Days*; the movement for women's liberation; and later in the 1970s and into 1980s, the Centres for Marxist Education, the revival of the disarmament campaign as END, and the Socialist Society.

28 The major texts of the 'Nairn Anderson theses' were, in chronological order: Perry Anderson, 'Origins of the Present Crisis', and Tom Nairn, 'The British Political Elite', *NLR*, I/23(January/February), 1964; Nairn, 'The English Working-class', *NLR*, I/24(March/April), 1964; Nairn, 'The Nature of the Labour Party', Part I, *NLR*, I/27(September/October), 1964, and Part II, *NLR*, I/28(November/December), 1964.

29 Quotes here are from Anderson, 'Origins', p. 43 and Nairn, 'The Nature of the Labour Party', Part 1, p. 51.

30 The main texts in the exchange were E.P. Thompson, 'The Peculiarities of the English', *Socialist Register*, London: Merlin, 1965; Perry Anderson, 'Socialism and pseudo-empiricism', *NLR*, I/35(January/February), 1966. See also Anderson, 'The Left in the Fifties', *NLR*, I/29(January/February), 1965; and Thompson, 'The poverty of theory, or an orrery of errors', in *The Poverty of Theory and other essays,* London: Merlin, 1978. Only in the 1980s, with Anderson's more considered – though still critical – reassessment of Thompson's treatment of class in *Arguments within English Marxism* (London: Verso, 1980) would they appear in sharper relief. The ferocity of the debate meanwhile had echoes in the broader humanism/structuralism controversy within British Marxist historiography in the 1970s. See Richard Johnson, 'Edward Thompson, Eugene Genovese and socialist humanist history', *History Workshop Journal*, 6, Autumn, 1978; and responses from Keith McClelland, 'Some comments on Richard Johnson' and G. Williams, 'In defence of history', *History Workshop Journal*, 7, 1978.

31 For more detail and participant accounts of the origins of *Socialist Register* see Marion Kozak, 'How it all began: a footnote to history', *Socialist Register*, London: Merlin, 1995; Ralph Miliband, 'Thirty Years of the Socialist Register, *Socialist Register*, London: Merlin, 1994. Michael Newman's *Ralph Miliband and the Politics of the New Left* treats the founding of the *Register* in detail on pp. 113-25.

32   Ralph Miliband, 'John Saville: a representation', in David Martin and David Rubinstein, eds., *Ideology and the Labour Movement: Essays presented to John Saville*, London: Croom Helm, 1979. p. 26.

33   Newman, *Ralph Miliband*, p. 94.

34   Newman, *Ralph Miliband*, pp. 116-9.

35   Letter from Thompson to Miliband, October 1963 and Miliband's reply, 29 October 1963, Miliband Papers, University of Leeds Special Collections, File CO/45.

36   Letter from Miliband to John Saville, 25 May 1963, Miliband Papers, File SR/1.

37   Letter from Miliband to Perry Anderson, 9 March 1963, Miliband Papers, File CO/3.

38   Ralph Miliband, 'A rethinking sermon', *New Statesman*, 7 November 1959.

39   Letter from Miliband to Thompson, 10 May 1963, Miliband Papers, File SR/1.

40   Letters, Miliband to Thompson, 10 May 1963, File CO/45; Miliband to Saville, 15 May 1963, File SR/1.

41   Letter, Miliband to Saville, 4 November 1963, Miliband Papers, File SR/1.

42   Miliband, 'Thirty Years of the Socialist Register', p. 2.

43   Editorial, 'Introducing Socialist Register', *Socialist Register*, London: Merlin, 1964.

44   Quoted in Newman, *Ralph Miliband*, p. 122.

45   Ralph Miliband and John Saville, 'Labour Policy and the Labour Left'; Michael Barratt Brown, 'Nationalization in Britain'; and V.L.Allen, 'Trade Unions in Contemporary Capitalism', all in *Socialist Register*, 1964; Dorothy Wedderburn, 'Facts and Theories of the Welfare State'; and Ralph Miliband, 'What Does the Left Want', both in *Socialist Register*, London: Merlin, 1965.

46   Thompson, 'Peculiarities of the English'.

47   Letter from Tom Nairn to Miliband, 28 Dec 1961, Miliband Papers, File CO/3.

48   Quoted in Newman, *Ralph Miliband*, p. 118.

49   See in particular Ralph Miliband, 'The new revisionism in Britain', *NLR*, I/150(March/April), 1985; and the critique of Laclau and Mouffe's *Hegemony and Socialist Strategy*, London: Verso, 1985, by Norman Geras, 'Post-Marxism?', *NLR*, I/163(May/June), 1987. Miliband and NLR editors were also jointly involved in the organisation of the Socialist Society in the early 1980s.

50   Victor Kiernan, 'Notes on the intelligentsia', *Socialist Register*, London: Merlin, 1969.

51   See correspondence with James Weinstein, Miliband Papers, File SR/1. The published piece was Franklin Hugh Adler, 'Black Power', *Socialist Register*, London: Merlin, 1968.

52   Ralph Miliband, *Marxism and Politics*, Oxford: Oxford University Press, 1977, p. 41.

53   Mills, 'Letter to the New Left', p. 22.

REGISTERING CLASS AND POLITICS: FIFTY YEARS OF THE *SOCIALIST REGISTER*

LEO PANITCH

I

Perhaps the most notable feature of the Register's output is how consistent was its perspective over the years. Consistency is not necessarily the most admirable of virtues, since it may well indicate a stubborn blindness to changes that are occurring in the world. On the other hand, it may also indicate a refusal to indulge in passing fads and fashions. We avoided this ….

These words are Ralph Miliband's, from his survey in the 1994 *Socialist Register* of its 'direction, policy and output since its first appearance' thirty years earlier.[1] They may still serve as a useful marker for reflecting, on the occasion of its fiftieth anniversary, on the *Register's* longevity despite the many defeats, disillusionments and retreats experienced by the left.

Miliband used to say that the *Register* 'should be hard to write for, as well as hard to read' – by which he meant that since the kind of essays it published demanded considerable effort on the part of the reader, contributors had a responsibility to work hard at producing essays that were not only of high analytical quality but also as readable as possible. While free of the procedural rigmarole associated with academic refereed journals, the commitment to both literary and analytic quality meant it was hard work to edit too, in various senses: deciding who could best tackle a given topic as each volume was planned; assessing whether drafts submitted showed enough potential to go ahead with; providing careful and extensive editorial commentary on each essay; and making sure that the style of writing was clear and accessible at a time when the opacity and clumsiness of much intellectual discourse affected the left like a plague.[2]

While Miliband was the main force behind the *Register*, it would never have been born nor survived its first decade without the part played by

John Saville as co-editor as well as frequent contributor – although Miliband used to tease him for an editorial approach that was 'a bit too Bulletin of the Society for Labour History oriented'.[3] As Saville in fact became increasingly preoccupied with the *Dictionary of Labour Biography* in the 1970s, Miliband found himself handling most of the detailed editorial tasks for the *Register* (while continuing in close consultation with Saville on themes and contributors). It was no easy thing to turn out such a high quality 300-400 page volume year after year, without any office or staff (albeit aided by the remarkable copy-editing skills of Martin Eve at Merlin Press, who would drive over to Miliband's house in North London on his motor bike to pick up essays when they were ready, and not too long after return with galleys to be checked).[4] The problems of finding the time and energy to do this largely as a one man operation came to a head by the early 1980s.[5] It became more and more difficult to get the annual volume to the bookstores with much time left in the year on its cover; and to ensure that no year was skipped, Martin Eve (with the help of David Musson) actually took on the editorship of the 1982 volume.

It was in the summer of that year that the question was first raised with Marcel Liebman and me (as well as George Ross, who demurred) of eventually joining Miliband and Saville as co-editors of the *Register*. Liebman was Miliband's oldest friend and intellectual comrade, and Ross and I were the two former graduate students at the LSE with whom he had forged the closest personal as well as intellectual ties. The seeds were also set around that time for the transition to producing each volume around a specific theme. Liebman became a co-editor for the first themed volume in 1984 on *The Uses of Anti-Communism*; and, after having helped a bit with the previous two volumes, I finally came on board as a co-editor for the following volume, *Beyond Social Democracy*. 'It is very unlikely we shall go on adding editors at this rate', our preface to that *Register* quipped. In fact, the reverse would occur all too soon and all too tragically with Liebman's death in 1986. The main tasks of editorship had already been shared between Miliband and myself from early 1985 on, with *Beyond Social Democracy* prepared as a special double issue for 1985/86 so as to allow us to put in place a more timely production schedule. This was maintained through our very close editorial partnership until Miliband's untimely and unexpected death at 70, just two months after we finished the preface for the thirtieth volume of the *Register* in 1994.

Daunted by suddenly carrying sole editorial responsibility, I edited the 1995 volume with the help of Ellen Wood and John Saville (who had taken his name off the masthead in 1990 but continued to contribute essays and advise on editorial direction). Less concerned about the too-many-cooks syndrome than Miliband and Saville had been, I then moved to establish the *Register*'s first editorial collective. Its membership initially consisted of active working groups in Toronto and Manchester, with corresponding editors spread from Hong Kong and Johannesburg to Boston and San Francisco. The new editorial collective – which mapped the themes of five future volumes ('the last five year plan of the 20th century', we called this) – was a crucial lifeline for me until Colin Leys became co-editor for the 1998 volume, exactly 20 years after his first *Register* essay had appeared.[6] Our collaboration on the *Register* continued over the subsequent twelve volumes, very much aided by Alan Zuege's outstanding editorial assistance. Leys retired as co-editor after playing the leading role in producing the 2010 volume on *Morbid Symptoms: Health under Capitalism*. Greg Albo and Vivek Chibber – already primed by serving as associate editors since 2008 – became the new co-editors.

With Albo also in Toronto (as Leys had been for much of his tenure as co-editor), and with Chibber in New York, this seemed to further confirm Göran Therborn's observation in 2007 that 'the resilience of the small North American left stands out, in comparison with the larger but much softer and more often disheartened forces of Europe'. Indeed, one of his measures for this was that the '*Socialist Register* was launched in the mid-1960s as a very British enterprise, but is now, in the new millennium, edited from Toronto'.[7] Yet without dissenting from the overall continental comparison, this could be misinterpreted as regards the *Register*. This is not only because its publisher continues to be Merlin Press in the UK (with Tony Zurbrugg, having taken it over not long before Martin Eve's death in 1999, providing unwavering support with the creative help of Adrian Howe and Louis Mackay). Nor is it only because of the many members of the editorial collective located in the UK and elsewhere in Europe. It is also because it gives too short shrift to the *Register*'s international focus from the beginning. Miliband's wide connections abroad were a key source for many contributors to the *Register*, which also always had a large readership outside the UK. Indeed this was why it seemed perfectly natural, when the idea of adding new co-editors came up in the early 1980s, for Miliband to think that Liebman's residency in Belgium or mine in Canada were not serious obstacles. Indeed, Miliband himself was just then embarking on spending part of each year at North American universities. But as George Ross once told me, 'if you want to be read in Alexandria, Egypt, publish in the *Register*; if you want to be read in Cambridge, Massachusetts, don't'.

II

When the 1964 preface, in announcing 'a series of annual volumes of socialist analysis and discussion', expressed the belief that 'the possibility of fruitful discussions is now greater than for a long time past', the editors were clearly thinking beyond the UK. Insofar as it was 'now better realized among socialists that dogmatic reiteration cannot, any more than crass empiricism, provide answers to the problems of the present', this was a recognition of the *general* limitations of both Communist and Social Democratic parties, especially as venues of socialist analysis, discussion and education. The perception that the *Register* was 'a very British enterprise' was certainly understandable in light of its genesis in the British New Left. It is also understandable in light of all the attention the *Register* paid to analyzing the Labour Party and the labour movement in the UK, on which topics the first two volumes had five essays each. That said, the overwhelming majority of the 37 essays in these first two volumes were focused elsewhere. The lead essays in 1964, on Maoism by Isaac Deutscher and Nasserism by Anouar Abdul-Malek, set the tone for the *Register*'s consistent sobriety about third world revolutions. There was also an essay on Italian Communism by Andre Gorz (writing under the pseudonym of Michel Bosquet) and another on West Germany ('The Reactionary Democracy' by Jean-Marie Vincent), as well as wide-ranging comparative essays on 'The Economics of Neo-capitalism' by Ernest Mandel, 'Imperialism Old and New' by Hamza Alavi, and the break-up of the Second International ('1914: the Great Schism') by Marcel Liebman. The 1965 volume contained four essays on Russia and Eastern Europe (including one by Georg Lukács on Solzhenitsyn), three on the Arab world, one on the US (by Harry Magdoff), as well as a broadly comparative essay on welfare states (by Dorothy Wedderburn).

Another essay in that volume was by Hamza Alavi, on peasants and revolution in Russia, China and India, and the continuing close attention the *Register* would pay to new revolutionary developments in the third world, without romanticizing them, was exemplified by essays in subsequent volumes by John Saul and Giovanni Arrighi on 'Nationalism and Revolution in Sub-Saharan Africa', Eric Hobsbawm on 'Guerillas in Latin America', and Basil Davidson on 'The African Prospect'. And as seen in the essays by Lucio Magri on 'The May Events and Revolution in the West' and Anthony Arblaster on 'Student Militancy and The Collapse of Reformism', the *Register* would remain no less sober about the student revolts in the 1960s, not to mention about the problems with trying to emulate Che or Mao, or Lenin and Trotsky for that matter. The major role the *Register* would play in developing Marxism's conceptual apparatus in relation 'to the problems of the present' was initiated with Miliband's famous essay on 'Marx and the State' in the 1965 volume, and then sustained by his highly critical assessment in 1970 of 'Lenin's *The State and Revolution*'. This 'sacred text' of Marxist thought – the very notion of which was 'alien to the spirit of Marxism, or at least should be' – especially deserved such critical scrutiny, since 'far from resolving the problems with which it is concerned, [it] only serves to underline their complexity'. Essays by Andre Gorz on 'Reform and Revolution', Rossanna Rossanda on 'Class and Party', J.P. Sartre on 'Masses, Spontaneity, Party', and Hal Draper on 'The Death of the State in Marx and Engels' further added to the *Register*'s assessment and renewal of Marxist theory. The early volumes also contained a series of critical essays on Engels, highlighted by Donald Hodges' searing critique of the 'allegedly' scientific philosophy of nature ('To him we owe the Soviet identification of Marxism with a scientific world outlook').

Looking back from today's vantage point, all this goes very far in explaining why the *Register* was not caught out or disheartened by the widespread but extremely thin intellectual dismissal of Marxism in later decades, nor by the ignominious collapse of communist regimes, the servile accommodation of social democracy to neoliberalism, and the disappointment of so many third world revolutions before the twentieth century was over. Indeed, in light of the tendency these days to measure the weakness of the left over the past quarter century with its alleged strength the quarter century before, it is important to recall that the *Socialist Register* was born at a time when the notion of socialist decline was already 'pretty well taken for granted', as Miliband's essay for the first volume put it. It is also important for understanding the legacy of the early *Register* to recall how he addressed this: '[It] presumably means that at some particular point of time, at some point of the historical curve, socialist prospects were better, more hopeful ... One would therefore expect the evidence for it to be blindingly obvious, or at least very easily obtainable. But it is not. In fact, the evidence points mostly the other way'.[8]

Miliband then marshaled the following evidence. However admirable and heroic were many movements and struggles from Chartism to the Paris Commune in Marx's time, 'it is no disparagement of these pioneering endeavours to note the incoherence and divisions, the fragility of organization and the confusion of aims ... [or] the fact that the established order of which capitalism had become a part found it discouragingly easy, despite its limited means, to repel the challenge against it'. And while the decades before the First World War witnessed the growth of working-class parties and unions, it was still the case that 'a large part of the working classes, most workers on the land, the bulk of the lower middle class and much the larger part of the intelligentsia still gave more or less active support to a variety of resolutely anti-socialist parties and causes', including strong support for 'imperialist ventures and conquests'. Meanwhile, the new mass organizations themselves not only quickly fell victim to 'the bureaucratic curse', but also were 'riddled with energetic climbers, more concerned with place than purpose'. The interwar years – 'usually most favoured as providing an illustration of the thesis of socialist decline' – witnessed 'the survival of the Bolshevik revolution' but 'the absence of revolution almost everywhere else, particularly in Germany', leaving a deleterious image 'stamped upon socialism by its consolidation in a country so profoundly backward as Russia'. This could not be erased by those who made the 'acceptance of a grotesquely roseate view of the Soviet regime … the first criterion of socialist rectitude'. And while many labour movements in the 1930s grew in 'numbers, organization, and influence … the thirties have a high claim to be considered as the most terrible period of defeat in this century for the international Socialist and Labour movements'. The Nazis' 'capture of Germany' involved crushing with relative ease 'a divided and demoralized labour movement', and this was soon followed by the ineffective opposition to appeasement by labour movements in other countries. Moreover, it was 'only in the world of historical make-believe that most British intellectuals and academics were then on the left, or that Cambridge University went off en masse to fight for Republican Spain. The reality was altogether different'. And if it was true that in the United States in the 1930s socialist ideas 'gained a wider currency than ever before, notably among intellectuals and academics' at a time when 'trade unionism made spectacular gains', the 'feuding socialist groups never achieved any degree of popular support' while the unions 'found acceptable the New Deal's explicit aim of putting capitalism back on its feet'. And here was the punch line:

> What is true about the thirties is that the committed minorities were much more confident than the equivalent (and probably larger) minorities of the recent past that capitalism was more or less on its last legs, and that socialism was not only round the corner, but that, as proved by Soviet experience, it must soon usher in the reign of sweetness and light, with minor difficulties mostly caused by a handful of enemies of the people. This no doubt gave many socialists a sense of certitude which their successors have found it difficult to share. But since some part, at least, of the socialist confidence of the thirties was based on wishful thinking and undemanding faith, the loss of it may be less regrettable than is often

suggested. Socialism is not a religious movement. An awareness of its problems as well as of its promise may be a more solid and lasting basis of commitment than a belief in its magic properties as a cure-all.

A key strategic lesson Miliband wanted *Register* readers to draw from his observations on the 1930s concerned 'the relationship between economic crisis and socialist commitment – or rather the lack of such relationship'. If deprivation alone was the catalyst, socialism would have conquered capitalism long ago. On the other hand, the very 'character of capitalist "affluence"' left plenty of room for socialist pressure and persuasion 'to drive home the lesson that a system whose dynamic is private appropriation and profit makes impossible the rational and human organization and use of the tremendous resources it has brought into being'. This perspective was further sustained by Hamza Alavi's essay which immediately followed Miliband's in the first volume. It posed a fundamental challenge to the Leninist theory of imperialism as well as to various postwar Marxist explanations for 'the continued functioning of the economies of the advanced capitalist countries which have helped to "postpone the crisis"'.

> Sophisticated Marxists would qualify the prediction of the final crisis by a warning against interpreting the theory of crisis in a mechanical fashion. We should take into account, they would say, the influence of counteracting tendencies which could *temporarily* offset the basic tendencies working towards the final crisis. It is the timing of the crisis which, they would argue, cannot be foretold with accuracy; its inevitability is not questioned. Such qualification smacks of sophistry when we are considering a time span not of a few years but of decades. It is a hundred years since Marx wrote; and nearly half a century since Lenin wrote of the eve of the socialist revolution. Such a prolongation of the life of capitalism calls for a more searching analysis of the changes which have taken place since then … We do not suggest that capitalism shall be free of crises – for the conditions postulated in theory for the achievement of growth with stability cannot be realized within its framework. What we do suggest is that there is no *necessity* for a dramatic major crisis which would ensure the automatic collapse of capitalism.

Marxist economists who had shifted their perspective from a 'breakdown thesis' to a 'stagnation thesis' had recognized this much, but the main remit of Alavi's argument was the importance of recognizing the 'vast expansion' of capitalist production, and the rise in working- and middle-class incomes which allowed capitalists 'to realize the value of this increased production'. The development of 'more searching economic analyses of modern capitalism' would be important for destroying 'illusion and complacency' on the left, and for helping to put 'much greater emphasis on the conscious mobilization of the people for bringing about socialism – the contradictions of capitalism will not necessarily do the job for us'.[9] These very words could have been used to sum up the overall perspective of the *Register*'s recent volumes on *The Crisis This Time* in 2011 and *The Crisis and the Left* in 2012.

III

No less crucial to the *Register*'s perspective has been its clear-headed recognition that social democracy and the Keynesian welfare state would not do the job either. Thus Miliband insisted in the 1964 *Register* that what 'Fabian-minded socialists have always found ... difficult to understand' was that socialism was 'not about the improvement in the condition of the working class, but about the abolition of that class'.[10] In her essay on the welfare state in the 1965 *Register*, Dorothy Wedderburn presciently pointed out that 'a social reform won at a particular point of time can become adapted, modified, less effective as a result of market forces acting upon it. We cannot insulate our socialist victories from the complex operations of the capitalist system'. This was already happening to social insurance, where the acceptance of the 'wage-relation as a basis for fixing social security benefits', especially in the area of pensions, increasingly involved accepting 'the judgment of, and the inequalities in, the market'.[11] For his part, John Saville – noting Richard Titmuss's new evidence that what had been taking place in the 1950s was 'not a leveling of incomes, but its opposite' – laid a good deal of the blame for this at the feet of Fabian intellectuals who conceded too much to *The Economist* and other conservative voices. Arthur Lewis was only speaking in terms of 'the general clichés of those years' when he wrote in 1955 of almost reaching the limits of redistributive policies 'not only in the sense that the incomes of the rich, after taxation, are now comparatively small; but also in the sense that we are in danger of destroying the incentive to take risks'.[12] In fact, by the time the leadership of the Labour Party had 'voted themselves out of office in 1951 to the bewilderment and disillusionment of their ordinary supporters', the leadership was already by then 'tired and exhausted, and without a shred of inspiration'. The inflated claims about the 1945 government's accomplishments ran up against 'the common sense skepticism of the working class', for whom 'evidence of a massive shift in income distribution was not exactly overpowering'. When another Labour government was finally re-elected the same year the *Register* was launched, its editors could justifiably point to 'the hopelessly wrong conclusions which the revisionists deduced from post-war economic and social trends [that] led them to argue for further accommodation to capitalist society, in order to allow capitalism to continue its good works'.[13]

Miliband argued in his 1965 *Register* essay that the left still had 'no option but to try and implant socialist proposals in the thinking of the Labour movement, and to fight for their adoption as party policy. Realistic alternatives do not exist'. But he would himself leave the Labour Party a year later, above all in disgust with the Wilson government's support of the US in Vietnam.[14] By the time the second edition of his *Parliamentary Socialism* was published in 1973, Miliband made it clear in his new postscript that it was the view that the Labour Party could be turned into a serious socialist party that was really unrealistic.[15] The 1973 *Register* featured an essay by Richard Hyman that showed how debilitating was the Labour leadership's entirely negative attitude to the rank-and-file industrial militancy of the time, given the fragile and contradictory state of working-class consciousness. Indeed, in this light, even the defensive slogan of 'Hands off the Unions' which was the 'favorite response of union leaders, "left" MPs, and the Communist Party ... is doomed to failure by the current requirements of British capitalism: the power of trade unionism *must* escalate if it is not to be eroded'.[16] The 1973 volume contained another essay by Hilary Rose which addressed similarly unhelpful attitudes to 'the upsurge of a new form of political action, called variously community politics or community action: organizing around the neighbourhood and the home became a significant political activity'. Looking especially at claimants unions in the UK which had become 'one vital strand within a nexus of activities focused on the home and street', she observed that, like the black and women's movements, 'their critique is cultural rather than merely economistic and contains an edge of anger ... partly in response to changing economic conditions, but also in response to the failure of the Labour Party and the neglect by many – if not most – Marxist groups of those not directly engaged "at the point of production"'. Yet this early *Register* essay also already discerned the political 'tragedy' lurking in these new movements, being one of the first to cite the subsequently famous pamphlet by Jo Freeman (just published in December 1972 under the pseudonym 'Joreen') on their 'tyranny of structurelessness'. This concealed the leadership that lay in the 'friendship networks at the core of the movement' which often excluded 'the very people who potentially could be of help to the movement'; at the same time, it denied 'the movement the possibility of developing more complex forms of organization with which to meet the increasing opposition of the Welfare State'.[17]

Notably, the 1973 *Register* also had an essay by Ken Coates which directly challenged Miliband's view that it was unrealistic to try to turn Labour into a serious socialist party. A new left in the Labour Party (whose most prominent voice was Tony Benn, with whom Coates was closely aligned) was just emerging, inspired by the rank-and-file militancy and community politics of the time. While agreeing that the current Labour leadership's 'pragmatism inspires no sacrifices, blazes no trails, bodes no fundamental changes, and meets no deep spiritual needs', Coates nevertheless insisted on asking: 'If the Labour Party cannot be turned into a socialist party, then the question which confronts us all is, how can we form a socialist party? If we are not ready to answer this question, then we are not ready to dismiss the party that exists.'[18] Miliband directly addressed this argument in his famous 'Moving On' essay in the 1976 *Register*. He noted that twenty years after 1956 'the main problem for the socialist left in Britain is still that of its own organisation into an effective political formation, able to attract a substantial measure of support and to hold out a genuine promise of further growth'. He also granted that 'insofar as it cannot be conclusively proved that the Labour Party will not in any serious sense be turned in socialist directions, the chances are that the controversy will go on for a long time to come' – only immediately adding, 'without leading anywhere'. Indeed, he insisted that 'the belief in the effective transformation of the Labour Party into an instrument of socialist policies is the most crippling of all illusions to which socialists in Britain have been prone'.[19] Nor did the essay brook any illusions about either the Communist Party or any of the newer groupings to its left – but this hardly made the argument that 'there is no alternative' to the Labour Party 'in any way conclusive'. It was unwarranted to imagine that 'the peculiar link' that gave the party a 'quasi-monopoly' with the trade unions ruled out the growth of any serious alternative, since the history of socialist parties had shown that 'not only is such a link unnecessary: it is in many ways undesirable'. Despite 'many formidable obstacles', what was required 'was the formation of a socialist party free from the manifold shortcomings of existing organisations and able to draw together people from such organisations as well as people who are now politically homeless … which would at first be necessarily fairly small but which would have a capacity for growth such as the existing formations on the left of the Labour Party do not have and are not likely to acquire'.[20]

IV

In a certain sense Miliband was here only bringing to a logical conclusion what '[f]rom the first volume of *The Register* in 1964, its editors [had] constantly sought to encourage', as David Coates later put it, namely 'the emergence of a form of left-wing politics free of traditional parliamentarism on the one side, and of the Stalinism of Communist (and the Leninism of Trotskyist) politics on the other'.[21] But the *Register's* growing concern through the 1970s with the need for socialists to more urgently address the arduous and intricate task of developing socialist parties of a new kind had to do with the recognition that the existing ones were unable, as Miliband put it in 'Moving On', 'to provide a credible and effective rallying point' against the danger of a 'marked and accelerating drift to the right'.

Andrew Gamble's lead essay in the 1979 volume on 'The Free Market and the Strong State' clearly outlined how 'the new ideologues of the right and the band of vociferous converts and roving spokesmen for management that consort with them' were embarking on a major attempt 'to appeal to that section of the working-class electorate for whom the policies and organizations of social democracy have become increasingly unpopular'.[22] It was the inadequate response to this among unions as well as existing working-class parties which also set the stage for many intellectuals' widespread dismissal of labour as a transformative or even a progressive social force. E.P. Thompson had already warned against this in the 1973 *Register*, in his 100 page-long 'Open Letter to Leszek Kolakowski', whose explicit turn against Marxism was in many ways the forerunner of the path taken by a great many intellectuals in the West a decade later. Thompson noted how the old 'pathetic fallacy of intellectuals that by their own thinking they can change the world' was now being reflected in a generation of American radical students for whom 'the entire white working-class was being "written off"'. He argued that there were 'real reasons for this: but this writing-off did damage to intellectual growth itself. And in such situations both despair and rebellion can lead to the same terminus.'[23]

Raymond Williams' lead essay in the 1981 volume warned that the 'don't rock the boat, let's unite to get Thatcher out' stance of the Labour leadership was precisely the kind of 'opportunist negativism' that was likely to sow new confusions and further get in the way of developing 'sustained popular understanding and support' for a socialist alternative.[24] This was also the remit of Stuart Hall's original interpretation of the rise of Thatcherism. Picking up a central theme in the *Register* since its inception, i.e. that there was nothing inevitable about socialist advance, Hall's lead essay in the 1982 volume argued that far from socialism being 'the natural centre of gravity of working-class ideas', it was necessary to 'stress the centrality of the domain of the ideological-political ideas and the struggle to win hearts and minds to socialism'. And while one could 'recognise a certain kind of Marxist "traditionalism" behind this notion of the "inevitable triumph of socialist ideas"... actually, it is even more deeply rooted in the non-Marxist, "labourist", traditions. Vulgar economism comes in many disguises.'[25] As my own essay in the 1985/86 *Register* put it, it was precisely because 'class identity, class consciousness, class politics, were indeed but one of a number of possible forms of collective expression even in a capitalist society ... by no means an automatic outcome of economic locations in productive relations alone' that it was also necessary to stress 'ideological and cultural factors in the formation of social and political subjects'. Indeed those intellectuals who were concentrating on the shortcomings of Marxism ignored the fact that (apart from their misinterpretations) this obviously could have little salience in explaining the impasse of working class politics in those countries where social democratic parties and unions had either never adopted or long since rejected any association with Marxist thought. It was necessary in this context to also pay attention to the ways in which they had constrained rather than encouraged a broad rather than particularistic working-class consciousness. Above all, it was necessary for the left to give priority now to fostering working-class capacities 'to provide leadership in their wider communities in relation to multifarious forms of subordination, deprivation, and struggle'.

[A] politics that envisions creating a working class majority in terms of collective socio-political identity does not need to mean that other identities – of gender, or race, of ethnicity – have to be effaced ... it is possible for working people to think of themselves as workers and to act politically in a way that allows for, in fact obtains strength from, a simultaneous expression of their other collective identities in so far as a popular socialist culture provides a common terrain of understanding, purpose and activity.[26]

The 1990 volume on *The Retreat of the Intellectuals* rededicated the *Register* to the task of 'creating an intellectual and ideological climate very different from that which has prevailed on the left in the past decade'. As the preface explained, the 'particularly pronounced' retreat from Marxism through the 1980s had been accompanied by 'a more general retreat from socialism conceived as a radical alternative to capitalism. The very notion of capitalism has come to be exceedingly blurred in much left discourse; and the notion of a radical alternative to capitalism has been correspondingly devalued in

the eyes of many intellectuals who had previously been committed to it.'
No less blurred was the understanding of class. As Terry Eagleton's essay
so incisively argued regarding 'the celebrated triptych of "class, race and
gender", a formula which has rapidly assumed for the left the kind of
authority which the Holy Trinity exerts for the right'.

> [This] formula comes near to involving what the philosophers might call
> a category mistake … The social constitution of categories like black and
> female is, like social class, a wholly relational affair; but nobody is black
> because someone else is white, in the sense that some people are only
> landless labourers because there are gentlemen farmers around the place.
> This distinction may not be of great political importance, but sloppy
> thinking about such crucial issues is always perilous.[27]

What the *Register* consistently represented for socialist intellectuals in
this context was evinced by John Saville's 'anatomy' of the 'intellectual
feebleness and absence of a steadfastly critical approach' of *Marxism Today*.
This formerly very old-fashioned monthly journal of the Communist Party
had responded to Thatcherism, as well as to broader neoconservative,
neoliberal, postmodern and post-Fordist trends of the 1980s, with 'the
shallow and superficial trivia known as New Times' (including an 'editorial
direction that thought it proper to devote two pages to fashion against
one to politics' in one issue). Political movements of the left especially
needed to 'be able to rely upon their writers and intellectuals to provide
interpretations and judgements' which consistently sought 'to situate the
individual within historical time; to relate the past to the present and offer
a variety of perspectives for the future; to make sense of individual purpose,
a matter of self-enlightenment, within a wider social-political framework
and setting'. Precisely because the left had 'often been wrong, confused and
blinded by a dogmatic reference to the past which has encouraged a false
or one sided understanding of the present, and mistaken prognosis of things
to come', what was all the more needed now for a really serious 'review of
the contemporary world' was to provide an 'informed, relevant and sharply
critical approach to the dominant ideas and policies of those in power, and
to those who uphold them'.[28]

V

This remained the aim and purpose of the *Register* amidst the realization
of a truly global capitalist order by the end of the twentieth century. The
1991 volume on *Communist Regimes: The Aftermath* had already analyzed the

capitalist transformations of those regimes,[29] while the sheer breadth as well as depth of the neoliberal restructuring of economies, class structures and state apparatuses elsewhere justified the title of Robert Cox's essay, 'Global Perestroika', for the 1992 *Register*. The concept of 'disciplinary neoliberalism', which Stephen Gill introduced in that volume, captured very well the EU's impositions on Eastern European countries of the kind of conditionalities the IMF had applied to Latin America in the 1980s. It also appeared to meld with global American military discipline, as trumpeted after the Gulf War by George Bush Sr with the phrase 'New World Order'. But the attachment of a question mark to this phrase in the title of the 1992 volume reflected our questioning of the notion that neoliberal capitalism, or for that matter the US imperial embrace, was entirely externally imposed on states, rather than promoted by capitalist forces within them. That this even included social democracy's strongest citadels made the essay by Rudolph Meidner in the 1993 *Register* on 'Why did the Swedish Model Fail?' especially significant. Of 'decisive importance', he showed, was the internationalization of the Swedish economy, as the very large private companies favoured by Social Democratic governments grew into multinationals that increasingly invested abroad the handsome profits they secured through the trade union policy of solidarity wage restraint.[30] Insofar as Sweden was now emulated by liberals and social democrats abroad, it was not for its balance between social control and private ownership but rather for its success at sustaining the competitiveness of its capitalists in international trade and investment through a labour market strategy of skills training and workplace flexibility.

The preface to the 1994 volume on *Between Globalism and Nationalism*, the last before Miliband's death, asserted that 'the *Register* is performing an important service in probing and challenging [the] assumption' that globalization was a process that diminished or marginalized states. The false dichotomy between markets and states that had become so prevalent not only in mainstream discourse but also on the left was a symptom of all that had already been forgotten about the advances made in the Marxist theory of the state in the 1970s. But it demonstrated as well the need for further advances. My essay on 'Globalization and the State' sought to develop the concept of the internationalization of the state to capture the growing orientation of state policies and the responsibilities of state institutions towards facilitating and managing a global capitalist order. This was complemented by Greg Albo's path-breaking critique of 'progressive competitiveness' as a left version of 'supply-side' and 'competitive austerity policies', while at the same time outlining the components of a genuine policy alternative which would focus on the reintegration of national economies through employment planning, the redistribution of work and democratic workplaces.[31]

A further concern of the *Register* at this time was to better understand the capitalist transformations taking place in many states of the Global South in defiance of the expectations of dependency theory, while avoiding the starry-eyed adulation of East Asia's state-led economic development that had grown so common on the left. This had been the remit of Paul Cammack's celebrated essay on 'Statism, New Institutionalism, and Marxism' in the 1990 volume, and it would remain a central concern, since even as late as 2005, as Vivek Chibber pointed out in his first essay for the *Register*, this adulation was still 'not only to be found among political elites. It also emanates from a powerful and articulate wing of the anti-globalization movement – critical intellectuals, NGOs, and trade unions.'

> In a period when free market policies have little credibility, but labour is not strong enough to pose a serious challenge to private property, some kind of statist development project appears to many to be the 'transitional programme' of our time. Defending a space for national capitalist development, under the direction of domestic groups, at least seems consistent in *principle* with conscious direction of the economy – even if under the hegemony of the national bourgeoisie ... In this, the national bourgeoisie was inevitably contrasted with the local 'compradors', who, because of their links with metropolitan firms, were seen as irredeemably tied to imperial interests ... But capitalists seem to have been happy to play both roles simultaneously – trying to protect their domestic market, while striving for lasting ties with metropolitan firms.[32]

Many of the most original and influential analyses of neoliberal globalization have appeared in the *Register*, spanning academic disciplines and specialized debates so as to provide a critique of the dominant intellectual and political fashions, and to encourage analyses that transcended orthodox left perspectives.[33] This built on the contributions to Marxist political economy the *Register* had published in previous decades by such luminaries as Michael Barratt Brown, Ernest Mandel, Harry Magdoff, Ben Fine, Laurence Harris, Andrew Glyn, Simon Clarke and others. But this now was undertaken in a more focused way with essays on the nature, consolidation and contradictions of neoliberal capitalism by authors like Elmar Altvater and Birgit Mahnkopf, Gerald Epstein and James Crotty, Gerard Dumenil and Dominique Levy, Mino Carchedi, David Harvey, Ursula Huws, David McNally, Hugo Radice, Alfredo Saad-Filho, Anwar Shaikh and others. This included enriching Marxism's capacity to understand the transformations states in the advanced capitalist world were going through while promoting and sustaining capitalist globalization as well as managing its contradictions. Not only their continuing cooperation in doing all this but the deep structural linkages among them that were developed in the process, with the American state consistently remaining at the core, increasingly led us to put particular emphasis on encouraging new understandings of the nature of imperialism that finally escaped the out-dated Marxist analyses of the old inter-imperial rivalries. This culminated in the *Register's* much-celebrated and widely-translated volumes on *The New Imperial Challenge* in 2004 and *The Empire Reloaded* in 2005. As our preface to the first of these volumes put it, our goal was to 'help make socialist theory and analysis realistic, and socialist activism focused and coherent, in the opening years of a new century marked by US-led globalization and a new and more overt form of US imperialism'.

The need for theory to inform practice is particularly acute at times of rapid and comprehensive change such as we are now experiencing. Perhaps the arbitrary division of time into centuries makes any 'turn of the century' seem a moment of exceptional change, yet it is striking that so many socialist thinkers had precisely the same feeling a hundred years ago, when imperialism was also a chief focus of their concern. Many non-Marxists as well as Marxists at that time saw global capitalism as in flux, or in crisis, and imperialism as its newly-defining moment. The range of thinkers involved then, and the scope of the work they undertook, should have warned us not to embark lightly on the similar task we were proposing to undertake a hundred years later, but it was only when we started commissioning contributions that we realized fully how much it was a task for many volumes, by many authors.

The concern to sustain the most positive aspects of the Marxist legacy while jettisoning those which had increasingly got in the way of both the intellectual and political advance of the left had in fact motivated the new editorial collective from the beginning. Its inspiration and contribution in this respect was especially evident when the 1998 volume on *The Communist Manifesto Today* was launched at a very large event at Conway Hall in London, called 'Celebrating and Moving On', which Sheila Rowbotham took the lead role in organizing for the *Register* collective. Her lead essay for the 1998 volume involved the brilliant conception of a letter written to Marx from a socialist feminist who had been active in many of the same struggles in the 1840s. Having chanced across the *Manifesto* in a shirt pocket in the laundry of the Wisconsin phalanx to which she had escaped after the repression that followed the European revolutions, the letter penned to 'Dear Dr Marx' tells him of her disappointment at the *Manifesto*'s 'exclusion of all reference to women's part in our own emancipation'. The letter proceeds to remind him of much socialist feminist activity in Europe and to inform him of much else that socialist feminist women were up to in North America.[34] The programme for the Conway Hall event which Rowbotham produced featured the performance of a play she wrote for the occasion, 'The Tale That Never Ends', as well as the reading by Julie Christie of a Pablo Neruda poem, 'The Standard Oil Company':

> Their obese emperors from New York
> are suave smiling assassins
> who buy silk, nylon, cigars
> petty tyrants and dictators.
> They buy countries, people, seas, police, county councils,
> distant regions where the poor hoard their corn
> like misers their gold ...

VI

In our essay on the *Manifesto*'s political legacy 150 years on, Leys and I noted that 'stubborn historical facts' about capitalism were breaking through 'the illusions fostered by neoliberal rhetoric – and equally through the pseudo-left illusions of "new times", "radicalism of the centre" and all similar dreams of a capitalist world miraculously freed from alienation, immiseration and crises'. Yet with Tony Blair's recently-elected New Labour government not only signalling a rather enthusiastic (if also cynically pragmatic) accommodation to Thatcherism and the American imperium, but joining the dozen other social democratic governments in Europe unable, or at least unwilling, to break with neoliberal policies, we also noted that '[t]he tide of reaction is still flowing, but with diminishing confidence and force, while the counter-flow of progressive feeling and ideas gathers strength but has yet to find effective political expression'.[35]

Among the various reasons for this, we were acutely aware, was the debilitating loss of socialist vision and conviction in the wake of the retreats of the 1980s. How to move beyond 'identity politics' by resuscitating socialist feminism's promise to renew Marxist analysis and working-class politics; how to develop socialist ecological analyses and practices that avoided either catastrophism or mere piecemeal reformism; how to support the widespread growth of the anti-globalization protest movement while recognizing that it was not in fact possible to 'change the world without taking power';

how to encourage new socialist parties committed to overcoming the old limitations of both parliamentarism and vanguardism: these remained the guiding concerns of the *Register*.

The advances socialist feminism made in the 1970s largely took place outside of the pages of the *Register*, apart from a few exceptions like Hilary Rose's essay discussed above, or Hal Draper and Anne Lipow's 1976 essay documenting what socialist feminists could still learn from Zetkin and Luxemburg. By the early 1980s the *Register* had become much more a site of socialist feminist analysis, as seen in Jane Jenson's 1980 essay on 'The French Communist Party and Feminism', as well as Dorothy Smith's lead essay in 1983 on 'Women, Class and Family' and Varda Burstyn's 'Masculine Dominance and the State' in the same volume. This continued through the decade, with such essays as Elizabeth Wilson's on 'Thatcherism and Women' and Zillah Eisenstein's on 'Liberalism, Feminism and the Reagan State' in 1987, and Johanna Brenner's on 'Feminism's Revolutionary Promise' in 1989. Notably, Brenner's subtitle, 'Finding Hope in Hard Times', expressed the frustration felt by many socialist feminists who, just as they were 'trying to cope with what we experience as decline if not defeat of feminism, or at least of feminism as a grass-roots movement within which radicals could organize, some on the left are finding in feminism and other "new movements" revolutionary subjects to replace the working-class'.[36] This presaged the *Register*'s critical engagement with this aspect of the 'retreat of the intellectuals', including Linda Gordon's 'The Welfare State: A Socialist-Feminist Perspective' and Eleanor Macdonald's 'Derrida and the Politics of Interpretation' alongside Ellen Wood's 'The Uses and Abuses of Civil Society' and Amy Bartholomew's 'Should a Marxist Believe in Marx on Rights?' in the 1990 volume. This continued with Marsha Hewitt's 'Illusions of Freedom: The Regressive Implications of Post-Modernism' and Lynn Segal's 'False Promises: Anti-Pornography Feminism' in 1993, Frances Fox Piven's 'Globalizing Capitalism and the Rise of Identity Politics' in 1995 and Barbara Epstein's 'The Marginality of the American Left: The Legacy of the 1960s' in 1996. Meera Nanda, who had worked as a molecular biologist with science for the people movements in India in the 1970s and 1980s, offered a particularly powerful critique in the 1997 volume of 'the neo-traditionalism condoned, tolerated and, indeed, often celebrated by feminist and postcolonial science critics … Most progressive intellectuals in the West at the close of the twentieth century have come to see scientific rationality as the "mantle of those in power, those with authority." But coming from where I come from, I can see the missing half of the dialectic: scientific rationality *also* contains the resources to challenge those in power, those with authority.'[37]

Perhaps most important was the *Register*'s determination not to hive off socialist feminist analysis as something separate from our 'main business'. It increasingly informed the *Register*'s approach to political economy, as was evident from Ursula Huws' 'Material World: The Myth of the Weightless Economy' and Wally Seccombe's 'Contradictions of Shareholder Capitalism: Downsizing Jobs, Enlisting Savings, Destabilizing Families' in the 1999 volume on *Global Capitalism versus Democracy*. And it was especially evident in the 2001 volume on *Working Classes, Global Realities* (edited with the help of Greg Albo and David Coates), where a great many of the essays probed the contemporary relationship between class and gender in a broad range of both developing and advanced capitalist countries, and the challenges for working-class solidarity and socialist strategy that women's participation in the labour force and in trade unions exposed. Brigitte Young's essay on 'The "Mistress" and the "Maid" in the Global Economy' explored how the flexibilization of the labour market had produced greater equality between educated middle-class women and men while creating greater inequality among women, not least through the way the growing participation of professional women in the labour market was accompanied by the largely 'invisible' development of paid work in the private household by growing numbers of migrant women. Rosemary Warskett's essay on 'Feminism's Challenge to Unions', in assessing the effect that feminism as an ideology as well as women's increasing membership and rise to senior positions had on trade unions, observed that while many gains had been made, this nevertheless stood in 'stark contrast to a vision of transforming the hierarchical nature of the work-place, with its authoritarian division of tasks and separation of intellectual and physical labour. The earlier socialist-feminists' vision of changing union organization so as to promote the value of all people's work in terms of self-activity and human liberation is removed from the agenda, and equity, in terms of what white men have, becomes the ultimate objective'.[38]

Sustaining this vein of socialist feminist analysis remained an important priority for the *Register* in the new millennium, as seen in essays by Barbara Ehrenreich, Fran Piven, Barbara Harriss-White, Lynn Segal, Paula Tibandebage and Maureen Mackintosh, and Pat and Hugh Armstrong, among many others. The *Register* thus stood steadfast against what Meg Luxton and Joan Sangster in the 2013 volume identified as 'the problems of amnesia'. In countering the claim that 'second-wave feminism came to share a "subterranean elective affinity" with neoliberalism', they argued instead that 'liberal feminism's compatibility with neoliberalism is an explicit, structural compatibility, and that it has been able to achieve almost hegemonic status as "second-wave feminism" only to the degree that socialist feminism has been ignored or defeated'. Recognizing this was essential 'to avoid an American-centric understanding of feminism, and to move beyond taken-for-granted assertions about intersectionality to develop an analysis of class relations that thoroughly integrates gender and race and other systems of discrimination and oppression'.[39]

The 2000 volume on *Necessary and Unnecessary Utopias* contained not only Frigga Haug's 'On the Necessity of Conceiving the Utopian in a Feminist Fashion' and Johanna Brenner's 'Utopian Families', but also essays by Diane Elson on 'Socialized Markets, not Market Socialism', and Kate Soper on 'Other Pleasures: The Attractions of Post-consumerism'. Soper's socialist environmentalism was also indicative of the increasing attention the *Register* was paying to the ecological question. This was by no means a new concern, as seen by Peter Sedgewick's 1966 essay on 'Natural Science and Human Theory', Hilary and Steven Rose's 'The Radicalisation of Science' in 1972, S. M. Miller's analysis of the American left's new environmentalist politics in 1980, or Michael Bodemann's essay on the German Green Party in the 1985/86 volume. But it was only with the 1993 volume and David Harvey's lead essay on 'The Nature of Environment: Dialectics of Social and Environmental Change' that the *Register* could be seen as making a really significant contribution. This was followed by such essays as Larry Pratt and Wendy Montgomery's on 'Green Imperialism: Pollution, Penitence, Profits' in 1997, John Bellamy Foster's 'The Communist Manifesto and the Environment' in 1998, Soper's above-mentioned essay on post-consumerism in 2000, and Foster and Brett Clark's 'Ecological Imperialism: The Curse of Capitalism' in 2004. But it really took the 2007 volume on *Coming to Terms with Nature* for the *Register* to make a major impact in terms of advancing the ecological analysis of contemporary capitalism. This volume also made a much needed contribution to better understand the limitations of environmentalist politics, with Frieder Otto Wolf's 'Party-building for Eco-Socialists: Lessons from the Failed Project of the German Greens' and Greg Albo's 'The Limits of Eco-Localism: Scale, Strategy, Socialism'.

But it has been the continuing political impasse of the left more generally that has continued to especially occupy the *Register*'s attention. As wave after wave of protests against neoliberal globalization took shape in the proclamation that 'Another World Is Possible' at the first annual World Social Forum in Porto Alegre, Brazil, Naomi Klein observed in her lead essay in the 2002 *Register* that 'Many people said that they felt history being made in that room. What I felt was something more intangible: the end of The End of History'.[40] Yet it was the very organizational intangibility of the alter-globalization movement that limited its capacity to effect real political change. Recalling Hilary Rose's citation in the *Register* of 'the tyranny of structurelessness' on a much smaller scale four decades earlier, Stephanie Ross's essay in the 2003 *Register* identified the key problems with the anti-globalization movement's 'variety of decentralized decision-making structures'. Such structures could not 'ensure equal and effective participation' since they tended to be 'fluid in terms of membership and loose in terms of the extent to which participants are bound by the decisions made … Consensus produces its own tyranny, that of *endurance*, in which "the last ones left at the table get to make the decision"'.[41] The admirable impulse to international solidarity that so inspired the anti-globalization movement also donned rose-coloured glasses, the wearing of which the *Register* has always resisted, as it did now with Judy Hellman's 'Real and Virtual Chiapas: Magic Realism and the Left' in 2000, and Sergio Baierle's 'The Porto Alegre Thermidor: Brazil's "Participatory Budget" at the Crossroads' in 2003.

Hilary Wainwright's 'Once More Moving On: Social Movements, Political Representation and the Left' in 1995 and her 'Building New Parties for a Different Kind of Socialism' in 1996, had already sharply posed the question of whether the 'political methodology' of the new social movements might be able to make new headway in developing popular democratic capacities and contesting for state power to the end of transforming it for socialist purposes.[42] She hoped that their 'principles of organisation, approaches to power, views of knowledge and of whose knowledge matters' could be adapted in ways that would inform the development of parties of a new kind. Unfortunately the ANC in South Africa and PT in Brazil which seemed to embody exemplary alliances between grassroots movements, trade unions and parties would soon disappoint the socialist hopes so many had invested in them. The *Register* has closely probed the reasons for this in South Africa, from Patrick Bond and Mzwanele Mayekiso's, 'Reflections from the South African Struggle' in 1996 to John Saul's 'On Taming a Revolution: The South African Case' in 2013. And its coverage of the PT runs from Huw Beynon's 'Democracy and the Organization of Class Struggle in Brazil' in 2001 and Baierle's 'Porto Alegre Thermidore' in 2002 to João Pedro Stédile's 'The Class Struggles in Brazil: The Perspective of the MST' in 2008 (not to mention the two essays on Brazil in this volume). The contrasting assessments in the 2008 volume of Hugo Chavez's Bolivarian revolution offered by Margarita López Maya's 'Venezuela Today: A "Participative and Protagonistic" Democracy?' and Marta Harnecker's 'Blows and Counterblows in Venezuela' are also particularly worth going back to in light of Chavez's death this year.

Careful assessment of the possibilities and limitations of the most significant new socialist parties and governments around the world has remained the hallmark of the *Register*. This is why it seemed especially appropriate to close out the *Register*'s first half century in 2013 with *The Question of Strategy*, featuring essays on 'Rethinking Unions, Registering Socialism' and 'Socialist-feminist Strategy Today' alongside essays on 'Strategy and Tactics in Popular Struggles in Latin America' and 'Twenty-first Century Socialism in Bolivia', as well as on the Occupy movement in the US and the new European parties of the left, from Rifondazione in Italy to Die Linke in Germany to Syriza in Greece. That the broad questions this volume raised has generated a new discussion of 'the return of the question of the party' is a welcome tribute to the *Register*'s ongoing contribution.[43]

VII

It is impossible to conclude this survey of the *Register*'s perspective on class and politics over the past five decades without noting the irony that this fiftieth volume should contain an observation that 'most working-class voters view the possibilities of a Miliband-led Labour government with at least tepid optimism'. This is in the essay by Andrew Murray, the chief of staff in Britain's largest union, on whether socialists should be supporting the new Left Unity initiative to form a new working-class party rather than still engage in trying to change the Labour Party. Murray's observation, offered in favour of staying in the party, speaks more generally to the electoral base that social democratic parties retain in the working class today (so far only broken in Greece during the current capitalist crisis, with Syriza's meteoric rise and Pasok's abject decline).

Murray's essay makes the most spirited socialist case for staying in the Labour Party since Ken Coates's essay in the 1973 *Register*. But to say that the Labour Party even today remains the tepid choice of most working-class people is only, as Ralph Miliband put it in his 'Moving On' essay, 'to open the discussion, not to conclude it'. The question Raymond Williams posed in the 1981 *Register* on whether the continuing electoral appeal of social democracy's 'opportunist negativism' is likely to sow new confusions and further get in the way of developing 'sustained popular understanding and support' for a socialist alternative still rings true. It was the strength of what Williams criticized as the 'let's unite to get Thatcher out' appeal that drew Miliband's sons (both born after the *Register* was founded) into the Labour Party in the 1980s. When Labour finally formed a government again almost twenty years later, there were many who claimed that these types of criticisms had no contemporary relevance. But as David Coates put it in his 2003 anthology of *Register* essays, *Paving the Third Way*:

> Part of the New Labour appeal is its telling of the party's own history. But much of that telling is itself partial, misleading, self-indulgent, and persistently distorting of the nature and limits of earlier Labour leaderships. New Labour is not as new as it likes to think ... earlier and current revisionisms have features in common, and operate within parameters and logics that were evident long before the current leadership even joined the Party, let alone led it. The limits of Old Labour paved the way for the limits of New Labour ...[44]

As it turned out, the Miliband who defeated the other for the party leadership was always more uncomfortable with New Labour's accommodation to Thatcherism and the City of London, although even the latter never was so 'unthoughtful' as to express himself like Peter Mandelson did in avowing that he was 'intensely relaxed about people getting filthy rich as long as they pay their taxes'.[45] The votes of trade union activists in the party's electoral college made the difference in the election of the Miliband who blamed the New Labour philosophy (and the invasion of Iraq) for the defeat in the General Election, and demanded that the theme of inequality once again become a central political issue of British politics. And Ed Miliband has even from time to time actually touched on the core relationship between class and politics that underlies this inequality, as in his preface to an e-book by the 'Blue Labour' group of intellectuals:

> Historically, debates within Labour have often been conducted on the basis of a choice between 'more state and less market' or 'more market and less state' ... both the statists and the pro-market voices underplayed the importance of the aspect of our lives and our communities that must be protected from the destructive effects of both markets and the unresponsive state .... Labour originally grew out of a vast movement of voluntary collectivism. We should remember the co-operatives, mutual associations, adult schools and reading circles that constitute a proud tradition of mutual improvement and civic activism ... we need to rediscover the tradition for labour as a grassroots community movement – not for the sake of nostalgia for the past, but to strengthen our party's capacity to bring about real change to people's lives.[46]

Yet it was the same new leader who, in a speech to the annual Trade Union Congress in September 2011, took it upon himself to tell the assembled delegates: 'Strikes are always the consequence of failure. Failure we cannot afford as a nation. Instead your real role is as partners in the new economy.' This was, of course, a message designed to be heard by the assembled media, and through them by bankers, managers and investors, but perhaps above all by a Parliamentary Labour Party overwhelmingly made up of MPs whose political inclinations were instilled by New Labour in its ascendancy. But whatever the constraints on the new leader, his words to the TUC were indicative of something much deeper, namely what Ralph Miliband meant by the 'whole philosophy of politics', which someone who aspires to become a leader of a social democratic party must imbibe – or give up such aspiration unless he secretly intends to irrevocably split the party once he comes into office. The joke widely circulated during the party leadership campaign – which went something like 'Ralph Miliband always said the Labour Party leadership would betray the working class, and he produced two sons to prove it' – was above all inapt because 'betrayal' was a word the father very seldom used, except to challenge its misuse, even with respect to such a momentous event as the calling off of the 1926 General Strike 'without guarantees of any kind, either for the miners, or against the victimization of other workers'. The notion of betrayal, he argued,

> should not be allowed to reduce the episode to the scale of a Victorian melodrama, with the Labour leaders as the gleeful villains, planning and perpetrating an evil deed. The Labour movement *was* betrayed, but not because the Labour leaders were villains, or cowards. It was betrayed because betrayal was the inherent and inescapable consequence of their whole philosophy of politics – and it would be quite foolish to think that their philosophy was the less firmly held for being unsystematically articulated ... Most important of all ... was the belief common to both industrial and parliamentary leaders, that a challenge to the Government through the assertion of working class power was *wrong*. Try though they might to persuade themselves and others that they were engaged in a purely industrial dispute, they knew it was more than that, and it was this that made them feel guilty, uneasy, insecure.[47]

To be sure, Ralph Miliband always insisted there was room for manoeuvre within the capitalist state. Even in conditions of a crisis in capital accumulation, it was possible for a radical leader 'to treat these conditions as a challenge to greater boldness, as an opportunity to greater radicalism'; and he argued that in doing so, such a leader was 'likely to receive the support of many people, hitherto uncommitted or half-committed, but willing to accept a resolute lead'. But he rejected explanations of the failure to do this that were based on the 'personal attributes of social-democratic leaders', insisting that 'the question cannot be tackled in these terms', nor even just in terms of 'the tremendous weight of conservative pressures'. Rather it needed to be tackled in terms of 'the fact that the ideological defenses of these leaders have not generally been of sufficient strength to enable them to resist with any great measure of success conservative pressure, intimidation and enticement'.[48] What is especially notable about the 'Blue Labour' intellectuals today is that they have so little to offer the new leader of the Labour Party by way of such ideological defences. Indeed, while reasserting the need for the Party to rediscover the social activism of the old labour movement, they trumpet the old collectivist values and practices only so long as they are attached to the promise of class harmony rather than finding more effective ways of promoting class struggle.

We shall have to see which of the alternative scenarios Murray sets out for a post-2015 Labour government led by Ed Miliband actually comes to pass. Even the most positive one, which envisages that this government could 'generate – even in spite of itself – an arena of struggle over its direction which could bring benefits in terms of strengthening the movement, and could create circumstances for the working class to recover a measure of confidence', would inevitably produce a split in the Labour Party, starting at the very top. This calls to mind my own first contribution to the *Register* in 1979, which also took the view that to be viable a new socialist party would need to take with it some left Labour MPs, many constituency activists, and even some unions from the Labour Party:

> One important reason for making the attempt to found an even remotely viable socialist alternative is that it would act as pole of attraction for those socialist elements within the Labour Party to break out of the vicious circle of both trying to change the party and maintain its defensive unity, and put their energy, their talents, and the respect and legitimacy they enjoy in the eyes of many trade unionists to more positive use ... [But] it need not inherit by this token the same structure or all the burdens that come with the Labour Party tradition. With different leaders, a different ethos and with a positive attitude to Marxism, these elements would necessarily combine in a different way ... [which] need not carry with it the same separation between parliamentary and extra-parliamentary activity, and the same division of labour between industrial and political leadership.[49]

This is not at all a case for reverting to Leninist forms of party organization. Murray's sharpest line is that 'there is absolutely *nothing* that can be adduced for or against Leninism from the crisis eroding the SWP, any more than the results obtained by the experiments of the Large Hadron Collider need verifying by observing the Duracell Bunny'. This does not negate Ralph Miliband's argument in 'Moving On' that those who took the Bolshevik revolution as 'their common point of departure and of arrival, the script and scenario which determines their whole mode of being' were doomed to marginality. But as he went on to say: 'This is not why any of the groupings of the "ultra-left" have failed to become mass parties or even large parties; it is why they have scarcely become parties at all … [T]he main cause of their lack of attraction is not their sectarianism, dogmatism, adventurism and authoritarianism but their basic perspective which produces their isolation; and it is their isolation which at least in part if not wholly produces their unpleasant characteristics.'[50] That these parties, wherever they still exist, are more or less in their death throes almost everywhere, can only help clear the ground for new forms of party organization more suitable to twenty-first century conditions to be seeded and take root.

At the same time, it must surely also be finally recognized by now that so much of the thinking that produced the retreat of the intellectuals in the 1980s failed to appreciate how the strategic choices of party and union leaders were determined by highly pragmatic calculations rather than the writings of Marx, or this or that Marxist theorist. For a really serious socialist intellectual like Andre Gorz, it took less than a decade after his *Farewell to the Working Class* was published in the early 1980s before he made it perfectly clear that he still thought that no strategy for socialism was possible without a strategy for labour at its core: without powerful and committed organizations of workers, social movements drawn from a 'non-class of non-workers' would be ineffective agents of change. But this also meant that organizations of workers had a 'particular responsibility', since the success or failure of other social movements depended on labour taking 'a common course of action with them'.[51] This is more than ever true today, when it is clearer that, as much as socialist parties of a new kind are needed in the twenty-first century, so are unions of a new kind (such as the New Trade Union Initiative in India, whose highly creative community organizing and rapid growth will be explored in the *Register*'s next volume). But it is doubtful that creative and combative labour movements can emerge on any large scale without new socialist organizations emerging and their activists playing a key role.

Of course, we must ask what a strategy for labour means today amidst the vast restructuring of work taking place on a global scale. The decline of jobs in the manufacturing sector does not represent a 'hollowing out' of advanced capitalist economies, or even of manufacturing as an important element in them. If some old industries are dying, others are on the rise. The lowly paid retail service sectors where the fastest growing occupations are often located takes place alongside the rapid growth of business services as well as new bio-medical, communications and entertainment industries, and the development of classic labour-capital relations in health and education. As Ursula Huws so clearly shows in this volume, the growth of work in these sectors, whether highly or lowly remunerated, does not at all reflect the end of the material economy: 'There are few jobs that do not require workers to bring their own knowledge, judgement and intelligence to the task in hand, and even fewer that do not involve some physical activity, even if this just entails speaking, listening, watching a screen or tapping keys'. That the growth of precarious work is taking place in all sectors, and in the advanced capitalist world as much as elsewhere, is an inevitable consequence of the actual realization of capitalist globalization by the beginning of the twenty-first century.

But what precariousness means in very different social contexts can itself be quite different, especially in terms of the consequences it may hold for the people concerned. It is certainly incorrect to treat the 'precariat' as a different social category, conceptually and actually, than the working class. In fact what we are witnessing in many respects is the very kind of precarity of work – and of life – that led to the designation of dispossessed workers as a proletariat in the nineteenth century, as Bryan Palmer points out in his contribution to this volume. To address the question of the organizational and political implications of this mainly in terms of the declining industrial base of working-class movements is rather myopic, since it misses the long-standing unionization of many 'service' workers from municipal workers in early decades of the twentieth century to teachers and nurses in the 1960s and '70s to the Walmart working class today. It is useful to recall that it was only through their unionization that industrial workers overcame their earlier precarity. And it is absolutely necessary not to romanticize this by imagining they had some sort of inherent aptitude for organization or political radicalism. It is also a mistake to analyze working-class formation and identity in terms of wage work alone. Working classes are constituted by households, extended families, neighbourhoods, communities in which workers who sell their labour power for a wage are embedded and thus intertwined with a broad range of non-waged work. Moreover, changing urban housing and transportation patterns in the twentieth century were often more important to the decline of working–class identities than was deindustrialization or occupational shifts. We need to be sensitive to the ways all this is changing again, and what it means for working–class formation.

The question of whether new configurations of class are conducive to the development of socialist alternatives is really what this fiftieth volume of the *Register* is all about – and the fifty-first will be as well.

NOTES

1   Ralph Miliband, 'Thirty Years of the Socialist Register', *Socialist Register 1994*, London: Merlin Press, p. 4.

2   Despite the very many differences that Miliband certainly had with George Orwell, his 'Politics and the English Language' must have held a strong appeal, especially in identifying the four questions that 'a scrupulous writer, in every sentence that he writes, will ask himself … What am I trying to say? What words will express it? What image or idiom will make it clearer? Is this image fresh enough to have an effect? And he will probably ask himself two more: could have I put it more shortly? Have I said anything that is avoidably ugly?' Miliband would likely have agreed as well with Orwell's claim in his essay 'Why I Write' that, apart from 'sheer egoism' and 'aesthetic enthusiasm', writers were motivated by two main things: 'Historical impulse: Desire to see things as they are, to find out true facts and store them up for the use of posterity'; and 'Political purpose: Desire to push the world in a certain direction, to alter people's idea of the kind of society they should strive after'. 'Why I Write' and 'Politics and the English Language', both written in 1946, were published together in a collection with two other essays as George Orwell, *Why I Write*, London: Penguin, 2004. The quotations here are at pp. 4-5 and 113.

3   Marion Kozak, 'How It All Began: A Footnote to History', *Socialist Register 1995*, London: Merlin Press, 1995, p. 274. See also Colin Leys, '"Honest Socialists": John Saville and the *Socialist Register*', in David Howell, Dianne Kirby and Kevin Morgan, eds., *John Saville: Commitment and History*, London: Lawrence & Wishart, 2011.

4   See Walter Kemsley, ed., *Martin Eve Remembered*, Rendelsham: Merlin Press, 1999, esp. pp. 43-4.

5   For a fuller account of these difficulties, see Michael Newman's excellent biography, *Ralph Miliband and the Politics of the New Left*, London: Merlin Press, 2002, pp. 285-8.

6   Colin Leys, 'Capital Accumulation, Class Formation and Dependency: The Significance of the Kenyan Case', *Socialist Register 1978*, London: Merlin Press, 1978.

7   Göran Therborn, 'After Dialectics: Radical Social Theory in a Post-Communist World', *New Left Review*, 43(Jan/Feb), 2007, p. 99. The fact it was edited in Toronto *specifically* had much to do with the uniquely supportive environment that York University provided. Straddling the Atlantic between editors and publisher, as well as readers and writers, has occasioned much agonizing over British versus American styles, with a Canadian compromise usually settled on.

8   Ralph Miliband, 'Socialism and the Myth of the Golden Past', *Socialist Register 1964*, London: Merlin Press, 1964, pp. 92ff.

9   Hamza Alavi, 'Imperialism Old and New', *Socialist Register 1964*, pp. 113-5.

10   Miliband, 'Socialism', p. 102.

11   Dorothy Wedderburn, 'Facts and Theories of the Welfare State', *Socialist Register 1965*, London: Merlin Press, 1965, pp. 143-4.

12   John Saville, 'Labour and Income Redistribution', *Socialist Register 1965*, p. 155.

13   Saville, 'Labour'. pp. 157-61.

14   See Newman, *Ralph Miliband and the Politics of the New Left*, pp. 108-13.

15   Ralph Miliband, *Parliamentary Socialism*, London: Merlin Press, 1973 [1961], p. 372.

16   Richard Hyman, 'Industrial Conflict and the Political Economy', *Socialist Register 1973*, London: Merlin Press, 1973, pp. 130-1.

17   Hilary Rose, 'Up and Against the Welfare State: The Claimants Unions', *Socialist Register 1973*, pp. 199-200.

18   Ken Coates, 'Socialists and the Labour Party', *Socialist Register 1973*, p. 155.

19   Ralph Miliband, 'Moving On', *Socialist Register 1976*, London: Merlin Press, 1976, p. 128. The following quotations are from pp. 130-1 and 137-9.

20   Miliband, 'Moving On', p. 140.

21   David Coates, ed., *Paving The Third Way: The Critique of Parliamentary Socialism*, London: Merlin Press, 2003, p. 3.

22   Andrew Gamble, 'The Free Economy and the Strong State: The Rise of the Social Market Economy', *Socialist Register 1979*, London: Merlin Press, 1979, p. 3.

23   E.P. Thompson, 'An Open Letter to Leszek Kolakowski', *Socialist Register 1973,* p. 84. To Kolakowski's apparent endorsement of this 'writing-off' when he said 'Let us imagine what "the dictatorship of the proletariat" would mean if the (real, not imaginary) working class took over exclusive political power now in the U.S.', Thompson retorted: 'The absurdity of the question appears (in your view) to provide its own answer. But I doubt whether you have given to the question a moment of serious historical imagination: you have simply assumed a white working class, socialized by capitalist institutions as it is now, mystified by the mass media as it is now, structured into competitive organizations as it is now, without self-activity or its own forms of political expression: i.e. a working class with all the attributes of subjection within capitalist structures which one then "imagines" to achieve power without changing either those structures or itself: which is, I fear, a typical example of the fixity of concept which characterizes much capitalist ideology' (pp. 99-100, n. 69).

24   Raymond Williams, 'An Alternative Politics', *Socialist Register 1981*, London: Merlin Press, 1981, p. 2.

25   Stuart Hall, 'The Battle for Socialist Ideas in the 1980s', *Socialist Register 1982*, London: Merlin Press, 1982, pp. 1-2.

26   Leo Panitch, 'The Impasse of Social Democratic Politics', *Socialist Register 1985/86*, London, Merlin Press, 1985, pp. 63, 95.

27   Terry Eagleton, 'Defending the Free World', *Socialist Register 1990*, London:

Merlin Press, 1990, pp. 88-9.

28   John Saville, 'Marxism Today: An Anatomy', *Socialist Register 1990*, pp. 35, 58.

29   Among the essays in this volume were 'Perestroika and the Neoliberal Project' by Patrick Flaherty, 'Marketization and Privatization: The Polish Case' by Thadeus Kowalik, 'Privilegentsia, Property and Power' by Daniel Singer, as well as 'Perestroika and the Proletariat' by Sam Gindin and myself (based on a trip to meet with Russian autoworkers we had just made). In his essay critiquing proponents of market-socialist reform, Michael Lebowitz set out for the first time his important argument that rather than focusing upon productive forces as the condition for the development of a common system of production, what was required was 'not merely exhortation but the *actual creation of* democratic and decentralised forms in which people change themselves in the course of changing circumstances' so as to overcome the self-orientation, including towards their own labour power, that working people acquired under capitalism, and which market socialist forms further fostered. 'When we consider the cynicism, the retreat into private lives, the everyday accommodation to anti-social and illegal acts, the ripping off of social property, etc. described by so many observers, we are quite justified in wondering whether [Actually Existing Socialism] offers any prospects for the passage to a communist society. Indeed, the question which emerges is whether it is possible to get there from here? Is it, rather, necessary for people to retrace their steps back to capitalism and then to attempt, through the inevitable struggles which emerge from the contradiction between human beings and an inhuman existence, to try again?' 'The Socialist Fetter: A Cautionary Tale', *Socialist Register 1991*, London: Merlin Press, 1991, pp. 367-8.

30   The trade unions' famous wage earner's plan, which went under Meidner's name and intended to achieve the gradual socialization of capital in exchange for wage restraint, had by this point been so watered down by successive Social Democratic governments concerned with sustaining their partnership with capital that 'the whole scheme must now be considered a rather symbolic gesture. The strong Swedish labour movement had proved its inability to encroach upon private ownership, the very core of the capitalist system ... The Swedish system, balancing private ownership and social control, has broken down because real power has shifted from labour to the owners of capital'. Rudolph Meidner, 'Why Did the Swedish Model Fail?', *Socialist Register 1993*, London: Merlin Press, 1993, pp. 225-6.

31   Greg Albo, 'Competitive Austerity and the Impasse of Capitalist Employment Policy', *Socialist Register 1994*.

32   Vivek Chibber, 'Reviving the Developmental State? The Myth of the "National Bourgeoisie"', *Socialist Register 2005*, London: Merlin Press, 2004, pp. 144-5.

33   As the introduction to a collection of these essays that Merlin Press published in 2004 put it, their effect when taken together allowed globalization to be understood 'in its totality: not as a mere series of "reforms" giving free rein to transnational companies but as a radical programme to reshape the entire economic, political, legal and ideological landscape of capitalism. They link the economics of global capitalism both to its geopolitical dimensions and to

its intimate repercussions on daily life.' Leo Panitch, Colin Leys, Alan Zuege and Martijn Konings, eds. *The Globalization Decade: A Critical Reader*, London: Merlin Press, 2004.

34 Sheila Rowbotham, 'Dear Dr. Marx: A Letter from a Socialist Feminist', *Socialist Register 1998*, London: Merlin Press, 1998. The text of Rowbotham's play performed at the Conway Hall event, 'The Tale that Never Ends' was published in the *Socialist Register 1999*, London: Merlin Press, 1999.

35 Colin Leys and Leo Panitch, 'The Political Legacy of the Manifesto', *Socialist Register 1998*, p. 18.

36 Johanna Brenner, 'Feminism's Revolutionary Promise: Finding Hope in Hard Times', *Socialist Register 1989*, London: Merlin Press, 1989, p. 245.

37 Meera Nanda, 'Restoring the Real: Rethinking Social Constructivist Theories of Science', *Socialist Register 1997*, London: Merlin Press, 1997, pp. 305-6.

38 Rosemary Warskett, 'Feminism's Challenge to Unions in the North', *Socialist Register 2001*, London: Merlin Press, 2001, p. 337. See also Anna Pollert's 'The Challenge for Trade Unionism: Sectoral Change, "Poor Work" and Organising the Unorganised', *Socialist Register 1995*.

39 Joan Sangster and Meg Luxton, 'Feminism, Co-optation and the Problems of Amnesia: A Response to Nancy Fraser', *Socialist Register 2013*, Pontypool: Merlin Press, 2012, p. 289.

40 Naomi Klein, 'Farewell to the "End of History": Organisation and Vision in Anti-Corporate Movements', *Socialist Register 2002*, London: Merlin Press, 2002, p. 1.

41 Stephanie Ross, 'Is This What Democracy Looks Like?', *Socialist Register 2003*, London: Merlin Press, 2003, pp. 284, 293.

42 Hilary Wainwright, 'Once More Moving On: Social Movements, Political Representation and the Left', *Socialist Register 1995*, pp. 84, 90.

43 See the various papers on Mimmo Porcaro's essay in the 2013 *Register* by Mario Candeias, Jan Rehman, John Milios and Haris Triandafilidou, and Porcaro's response, posted during August 2013 at http://rosalux.de/english as well as in *The Bullet*, available at http://socialistproject.ca.

44 Coates, *Paving The Third Way*, p. 2.

45 The word 'unthoughtful' was much later used by Mandelson himself to characterize this comment. See Shiv Malik, 'Peter Mandelson gets nervous about people getting "filthy rich"', *The Guardian*, 26 January 2012.

46 Ed Miliband, 'Preface', in Maurice Glasman, Jonathan Rutherford, Marc Stears, Stuart White, eds, *The Labour Tradition and the Politics of Paradox*, Oxford: London Seminars/Soundings, 2011, pp. 6-8, available at http://lwbooks.co.uk/journals/soundings.

47 Miliband, *Parliamentary Socialism*, p. 144.

48 Ralph Miliband, *The State in Capitalist Society*, Pontypool: Merlin Press, 2009 [1969], pp. 73, 141-2.

49 Leo Panitch, 'Socialists and the Labour Party: A Reappraisal', *Socialist Register 1979*, London: Merlin Press, 1979, pp. 72-3.

50 Miliband, 'Moving On', p. 138.

51 Andre Gorz, *Critique of Economic Reason*, London: Verso, 1989, pp. 231-3.

Socialist Register is now available online

Individual subscribers:

Permanent online access to the current volume, plus access to all
previous volumes for the period of the subscription.

Details at www.merlinpress.co.uk

Institutional subscribers:

Options:
A. To buy current volume only:
1. Permanent online resource
2. Permanent online access plus hardback printed copy. Mixed Media

B. For ongoing subscriptions: ISSN 0081-0606
3. Ongoing online access with permanent access to the current volume
and access to previous volumes for the period of the subscription.
4. As 3 plus hardback printed copy.

Prices and other information available at www.merlinpress.co.uk (or order
through a subscription agent)
e-mail: orders@merlinpress.co.uk

The Merlin Press
Unit 4 Talgarth Business Park
Talgarth, Brecon, Powys
LD3 0PQ, Wales

www.merlinpress.co.uk